International Relations in Southeast Asia

The **Institute of Southeast Asian Studies (ISEAS)** was established as an autonomous organization in 1968. It is a regional research centre dedicated to the study of socio-political, security and economic trends and developments in Southeast Asia and its wider geostrategic and economic environment. The Institute's research programmes are the Regional Economic Studies (RES, including ASEAN and APEC), Regional Strategic and Political Studies (RSPS), and Regional Social and Cultural Studies (RSCS).

ISEAS Publishing, an established academic press, has issued more than 2,000 books and journals. It is the largest scholarly publisher of research about Southeast Asia from within the region. ISEAS Publishing works with many other academic and trade publishers and distributors to disseminate important research and analyses from and about Southeast Asia to the rest of the world.

International Relations in Southeast Asia

Between Bilateralism and Multilateralism

Edited by
N. Ganesan and Ramses Amer

ISEAS

INSTITUTE OF SOUTHEAST ASIAN STUDIES
Singapore

First published in Singapore in 2010 by ISEAS Publishing
Institute of Southeast Asian Studies
30 Heng Mui Keng Terrace
Pasir Panjang
Singapore 119614

E-mail: publish@iseas.edu.sg
Website: <http://bookshop.iseas.edu.sg>

The responsibility for facts and opinions in this publication rests exclusively with the authors and their interpretations do not necessarily reflect the views or the policy of the publisher or its supporters.

ISEAS Library Cataloguing-in-Publication Data

International relations in Southeast Asia : between bilateralism and
    multilateralism / edited by N. Ganesan and Ramses Amer.
1.   Southeast Asia—Foreign relations.
I.   Ganesan, N. (Narayanan), 1954-
II. Amer, Ramses.
DS526.8 I61   2010

ISBN 978-981-4279-57-4 (soft cover)
ISBN 978-981-4279-58-1 (PDF)

Typeset by International Typesetters Pte Ltd
Printed in Singapore by Utopia Press Pte Ltd

Contents

Preface

This book is the end product of a project on bilateralism and multilateralism in Southeast Asia. The contributions to this edited volume have been developed through a process involving presentations of papers at two international workshops held in Hiroshima and Kuala Lumpur in December 2007 and October 2008, respectively.

The contributors to this book have strictly adhered to an agreed timetable to deliver their individual contributions to this book. In so doing they have integrated feedback from the editors, from discussants at the two workshops and from other participants in the workshops. Finally, the entire manuscript benefitted from the feedback of three anonymous referees who reviewed it for ISEAS.

The project was generously funded by the Hiroshima Peace Institute (HPI) through the Hiroshima City Government, which also hosted the first workshop. Additional financial support to the two Workshops has been provided by the Asian Political and International Studies Association (APISA), Council for the Development of Social Science Research in Africa (CODESRIA) and the Konrad Adenauer Stiftung (KAS). APISA hosted the second workshop in Kuala Lumpur, Malaysia.

We acknowledge the supportive role of Associate Professor Hari Singh, the Executive Secretary of APISA for economic support, hosting, and his contribution as participant in the two workshops. We also acknowledge the supportive role of Dr Colin Duerkop of KAS for financial support and participation in the first workshop.

We would like to acknowledge the important contribution made by the discussants at the two workshops: Professor Patricio Abinales and Professor Omar Farouk at the Hiroshima workshop and Professor Johan Saravanamuttu and Dr Lam Peng Er at the Kuala Lumpur workshop.

Last but not least we would like to express our appreciation for the efforts and role played by Yukiko Yoshihara from the HPI throughout the project and in particular in connection with the first workshop. We also express our appreciation to Patricia Marin for her key role in the organization of the second workshop in Kuala Lumpur.

The chapter by Natasha Hamilton-Hart on Singapore-Indonesia relations appeared as "Indonesia and Singapore: Structure, Politics and Interests" in the journal *Contemporary Southeast Asia* 31, no. 2 (August 2009): 249–71, first published by ISEAS Publishing.

N. Ganesan and Ramses Amer
Editors

Hiroshima and Stockholm, October 2009

List of Abbreviations

ACMECS	Ayeyawady–Chao Phraya–Mekong Economic Cooperation Strategy
APEC	Asia Pacific Economic Cooperation
APISA	Asian Political and International Studies Association
ARF	ASEAN Regional Forum
ASA	Association of Southeast Asia
ASEAN	Association of Southeast Asian Nations
BIMP-EAGA	Brunei-Indonesia-Malaysia-Philippines East ASEAN Growth Area
CGDK	Coalition Government of Democratic Kampuchea
CIQ	Customs, Immigration, and Quarantine
CODESRIA	Council for the Development of Social Science Research in Africa
CPM	Communist Party of Malaya
CPT	Communist Party of Thailand
CPV	Communist Party of Vietnam
DCA	Defence Cooperation Agreement
DK	Democratic Kampuchea
EAGA	East ASEAN Growth Area, see also BIMP-EAGA
FUNCINPEC	Front Uni National pour un Cambodge Indépendant, Neutre, Pacifique et Coopératif (National United Front for an Independent, Neutral, Peaceful, and Cooperative Cambodia)
GAM	Gerakan Aceh Merdeka (Free Aceh Movement)
GDP	Gross Domestic Product
HPI	Hiroshima Peace Institute
ICJ	United Nations International Court of Justice
ISEAS	Institute of Southeast Asian Studies

JBC	Joint Boundary Committee
JCM	Joint Commission for Bilateral Cooperation
JESPA	Japan Singapore Economic Agreement for a New Age Partnership
JI	Jemaah Islamiah
KAS	Konrad Adenauer Stiftung
KNUFNS	Kampuchean National Front for National Salvation
KPNLF	Khmer People's National Liberation Front
KTM	Keretapi Tanah Melayu (Malayan Railway)
MILEX	Military expenditure
MILF	Moro Islamic Liberation Front
MNLF	Moro National Liberation Front
MOFA	Vietnam Ministry of Foreign Affairs
NGC	National Government of Cambodia
NGO	non-governmental organization
OIC	Organisation of the Islamic Conference
PAP	People's Action Party
PAS	Parti Islam SeMalaysia (Pan-Malaysian Islamic Party)
PDK	Party of Democratic Kampuchea
POA	Points of Agreement
PRC	People's Republic of China
PRG/DRV	Provisional Revolutionary Government/Democratic Republic of Vietnam
PRK	People's Republic of Kampuchea
PTA	preferential trade agreement
RBC	Regional Border Committee
RELA	Ikatan Relawan Rakyat Malaysia (Malaysian People's Volunteers Corps)
RSAF	Republic of Singapore Air Force
RMAF	Royal Malaysian Air Force
SEATO	Southeast Asia Treaty Organization
SOC	State of Cambodia
TAC	Treaty of Amity and Cooperation
TBC	Township Border Committee
UMNO	United Malays National Organisation
UNCLOS	United Nations Law of the Sea Conference
UNHCR	United Nations High Commissioner for Refugees
UNTAC	United Nations Transitional Authority in Cambodia
WTO	World Trade Organization
ZOPFAN	Zone of Peace, Freedom and Neutrality

Contributors

N. Ganesan is Professor of Southeast Asian politics at the Hiroshima Peace Institute in Japan, where he has been since 2004. His research interests are in intrastate and interstate sources of tension and conflict in Southeast Asia.

Ramses Amer, Associate Professor and Ph.D. in Peace and Conflict Research, is Senior Research Fellow at the Center for Pacific Asia Studies (CPAS), Department of Oriental Languages, Stockholm University. Major areas of research include security issues and conflict resolution in Southeast Asia and the wider Pacific Asia, and the role of the United Nations in the international system.

Pavin Chachavalpongpun is Fellow and Lead Researcher for Political and Strategic Affairs at the ASEAN Studies Centre, Institute of Southeast Asian Studies, Singapore. Pavin received his Ph.D. in 2002 from the School of Oriental and African Studies, University of London. His research interests include Thai politics and foreign policy, Thailand's relations with Myanmar, Laos and Cambodia, and interstate relations among ASEAN members.

Isagani de Castro Jr. covered ASEAN affairs for the Manila bureau of *Asahi Shimbun*, one of Japan's major newspapers, from 1996 to 2007. He started his journalism career in 1987 with *Business Day*, Southeast Asia's first business daily, where he covered the diplomatic beat. He is currently editor for content of www.abs-cbnNEWS.com, a major news website in the Philippines.

Natasha Hamilton-Hart is an Associate Professor in the Southeast Asian Studies Programme, National University of Singapore. Her research interests are in the areas of international relations and political economy of Southeast Asia.

Ikrar Nusa Bhakti is Professor at the Research Centre for Politics of the Indonesian Institute for Sciences (LIPI). His research interests are in Indonesian domestic politics and foreign policy.

K.S. Nathan is currently Professor and Head of the Centre for American Studies (KAMERA) in the Institute of Occidental Studies (IKON), Universiti Kebangsaan Malaysia, Bangi. He is also the Deputy Director of the institute. His teaching and research interests include U.S. foreign policy, ASEAN's relations with major external powers, Malaysian politics and foreign policy, Malaysia-Singapore relations, and regional security in Southeast Asia.

Nguyen Vu Tung joined the Institute for International Relations (IIR, renamed in 2008 as Diplomatic Academy of Vietnam, DAV) in 1990. He graduated from the College of International Affairs (Hanoi) in 1986, earned a Master of Arts in Law and Diplomacy from the Fletcher School of Law and Diplomacy (TUFTS University, Massachusetts) in 1996, and received his Ph.D. in Political Science from Columbia in 2003. His main areas of teaching, research, and publications include international relations theories, international relations in Southeast Asia, and Vietnamese foreign policy and relations with the United States and ASEAN.

Sheldon W. Simon is Professor in the School of Politics and Global Studies at Arizona State University. His research interests encompass Asian international politics, security, and regional organizations.

Etel Solingen is Chancellor's Professor of Political Science at the University of California, Irvine. Her most recent book, *Nuclear Logics: Contrasting Paths in East Asia and the Middle East* (Princeton University Press, 2007) was the recipient of the 2008 Woodrow Wilson Foundation Award by the American Political Science Association for the best book on government, politics, or international affairs, and of the 2008 Robert Jervis and Paul Schroeder Award for the Best Book on International History and Politics. She also authored *Regional Orders at Century's Dawn:*

Global and Domestic Influences on Grand Strategy (Princeton University Press, 1998) and *Industrial Policy, Technology, and International Bargaining: Designing Nuclear Industries in Argentina and Brazil* (Stanford University Press, 1996).

Meredith L. Weiss is Assistant Professor of Political Science at the University at Albany, State University of New York. She is the author of *Protest and Possibilities: Civil Society and Coalitions for Political Change in Malaysia* (Stanford, 2006) and co-editor of *Social Movements in Malaysia: From Moral Communities to NGOs* (RoutledgeCurzon, 2003, 2004). Her current research focuses on issues of student activism, collective identity, electoral alignments, and political mobilization in Southeast Asia.

Introduction

N. Ganesan and Ramses Amer

The central theme of this book is the utility of bilateralism and multilateralism in Southeast Asian international relations. The intention was to examine a sufficient number of empirical cases in the Southeast Asian region since the mid-1970s so as to establish a pattern of interactions informing a wider audience of interactions unique to the region. Through these case studies, we seek to identify how this pattern of interaction compares with similar experiences elsewhere vis-à-vis the theoretical underpinnings of multilateralism and bilateralism. Consequently, this book also examines the theoretical drift in international relations literature at the broadest level and the overall drift of Southeast Asian international relations between the nations themselves and the Association of Southeast Asian Nations (ASEAN).

Since the post–Cold War period, multilateralism has gained prominence as an approach for forging international consensus on a number of issues. Multilateralism quite simply refers to three or more countries coming together to deal with issues of common interest, whether they be positive or negative. During the Cold War, forging multilateral consensus on issues tended to be much more difficult given the ideological differences between the Soviet-led bloc and the U.S.-led bloc. The level of mutual distrust between those two blocs was so evident that each considered the other its antithesis. To further complicate the situation in Pacific Asia, deep conflicts emerged between communist countries, which pitted the Soviet Union against China, and Vietnam against both Cambodia and China.

With the end of the Cold War and the implosion of the Soviet Union in 1991, there has been far better accommodation between the communist/ socialist countries and the liberal democratic states. This accommodation witnessed a greater willingness on the part of the international community to seek common solutions to common problems, from civil war in Cambodia to collapsed states like Somalia and hunger in Ethiopia. The period also witnessed the international community's willingness to assign immediate tasks to international regimes for resolution. This mood in turn led to the empowerment of international agencies, in particular those associated with the United Nations. During the presidency of George W. Bush, the United States largely reversed its commitment to multilateralism, displaying a preference to act unilaterally or in alliance with like-minded countries such as the United Kingdom. Whether or not such an approach is conducive in the longer term is questionable as it dissipates diplomatic goodwill and costs too much to be sustainable as a permanent policy position. Besides, the world has become considerably smaller and much more interdependent to the point that unilateralism is neither a realistic nor sustainable policy.

The global developments also had an impact on the international relations of Southeast Asia. The region was deeply divided during the Cold War and was also the scene of severe conflicts linked to the Cold War, like the Vietnam War. Similarly, the Cambodian conflict sharply divided the region during the 1980s between ASEAN on the one hand and the communist countries of Vietnam, Laos, and Cambodia on the other. However, with the end of the Cold War and the resolution of the Cambodian Conflict in 1991, the ideological divide between communist and non-communist countries receded and rapprochement became possible. This process led to the expansion of ASEAN in the 1990s to include all ten Southeast Asian countries. Subsequently, ASEAN shed its ideological garb and introduced a number of multilateral initiatives on its own. These included the ASEAN Free Trade Area in 1993, the ASEAN Regional Forum (ARF) in 1994, and the ASEAN Plus Three forum — including China, Japan, and South Korea — in 1998 that eventually culminated in the East Asian Summit Meeting in December 2005 in Kuala Lumpur, Malaysia. Multilateralism arose from this inward strengthening of ASEAN structures, membership, and outward expansion of its protocol, and came to take root in the region.

Just as there was greater regional cooperation, there were also a number of instances of extremely tense bilateral relations between

ASEAN member states. Also, the domestic political situation in some Southeast Asian countries deteriorated in the 1990s due to certain developments in Cambodia and Myanmar. Likewise, the Asian financial crisis had considerable impact on Indonesia and Thailand in particular. ASEAN's multilateralism appeared impotent in solving the problems of countries within the regional footprint. In fact, the attitude was one of not wanting to get involved in the situation in the first place. Hence, in contrast to an emerging consensus and the onset of multilateralism, it seemed as if ASEAN was unprepared to utilize multilateral initiatives at the regional level to resolve problems within individual countries, or for that matter, those between member states. Although ASEAN had established structures, such as the ASEAN Troika, they have not been called upon to arbitrate or intervene in such situations. Hence, ASEAN and its institutional mechanisms were either dormant or seemed to perform different functions during good times as opposed to turbulent ones. This observation also raises a fundamental question as to whether ASEAN's role is to create and establish norms for its members or whether such a role definition involves being an active mediator and actor in resolving interstate disputes in the region.

Structurally, there was also a tendency for ASEAN to be shunned as the platform of choice for dispute resolution. Countries experiencing internal difficulties or problems with proximate states were invariably disinterested in ASEAN auspices for dispute resolution. While part of the reason for this hesitation can be attributed to the relatively young states' (gaining independence after World War II) fear of surrendering sovereignty, appealing to ASEAN for assistance or arbitration does not even appear to have been seriously considered. In fact, the typical situation involved invoking a veil of secrecy and trying to resolve the situation internally, using force if necessary, or undertaking strictly bilateral negotiations between affected countries. Indeed this trend continues to be true today. Curiously, the reasons for this practice have never really been studied and the continued utilization of this approach is injurious to meaningful multilateralism where resources are collectively pooled to address common regional concerns. Additionally, the seemingly exclusive nature of bilateral conflict resolution does not appear to allow for the emergence of a region-wide diplomatic protocol. The evolution of such a protocol would significantly enhance dispute resolution within a common framework that could then be codified to endorse softer and more positive cultural practices which in turn would prevent miscalculations and inhibit adventurous behaviour between states. This observation refers back to the nature of ASEAN's mandate and its relationship vis-à-vis regional mechanisms as well as the preference for bilateral initiatives to settle interstate disputes among ASEAN member states.

This project sought to examine a number of cases of bilateral tensions between ASEAN member states so as to determine the causes of persistent bilateral tensions. After a listing of reasons, the next stage of the research examines how the tensions have been managed and possibly resolved. An added question then arose, namely, why countries with bilateral tensions did not choose ASEAN or its institutions as the vehicle for dispute resolution. Another issue that has been researched is the role of ASEAN and its mechanisms for dispute settlement in the context of the bilateral disputes. The case studies will allow for hypothesis testing and cross-comparative treatment of findings from them. The latter will be especially useful in identifying a workable protocol with applied utility to resolve future disputes. As for the countries involved in bilateral disputes, nine sets of bilateral relationships have been chosen; they are in alphabetical order: Cambodia-Vietnam, Indonesia-Malaysia, Indonesia-Philippines, Indonesia-Singapore, Malaysia-Philippines, Malaysia-Singapore, Malaysia-Thailand, Myanmar-Thailand, and Thailand-Vietnam. These nine sets of bilateral relationships are a sufficient sampling of the entire region and representative of both mainland and maritime Southeast Asia. That the sampling actually correlates to a good representation of the region is indicative of the pervasiveness of bilateral tensions in the region. In order to frame the research within the international and regional context, one chapter examines the general nature of international relations and another chapter examines Southeast Asian international relations in particular.

This book is divided into three main sections for geographical and methodological reasons. The first section has two chapters; the first, by Etel Solingen, details the evolution of bilateralism and multilateralism in international relations theory, and the second, by Sheldon Simon, examines the general dynamics of international relations in Southeast Asia and, more specifically, the evolution of multilateralism in the region. The second section deals with mainland Southeast Asia and comprises four case studies of bilateral relations — Vietnam-Thailand by Nguyen Vu Tung, Cambodia-Vietnam by Ramses Amer, Thailand-Myanmar by Pavin Chachavalpongpun, and Thailand-Malaysia by N. Ganesan. The third section comprises five cases from maritime Southeast Asia — Indonesia-

Malaysia by Meredith Weiss, Indonesia-Singapore by Natasha Hamilton-Hart, Malaysia-Philippines by Isagani de Castro, Malaysia-Singapore by K.S. Nathan, and Indonesia-Philippines by Ikrar Nusa Bhakti. The book then ends with a concluding chapter that places the findings from the book in relation to the international relations literature.

The chapter writers for the case studies were provided common frames of references as well as a number of common questions. The first of these guidelines was that authors should try to place the relationships in question within a time frame. They were asked to focus on more contemporary developments after a brief historical overview of the relationship. Contemporary developments were then specified as those occurring after the conclusion of the Second Indochina Conflict in 1975. Despite the fact that the Third Indochina Conflict involving the Vietnamese military intervention in Cambodia and the subsequent Cambodian Conflict as well as the conflict between China and Vietnam did not finally draw to a close until 1991, there is general agreement that 1975 marked a major watershed in Southeast Asian international relations. Case study chapter writers have also been asked to identify the most important and sensitive issues in the bilateral relationship they were examining. Finally, they have been tasked to identify how these issues are typically dealt with at the bilateral level and whether there had been recourse to multilateralism.

PART I

On International Relations

1

Multilateralism, Regionalism, and Bilateralism: Conceptual Overview from International Relations Theory

Etel Solingen

The different chapters in this volume discuss different dimensions of bilateralism and multilateralism in Southeast Asia. Unfortunately, definitions of these particular forms of international cooperation and competition abound and different meanings can be attached to them. This terminological variance can hinder our understanding of the phenomena under study. This chapter attempts to provide a general overview of some basic concepts underlying this collaborative project as they have been dealt with in the international relations literature. Arriving at common definitions is not always easy but, at a minimum, the effort can help raise awareness of different interpretations of concepts across contexts. At best, the adoption of consensual terminology can help carry out a more convergent set of empirical studies, with a potentially more robust set of propositions and findings.

I provide an outline of seven core concepts as they have been used in representative literature in international relations: multilateralism, multilateral/regional institutions, regionalism versus regionalization, networks, forum shopping, and bilateralism. This literature spans security and political economy. Both can inform the discussion in several ways. First, the seven mentioned concepts may have been applied to one realm (economics, for instance) in the academic literature but often spilled over into the other (security). Gauging the utility of core concepts across issue-areas can provide important insights and extend our understanding of their distinct operation and meanings in each case. Second, in the real world of international politics, considerations of security and political economy are joined at the hip, in Southeast Asia and beyond. Third, it is important to understand whether the substantive evolution of multilateralism, regionalism, or any of these concepts tends to follow any sequential logic, so that economic bilateralism may beget security bilateralism, or vice-versa. These synergies are too important to disregard both in the conceptual literature and in empirical studies. Examples from ASEAN and the Asia-Pacific will be weaved through the conceptual discussion in this chapter.

Multilateralism: Definitional Issues

The initial memo sent out by this volume's editors, Professors Ganesan and Amer, defined multilateralism, as "quite simply ... three or more countries coming together to deal with issues of common interest, whether they be positive or negative." In characterizing the general state of international relations at the present time, they argued, "the world has become considerably smaller and much more interdependent, to the point that unilateralism is quite simply neither a realistic nor sustainable policy." Extending this general argument to Southeast Asia, the editors further argued that with ASEAN's internal strengthening and external expansion, multilateralism appeared to be taking root in this region as well. Evidence for that included expansion into the ASEAN-10 in the 1990s, conclusion of the ASEAN Free Trade Area in 1993, the ASEAN Regional Forum (ARF) in 1994, the ASEAN Plus Three forum in 1998, and the East Asian Community summit meeting in December 2005. In tandem with these developments, however, it is clear that tense bilateral relations among some ASEAN dyads remain, that ASEAN was unwilling to deal with an array of domestic debacles in different member countries, that mechanisms such as the ASEAN High Council and the ASEAN Troika were never activated to resolve problems, and that members looked elsewhere for dispute resolution mechanisms, typically bilateral ones.

The term multilateralism became fashionable in the 1990s in the international relations literature as well as in common diplomatic parlance. Yet it has been used in disjointed ways both within and across these two communities. Keohane defined multilateralism simply as "the practice of co-ordinating national policies in groups of three or more states".[1] The 1992 issue of *International Organisation* devoted several articles to the study of multilateralism, which were later compiled into John Ruggie's *Multilateralism Matters*.[2] Ruggie's own seminal article, which remains one of the most widely cited definitions of multilateralism, argues that the "nominal definition of multilateralism misses the qualitative dimension that makes multilateralism a distinct form."[3] The *kinds* of substantive relations established among parties are of greater importance than the nominal number of parties. These qualitative features are not completely captured by concepts such as international regimes (that may not be multilateral) or intergovernmental organizations (which are only a fraction of all forms of multilateralism). Thus, "what is distinctive about multilateralism is not merely that it coordinates national policies in groups of three or more states, which is something that other organizational forms also do, but that it does so on the basis of certain principles of ordering relations among those states".[4]

Ruggie differentiated between an older, generic institutional form that can be found in "institutional arrangements to define and stabilize the international property rights of states, to manage coordination problems, and to resolve collaboration problems",[5] and more recent formal multilateral organizations. He thus defines multilateralism as an "institutional form which coordinates relations among three or more states on the basis of 'generalized' principles of conduct — that is principles which specify appropriate conduct for a class of actions, without regard to the particularistic interests of the parties or the strategic exigencies that may exist in any specific occurrence".[6] Generalized organizing principles entail indivisibility among members regarding the range of behaviour in question. Successful cases of multilateralism generate what Keohane has labelled expectations of diffuse reciprocity,[7] that is, they yield a rough equivalence of benefits across members in the aggregate and over time. For Ruggie multilateralism is a demanding institutional form whereas international orders, regimes, and organizations may not be multilateral. It is demanding because states must restrain their strong tendency to pursue their interests unilaterally, and it requires them to abstain from bilateral or other instrumental alliances that may run counter to the expectations of a multilateral forum.

Ironically, what makes multilateralism so hard to establish might also make it more durable and adaptable, according to Ruggie. The expectation of diffuse reciprocity may make states more flexible: "arrangements based on generalized organizing principles should be more elastic than those based on particular interests and thus be more adaptable to changing circumstances".[8] Ruggie also observed that "a permissive domestic environment … is at least as important and, in some cases, more important."[9] When we look more closely at the post–World War II situation, for example, we find that it was less the fact of American *hegemony* that accounts for the explosion of multilateral arrangements than it was the fact of *American* hegemony. As we shall see in the next section, the nature of the domestic environment plays an important role in determining the substance and quality of multilateralism in Southeast Asia as well.

Caporaso argued that multilateralism was not extensively employed as a theoretical category and that it was rarely used as an explanatory concept, noting that much of the theoretical heavy-lifting in studies of multilateralism builds on theories of cooperation and institutions, which I review below.[10] Caporaso also argued that multilateralism is distinguished by three properties: (1) indivisibility, "scope over which costs and benefits are spread"; (2) generalized principles of conduct, "norms exhorting general modes of conduct among states"; and (3) diffuse reciprocity, "actors expect to benefit over the long term and over many issues."[11] These three properties should themselves be considered as indivisible rather than as additive, detachable ingredients of multilateralism. He also distinguished between multilateral institutions and the institution of multilateralism. On the one hand, multilateral institutions "focus attention on the formal organizational elements of international life and are characterized by permanent locations and postal addresses, distinct headquarters, and ongoing staffs and secretariats." In other words, we tend to refer to these as organizations (see next section). On the other hand, the institution of multilateralism "is grounded in and appeals to the less formal, less codified habits, practices, ideas, and norms of international society." It may express itself in concrete organizations but its significance cuts more deeply. These two forms may, of course, be related in various causal ways. A normative sense of how things should be — democratic values, for instance — may imbue and shape multilateral institutions.

Other work provides other definitional categories. For instance, Finnemore and Luck argue that multilateralism can be defined operationally or procedurally.[12] Ikenberry suggests that multilateralism operates at three levels of international order: system multilateralism, ordering or foundational multilateralism, and contract multilateralism.[13] He further distinguished between basic levels of multilateralism, or "multilateralism as it relates to the deep organization of units and their mutual recognition and interaction", and the intermediate level, which "can refer to the political-economic organization of regional or international order." Finally, a key question often raised is why states comply with multilateral agreements. A seminal article by Chayes and Chayes argued that states do so for fear of punishment by other member states, of transaction costs, and of bad image.[14]

Multilateralism and Institutions: Why, Which, What For?[15]

The study of multilateralism at the global and regional levels is informed more broadly by the study of institutions in international relations theory and beyond. Why do institutions come into being? For neorealism, institutions can be traced to powerful states that occasionally find them convenient instruments of statecraft. Given these imputed origins, the design of institutions resembles flimsy artefacts, arenas for exercising power, pliable superstructures coating the deeper foundations of power and hence subject to changes in those foundations, which render institutions ephemeral. Martin points out the specific advantages for hegemons, as institutions lower transaction costs, deflect challenges from weaker members, and increase stability under conditions of change in relative power.[16] As intervening variables at best, institutions have limited effects in neorealist interpretations. The most powerful states accrue disproportionately whatever benefits they yield. This approach has generated various critiques. For one, hegemons may have strong incentives to organize regional institutions but so may have others seeking to balance against hegemons or other institutions. ASEAN is a relevant example, as are other regional institutions spawned by ASEAN. Weaker states may bind themselves to institutions to enhance their power within them or for fear of being left behind. Williams finds multilateralism to be advantageous to weaker players because it provides non-discrimination, reciprocity, and self-restraint, which bilateral agreements generally do not.[17]

Constructivist approaches trace regional institutions to converging norms, legitimacy, and identity. "Logics of appropriateness", not interests or rational expectations, determine institutional purpose.[18] An institution's design embodies symbolic representations,[19] the norms that engendered them, and internal socialization.[20] For instance, institutions reflecting democratic identities of member states exhibit norms of transparency, consultation, and compromise.[21] Experience with shared rules facilitates the development of rule-based institutions, making collective identity more viable. In a constructivist framework the effects of institutions can be far reaching, changing actors' beliefs and identities, and hence, their definition of interests. As handmaidens of new actors, tasks, and objectives, institutions are purposive agents specifying authority patterns and allocating responsibilities. Institutions "constitute and construct the social world".[22] Their independent authority stems from the legitimacy of the rational-legal authority they embody and/or from technical expertise and information. Output and practices enhance their legitimacy sometimes at the expense of efficiency, although gauging the scope of legitimacy is problematic.[23] Constructivist approaches have been heavily relied upon to understand ASEAN as a multilateral institution.

For neoliberal institutionalism, states advance their interests by creating institutions to manage growing interdependence and overcome collective action problems. Institutions reduce uncertainty, enhance information about preferences and behaviour, lower transaction costs responsible for market failure, monitor compliance, detect defections, increase opportunities for cooperation, reduce the costs of retaliation, facilitate issue-linkages, and offer focal points or salient solutions.[24] State benefits from creating institutions are presumed to be greater than the transaction costs entailed in negotiation and enforcement.[25] Institutions are assumed to take different forms contingent on the type of collective action problem to be solved;[26] they constrain and can change the context, preferences, and beliefs over outcomes.[27] This brand of theory has proven less apt in explaining why certain points become "focal" but not others,[28] or why some solutions along the Pareto frontier — that leave everybody better off — are adopted over others.[29] Furthermore, investments are not always crucially about material resources, talk is not always cheap, and formalization can undermine cooperation.[30] Haggard found "little evidence for the theory that higher levels of interdependence generate the demand for deeper integration", or that trade generates prisoners' dilemmas that only institutions (or hegemons) can resolve.[31] Finally, institutions may not have the *state-level* Pareto-improving distributional effects often assigned to them in neoliberal institutionalism. Instead, they may be created and maintained because they benefit powerful domestic coalitions.

Haggard urges a proper understanding of preferences and capabilities of relevant domestic actors and of distributional effects within states, as a more productive path to understanding the emergence of multilateral institutions.[32] According to Thelen, functionalist theories "skirt the issue of the origins of institutions and the all-important matter of the material and ideological coalitions on which institutions are founded."[33] Domestic politics arguments apply different theories of preference formation and, in their rationalist form, reduce institutions to arenas for reaching political compromises that reflect changing domestic configurations and transnational coalitions.[34] Kahler suggests that the nature of domestic coalitions may explain varying positions toward legalization, or the extent to which institutions display heightened obligation, greater precision in rules, and delegation of rule interpretation and enforcement to third parties.[35] Thus, internationalizing coalitions — chiefly business — may be more prone to use legalization to enforce liberalization and ensure regional stability. By contrast, coalitions resisting internationalization — such as military and security bureaucracies — are arguably more likely to counter legalization due to high sovereignty costs or autonomy loss. The degree, nature, and scope of institutional effects can be gauged empirically, calibrated against the strength and preferences of primary domestic beneficiaries.

As I argued elsewhere, dominant ruling coalitions in ASEAN's Five launched a domestic model of economic growth through engagement in the global economy.[36] Their converging interest in collaborating regionally through ASEAN was geared to protect their model from interrelated domestic insurgencies and regional threats to their model's domestic dominance. Theirs was a very different conception of regional order than the one advanced by Indonesia's Sukarno, who rejected the global economy and institutions while inciting conflict with neighbours (*Konfrontasi*). Economic growth was at the heart of Suharto's strategy, embedded in the concept of "national resilience" (*ketahanan nasional*). Regional stability was a natural related cornerstone, allowing ASEAN rulers to wield national and collective resilience to mutual benefit. This model relied initially on state-directed lending and crony conglomerates, variously favouring foreign direct investment, manufacturing, and natural resource exports while compensating import-substituting and rural interests.[37] An embedded social bargain provided high per capita growth, employment, investments in health and education, and increasing returns to small businesses and farmers. The bargain was pivoted on gradual and selective internationalization. Intra-regional trade was rather limited and regional integration not a priority.

ASEAN leaders also sought to socialize proto-internationalizing leaders in the continental Southeast Asian models in Cambodia, Laos, and Burma. Challenges to the tradition of non-intervention intensified with Myanmar's military junta's repeated repression and detention of opposition politician Aung San Suu Kyi. Military expenditures (MILEX) relative to gross domestic product (GDP) declined sharply across ASEAN states as the export-led model took root, from slightly above 5 per cent at their height in the 1970s, during the Cold War, to an average of 2.8 per cent in 1990.[38] They plummeted from a high of 5.4 per cent of GDP in the early 1960s (under Sukarno) to 1.2 per cent by the 1980s under Suharto in Indonesia. Thailand halved MILEX/GDP from 5 to 2.5 per cent, Malaysia reduced it from 5.6 to 3.9 per cent, Singapore and Brunei from 6.7 to 4.8 per cent, and Vietnam (after adopting the ASEAN model) from 19.4 to 4.7 per cent. The model's relative moderation in MILEX/GDP is suggested by two observations: (1) Growth in military expenditures remained far behind growth in GDP; and (2) MILEX/GDP in this region was lower than the 5 per cent average for industrializing regions in the 1980s, and about one-fourth to one-fifth that of Middle Eastern states. Buzan and Segal, as many others, argued that there have been "no highly focused competitive arms accumulations" or arms races in Southeast Asia.[39] The 1995 Southeast Asian Nuclear Weapon Free Zone Treaty, finalized a decade later, includes the right to trigger fact-finding missions and calls for referral to the International Court of Justice when disputes remain unresolved for over one month.[40]

In 1999 ASEAN leaders agreed to constitute an ASEAN Troika, an ad hoc body of foreign ministers able to address urgent concerns with regional peace and stability. The Troika was to operate in accordance with core principles of consensus and non-interference, and make recommendations to ASEAN Foreign Ministers. Indonesia and the Philippines swiftly rejected the Troika as a mechanism to address secessionist conflicts. Nor was the Troika activated in repeated impasses regarding Myanmar, or in the latter's border clash with Thailand. Thus, none of the more formal mechanisms have taken root yet. ASEAN's secretariat continues to be subordinated to national secretariats, no precise legal obligations have emerged, and parties have not resorted to the TAC's (Treaty of Amity and Cooperation) High Council dispute settlement, turning instead to the International Court of Justice. In October 2003 ASEAN approved the Bali Concord II and its three pillars: an ASEAN Security Community (proposed by Indonesia), an ASEAN Economic Community (proposed by Thailand), and an ASEAN Socio-cultural Community.

The synergies between economics and security were evident in formal statements: "For the sustainability of our region's economic development we affirmed the need for a secure political environment based on a strong foundation of mutual interests generated by economic cooperation."[41] The Concord II also reaffirmed ASEAN's commitment to enhance "economic linkages with the world economy", ASEAN competitiveness and investment environment, and adherence to the TAC as a fully functioning and effective code of conduct. As Bandoro argued, "the world will judge the impact of ASEAN's ninth summit on making Southeast Asia more attractive for foreign investment and its contribution to the stability and security of the region."[42] The Concord II refers to ASEAN as a "concert of Southeast Asian nations", pursuing the objectives of ASEAN Vision 2020 but not "a defence pact, military alliance or a joint foreign policy." The emphasis on the TAC's High Council as a "principal instrument" has yet to be realized. ASEAN's informal makeup is geared to "conflict-avoidance" rather than "conflict-resolution" or "dispute settlement".[43]

Neither moderate institutionalization towards formality nor ASEAN's growing embeddedness into seemingly significant broader regional frameworks such as the ARF can be imputed with improving bilateral relations among ASEAN members. Vietnam and Indonesia agreed on a maritime boundary in the South China Sea. Thailand and Burma resolved their interlocked border, drugs, and refugee disputes in 2001. In early 2003, Malaysia and Singapore agreed to settle the Pedra Branca dispute (Pulau Batu Putih, South Ledge, and Middle Rocks) through third party adjudication by the International Court of Justice, signalling that other disputes (over water, for instance) might be similarly settled. Prime Minister Abdullah Ahmad Badawi, who moved Malaysia away from Mahtahir's hybrid strategies, began nurturing closer relations with Singapore, allowing the latter's state-linked companies to invest in Malaysia. Malaysia and Indonesia resolved the long-standing dispute over Sipadan-Ligitan through the International Court of Justice as well, and Mahathir labelled relations between Thailand and Malaysia "the best model for the world".[44]

Finally, notwithstanding some limited police cooperation and multiple statements condemning terrorism, ASEAN never achieved strong multilateralism on terrorism, despite common fears that terrorism could stifle foreign investment and economic growth, pillars of their export-led strategy. The most effective cooperation on counter-terrorism has been bilateral (in particular Singapore with the Philippines but also Malaysia with Thailand and the Philippines), trilateral (Indonesia, Malaysia, Philippines), or between individual states and extra-regional actors. According to Jones and Smith, in the realm of counter-terrorism, ASEAN states — Singapore, Indonesia, the Philippines — have revealed a greater tendency to rely on bilateral cooperation with extra-regional states, particularly the US and Australia, than among states in the region.[45] Indeed, security services appear to compete more than collaborate, as domestic politics (such as concerns with Muslim constituencies in Indonesia) and obsessive concerns with national sovereignty foil both bilateral and multilateral regional security strategies. On narcotics, "coalitions of the willing" have superseded ASEAN's activities to make the region drug-free by 2012, including the quadrilateral forum between Thailand, Laos, Burma, and China. Thailand and the Philippines, not ASEAN, became involved in peacemaking efforts on Aceh, as was the case for efforts by Malaysia on Mindanao.

Regionalism

The concepts of regionalism and regionalization have also gained increased usage and, over time, some convergence in their meaning, although often varying across the positivist-constructivist divide. Haggard defined "regionalism" as economic integration or political cooperation, and regionalization — in the economic sense — as "an economic process in which trade and investment within a given region — however defined — grow more rapidly than the region's trade and investment with the rest of the world."[46] Hurrell distinguished between regionalism as description and as prescription, breaking it down into five analytically distinct categories: (1) regionalization, (2) regional awareness and identity, (3) regional interstate cooperation, (4) state-promoted regional integration, and (5) regional cohesion.[47] He defined "regionalization" as "the growth of societal integration within a region and the often undirected processes of social and economic interaction."[48] This is akin, he argued, to what used to be known as informal integration and was later referred to as "soft regionalism". It can also involve "increasing flows of people, the development of multiple channels and complex social networks by which ideas, political attitudes, and ways of thinking spread from one area to another, and the creation of transnational regional civil society." Mansfield and Milner defined regionalism as "the disproportionate concentration of economic flows or the coordination of foreign economic policies among a group of countries in close geographic proximity to one another."[49] They also extended the concept to apply to the concentration of political-military relations among geographically proximate states.

Marchand, Boas, and Shaw emphasize the globalizing, restructuring context of regionalization, which has an explicit *spatial* articulation.[50] Regionalization can, but need not necessarily, be state-led; other actors can be no less important, including NGOs, media, companies, and the informal sector. Regionalization can thus reflect counter-forces responding against globalization. By contrast, regionalism concerns ideas, identities, and ideologies related to a regional project. It is clearly a political project but not necessarily *state-led*. They also introduce the concept of region-ness/regionality to refer to the relative convergence of cultural affinity, political regimes, security arrangements and economic policies, and the creation of a regional identity. For Breslin and Higgott regionalism involves state-led cooperative projects, intergovernmental dialogues and treaties, whereas regionalization is a process driven mainly by market forces in the form of trade and investment flows.[51] Okawara and Katzenstein described regionalization as "geographic manifestations of political, military, economic or social processes" that can be both societal and governmental.[52] Ernst defined regionalization as "the integration, across national borders but within a macro-region, of markets for goods, capital, services, knowledge, and labor."[53]

Taking the term beyond the economic domain, Fawcett defined regionalism as aiming:

> to pursue and promote common goals in one or more issue areas. Understood thus, it ranges from promoting a sense of regional awareness or community (soft regionalism), through consolidating regional groups and networks, to pan- or sub-regional groups formalized by interstate arrangements and organizations (hard regionalism).... If regionalism is a policy or project, regionalization is both project and process. At its most basic it means no more than a concentration of activity at a regional level.[54]

Pempel offers similar distinctions. Regionalism "involves primarily the process of institution creation" involving top-down activities, deliberate projects involving government-to-government cooperation, designed to deal with common transnational problems, and often formalized in semi-permanent structures.[55]

By contrast, regionalization is a bottom up, societally driven process, the result of social construction, and not necessarily involving governmental bodies. Katzenstein defined regionalism in terms of institutionalized practices, and regionalization as "a process that engages actors".[56] For Munakata, regionalism refers to institutional frameworks set up by governments to promote regional economic integration, where various arrangements entail different levels of commitment by members.[57] She considers free trade agreements a solid form of regionalism. By contrast, regional consultative bodies that lack legally binding agreements — even if they promote economic integration — are a looser form of regionalism.

Networks

Another multilateral arrangement worth mentioning in this conceptual menu is that of networks, which are often differentiated from hierarchic and market structures. According to Kahler, the analysis of networks enables us to study and measure structures and patterns of relational ties between agents.[58] Networks are formed by states, ruling coalitions, transnational parties, regional institutions, and individuals. Networks are not necessarily aggregated in multilateral institutions but can help create such institutions, and can clearly emerge in their midst. An example of the latter is provided by the democratic regimes in Thailand and the Philippines, which acted as a network within ASEAN at some points in time. In this case, a bilateral network operated within a multilateral context. In other words, networks can be nested in or overlap with international or regional institutions. Sometimes these networks can be transformed into mini-lateral institutions within a broader multilateral institutional framework. Networks linking ruling coalitions oriented toward the global economy can transcend individual nation states and cooperate against domestic adversaries in individual countries who are interested in protectionism and import-substitution. Networks among sub-national actors in trade, environmental, scientific, crime, and other arenas can collaborate or compete; they can buttress state policies or undermine them; they can be marginal or powerful.

The study of networks focuses attention on the *relationship* rather than the unit (or node). At the same time, the structure of a network may illuminate why certain nodes acquire more centrality than others. In Southeast Asia, some consider Singapore to be a critical node in different networks related to economics and security. Others consider Malaysia, Singapore, and Indonesia to be key nodes in various ASEAN networks. Networks are important for understanding mutual dependence, the transmission of material and ideational resources across them, and the way in which networks can constrain states, ruling coalitions, or individuals.[59] Networks are available for the transmission of public goods (health and environmental groups) or public bads (terrorism, drugs). ASEAN itself may be conceived as a network but many functional sub-groups within ASEAN are also networks. These are networks nested in an institution but not every network exhibits formalized relations, although both can be instances of international governance. Networks can also come into existence because states or ruling coalitions or private groups prefer to circumvent formal bilateral or multilateral arrangements. Networks can promote cooperation but also conflict, for instance when nodes vie for control of particular transnational ethnic or crime-related networks. Informal networks can sometimes be more influential than formal institutions.

Forum Shopping

With so many options across the bilateral, regionalism/regionalization, and global multilateral spectrum, the rise of a new literature on forum shopping should be unsurprising. Which way do/should actors go? The concept of forum shopping is grounded in legal studies on venue choice in jurisdictionally compound settings,[60] and has found a home in the international relations literature on institutions. Where there are multiple institutional options available, actors can "forum" shop and strategically select the ones that fit their material or ideational preferences best.[61] Busch applies the term more specifically to the choice among different dispute settlement mechanisms.[62] Jupille finds forum shopping to be a consequence of the contemporary governance of international trade characterized by complex — overlapping and consequential — institutionalization, which creates opportunities.[63] Kellow and Zito studied how European actors can select from multiple international and European Union arenas in order to exploit and manipulate the agenda in advantageous ways.[64]

Thus, forum shopping can rely on precedent setting within one forum and use it to advance the agenda in another, more restrictive arena. There are strong incentives to form similar groups to counter the enhanced effectiveness of those using forum shopping.[65] Hafner-Burton studied forum shopping for human rights in the context of trade agreements, and found that states choose institutions that yield more satisfactory outcomes at reasonable costs, seeking almost always to economize rather than optimize.[66] Looking at international environmental law, Gillespie found that when disgruntled members of one international organization go forum shopping for others there is a risk of anarchy and damage to international law and community order.[67] Jupille found that forum shopping reduces problem-solving efficiency, shapes substantive policy outcomes, and tends to favour skill and power, thus undermining the rule of law.[68]

Pekkanen, Solis, and Katada argued that traditional schools in international relations and international political economy do not explain particularly well what forum is eventually chosen.[69] Some systemic theories would predict that states act in their own interests. More specifically, hegemonic stability theory would predict that hegemons declining in their relative economic position in the international system would be more likely to turn to regional and bilateral agreements and away from exclusively supporting multilateralism as in the World Trade Organization (WTO). Yet the shortcomings of this theory are very significant. For instance, Japan's move from a rejection of preferential regionalism till the mid-1990s to its embrace of FTA diplomacy by the late 1990s took place without fundamental changes in its economic capabilities. A second set of explanations for the politics of forum shopping is derived from positive political economics, domestic politics, sectoral interests, and leader's calculations of political survival. Pekkanen, Solis, and Katada find this approach deficient as well.[70] Nor do explanations for forum shopping suggesting that increased regional interdependence pushes states toward regional and bilateral agreements and away from exclusive support for multilateralism fare well, in their view. Instead, they propose a framework that defies the basic understanding stipulated in an earlier section that multilateralism is invariably about generalized principles of conduct and bilateralism invariably about specific reciprocity. A bilateral forum can be based on a generalizable principle of conduct, for instance one imported from a multilateral institution. States thus face a trade-off between the scope and flexibility of the underlying rules of different forums. Scope refers to the extent to which the underlying rules promise to maximize gains from trade by exacting liberalization commitments from a near-universal membership. Flexibility refers to the extent to which the underlying rules allow for sectoral exclusions, escape clauses, membership selection, and issue selection. This scope-flexibility trade-off, in their view, is the most important characteristic of forums. Since states seek to minimize political disruptions at home at the expense of optimizing economic gains abroad, states are forced to balance between scope and flexibility. A multilateral forum entails greater scope than its alternatives — large gains from trade and reduced transaction costs through standardization of rules — but also reduces flexibility. A bilateral forum falls significantly short in the scope dimension — small market gains, idiosyncratic rules — but scores high on flexibility (can exclude sectors, select issues, and, above all, choose suitable partners). Finally, regional forums lie somewhere in between those two extremes.

Busch also seeks to explain how states choose between institutions if they decide to file for dispute settlement.[71] The answer lies, in his view, in whether or not complainants wish to set a regional or multilateral precedent or no precedent at all. The key to forum shopping is whether the complainant favours a more "liberal" ruling (i.e., one promoting "freer trade") than what the PTA (preferential trade agreement) or WTO is expected to hand down, in relation to the status quo policies of the defendant *and* third parties. Since the complainant is also concerned about how this ruling might influence third parties, not just the defendant, the choice of forum is often counter-intuitive.

Thus, in addition to how the two dispute settlement institutions are expected to rule, the relative weight that the complainant places on its regional or multilateral trade influences the choice of forum. Again, this literature largely draws on political economy, but some of its insights are applicable to security and other issue areas. For instance, Hafner-Burton and Montgomery tested the proposition that mutual membership in PTAs significantly decreases the propensity of member states to sanction each other. They found that such membership has no clear effect on the propensity of states to sanction each other.[72] Increases in trade dependence independent of PTAs does decrease sanctioning behaviour, while relative differences in social power structures (created by PTA membership) or economic power (GDP) make sanctioning more likely.

Bilateralism

I have thus far reviewed various concepts used to refer to collective arrangements, including multilateralism, international and regional institutions, and regionalism. What about bilateralism? Ruggie identified the Nazi system as a typical form embodying bilateralism as its organizing principle.[73] Shortly after taking power, the Nazi government implemented a scheme of bilateralist trade agreements and monetary clearing arrangements devised by Hjalmar Schacht in 1934. Its essence was "reciprocal arrangements" with trading partners around the world that rendered those partners even more dependent on Germany. This example is important because a nominal definition of multilateralism would not exclude the Schachtian system, which was inherently discriminatory, unequal, and fundamentally bilateral. Yet not all bilateralism shares these traits. Pempel defined bilateralism as:

> two countries ... [ceding] particular privileges to one another that they do not give to other countries. Bilateralism also involves the normative belief among policymakers from both countries that dealings between them on most issues should be primarily dealt with through one-to-one governmental links; they should not generally involve the private sector, nor should they be settled in multilateral arenas.[74]

Dent defined economic bilateralism as an extension of regionalization, where two states are involved in enhancing cooperative and integrative arrangements.[75] Bilateralism, according to Ruggie, is premised on specific reciprocity, by which he means the simultaneous balancing of specific quid pro quos by each party with every other at all times (in contrast to multilateralism's diffuse reciprocity).[76]

The United States has forged bilateral arrangements across the Asia-Pacific region, in both economics and security, a system that followed a "hub and spokes" model. The five bilateral alliances (Australia, Japan, South Korea, the Philippines, and Thailand) are prominent examples.[77] In the security arena, Weber found bilateralism to be generally positive for great powers because they can threaten to leave the alliance and demand advantageous terms from less powerful countries.[78] Furthermore, Dent found bilateral arrangements to be easier to arrange than multilateral ones; stronger and more resourceful countries find them preferable because they tend to gain better terms than those of multilateral forums, with their checks and balances.[79]

Has economic bilateralism evolved differently from bilateralism in security affairs? Bilateral agreements once followed bilateral security alliances,[80] but bilateral trade agreements have now multiplied across the board, at a faster rate than regional and multilateral agreements. According to Krugman, bilateral and regional agreements are more protectionist towards third parties, affecting world trade negatively.[81] For others like Hanke, the rise of bilateralism is dangerous, potentially leading to a situation similar to the 1930s. Bhagwati, among the strongest opponents of the bilateralist trend in trade policy, argues that it could create ominous systemic problems in the global trading system, constituting a stumbling block to free trade.[82] Bond and Syropoulos found that trade liberalization in a customs union may make countries more aggressive in trade with external countries and undermine global free trade.[83] Aggarwal and Urata emphasize that bilateral agreements in the Asia Pacific region could decrease APEC's authority and exclude economies that compete or threaten U.S. interests.[84] Furthermore, it does not appear — at least in the short term — that bilateral FTAs will lead to more multilateral agreements. In contrast, Yarbrough and Yarbrough found that, notwithstanding the negative characterization of bilateralism for enhancing global trade liberalization, they could be a way of dealing with enforcement challenges.[85] Bilateralism can be one component in negotiating trade agreements that might not be implemented otherwise. Riezman identified cases in which bilateral trade agreements increase global free trade.[86] Others find bilateral agreements to increase competition. Bergsten argued that the trend towards bilateral/regional agreements will promote "competitive liberalization",[87] and Schott found bilateral agreements able to create opportunities to increase exports and reinforce crucial economic reforms.[88]

The debate over the mutually exclusive or mutually incompatible relationship between bilateralism and multilateralism is neither new nor settled. Acharya found bilateral agreements to have provided some foundation for multilateralism and regionalism in the Asia-Pacific region.[89] Others take a more nuanced view, arguing that bilateralism can increase multilateral ties sometimes but not others. In the case of Japan, Katzenstein and Okawara found bilateralism and multilateralism to be complementary to each other.[90] Dent distinguished between region-convergent and region-divergent bilateralism. The former may provide a sub-structural or "latticed" foundation for regionalism to develop. The latter can:

(1) undermine the integrity or capture key aspects of regional organizations
.... (2) increase convoluted patterns of reactive counter-balancing
manoeuvres amongst the region's constituent states, leading to potentially
hazardous inter-state rivalry ... (3) further exaggerate or reinforce power
asymmetries within a region, which in turn may work against regional
community-building, and ... (4) exacerbate the existing development
divide within a regional organization.[91]

Dent found a new pattern of bilateralism in Southeast Asian economic
diplomacy. From an extra-regional standpoint, an increasing number of
ASEAN states have gravitated toward Asia-Pacific bilateral free trade
agreements, with Singapore and Thailand at the forefront. From an
intra-regional standpoint, there appears to be an emerging Singapore-
Thailand bilateral alliance on matters of economic regionalism. This
bilateralism — based on both the deeper strategic intentions embedded
in their foreign economic policies and wider international political
economy considerations — is underpinning region-divergent outcomes
within Southeast Asia.

Why have bilateral trade agreements increased substantially? Ravenhill
explained this rise by pointing to an "increasing awareness of the
weakness of existing regional institutions and initiatives, perceptions of
positive demonstration effects from regional agreements in other parts
of the world, and changing domestic economic interests."[92] Tellis found
that India pursued increased bilateral ties with the United States in
part to increase India's capacity to defeat security threats.[93] Mansfield
and Reinhardt argued that developments at the heart of GATT/WTO
encourage members to form PTAs to gain bargaining leverage within
the multilateral regime.[94] Growth in GATT/WTO membership, periodic
multilateral trade negotiation rounds, participation — and losses in
— formal GATT/WTO disputes, have all arguably pushed members into
PTAs. According to Elkins, Guzman, and Simmons the spread of bilateral
investment treaties is driven by international competition for foreign direct
investment among potential host countries — typically developing ones
— who are more likely to sign bilateral investment treaties when their
competitors have done so.[95] This study also found some evidence that
coercion and learning play a role, but less support for cultural explanations
based on emulation. Kwei found trade-dependent countries in Asia
to be more likely to seek out bilateral agreements, except China, given its
size and rate of growth.[96] Competition for FDI as well as expected market
access gains in the United States have arguably driven the proposed US-

Thai FTA.[97] Aggarwal and Urata traced the spread of bilateral agreements to economic, political and institutional factors.[98] Regarding potential beneficiaries, Pempel and Urata found the bilateral agreement between Japan and Singapore (JESPA) to exemplify how powerful industries or countries can secure benefits that would otherwise be less likely in a multilateral setting.[99]

There are different views on the connection between growing regionalism and global multilateralism. For Kemp and Wan any group of countries can establish a PTA that does not degrade the welfare of either members or third parties; incentives exist for this arrangement to expand until it includes all states under global free trade.[100] Krugman and Summers note that because regional institutions reduce the number of actors engaged in multilateral negotiations, they also mute problems of bargaining and collective action (reduce transaction costs).[101] Others have highlighted the potential of these agreements to promote and consolidate domestic economic reforms which, in turn, enhance further multilateral openness. Others, such as Bhagwati, suggest that PTA expansion into universal free trade may not be guaranteed, particularly not in a welfare-enhancing way.[102] Bond and Syropoulos see the formation of customs unions as rendering multilateral trade liberalization more difficult by undercutting enforcement.[103] Krugman finds regional blocs to lead to higher external barriers and lower world welfare. Yet others, such as Bagwell and Staiger, impute PTAs with contradictory effects on the global trading system, concluding that "it is precisely when the multilateral system is working poorly that preferential agreements can have their most desirable effects on the multilateral system."[104]

An important research agenda, both conceptually and empirically, should include an understanding of the extent to which some of these debates are replicated in the study of security bilateralism.

Conclusions

This chapter has reviewed seven core concepts straddling the bilateral-multilateral spectrum in international relations: multilateralism, multilateral/regional institutions, regionalism versus regionalization, bilateralism, forum shopping, and networks. Another concept that is gaining some currency in the analysis and praxis of multilateralism is the concept of "democratic clubs", gathering democratic states only (the Organisation for Economic Development is often mentioned but there are also regional and sub-regional ones). These clubs need not be global or regional institutions; they can also operate as networks. The rationale sometimes given for these international forms lies in the perception that democratic states share basic features: they are more reliable allies; do not wage wars against each other; are more prone to join international institutions (particularly those with fellow democracies) and to abide by their international commitments; and prone to reduce civil war tensions.[105] By contrast, non-democracies are found to be more prone to "gamble for resurrection" by going to war; to lengthen wars; to tolerate higher war costs; and to defect from, or violate, international commitments. Anocracies (somewhere between democracies and non-democracies) are found to be more susceptible than the other two types to political instability and armed conflict, to genocide/politicide events and terrorist attacks, and to international crises.[106]

ASEAN offers a fruitful arena to explore the utility (or lack thereof) of the international relations concepts explored in this chapter. Does the ASEAN experience in the early twenty-first century suggest enhanced multilateralism, regionalism, regionalization, networks, forum shopping, or bilateralism? And what explains greater reliance on one form or another? Can enhanced multilateralism and bilateralism coexist, or are they of a zero-sum nature? How do domestic politics in each of these countries influence their preference for any of these various forms discussed here? Are ruling coalitions more strongly oriented to the global economy more prone to rely on cooperative forms of multilateralism than more inward-looking coalitions? Do levels of compliance differ across these different forms? For instance, is compliance with bilateral agreements higher or lower than with sub-regional or multilateral ones? Do levels of effectiveness vary across these different forms? Are the observed trends similar in the realm of security, economics, environmental, and other arenas, or do they instead exhibit different tendencies? Are there synergies among multilateral forms of cooperation? Does bilateralism beget more bilateralism, or is instead conducive to multilateral forms? Does bilateralism in economic relations spill-over to security relations or vice versa? Are there any signs that democratic clubs or networks could ever become important phenomena in Southeast Asia? And if so, how would this affect ASEAN itself? Is unilateralism, a category excluded from the menu in this enterprise, obsolete in this region? Are informal networks more influential than formal multilateral institutions? These are some of the questions that different chapters in this book can address, providing an important empirical foundation for exploring the state of conceptualization in the discipline of international relations.

NOTES

I would like to acknowledge the Social Science Research Council's Abe Fellowship Program for initial support for research on Southeast Asian multilateralism. I also benefited from comments by the editors and participants at the Hiroshima Peace Institute conferences in Hiroshima and Kuala Lumpur and from Maryam Komaie's excellent research assistance.

1   Robert O. Keohane, "The Contingent Legitimacy of Multilateralism", in *Multilateralism Under Challenge?* edited by Edward Newman, Ramesh Thakur, and John Tirman (New York: United Nations University Press, 2006), p. 731.

2   See John Gerard Ruggie, ed., *Multilateralism Matters: The Theory and Praxis of an Institutional Form* (New York: Columbia University Press, 1993).

3   John Gerard Ruggie, "Multilateralism: The Anatomy of an Institution", *International Organization* 46, no. 3 (1992), p. 566.

4   Ibid., p. 567.

5   Ibid., p. 567.

6   Ibid., p. 571.

7   See Keohane, "The Contingent Legitimacy of Multilateralism", pp. 56–76.

8   Ruggie, "Multilateralism: The Anatomy of an Institution", p. 594.

9   Ibid.

10 James Caporaso, "International Relations Theory and Multilateralism: The Search for Foundations", *International Organization* 46, no. 3 (1992): 601.

11 Ibid., p. 602.

12 Martha Finnemore, "Military Intervention and the Organization of International Politics", in *Collective Conflict Management and Changing World Politics*, edited by Joseph Lepgold and Thomas G. Weiss (Albany, NY: State University of New York Press, 1998), pp. 181–204; and Edward Luck, "The United States, International Organization, and the Quest for Legitimacy", in *Multilateralism & US Foreign Policy: Ambivalent Engagement*, edited by Stewart Patrick and Shepard Forman (Boulder, CO: Lynne Rienner), pp. 47–74.

13 G.J. Ikenberry, "Is American Multilateralism on the Decline?" *Perspectives on Politics* 30, no. 1 (2003): 534.

14 See Abram Chayes and Antonia Handler Chayes, *The New Sovereignty: Compliance with International Regulatory Agreements* (Cambridge: Harvard University Press, 1995).

[15] This sections builds on Etel Solingen, "The Genesis, Design and Effects of Regional Institutions: Lessons from East Asia and the Middle East", *International Studies Quarterly* 52, no. 1 (2008): 261–94. For an overview of the literature on international institutions, see Arthur A. Stein, "Neoliberal Institutionalism", in *The Oxford Handbook on International Relations*, edited by Christian Reus-Smit and Duncan Snidal (New York: Oxford University Press, 2008), pp. 201–21.

[16] Lisa Martin, "Interests, Power, and Multilateralism", *International Organization* 46, no. 4 (1992): 783.

[17] See Phil Williams, "Multilateralism: Critique and Appraisal", in *Multilateralism and Western Strategy*, edited by Michael Brenner (New York: St. Martin's Press), pp. 209–31.

[18] James G. March and Johan P. Olsen, "The Institutional Dynamics of International Political Orders", *International Organization* 52, no. 4 (1998): 943–69.

[19] Michael Barnett and Martha Finnemore, "The Politics, Power, and Pathologies of International Organizations", *International Organization* 53, no. 4 (1999): 699–732.

[20] Alastair Iain Johnston, *Social States: China in International Institutions, 1980–2000* (Princeton, NJ: Princeton University Press, 2008).

[21] See Thomas Risse-Kappen, *Cooperation Among Democracies: The European Influence on US Foreign Policy* (Princeton, NJ: Princeton University Press, 1995); and Anne-Marie Slaughter, "International Law in a World of Liberal States", *European Journal of International Law* 6, no. 1 (1995): 503–38.

[22] Barnett and Finnemore, "The Politics, Power, and Pathologies of International Organizations".

[23] Peter A. Hall and Rosemary C.R. Taylor, "The Potential of Historical Institutionalism: A Response to Hay and Wincott", *Political Studies* 46, no. 5 (1998): 958–63.

[24] See Oliver E. Williamson, *The Economic Institutions of Capital: Firms, Markets, Relational Contracting* (New York: The Free Press, 1985); Douglas C. North, *Structure and Change in Economic History* (New York: W.W. Norton, 1981); and Robert O. Keohane, *After Hegemony* (Princeton, NJ: Princeton University Press, 1984).

[25] Walter W. Powell and Paul J. DiMaggio, *The New Institutionalism in Organizational Analysis* (Chicago: The University of Chicago Press, 1991).

[26] Barbara Koremenos, Charles Lipson, and Duncan Snidal, "The Rational Design of International Institutions", *International Organization* 55, no. 2 (2001): 761–800.

[27] Judith Goldstein and Robert Keohane, eds., *Ideas and Foreign Policy: An Analytical Framework* (Ithaca, NY: Cornell University Press, 1993).

[28] Alastair Iain Johnston, "Treating International Institutions as Social Environments", *International Studies Quarterly* 45, no. 4 (2001): 487–515.

29 Stephen D. Krasner, "Global Communications and National Power: Life on the Pareto Frontier", *World Politics* 43, no. 3 (1991): 336–66.

30 Charles Lipson, "Why Are Some International Agreements Informal?" *International Organization* 45, no. 4 (1991): 495–538.

31 Stephan Haggard, "Regionalism in Asia and the Americas", in *The Political Economy of Regionalism*, edited by Edward D. Mansfield and Helen V. Milner (New York: Columbia University Press, 1997), pp. 20–49.

32 Ibid.

33 Kathleen Thelen, "Historical Institutionalism in Comparative Politics", *Annual Review of Political Science* 2 (1999), p. 400.

34 Ellis S. Krauss, "Japan, the US, and the Emergence of Multilateralism in Asia", *The Pacific Review* 13, no. 3 (2000): 473–94.

35 Miles Kahler, "Networked Politics: Agency, Power and Governance", in *Networked Politics: Agency, Power, and Governance*, edited by Miles Kahler (Ithaca, NY: Cornell University Press, 2009).

36 See Etel Solingen, "Southeast Asia in a New Era: Domestic Coalitions from Crisis to Recovery", *Asian Survey* 44, no. 2 (2004): 189–212; Etel Solingen, "ASEAN Cooperation: The Legacy of the Economic Crisis", *International Relations of the Asia-Pacific* 5, no. 1 (2005): 1–29; Etel Solingen, "The Genesis, Design and Effects of Regional Institutions.

37 For details on this model, see Andrew MacIntyre, *Business and Politics in Indonesia* (Sydney: Allen & Unwin, 1991); Etel Solingen, "ASEAN, Quo Vadis? Domestic Coalitions and Regional Cooperation", *Contemporary Southeast Asia* 21, no. 1 (1999): 30–53; and Kanishka Jayasuriya, "Southeast Asia's Embedded Mercantilism in Crisis: International Strategies and Domestic Coalitions", in *Non-Traditional Security Issues in Southeast Asia*, edited by A.T.H. Tan and J.D.K. Boutin (Singapore: Institute of Defence and Strategic Studies, 2001), pp. 26–53.

38 SIPRI Yearbooks, *IISS's The Military Balance*, 1995/96, pp. 266–67 and 1997/98, p. 295. On MILEX/GDP in ASEAN and on cross-regional comparisons, see Etel Solingen, "Mapping Internationalization: Domestic and Regional Impacts", *International Studies Quarterly* 45, no. 4 (2001): 517–56.

39 Barry G. Buzan and Gerald Segal, "Rethinking East Asian Security", *Survival* 36, no. 2 (1994): 3–21.

40 Amitav Acharya and Sola Ogunbanwo, "The Nuclear-Weapons-Free Zones in Southeast Asia and Africa", in *Armaments, Disarmament, and International Security*, SIPRI Yearbook (Stockholm: Stockholm International Peace Research Institute, 1998).

41 Press Statement by the Chairperson on the 9th ASEAN Summit and the 7th ASEAN+3 Summit, ASEAN Secretariat, 7 October 2003 <http://www.aseansec.org/15259.htm> (accessed 23 February 2009).

42 Bantarto Bandoro, "ASEAN's Bali Summit", *The Jakarta Post*, 1 October 2003.

43 Members have not resorted to dispute settlement under the TAC, favouring
    bilateral management of conflicts and the International Court of Justice. For
    ASEAN's basic documents, see <http://www.asean.or.id>.
44 "Mahathir Hails Malaysian-Thai Cooperation as 'Best Model' for World",
    Bernama (Kuala Lumpur), 27 July 2003.
45 David Martin Jones and Mark L.R. Smith, "Making Process, Not Progress:
    ASEAN and the Evolving East Asian Regional Order", *International Security*
    32, no. 1 (2007): 148–84.
46 Stephan Haggard, "Comment", in *Regionalism and Rivalry: Japan and the United
    States in Pacific Asia*, edited by Jeffrey A. Frankel and Miles Kahler (Chicago:
    University of Chicago Press, 1993), pp. 48–49.
47 Andrew Hurrell, "Regionalism in Theoretical Perspective", in *Regionalism
    in World Politics: Regional Organization and International Order*, edited by
    Louise Fawcett and Andrew Hurrell (Oxford: Oxford University Press, 1995),
    pp. 39–40.
48 Ibid.
49 Edward D. Mansfield and Helen V. Milner, eds., *The Political Economy of
    Regionalism* (New York: Columbia University Press, 1997), p. 3.
50 Marianne H. Marchand, Morten Boas, and Timothy M. Shaw, "The Political
    Economy of New Regionalisms", *Third World Quarterly* 20, no. 5 (1999):
    900.
51 Shaun Breslin and Richard Higgott, "Studying Regions: Learning from
    the Old, Constructing the New", *New Political Economy* 5, no. 3 (2001):
    333–52.
52 Peter J. Katzenstein and Nobuo Okawara, "Japan, Asian-Pacific Security, and
    the Case for Analytical Eclecticism", *International Security* 26, no. 3 (2001/2002):
    p. 166.
53 Dieter Ernst, "Searching for a New Role in East Asian Regionalization:
    Japanese Production Networks in the Electronics Industry", in *Beyond Japan:
    The Dynamics of East Asian Regionalism*, edited by Peter J. Katzenstein and
    Takashi Shiraishi (Ithaca: Cornell University Press, 2006), p. 163.
54 Louise Fawcett, "Exploring Regional Domains: A Comparative History of
    Regionalism", *International Affairs* 80, no. 3 (2004): 433.
55 T.J. Pempel, "Introduction: Emerging Webs of Regional Connectedness", in
    Remapping East Asia: The Construction of a Region, edited by T.J. Pempel (Ithaca:
    Cornell University Press, 2005), pp. 19–20.
56 Peter J. Katzenstein, "East Asia: Beyond Japan", in *Beyond Japan: The Dynamics
    of East Asian Regionalism*, edited by Peter J. Katzenstein, and Takashi Shiraishi
    (Ithaca: Cornell University Press, 2006), p. 1.
57 Naoko Munakata, "Has Politics Caught Up with Markets? In Search of East
    Asian Economic Regionalism", in *Beyond Japan: The Dynamics of East Asian
    Regionalism*, edited by Peter J. Katzenstein and Takashi Shiraishi (Ithaca:
    Cornell University Press, 2006), p. 130.

58   See Kahler, "Networked Politics: Agency, Power and Governance".
59   Emilie M. Hafner-Burton, Miles Kahler, and Alexander H. Montgomery, "Network Analysis for International Relations", *International Organization* 63, no, 3 (Summer 2009).
60   Joseph Jupille, *Trading Rules: Forum Shopping Within and Among International Institutions* (Draft Prospectus, 2006).
61   Gunnar Nielsson, "The Parallel National Action Process: Scandinavian Experiences", in *International Organization: A Conceptual Approach*, edited by P. Taylor and A. Groom (London: Frances Pinter, 1978), pp. 270–316; Aynsley Kellow, *International Toxic Risk Management: Ideals, Interests and Implementation* (Cambridge: Cambridge University Press, 1999); G. Dudley and R. Richardson, "Arenas without Rules and the Policy Change Process: Outsider Groups and British Roads Policy", *Political Studies* 44, no. 4 (1998): 727–47; and Aynsley Kellow and Anthony R. Zito, "Steering Through Complexity: EU Environmental Regulation in the International Context", *Political Studies* 50, no. 1 (2002): 43–60
62   Marc L. Busch, "Overlapping Institutions and Global Commerce: Forum Shopping for Dispute Settlement in International Trade", *International Organization* 61, no. 4 (2007): 735–61.
63   See Jupille, *"Trading Rules"*.
64   See Kellow and Zito, "Steering Through Complexity".
65   See Kellow, *International Toxic Risk Management*.
66   Emilie Hafner-Burton, "Forum Shopping for Human Rights: The Transformation of Preferential Trade". Manuscript was drafted for participation in the workshop on "Forum Shopping and Global Governance" at the European University Institute, Florence, Italy, 23–24 April 2004.
67   Alexander Gillespie, "Forum Shopping in International Environmental Law", *Ocean Development and International Law* 33, no. 1 (2002): 17–56.
68   Jupille, *"Trading Rules"*.
69   Saadia Pekkanen, Mireya Solis, and Saori Katada, "The Politics of Forum Shopping in International Trade: The Case of Japan". Paper presented at the Annual Meeting of the American Political Science Association (APSA), 1–4 September 2005.
70   Ibid.
71   See Busch, "Overlapping Institutions and Global Commerce".
72   Emilie M. Hafner-Burton and Alexander H. Montgomery, "Power or Plenty: How do International Trade Institutions Affect Economic Sanctions?" Paper prepared for presentation in the annual conference of the International Studies Association, San Diego, 22–25 March 2006 <http://www.princeton.edu/~pcglobal/conferences/institutions/papers/hafnerburton_F900.pdf> (accessed 23 February 2009).
73   See Ruggie, "Multilateralism: The Anatomy of an Institution", pp. 561–98.

74   T.J. Pempel, "Challenges to Bilateralism: Changing Foes, Capital Flows, and Complex Forums", in *Beyond Bilateralism: U.S.-Japan Relations in the New Asia Pacific*, edited by Ellis Krauss and T.J. Pempel (Stanford: Stanford University Press, 2004), pp. 1–36.

75   Christopher Dent, "The New Economic Bilateralism in Southeast Asia: Region-Convergent or Region-Divergent?" *International Relations of the Asia Pacific* 6 (2006), pp. 81–111.

76   Ruggie, "Multilateralism: The Anatomy of an Institution".

77   David L. Shambaugh, "China Engages Asia: Reshaping the Regional Order", *International Security* 29, no. 3 (2004): 64–99.

78   Steven Weber, "Shaping the Postwar Balance of Power: Multilateralism in NATO", *International Organization* 46, no. 3 (1992): 633–80.

79   Dent, "The New Economic Bilateralism in Southeast Asia".

80   Douglas A. Irwin, "Multilateral and Bilateral Trade Policies in the World System: A Historic Perspective". In *New Dimensions in Regional Integration*, edited by Jaime De Melo and Arvind Panagariya (Cambridge: Cambridge University Press, 1993), pp. 90–119.

81   Paul R. Krugman, "Is Bilateralism Bad?" in *International Trade and Trade Policy*, edited by Elhanan Helpman and Assaf Razin (Cambridge, MA: MIT Press, 1991), pp. 9–23.

82   Jagdish Bhagwati, "U.S. House of Representatives Committee on Financial Services Testimony" (USA: Subcommittee on Domestic and International Monetary Policy, Trade and Technology, 1 April 2003), p. 1991.

83   Eric W. Bond and Constantinos Syropoulos, "The Size of Trading Blocs: Market Power and World Welfare Effects", *Journal of International Economics* 40 (1996), pp. 411–38; and Constantinos Syropoulos, "Customs Unions and Comparative Advantage", *Oxford Economic Papers* 51, no. 2 (1999): 239–66.

84   Vinod K. Aggarwal and Shujiro Urata, eds., *Bilateral Trade Arrangements in the Asia-Pacific: Origins, Evolution, and Implications* (New York: Routledge, 2006).

85   Beth Yarbrough and Robert Yarbrough, "Reciprocity, Bilateralism, and Economic Hostages: Self-Enforcing Agreements in International Trade", *International Studies Quarterly* 30, no. 1 (1986): 7–21.

86   Raymond Riezman, "Can Bilateral Trade Agreements Help Induce Free Trade?" *Canadian Journal of Economics* 32 (2000): 751–66.

87   Fred C. Bergsten, "Competitive Liberalization and Global Free Trade: A Vision for the Early 21st Century", APEC Working Papers no. 96-15 (Washington, DC: Institute for International Economics, 1996).

88   Jeffrey J. Schott, "Free Trade Agreements: US Strategy and Priorities", unpublished manuscript (Washington, DC: Institute for International Economics, 2004).

[89] Amitav Acharya, "A Survey of Military Cooperation among the ASEAN States: Bilateralism or Alliance?" Occasional Paper No. 14 (Toronto: Centre for International and Strategic Studies, 1990).

[90] Katzenstein and Okawara, "Japan, Asian-Pacific Security, and the Case for Analytical Eclecticism".

[91] Dent, "The New Economic Bilateralism in Southeast Asia", p. 86.

[92] John Ravenhill, "The New Bilateralism in the Asia Pacific", *Third World Quarterly* 24, no. 2 (2002): 300.

[93] Ashley J. Tellis, "The Evolution of U.S.-Indian Ties: Missile Defense in an Emerging Strategic Relationship", *International Security* 30, no. 4 (2006): 113–51.

[94] Edward D. Mansfield and Eric Reinhardt, "Multilateral Determinants of Regionalism: The Effects of GATT/WTO on the Formation of Preferential Trading Arrangements", *International Organization* 57, no. 4 (2003): 829.

[95] Zachary Elkins, Andrew T. Guzman, and Beth A. Simmons, "Competing for Capital: The Diffusion of Bilateral Investment Treaties 1960–2000", *International Organization* 60, no. 4 (2006): 811–46.

[96] Elaine Kwei, "Chinese Trade Bilateralism: Politics Still in Command", in *Bilateral Trade Arrangements in the Asia-Pacific: Origins, Evolution, and Implications*, edited by Vinod K. Aggarwal and Shujiro Urata (New York: Routledge, 2006), pp. 117–39.

[97] Smitha Francis and Murali Kallumal, "US Bilateralism in South East Asia: A Sectoral Analysis of Market Access Issues in the Proposed Thai-US Free Trade Agreement". Paper Presented at the 2nd International Workshop on the ASEAN Expert Collaboration for FTA Negotiations with the U.S., co-organized by International Development Economics Associates (IDEAs), the Good Governance for Social Development and the Environmental Institute (GSEI), and the Institute of Asian Studies, Faculty of Political Science, Chulalongkorn University, Bangkok, 3–4 August 2006.

[98] Aggarwal and Urata, *Bilateral Trade Arrangements in the Asia-Pacific*.

[99] T.J. Pempel and Shujiro Urata, "Japan: A New Move Toward Bilateral Free Trade Agreements", in *Bilateral Trade Arrangements in the Asia-Pacific: Origins, Evolution, and Implications*, edited by Vinod K. Aggarwal (London: Routledge, 2006), pp. 75–94.

[100] Murray C. Kemp and Henry V. Wan, Jr., "An Elementary Proposition Concerning the Formation of Customs Unions", *Journal of International Economics* 6, no. 1 (1976): 95–97.

[101] Paul Krugman, "Regionalism Versus Multilateralism: Analytical Notes", in *New Dimensions in Regional Integration*, edited by Jaime de Melo and Arvind Panagariya (New York: Cambridge University Press, 1993), pp. 58–79; and Lawrence H. Summers, "Regionalism and the World Trading System", in *Policy Implications of Trade and Currency Zones: A Symposium*, sponsored by

the Federal Reserve Bank of Kansas City (Kansas City, MO: Federal Reserve Bank, 1991), pp. 295–301.

[102] Jagdish Bhagwati, "Regionalism and Multilateralism: An Overview", in *New Dimensions in Regional Integration*, edited by Jaime de Melo and Arvind Panagariya (New York: Cambridge University Press, 1993), pp. 22–51.

[103] Bond and Syropoulos, "The Size of Trading Blocs: Market Power and World Welfare Effects".

[104] Kyle Bagwell and Robert W. Staiger, "Regionalism and Multilateral Tariff Cooperation", NBER Working Paper 5921 (Cambridge, MA: National Bureau of Economic Power, 1997), pp. 594–95.

[105] For an overview of these findings, see Etel Solingen, *Nuclear Logics: Contrasting Paths in East Asia and the Middle East* (Princeton: Princeton University Press, 2007); Etel Solingen, "The Global Context of Comparative Politics", in *Comparative Politics: Rationality, Culture, and Structure*, edited by Mark I. Lichbach and Alan S. Zuckerman (New York: Cambridge University Press, 2009), pp. 220–59; and Etel Solingen, "Economic and Political Liberalization in China: Implications for US-China Relations", in *Power and Restraint: A Shared Vision for the U.S.-China Relationship*, edited by Richard Rosecrance and Gu Guoliang (New York: Public Affairs, 2009), pp. 67–78.

[106] See Joseph Hewitt, Jonathan Wilkenfeld, and Ted Robert Gurr, *Peace and Conflict 2008: Executive Summary* (University of Maryland: Center for International Development and Conflict Management, 2008), p. 13. <http://www.cidcm.umd.edu/pc/executive_summary/pc_es_20070613.pdf> (accessed 23 February 2009).

REFERENCES

Acharya, Amitav. "A Survey of Military Cooperation among the ASEAN States: Bilateralism or Alliance?" Occasional Paper No. 14. Toronto: Centre for International and Strategic Studies, 1990.

Acharya, Amitav and Sola Ogunbanwo. "The Nuclear-Weapons-Free Zones in Southeast Asia and Africa". In *Armaments, Disarmament, and International Security*, SIPRI Yearbook. Stockholm: Stockholm International Peace Research Institute, 1998.

Aggarwal, Vinod K. and Shujiro Urata, eds. *Bilateral Trade Arrangements in the Asia-Pacific: Origins, Evolution, and Implications*. New York: Routledge, 2006.

Bagwell, Kyle and Robert W. Staiger. "Regionalism and Multilateral Tariff Cooperation". NBER Working Paper 5921. Cambridge, MA: National Bureau of Economic Power, 1997.

Bandoro, Bantarto. "ASEAN's Bali Summit". *The Jakarta Post*, 1 October 2003.

Barnett, Michael and Martha Finnemore. "The Politics, Power, and Pathologies of International Organizations". *International Organization* 53, no. 4 (1999): 699–732.

Bergsten, Fred C. "Competitive Liberalization and Global Free Trade: A Vision for the Early 21st Century". APEC Working Papers no. 96-15. Washington, DC: Institute for International Economics, 1996.

———. "Regionalism and Multilateralism: An Overview". In *New Dimensions in Regional Integration*, edited by Jaime de Melo and Arvind Panagariya. New York: Cambridge University Press, 1993.

Bhagwati, Jagdish. "U.S. House of Representatives Committee on Financial Services Testimony Subcommittee on Domestic and International Monetary Policy, Trade and Technology", 1 April 2003.

Bond, Eric W. and Constantinos Syropoulos. "The Size of Trading Blocs: Market Power and World Welfare Effects". *Journal of International Economics* 40 (1996): 411–38.

———. "Trading Blocs and the Sustainability of Interregional Cooperation". In *The New Transatlantic Economy*, edited by Matthew B. Canzoneri, Wilfred J. Ethier, and Vittorio Grilli. Cambridge: Cambridge University Press, 1996.

Breslin, Shaun and Richard Higgott. "Studying Regions: Learning from the Old, Constructing the New". *New Political Economy* 5, no. 3 (2001): 333–52.

Busch, Marc L. "Overlapping Institutions and Global Commerce: Forum Shopping for Dispute Settlement in International Trade". *International Organization* 61, no. 4 (2007): 735–61.

Buzan, Barry G. and Gerald Segal. "Rethinking East Asian Security". *Survival* 36, no. 2 (1994): 3–21.

Caporaso, James. "International Relations Theory and Multilateralism: The Search for Foundations". *International Organization* 46, no. 3 (1992): 599–632.

Chayes, Abram and Antonia Handler Chayes. *The New Sovereignty: Compliance with International Regulatory Agreements*. Cambridge: Harvard University Press, 1995.

Dent, Christopher. "The New Economic Bilateralism in Southeast Asia: Region-Convergent or Region-Divergent?" *International Relations of the Asia Pacific* 6 (2006): 81–111.

Dudley, G. and Richardson, R. "Arenas Without Rules and the Policy Change Process: Outsider Groups and British Roads Policy". *Political Studies* 44, no. 4 (1998): 727–47.

Elkins, Zachary, Andrew T. Guzman, and Beth A. Simmons. "Competing for Capital: The Diffusion of Bilateral Investment Treaties 1960–2000". *International Organization* 60, no. 4 (2006): 811–46.

Ernst, Dieter. "Searching for a New Role in East Asian Regionalization: Japanese Production Networks in the Electronics Industry". In *Beyond Japan: The*

Dynamics of East Asian Regionalism, edited by Peter J. Katzenstein and Takashi Shiraishi. Ithaca: Cornell University Press, 2006.

Fawcett, Louise. "Exploring Regional Domains: A Comparative History of Regionalism". *International Affairs* 80, no. 3 (2004): 429–46.

Finnemore, Martha. "Military Intervention and the Organization of International Politics". In *Collective Conflict Management and Changing World Politics*, edited by Joseph Lepgold and Thomas G. Weiss. Albany, NY: State University of New York Press, 1998.

Francis, Smitha and Murali Kallumal. "US Bilateralism in South East Asia: A Sectoral Analysis of Market Access Issues in the Proposed Thai-US Free Trade Agreement". Paper presented at the Second International Workshop on the ASEAN Expert Collaboration for FTA Negotiations with the US, co-organized by International Development Economics Associates, the Good Governance for Social Development and the Environmental Institute, and the Institute of Asian Studies, Faculty of Political Science, Chulalongkorn University, Bangkok, 3–4 August 2006.

Gillespie, Alexander. "Forum Shopping in International Environmental Law". *Ocean Development and International Law* 33, no. 1 (2002): 17–56.

Goldstein, Judith and Keohane, Robert, eds. *Ideas and Foreign Policy: An Analytical Framework*. Ithaca, NY: Cornell University Press, 1993.

Hafner-Burton, Emilie. "Forum Shopping for Human Rights: The Transformation of Preferential Trade". Manuscript was drafted for participation in the workshop on "Forum Shopping and Global Governance" at the European University Institute, Florence, Italy 23–24 April 2004, for presentation at the American Political Science Association in Washington, DC, 1–4 September 2005.

Hafner-Burton, Emilie M., Miles Kahler, and Alexander H. Montgomery. "Network Analysis for International Relations". *International Organization* 63, no. 3 (Summer 2009).

Hafner-Burton, Emilie M. and Alexander H. Montgomery. "Power or Plenty: How do International Trade Institutions Affect Economic Sanctions?" Paper prepared for presentation in the annual conference of the International Studies Association, San Diego, 22–25 March 2006. <http://www.princeton.edu/~pcglobal/conferences/institutions/papers/hafnerburton_F900.pdf> (accessed 23 February 2009).

Haggard, Stephan. "Comment". In *Regionalism and Rivalry: Japan and the United States in Pacific Asia*, edited by Jeffrey A. Frankel and Miles Kahler. Chicago: University of Chicago Press, 1993.

———. "Regionalism in Asia and the Americas". In *The Political Economy of Regionalism*, edited by Edward D. Mansfield and Helen V. Milner. New York: Columbia University Press, 1997.

Hall, Peter A. and Rosemary C.R. Taylor. "The Potential of Historical Institutionalism: A Response to Hay and Wincott". *Political Studies* 46, no. 5 (1998): 958–63.

Hurrell, Andrew. "Regionalism in Theoretical Perspective". In *Regionalism in World Politics: Regional Organization and International Order*, edited by Louise Fawcett and Andrew Hurrell. Oxford: Oxford University Press, 1995.

Ikenberry, G.J. "Is American Multilateralism on the Decline?" *Perspectives on Politics* 30, no. 1 (2003): 533–50.

Irwin, Douglas A. "Multilateral and Bilateral Trade Policies in the World System: A Historic Perspective". In *New Dimensions in Regional Integration*, edited by Jaime De Melo and Arvind Panagariya. Cambridge: Cambridge University Press, 1993.

Jayasuriya, Kanishka. "Southeast Asia's Embedded Mercantilism in Crisis: International Strategies and Domestic Coalitions." In *Non-Traditional Security Issues in Southeast Asia*, edited by A.T.H. Tan and J.D.K. Boutin. Singapore: Institute of Defence and Strategic Studies, 2001.

Johnston, Alastair Iain. "Treating International Institutions as Social Environments". *International Studies Quarterly* 45, no. 4 (2001): 487–515.

———. *Social States: China in International Institutions, 1980–2000*. Princeton, NJ: Princeton University Press, 2008.

Jones, David Martin and Mark L.R. Smith. "Making Process, Not Progress: ASEAN and the Evolving East Asian Regional Order". *International Security* 32, no. 1 (2007): 148–84.

Jupille, Joseph. *Trading Rules: Forum Shopping Within and Among International Institutions*. Draft Prospectus, 2006.

Kahler, Miles. "Conclusion: The Causes and Consequences of Legalization". *International Organization* 54, no. 3 (2000): 661–84.

———. "Networked Politics: Agency, Power and Governance". In *Networked Politics: Agency, Power, and Governance*, edited by Miles Kahler. Ithaca, NY: Cornell University Press, 2009.

Katzenstein, Peter J. "East Asia: Beyond Japan". In *Beyond Japan: The Dynamics of East Asian Regionalism*, edited by Peter J. Katzenstein and Takashi Shiraishi. Ithaca: Cornell University Press, 2006.

Katzenstein, Peter J. and Okawara, Nobuo. "Japan, Asian-Pacific Security, and the Case for Analytical Eclecticism". *International Security* 26, no. 3 (2001/2002): 153–85.

Kellow, Aynsley. *International Toxic Risk Management: Ideals, Interests and Implementation*. Cambridge: Cambridge University Press, 1999.

Kellow, Aynsley and Anthony R. Zito. "Steering Through Complexity: EU Environmental Regulation in the International Context". *Political Studies* 50, no. 1 (2002): 43–60.

Kemp, Murray C. and Henry V. Wan, Jr. "An Elementary Proposition Concerning the Formation of Customs Unions". *Journal of International Economics* 6, no. 1 (1976): 95–97.

———. *After Hegemony*. Princeton: Princeton University Press, 1984.

———. "Multilateralism: An Agenda for Research". *International Journal* 45 (1990): 731–64.

Keohane, Robert O. "The Contingent Legitimacy of Multilateralism". In *Multilateralism Under Challenge?* edited by Edward Newman, Ramesh Thakur, and John Tirman. New York: United Nations University Press, 2006.

Koremenos, Barbara, Charles Lipson, and Duncan Snidal. "The Rational Design of International Institutions". *International Organization* 55, no. 2 (2001): 761–800.

Krasner, Stephen D. "Global Communications and National Power: Life on the Pareto Frontier". *World Politics* 43, no. 3 (1991): 336–66.

Krauss, Ellis S. "Japan, the US, and the Emergence of Multilateralism in Asia". *The Pacific Review* 13, no. 3 (2000): 473–94.

Krugman, Paul R. "Is Bilateralism Bad?" In *International Trade and Trade Policy*, edited by Elhanan Helpman and Assaf Razin. Cambridge, MA: MIT Press, 1991.

———. "Regionalism Versus Multilateralism: Analytical Notes". In *New Dimensions in Regional Integration*, edited by Jaime de Melo and Arvind Panagariya. New York: Cambridge University Press, 1993.

Kwei, Elaine. "Chinese Trade Bilateralism: Politics Still in Command". In *Bilateral Trade Arrangements in the Asia-Pacific: Origins, Evolution, and Implications*, edited by Vinod K. Aggarwal and Shujiro Urata. New York: Routledge, 2006.

Lipson, Charles. "Why Are Some International Agreements Informal?" *International Organization* 45, no. 4 (1991): 495–538.

Luck, Edward. "The United States, International Organization, and the Quest for Legitimacy". In *Multilateralism & US Foreign Policy: Ambivalent Engagement*, edited by Stewart Patrick and Shepard Forman. Boulder, CO: Lynne Rienner, 2002.

MacIntyre, Andrew. *Business and Politics in Indonesia*. Sydney: Allen & Unwin, 1991.

Mansfield, Edward D. and Helen V. Milner, eds. *The Political Economy of Regionalism*. New York: Columbia University Press, 1997.

Mansfield, Edward D. and Eric Reinhardt. "Multilateral Determinants of Regionalism: The Effects of GATT/WTO on the Formation of Preferential Trading Arrangements". *International Organization* 57, no. 4 (2003): 829–62.

March, James G. and Johan P. Olsen. "The Institutional Dynamics of International Political Orders". *International Organization* 52, no. 4 (1998): 943–69.

Marchand, Marianne H., Morten Boas, and Timothy M. Shaw. "The Political Economy of New Regionalisms". *Third World Quarterly* 20, no. 5 (1999): 897–910.

Martin, Lisa. "Interests, Power, and Multilateralism". *International Organization* 46, no. 4 (1992): 765–92.

Munakata, Naoko. "Has Politics Caught Up with Markets? In Search of East Asian Economic Regionalism". In *Beyond Japan: The Dynamics of East Asian*

Regionalism, edited by Peter J. Katzenstein and Takashi Shiraishi, 130–57. Ithaca: Cornell University Press, 2006.

Nielsson, Gunnar. "The Parallel National Action Process: Scandinavian Experiences". In *International Organization: A Conceptual Approach*, edited by P. Taylor and A. Groom. London: Frances Pinter, 1978.

North, Douglas C. *Structure and Change in Economic History*. New York: W.W. Norton, 1981.

Okawara, Nobuo and Peter J. Katzenstein. "Japan and Asian-Pacific Security: Regionalization, Entrenched Bilateralism, and Incipient Multilateralism". *Pacific Review* 14, no. 2 (2001): 165–94.

Pekkanen, Saadia, Mireya Solis, and Saori Katada. "The Politics of Forum Shopping in International Trade: The Case of Japan". Paper presented at the Annual Meeting of the American Political Science Association, 1–4 September 2005.

Pempel, T.J. "Challenges to Bilateralism: Changing Foes, Capital Flows, and Complex Forums". In *Beyond Bilateralism: U.S.-Japan Relations in the New Asia Pacific*, edited by Ellis Krauss and T.J. Pempel. Stanford: Stanford University Press, 2004.

———. "Introduction: Emerging Webs of Regional Connectedness". In *Remapping East Asia: The Construction of a Region*, edited by T.J. Pempel. Ithaca: Cornell University Press, 2005.

Pempel, T.J. and Shujiro Urata. "Japan: A New Move Toward Bilateral Free Trade Agreements". In *Bilateral Trade Arrangements in the Asia-Pacific: Origins, Evolution, and Implications*, edited by Vinod K. Aggarwal. London: Routledge, 2006.

Powell, Walter W. and Paul J. DiMaggio. *The New Institutionalism in Organizational Analysis*. Chicago: The University of Chicago Press, 1991.

Ravenhill, John. "The New Bilateralism in the Asia Pacific". *Third World Quarterly* 24, no. 2 (2002): 299–317.

Riezman, Raymond. "Can Bilateral Trade Agreements Help Induce Free Trade?" *Canadian Journal of Economics* 32 (2000): 751–66.

Risse-Kappen, Thomas. *Cooperation Among Democracies: The European Influence on US Foreign Policy*. Princeton, NJ: Princeton University Press, 1995.

Ruggie, John Gerard. "Multilateralism: The Anatomy of an Institution". *International Organization* 46, no. 3 (1992): 561–98.

———, ed. *Multilateralism Matters: The Theory and Praxis of an Institutional Form*. New York: Columbia University Press, 1993.

Schott, Jeffrey J. "Free Trade Agreements: US Strategy and Priorities". Unpublished manuscript. Washington, DC: Institute for International Economics, 2004.

Shambaugh, David L. "China Engages Asia: Reshaping the Regional Order". *International Security* 29, no. 3 (2004): 64–99.

Slaughter, Anne-Marie. "International Law in a World of Liberal States". *European Journal of International Law* 6, no. 1 (1995): 503–38.

Solingen, Etel. "ASEAN, Quo Vadis? Domestic Coalitions and Regional Cooperation". *Contemporary Southeast Asia* 21, no.1 (1999): 30–53.

———. "Mapping Internationalization: Domestic and Regional Impacts". *International Studies Quarterly* 45, no. 4 (2001): 517–56.

———. "Southeast Asia in a New Era: Domestic Coalitions from Crisis to Recovery". *Asian Survey* 44, no. 2 (2004): 189–212.

———. "ASEAN Cooperation: The Legacy of the Economic Crisis". *International Relations of the Asia-Pacific* 5, no. 1 (2005): 1–29.

———. *Nuclear Logics: Contrasting Paths in East Asia and the Middle East*. Princeton: Princeton University Press, 2007.

———. "The Genesis, Design and Effects of Regional Institutions: Lessons from East Asia and the Middle East". *International Studies Quarterly* 52, no. 1 (2008): 261–94.

———. "Economic and Political Liberalization in China: Implications for US-China Relations". In *Power and Restraint: A Shared Vision for the U.S.-China Relationship*, edited by Richard Rosecrance and Gu Guoliang. New York: Public Affairs, 2009.

———. "The Global Context of Comparative Politics". In *Comparative Politics: Rationality, Culture, and Structure*, edited by Mark I. Lichbach and Alan S. Zuckerman. New York: Cambridge University Press, 2009.

Stein, Arthur A. "Neoliberal Institutionalism". In *The Oxford Handbook on International Relations*, edited by Christian Reus-Smit and Duncan Snidal. New York: Oxford University Press, 2008.

Summers, Lawrence H. "Regionalism and the World Trading System". In *Policy Implications of Trade and Currency Zones: A Symposium*, sponsored by the Federal Reserve Bank of Kansas City. Kansas City, MO: Federal Reserve Bank, 1991.

Syropoulos, Constantinos. "Customs Unions and Comparative Advantage". *Oxford Economic Papers* 51, no. 2 (1999): 239–66.

Tellis, Ashley J. "The Evolution of U.S.-Indian Ties: Missile Defense in an Emerging Strategic Relationship". *International Security* 30, no. 4 (2006): 113–51.

Thelen, Kathleen. "Historical Institutionalism in Comparative Politics". *Annual Review of Political Science* 2 (1999): 369–404.

Weber, Steven. "Shaping the Postwar Balance of Power: Multilateralism in NATO". *International Organization* 46, no. 3 (1992): 633–80.

Williams, Phil. "Multilateralism: Critique and Appraisal". In *Multilateralism and Western Strategy*, edited by Michael Brenner, pp. 209–31. New York: St. Martin's Press, 1995.

Williamson, Oliver E. *The Economic Institutions of Capital: Firms, Markets, Relational Contracting*. New York: The Free Press, 1985.

Yarbrough, Beth and Robert Yarbrough. "Reciprocity, Bilateralism, and Economic Hostages: Self-Enforcing Agreements in International Trade". *International Studies Quarterly* 30, no. 1 (1986): 7–21.

2

Southeast Asian International Relations: Is There Institutional Traction?

Sheldon W. Simon

Regionalism in contemporary Southeast Asia began inauspiciously in the 1950s with the Bandung Conference and the ill fated Association of Southeast Asia (ASA) and Malaysia-Philippines-Indonesia (Maphilindo) — separate efforts to organize mainland and insular Southeast Asia. Nor was the Southeast Asia Treaty Organization (SEATO) any more successful, a weak American attempt to create a multilateral Western alliance for Southeast Asia against Soviet and Chinese challenges to the region's political future. Only in the late 1960s did non-communist Southeast Asian states create an indigenous political organization — ASEAN — that has survived and even prospered over the past forty years, producing a number of spinoff organizations with expanded memberships including the great powers. The family consisting of ASEAN Plus Ones, ASEAN Plus Three, the ASEAN Regional Forum (ARF), the Asia Pacific Economic Cooperation (APEC) forum, and most recently the East Asia Summit constitute the most elaborate politico-security-economic combination of international bodies in the developing world. But how effective are they? Have ASEAN and its institutional offspring gained traction? Do they function as a security community? Have they aggregated political and economic interests collectively? Have they presented a united political front to other states? And have they worked together to resolve their internal security problems and protect each other against external threats?

Until the Asian financial crisis of 1997–98, ASEAN was generally considered the most successful multinational political organization among developing countries in the world.[1] ASEAN's international reputation was burnished in the 1980s by its ability to keep the United Nations focused on the necessity of repelling Vietnam's invasion and occupation of Cambodia. Hanoi's subsequent withdrawal — though achieved because of the Chinese-Soviet rapprochement — was seen as a major ASEAN victory. ASEAN also arranged annual meetings between the Association and the great powers (the United States, China, Japan, and the European Union) to discuss an agenda of political, economic, and security issues generated by the Southeast Asian states.

This record of Southeast Asian states playing well above their collective weights in global politics apparently came to an end in the late 1990s due to a series of regional challenges to which ASEAN has been unable to respond effectively. These included the region's financial crisis; the Indonesian-generated forest fire haze that periodically blankets Singapore, Malaysia, and the southern Philippines; the upheaval and elections in East Timor leading to its independence; and the 1997 Cambodian coup which overturned the results of a UN-sponsored and ASEAN-endorsed election. All of these created what the late Michael Leifer called "a clear failure of regional cooperation" and have led to a crisis of regional identity and credibility within ASEAN.[2] Nor has ASEAN been of help in resolving persistent sub-regional tensions, including the Thai-Myanmar confrontation over the latter's drug trafficking and allegations by Myanmar that Thailand provides sanctuary for Myanmar's Karen minority, who are fighting to create a separate homeland; Thai concerns about support from northern Malaysia to separatists in southern Thailand, some of whom seek to unite with their Malay brethren across the Malaysian border; discord between Kuala Lumpur and Jakarta over hundreds of thousands of illegal Indonesian workers seeking jobs in Malaysia and a similar problem with illegal Philippine labourers in Sabah; and the ongoing saga over the future of the Spratly Islands, where

China, Taiwan, Vietnam, Malaysia, the Philippines, and Brunei contest ownership and sometimes seize each other's fishing boats for alleged maritime territory violations.

The primary reason for ASEAN's inability to deal effectively with these issues is its normative attachment to the principle of non-interference. If regionalism is to be more than a process of multilateral policy coordination and negotiation of competing stakeholder interests, then a sense of collective intersubjective identity among the region's members is required. ASEAN has not yet achieved this identity, though efforts have been made in the middle of this decade to overcome this obstacle. The new ASEAN Charter adopted at the association's November 2007 fortieth anniversary summit constitutes a significant effort to modify the non-interference norm[3] (see the discussion below).

From its inception in 1967, ASEAN embedded a non-interference norm that stipulated consultation, consensus, and non-interference with respect to its members' internal affairs, as well as any disagreements with each other. The consensus requirement reassured members that sovereignty would remain inviolate, and the domination of the sovereignty principle meant that serious differences among members would be deferred to defuse conflict. Thus, ASEAN's approaches to conflict were not geared to external threats but rather to helping its members achieve regime security vis-à-vis their neighbours through confidence-building via consultations. This "soft security" approach has contrasted sharply with U.S. bilateral security arrangements in Asia, which are geared exclusively to external threats.[4]

Already weakened by the financial crisis and the challenges listed above, Southeast Asia now has to cope with the post–11 September world. Though national responses varied, generally the region has gone through four stages: initially shock and sympathy, then concern and anger over the U.S. wars in Afghanistan and Iraq, because both are Muslim countries. Anger at the American invasion of Afghanistan was followed by a third stage, discovery of a major bomb plot in Singapore (January 2002) and the signing of a U.S.-ASEAN anti-terrorist agreement in August 2002. Finally, there were the October 2002 and August 2003 Bali and Jakarta Marriott bombings — the worst terrorist acts in the region's history, killing over 200 people — which heralded unprecedented cooperation among regional and foreign law enforcement agencies in Southeast Asia. This new cooperation was reinforced by the 2004 bombing of the Australian Embassy in Jakarta and a second bombing in Bali in 2005.[5]

Paradoxically, the post–11 September terrorist challenge may provide ASEAN with an opportunity to restore cohesion and create a new security agenda, similar to the opportunity that emerged with Vietnam's occupation of Cambodia in the 1980s. Of course, the nature of the threat is different. Instead of a heavily armed state, today the threat is from individuals in relatively small groups operating transnationally that endanger an entire region, requiring governments to cooperate on a priority basis if the threat is to be suppressed. Whether ASEAN is up to this challenge remains to be seen. Clearly, the non-interference norm must be revisited, as the terrorist challenge necessitates regional collaboration in suppressing terrorist cells that operate transnationally.

Meanwhile, bilateral strife within Southeast Asia continues. Anti-Thai riots in Cambodia in early 2003, which led to the razing of the Thai Embassy, constitute a dramatic example of persistent historical animosities lying below the surface of common ASEAN membership. Cambodia's delays in creating a tribunal to deal with the former Khmer Rouge leaders (finally convened in 2007) and the country's endemic corruption have kept foreign loans, grants, and investments at bay and mire the country in poverty. There are rising tensions along Indonesia's land border with Malaysia in Borneo. Following the World Court's ruling in December 2002 that the disputed islands of Sipadan and Ligitan belonged to Malaysia, Jakarta has been looking for ways to guarantee its sovereignty over other disputed islands and to protect its vast maritime boundaries from smugglers, poachers, and pirates. Given its minimal navy, however, that may be impossible.

Indonesia and the Philippines resent Malaysia's expulsion of illegal foreign workers in order to free up more jobs for locals. Malaysia has rekindled animosities with Singapore over water arrangements, contested islands (as their navies monitor each other), and competing port facilities for international maritime commerce. In 2005–6, tensions arose between Thailand and Malaysia over southern Thai Muslim separatists of Malay ethnicity who might have crossed into northern Malaysia to escape the Thai army and police.[6]

In light of bilateral tensions within ASEAN, the Association's apparently meagre ability to deal with current regional challenges, including Indonesian forest fires; separatist movements in Indonesia, the Philippines, and southern Thailand; transnational arms smuggling; illegal population movements; drug trafficking; and terrorism, the question arises: *Whither security regionalism?*

The remainder of this chapter is devoted to assessing whether there are significant roles for ASEAN and the ASEAN Regional Forum (ARF) in meeting these challenges and how other regional arrangements are being created to fill the gaps. While it would be fair to say neither ASEAN nor the ARF are leading efforts to resolve the challenges listed above, neither are they irrelevant. The questions for their future effectiveness focus on the structural limits to their capabilities and identifying the norms that might enhance their roles in conflict resolution.

ASEAN: Has Expansion led to the "Peter Principle?"

If the five original members of ASEAN — Malaysia, Singapore, Thailand, the Philippines, and Indonesia — collaborating since the Association's 1967 inception, remain suspicious of each other and wary of multilateral cooperation, how has expansion to all ten Southeast Asian states affected the organization's cohesion? Unsurprisingly, this development has had a negative impact. In economic affairs, a two-tier system has been created whereby progress toward an ASEAN Free Trade Area posed one set of deadlines for the first six members (2003) and an indefinite delay for the four newest members (Vietnam, Laos, Cambodia, and Myanmar), though 2010 is the target date. With respect to security, when law enforcement investigations revealed that terrorists moved readily among several ASEAN states because of visa-free travel, porous borders, and corrupt immigration officials, ASEAN has done little to remedy the situation.[7] Intra-ASEAN differences over the long-standing norm of non-interference are difficult to overcome, even when all members face a common threat.

The peaceful settlement of international disputes is a core ASEAN norm. However, ASEAN expansion imposes new security burdens arising from unsettled maritime boundaries and overlapping maritime exclusive economic zones. Territorial disputes between Thailand-Vietnam, Vietnam-Cambodia, and Thailand-Myanmar challenge the ASEAN non-use-of-force norm embodied in the 1976 Treaty of Amity and Cooperation (TAC). For example, Thailand's and Myanmar's forces clash sporadically over ethnic minority insurgents along their common border, as well as Myanmar-based drug trafficking. Whether ASEAN's new members can be socialized into the interpersonal and informal way in which the association copes with its differences remains to be seen.[8]

Equally problematic is the viability of the non-use-of-force norm. While no ASEAN member contemplates outright war with its neighbours, regional arms build-ups are nevertheless conducted, with an eye toward maintaining a balance with ASEAN partners. Intra-ASEAN military cooperation, therefore, is at best tentative. Even Malaysia's suggestion for establishing an ASEAN peacekeeping force based on the experience of several ASEAN states' armed forces in Cambodia, East Timor, and the Balkans, were shelved, partly because it might be seen as an attempt to turn ASEAN into a military alliance and partly because it would be impolitic to insert such a force into an intra-ASEAN conflict. Practical considerations also stymie ASEAN military cooperation, since weapons systems are purchased from so many different national suppliers that interoperability would be problematic.[9]

An important ASEAN principle with respect to the war on terror is that no member will provide sanctuary or support to groups bent on undermining the government of an ASEAN state. While no ASEAN government supports subversion against a neighbour, governments have been unwilling or more probably unable to suppress groups that take refuge within their borders. Thai separatists flee to northern Malaysia; large numbers of Karen are located inside the Thai northern border; Philippine Moros are found in Malaysian Borneo; and Jemaah Islamiah (JI) cells, which target several ASEAN states, are entrenched in parts of Indonesia despite Jakarta's efforts at disruption. Moreover, JI recruits continue to train in southern Philippine camps run by the Abu Sayyaf, a terrorist group linked to JI.

The "ASEAN Way" of emphasizing quiet diplomacy, non-confrontation, and non-interference in domestic affairs has been supplemented (if not replaced) since 11 September and the Bali and Jakarta bombings by more proactive measures. Visa-free travel is being reconsidered among ASEAN states. At the November 2001 ASEAN summit, a Declaration of Joint Action to Counter Terrorism was adopted. Subsequently, in August 2002, a U.S.-ASEAN declaration to counter terror was also endorsed. While these declarations certainly acknowledge the ASEAN-wide challenge, much remains to be done. In May 2002, the ASEAN states agreed on an action plan that provided for enhanced cooperation in intelligence-sharing and the coordination of anti-terror laws. Singapore's proposal that each member form a special anti-terrorist team as a contact point was also accepted.[10] However, the ASEAN states remain slow to ratify twelve key anti-terrorist conventions, especially the treaty suppressing terrorist finances. Nevertheless, a breakthrough may have occurred at the January 2007 ASEAN summit that agreed on an ASEAN Convention on Counter-Terrorism. While all ASEAN leaders signed off on the Convention, it still must be ratified by each member state — a process that could take years.

ASEAN members could consider modest steps to harden their borders against the transnational flow of terrorists, their weapons, and their funds. Background checks for visas constitute one measure, though they may delay freedom of movement and commerce within ASEAN. Training immigration officials in detecting forged documents is another. Passing legislation requiring closer scrutiny of corporate accounts would bring the ASEAN states in line with the anti-money-laundering standards of the Financial Action Task Force (Singapore is the only ASEAN state that is currently a member of this organization). In spring of 2003, Thailand and the Philippines passed anti-money-laundering legislation. However, enforcement will be key to their effectiveness.

Maritime policing is another woefully inadequate area among ASEAN states. A favourite route for illicit arms traffic goes from southern Thailand westward across the northern Strait of Malacca to Aceh, as well as across the South China Sea to Sabah and the southern Philippines.[11] Collaboration among the littoral navies and coastguards, especially in the Strait of Malacca, is difficult. Hot pursuit of pirates has been hampered by the requirement that the pursuing state obtain permission in each instance from the country into whose waters the pirates flee. In 2004–5, the three states that straddle the Strait of Malacca (Indonesia, Malaysia, and Singapore) began to mount coordinated naval patrols as well as joint air patrols over the strait with one military officer from each country on board maritime patrol aircraft. However, the patrols are not joint endeavours in that each country's ships may only operate in its own maritime territory and must hand off any pursuit if a suspect vessel crosses into a neighbour's waters.[12] Although terrorist groups so far have not hijacked ships, one can imagine the devastation caused if a liquefied natural gas tanker were seized and blown up in the Strait of Malacca. Maritime insurance rates would skyrocket.[13] In addition to augmented Indian navy and U.S. Seventh Fleet patrols around the western and eastern entrances to the Strait of Malacca, the U.S. and Japanese coastguards could engage selected ASEAN navies in anti-piracy exercises and provide intelligence on suspicious activities in the Strait of Malacca and its approaches. During 2000, India deployed a destroyer to help escort high-value vessels through the strait.[14] And in 2006, Japan promised to provide equipment, ships, and training as part of its collaboration with ASEAN on counter-terrorism and maritime security.

In August 2007, Thailand indicated its readiness to join the trilateral naval straits patrol. And at the August 2007 Bali ARF, members agreed to assist the littoral states through training and technology because security in the strait is also crucial for user states. In September, the UN's International Maritime Organization set up a cooperative arrangement whereby user states and the shipping industry could jointly undertake and finance projects designed to make the strait safer through the installation and maintenance of navigational aids. Then, in April 2008, Thailand in discussions with Indonesia proposed joining the littorals' navy patrols in the straits.[15]

In January 2003, ASEAN police forces meeting in Jakarta not long after the Bali bombings proposed an anti-terrorism task force for each country to strengthen regional anti-terrorist collaboration. The model would be the cooperation that takes place between the Indonesian National Police and the police forces of other countries to arrest the perpetrators of terror and uncover their networks in the region. Malaysia and Indonesia argued that national legislation should be passed in each country to make terrorism an extraditable offense. Singapore balked, however, pointing to the different legal systems within ASEAN, though Singapore's primary concern was probably the safety of large numbers of wealthy ethnic Chinese who fled from Indonesia to Singapore in the wake of anti-Chinese riots in 1998.[16] A blanket extradition treaty among ASEAN states could lead Indonesia to claim that its ethnic Chinese citizens in Singapore committed economic crimes by fleeing with their resources.[17] Subsequently, in 2006–7, Singapore and Indonesia negotiated an agreement combining extradition arrangements and military training cooperation that has since been shelved when Indonesian parliamentarians raised concerns that Singapore would not enforce the extradition part of the treaty.

Other issues on ASEAN's table include the U.S. war in Iraq, the SARS epidemic, and Avian flu. The Iraq war split the Association — with Singapore, the Philippines, and, to a smaller degree, Thailand backing Washington, while Malaysia, Indonesia, and other ASEAN states either condemned U.S. actions or remained silent. The Philippines was among thirty countries openly backing the U.S. invasion and hence well positioned, so it believed, to obtain some reconstruction contracts in medical and educational domains. With respect to post-war reconstruction, Malaysia and Indonesia share the view that the United Nations should be given the major role.

The Myanmar Challenge: An ASEAN Litmus Test?

Another hopeful sign with respect to reconsideration of ASEAN's non-interference norm has been the association's discussion of the Myanmar military junta's treatment of opposition leader and Nobel laureate Aung San Suu Kyi. At its June 2003 annual ministerial meeting in Cambodia, ASEAN broke with its longstanding policy of not interfering in the internal affairs of member states by demanding Suu Kyi's release. Malaysian Prime Minister Mahathir summarized the members' dismay when he stated: "We don't criticize member states unless what one state does embarrasses us.... [W]hat they have done has affected us, our credibility. Because of that, we have raised our voices."

Mahathir went on to say that even Myanmar's expulsion from ASEAN was a possibility, since ASEAN has a right to demand standards of behaviour from its members. Mahathir's comments were particularly striking, since Malaysia had been instrumental in pushing for Myanmar's 1997 ASEAN admission in the face of strong objections from critics of the military regime. Expulsion may be a hollow threat, however, because there are no ASEAN provisions for excluding a state once it has membership. Moreover, unlike the United States and the European Union, which have imposed economic and political restrictions on Myanmar, neither ASEAN, India, nor China — the junta's primary economic partners — are willing to do so. Nevertheless, in 2006, ASEAN members persuaded Myanmar to forgo its scheduled chairmanship of the association so as not to alienate the association's European Union and American partners.

In August and September 2007, ASEAN was presented with yet another Myanmar crisis.[18] In August, the ruling junta suddenly and without warning raised fuel prices 500 per cent, threatening the livelihoods of much of the country's population. Protests originating with city dwellers spread to the highly revered Buddhist *sangha* (monks) who joined civilians in demonstrations against the regime that, at their height, involved several hundred thousand. These were followed by a swift, brutal crackdown leading to the arrest of thousands of monks and citizens and the torture and killing of an undetermined number.

World outrage was expressed by individual states and at the United Nations. Several ASEAN foreign ministers met at the UN to condemn the junta's tactics and endorse the intervention of a special UN human rights envoy, Ibrahim Gambari. While the ASEAN ministers deplored the violence and expressed "revulsion", they did not convene a special ASEAN meeting to deal with the outrage, nor did they imitate American and European sanctions against the junta. The only call for Myanmar's suspension from ASEAN came from a noted Singaporean academic, Barry Desker, with ties to his state's Foreign Ministry. Desker noted that the then draft ASEAN Charter calls for the promotion of democracy and human rights, while Myanmar's behaviour flaunts these putative commitments.[19] Although ASEAN leaders admit that the association's "constructive engagement" with Myanmar has failed, they warn that no future solution for the country's governance can exclude the military for it is the only institution that is organized to govern nationwide. At best, as Indonesian Foreign Minister Hassan Wirajuda put it: "That's why perhaps a transition in which there would be sharing of power between the military and civilian leaders" might be best, a transition that could last five years. The Thai Prime Minister, General Surayud Chulanont merely called for renewed dialogue between Aung San Suu Kyi and the military; and Lee Kuan Yew, Singapore's elder statesman, urged ASEAN to help Myanmar restore stability. Otherwise, "it will become a ticking time bomb" in Southeast Asia.[20] So, neither ASEAN, China, nor India is prepared to seriously pressure Myanmar's regime to reform.

Indonesia's Defence Minister Juwono Sudarsono went even further, insisting that Jakarta would not support an arms sales ban on Myanmar because ASEAN should try to nurture a younger generation of army officers who might be willing to loosen the junta's grip on power. The Foreign Minister, Hassan Wirajuda, stated that Indonesia could show the Myanmar junta how to move from a military dictatorship to a civilian government, a transition accomplished in 1998 in Indonesia after the financial crisis led to the demise of the Suharto government.[21] The problem, of course, is that Myanmar's military leaders have no interest in transition. The new "constitution" that the junta claims was approved in a May 2008 referendum that coincided with Cyclone Nargis simply enshrines the army's control.

In early May 2008, ASEAN was faced with a litmus test with respect to humanitarian intervention to meet the dire needs of one of its own members, requiring abandonment of the non-interference principle.[22] On 3 May, Cyclone Nargis whipped though Myanmar's Irrawaddy delta packing 155 mile per hour winds, the worst natural disaster to strike Southeast Asia since the December 2004 tsunami. However, in contrast to the Indonesian Government at that time which immediately welcomed international assistance for the devastated Sumatran province of Aceh, Myanmar's ruling military junta denied qualified aid workers access to the stricken region for several days and subsequently only permitted a small number to provide emergency supplies mainly via Myanmar's military which, in turn, distributed the aid to just a fraction of the 2.5 million people in need.

The new ASEAN Secretary-General Surin Pitsuwan seized the moment by ignoring the organization's non-interference principle and urging the junta to grant immediate access to international relief teams. Singapore and Thailand were among the first countries permitted by the junta to provide aid, and in fact ASEAN had already created a regional agreement in 2005 after the Indian Ocean tsunami on disaster management and emergency response.

In mid-May, the Myanmar authorities agreed to an ASEAN Emergency Rapid Assessment Team to determine the critical needs of the population, though its scheduled full report in mid-July suggests that it was less than rapid or critical. A pledging conference took place in Rangoon in late May, though the junta made clear that only medical teams exclusively from ASEAN states would be given preferential access. However, ASEAN's capacity to provide urgent medical aid was quite limited. Additionally, by late May, Myanmar's generals insisted that the emergency phase of cyclone relief was over and that the donors should focus on providing billions of dollars for reconstruction — to be given, of course, directly to the junta.

At the May/June 2008 Shangri-La Dialogue in Singapore, Malaysian Deputy Prime Minister Najib Razak insisted that ASEAN country militaries would be the most effective purveyors of humanitarian aid and that Myanmar should be assured "that our involvement is strictly humanitarian in nature and there is no other agenda we have in mind when we sent our military in the various disaster-stricken areas in other countries in the past." One ASEAN official interviewed in Yangon was asked whether Myanmar's military was cooperating fully with the aid effort. His reply was "How can I fully answer that without hurting the mission?"

A spinoff from this ASEAN experience and the growing frequency and severity of natural disasters has been the creation in Jakarta of an interim ASEAN Coordinating Centre for Humanitarian Assistance on Disaster Management. Operations were scheduled to begin at the end of 2008. Has ASEAN finally come of age in its efforts to provide aid in the wake of Cyclone Nargis? Despite the Myanmar junta's roadblocks preventing foreign aid from reaching those in need, ASEAN in collaboration with the UN was able to insert 250 assessment teams into the south for a village-by-village survey to determine how much food, water, and shelter were needed. However, despite plans for an ASEAN arrangement to deal with natural disasters after the December 2004 tsunami, no such arrangement was created. ASEAN was prepared neither to send experts nor equipment when the cyclone struck. Those on site who were prepared to provide massive assistance via navy ships — the United States, Great Britain, and France — were refused access by the junta.

ASEAN Secretary-General Surin placed the best possible face on all of this: "We have been able to establish a space, a humanitarian space, however small to engage with the Myanmar authorities." Subsequently he said that ASEAN has shown that it is up to the responsibility placed on it; that the new ASEAN was "baptized by Cyclone Nargis". Critics are less sanguine: The junta has returned to its old oppressive ways; and some say that ASEAN has allowed itself to be used by the ruling generals to provide the semblance of a positive response to the international community in order to escape international condemnation.

The ASEAN Charter: Does It Matter?

For the first forty years of its existence, ASEAN had no overarching legal document outlining the rights and obligations of membership. Although a number of norms have emerged over time such as the consensus principle, TAC (a non-aggression pact), the Zone of Peace, Freedom and Neutrality (ZOPFAN), the Southeast Asia Nuclear Weapon-Free Zone, and ASEAN's bedrock non-interference in domestic affairs principle, no charter or formal statement of community was written until 2007. Challenges such as the haze, SARS, and transnational crime have served as recent reminders that regional security is increasingly interdependent. These challenges are among the most important drivers for the creation of an ASEAN Community by 2015 via an ASEAN Charter.

Consisting of security, economic, and socio-cultural communities, the formal Charter provides ASEAN with a "legal personality". While early drafts of the Charter written by an Eminent Persons Group included a controversial section recommending sanctions — including expulsion — for those violating the Charter, this stringent condition was dropped. The Eminent Persons Group also recommended that ASEAN relax its consensus decision making style so that routine matters could be resolved by less than full agreement while unanimity would only be required for "important matters".[23] Yet ASEAN members' reticence to engage regionally does not bode well for the putative Charter. To wit, ASEAN treaties and statements lack formal binding commitments and mechanisms to monitor implementation. The December 2004 ASEAN Treaty on Mutual Legal Assistance in Criminal Matters does not provide for extradition and states that domestic laws take precedence over the treaty's provisions. Nonetheless, the EPG believed that the Charter would "put in place a system of compliance monitoring, and, most importantly, a system of compulsory dispute-settlement for non-compliance that will apply to all ASEAN agreements."[24] Nevertheless, as one high level official from an ASEAN state involved with the EPG in drafting the Charter explained: "the Charter should be seen less as a legal document than as a formal statement of ASEAN's hopes, a work in progress that will be interpreted according to each members' interests".[25] If this is true, one wonders how much the Charter goes beyond ASEAN's current practices.

Despite these caveats, at its November 2007 Singapore summit, ASEAN adopted a landmark Charter — its first full-scale legal commitment to human rights, democratic ideas, and an economic community, the latter advancing the goals of economic integration by five years to 2015. Other elements of the Charter disappoint: the principle of non-interference in members' internal affairs is maintained, undoubtedly at the insistence of the Indochinese countries and Myanmar. The consensus principle for decision making also continues, in effect giving any member a veto. Also, the Charter does not mention either expulsion or suspension of members found in serious breach of the Charter's provisions; and the Charter's statements on democracy and human rights provide no guidance for implementation. For the Charter to take effect, all ten members must ratify it. In October 2008, the last two ASEAN legislatures — the Philippines and Indonesia — ratified the document, though each body expressed reservations about the absence of democracy and human rights in Myanmar as well as the continued detention of opposition leader Aung San Suu Kyi.[26]

Arguably the most controversial part of the ASEAN Charter is the provision for a human rights body. Several members from authoritarian governments have expressed reservations, particularly Myanmar, Laos, Cambodia, and Vietnam, but also Brunei and Singapore. All are concerned that such a sensitive issue as human rights could lead to interference in their domestic politics. The consensus is that some kind of human rights body will be established, but that there will be no sanctions for violators; moral suasion will be human rights' primary implementation mode.[27]

The ASEAN Regional Forum: Is the Tail Wagging the Dog?

Just as ASEAN faces security problems that challenge non-intervention and sovereignty norms, so the ARF now confronts region-wide issues that make consensus difficult to achieve. The ARF emerged from ASEAN in the 1990s. The end of the Cold War left the Asia-Pacific searching for a new organizing principle for security. While traditional alliances remained, including bilateral treaties with the United States and the Five Power Defence Arrangement, these seemed inadequate to deal with security matters of a non-military nature, such as transnational crime, environmental hazards, and illegal population movements.[28] Moreover, "traditional" security issues persisted in the form of unresolved territorial disputes, divided states, nuclear weapons proliferation, and conflicting maritime jurisdictions resulting from the 1982 UN Law of the Sea, all of which have been addressed in discussion but not resolved.

Some kind of cooperative security enterprise linking the region to its major partners in Northeast Asia and North America was needed to fill the gap. Through the 1976 TAC, ASEAN members had already pledged among themselves to resolve intra-ASEAN disputes peacefully (or postpone their resolution). Underlying this vision of a larger security order was the hope that the treaty's peaceful resolution commitment could be extended to other states. This practice would constitute a kind of minimal diffuse reciprocity. That is, while ASEAN would not expect outsiders automatically to come to members' aid in times of crisis or come to their defence if attacked, at least outside countries could be asked to renounce the use of force in settling any conflicts they might have with the association's members. The unstated object of these concerns, of course, is China — the only "extra-regional" state with territorial claims in Southeast Asia. This is essentially a realist vision of the ARF. If successful, it would encourage the People's Republic of China (PRC) to explain and clarify its security policy and planning. China's neighbours, through the ARF, could then respond with their concerns about the PRC's policy, in hopes of modifying it and thus enhancing regional stability. In exchange for PRC transparency, other ARF members would reciprocate. For Beijing, the primary payoff would not be access to ASEAN defence plans, but rather to those of other members, such as Japan and the United States.

Fortunately for ASEAN, no exclusive Northeast Asian efforts were made to create a sub-regional counterpart to ASEAN, although the Six Party Talks dealing with North Korean nuclear weapons could evolve in that direction. In effect, ASEAN was able to fill this vacuum by offering to create a new region-wide entity modelled on the Association's process of consultation and dialogue. Because this approach fell well short of collective defence, it was not threatening to any potential adherent. Nor would a new regional forum interfere with individual states' security links to outsiders.

Purposefully imitative of the ASEAN Post Ministerial Conference, the ARF objective was to develop a predictable and constructive pattern of relationships in the Asia-Pacific, providing the whole region with opportunities for ASEAN-style dialogue. By themselves, the PMCs were viewed by Northeast Asians as insufficient for broad discussion of their sub-region's concerns on issues such as competitive arming, maritime exclusive economic zone rules, and the roles of China and Japan. Although ASEAN understood that these issues needed to be addressed, the association also desired to create a body that would acknowledge ASEAN's institutional status as *primus inter pares*. The ARF achieved this goal by ensuring that ASEAN states would be the venue for the ARF's annual meetings; that ASEAN would dominate the agenda; that inter-session study groups, each composed of two states, would always include an ASEAN member; and that the ASEAN consensus principle would prevail in ARF decisions.

By its second meeting, the ARF agreed on a three-stage progression toward comprehensive security in Asia, which would move from confidence building to preventive diplomacy, and finally on to the development of mechanisms for conflict resolution. The development of these mechanisms was subsequently renamed "elaboration of approaches to conflict" out of deference to China's concern that conflict resolution could be interpreted as justifying the ARF's interference in members' internal affairs. ASEAN PMCs, senior officers' meetings and ARF workshops have generated a cornucopia of transparency possibilities — that is, the discussion of security intentions. Both ASEAN and the ARF agree that security transparency is a prerequisite for more sophisticated preventive diplomacy and conflict resolution. Confidence-building measures that have been raised in ASEAN-related gatherings include notification of military exercises, hotlines among political and military leaders, extension of the Russian-U.S. Incidents-at-sea Agreement to the entire Asia-Pacific, and regional maritime, air surveillance, and safety regimes. These measures all fall within the trust and confidence-building category as defined by the ARF.[29]

The ARF has conducted an extensive security dialogue over the years encompassing human rights in Myanmar, problems on the Korean Peninsula, the South China Sea islands, weapons of mass destruction proliferation, and the implications of ballistic missile defence deployments. The ARF has called for support of the Nuclear Non-Proliferation Treaty and ratification of the Comprehensive Test Ban Treaty. It also addresses transnational security issues, especially piracy and illegal migration, as well as narcotics and small arms trafficking. These plenary discussions and inter-sessional meetings have had some practical results: annual defence policy statements and increased publication of defence white papers, which contribute to transparency; military exchanges at the staff college level; growing involvement and participation of defence officials in ARF deliberations; and the creation of an ARF Register of Experts/Eminent Persons who can be called upon by ARF members in conflict situations.[30] However, the ARF has no secretariat to provide continuity or engage in staff studies between its annual plenary discussions, special meetings, or inter-sessional group conclaves. Nevertheless, in 2006, the ASEAN Secretariat agreed to provide administrative support for ARF activities.

While the ARF has turned from exclusively confidence-building to the next stage of preventive diplomacy, the transition has been difficult. Reticence on the part of China, as well as some other members, reflect a concern that basic national security issues — such as the future of Taiwan — not be subject to ARF deliberations. By contrast, Canada, Australia, Japan, and the United States would like to see the ARF strengthened. The United States particularly hopes that the ARF will serve as an anti-terror cooperative mechanism. However, the ARF's consensus rule, adopted from ASEAN, has proven a serious obstacle to managing tensions that arise from the divergent strategic interests of ARF members.[31]

The ASEAN overlay on ARF procedures has provoked resentment among some participants, particularly South Korea, which believes that ASEAN's proprietary attitude has constrained any Northeast Asia dialogue within the forum. Moreover, even the numerous confidence-building measures implemented by the ARF are mainly declarations of transparency that do not involve constraints on behaviour. For example, there may be discussions among defence officials, but no agreement, on refraining from adding certain kinds of weapons into national arsenals. Nor can the ARF discuss intra-state conflicts because of Chinese objections.[32]

While Washington did not expect the ARF to be an action-oriented security organization, after 11 September 2001, the United States has urged the ARF to become more involved in devising ways to actively combat terrorism, such as shutting down terrorist finances through ARF transnational crime agreements. Another possibility would be to expand ARF undertakings on search-and-rescue operations to include simulating a ship hijacking in the Strait of Malacca that would require practical cooperation among littoral navies to rescue hostages.[33] Singapore's December 2003 participation in the U.S.-led multilateral Proliferation Security Initiative could be an initial step in that direction. Designed to stop the transfer of weapons of mass destruction to "states of concern" and terrorists, participating navies are simulating the cooperative interdiction of suspect ships.

To its credit, the ARF laid out an agenda for its members to block terrorist finances at its July 2002 Brunei summit, urging members to implement UN measures, which include blocking terrorists' access to national financial systems, freezing terrorists' financial assets, publicizing terrorist organizations whose assets have been seized, and creating national financial intelligence units to share information. These exhortations are exemplary, but they are not mandatory. There is no enforcement mechanism nor any sanctions against ARF members who choose not to comply.[34] Moreover, the ARF consensus principle obstructs joint agreements. This obstacle could be overcome if the ARF adopted an ASEAN procedure used to bypass a similar constraint. Called the "ASEAN Minus X" understanding, it permits a "coalition of the willing" — whereby those states that agree on a principle may proceed, while those that do not may refrain from participation.[35]

Other Forms of Regional Security Cooperation

While ASEAN and the ARF are the primary Asian regional security institutions, they are by no means the only ways in which Southeast Asian states engage in multilateral security cooperation. Interstate security cooperation takes place in both bilateral and multilateral arrangements outside of the ASEAN and ARF frameworks. The terrorist challenges posed by Al-Qaeda, JI, and other groups that transfer personnel, weapons, money and information across Southeast Asia's borders require a coordinated response among those states most affected. Intelligence sharing is particularly important, since captured JI members have provided authorities with useful information leading to further arrests or the discovery of new plots.

Several Southeast Asian states have increased anti-terrorist cooperation with one another. Intelligence organizations in Malaysia, Singapore, and the Philippines, are exchanging information about regional terrorist groups, as well as with U.S. intelligence agencies and the Federal Bureau of Investigation. Nevertheless, constraints still exist. In February 2003, Indonesian security officials arrested Mas Selamat Kastari, the alleged leader of JI in Singapore, based on information provided by the Singapore Government.[36] While incarcerated in Singapore, however, Mas Selamat escaped from the Whitley Road Detention Centre in February 2008 and was eventually captured in April 2009 in neighbouring Malaysia.

In May 2002, a Southeast Asian anti-terror pact was initialled by the Philippines, Indonesia, and Malaysia, to which Thailand and Cambodia subsequently adhered. The pact was activated in the aftermath of the Davao bombings, when Philippine officials claimed that Indonesian nationals were involved in collaboration with elements of the Moro Islamic Liberation Front (MILF), all of whom had trained in terrorist camps in North Cotabato.[37] Similarly, Thai authorities have acknowledged that JI members met in southern Thailand in January 2002, where a decision was made to attack soft targets in the region, such as nightclubs and restaurants.[38]

Possible linkages between the Bali and Davao bombings have led to intelligence and police cooperation between Malaysia, Indonesia, and the Philippines. Manila insists that the MILF is responsible for the Davao and other recent Mindanao attacks, although MILF leaders deny the allegations. It seems likely that some rogue MILF splinter groups may be among the perpetrators, but there is little evidence to suggest that the

MILF leadership, who are negotiating with the Philippines Government to resolve their conflict in Mindanao, are directing terrorist actions. Joined by Thailand and Cambodia, the five adherents to the Southeast Asia anti-terror pact agreed at a January 2003 gathering in Manila that they would establish a communication protocol to fight terror, piracy, money laundering, smuggling, and gun running. Whether these plans will facilitate collaboration among law enforcement authorities in the countries most susceptible to terrorist movements and actions remains to be seen, although Malaysian authorities have stated that they are regularly exchanging intelligence with Indonesia and the Philippines.[39]

Unsurprisingly, the most effective form of Southeast Asian security cooperation continues to be bilateral and focused on specific problems. Malaysian armed forces are patrolling waters between Sabah and the southern Philippines to intercept MILF militants fleeing Manila's crackdown. Australian police have been credited by Indonesia with providing the technical assistance needed to intercept cellular phone conversations, which led to the apprehension of many of the Bali bombers.[40] Moreover, bilateral military exercises occur annually between Indonesia and Thailand, the Philippines and Malaysia, Malaysia and Brunei, Singapore and Brunei, and Thailand and Brunei. Note, however, that these exercises involve only the first six ASEAN adherents and not the Indochinese states and Myanmar. The sharing of intelligence for law enforcement takes place at Malaysia's Counter-terrorism Centre and at Thailand's regional law enforcement institute.

Piracy is a continuing challenge in Southeast Asia, the possible marriage of piracy with terrorism causes considerable worry for the region. The deep water channels in Malacca and a number of Indonesian straits are so narrow that a single burning supertanker and its spreading oil slick could block the route for other tankers. Moreover, in these narrow straits, there may not even be enough room for naval escorts to screen tankers from attacks by small, fast craft.[41]

While Japan has proposed a regional coastguard to combat piracy, national sensitivities in the littoral states inhibit any broader collaboration. Many Southeast Asian countries are unwilling to prosecute pirates apprehended in their territorial waters for acts committed in other countries' jurisdictions. Most often, pirates are deported rather than prosecuted. Furthermore, since boundaries have not yet been drawn in some parts of the Malacca/Singapore Straits, jurisdiction over piracy is unclear.[42] Nevertheless, both Singapore and Malaysia are upgrading their air forces partly to enhance anti-piracy, anti-terrorist, and illegal immigration patrols. Both countries are acquiring air-to-air refuelling aircraft, and Singapore has manufactured its own unmanned aerial vehicle to extend surveillance over waters surrounding the island city-state. Malaysia has also produced its own reconnaissance aircraft, the *Eagle*, which is to be deployed in Sabah for coastal patrols.[43]

There were a significant number of attacks on tankers in the Strait of Malacca in 2003, though these seemed to be piracy rather than terrorism; however, from 2005 to 2006, piracy has significantly declined in the Strait of Malacca.[44] Hijacked tugboats could be used for terrorism, drug trafficking, or human smuggling. Taking these possibilities into account, Singapore requires tugboats to provide six hours advance notice before coming into port; and all small vessels have been prohibited from entering the special anchorages designated for chemical, oil, and liquefied natural gas carriers.[45] In 2005–6, the three littoral states — Singapore, Indonesia, Malaysia — formed a coordinated sea and air anti-piracy patrol arrangement for the Strait of Malacca that seems to be effective. It is the first such trilateral effort in Southeast Asia.

Conclusion

Most Southeast Asians believe their security is best maintained in the early twenty-first century not by isolating the region from great power activities, as originally envisaged in the 1970s ZOPFAN, but rather by engaging them in multilateral endeavours, such as the ASEAN Post Ministerial Conference, ASEAN Plus Three, and the ARF. While these measures were initially directed toward keeping China and the United States involved in assuring the region's security, ASEAN also welcomes participation by India and Japan.

India and Japan have exchanged high-level visits with virtually every Southeast Asian state. ASEAN members welcome India's efforts to strengthen ties with Myanmar as a way of balancing China's influence. Also, India is involved in the ASEAN Post Ministerial Conference. Although Delhi has not been able to turn ASEAN Plus Three into ASEAN Plus Four, it has been accepted into the ARF and the new East Asia Summit.

For the United States, ASEAN and the ARF security deficiencies are not a significant drawback. Washington's security strategy in East Asia continues to rely on bilateral relations and has developed a mix of bilateral and multilateral endeavours in Southeast Asia. In the war against terror the strongest bilateral tie is with the Philippines, where U.S. military assistance and training, now in their ninth year, are designed to enhance the Philippine armed forces' ability to suppress the Abu Sayyaf group in Mindanao.

On the multilateral dimension, little has been accomplished because neither ASEAN nor the ARF have been willing to tackle the core security issues affecting the region, be they external support for insurgencies, major refugee flows, or disputes over sovereignty of islands. Inclusive memberships in both organizations and the ASEAN consensus principle work against their security effectiveness.[46] Thus, Washington's only multilateral initiative in Southeast Asia is quite modest: the offer to fund a regional anti-terrorism training centre in Malaysia, which would focus on law enforcement and intelligence exchange, but not involve military training. As Stephen Leong of Malaysia's Institute of Strategic and International Studies said, not only would the centre show that ASEAN was involved in the anti-terror struggle, but it "will also help to boost the confidence for foreigners who want to invest or travel in the region especially after the Bali bombing." More recently the United States seems to be paying greater political attention to ASEAN. In the summer of 2006 Washington announced that it would appoint an Ambassador to ASEAN as an organization, and in April 2008 Deputy Assistant Secretary of State Scot Marciel was given that new designation, though he remains in Washington.[47]

Security regionalism in Southeast Asia remains, therefore, a weak reed. Absence of interoperability among the region's armed forces, embedded suspicions about neighbours' motivations, and an unwillingness or inability to set up effective arrangements to cope with transnational challenges all tend to move security cooperation by default to the bilateral — or at most trilateral — level, where more effective collaboration exists. This principle appears equally true for U.S. security arrangements in Southeast Asia. Bilateral military exercises and bilateral anti-terrorist and law enforcement collaboration dominate. Multilateral exercises, such as Cobra Gold in Thailand, while valued, are viewed by Southeast Asians as less useful than bilateral security links to the United States.[48] There is little to suggest that this situation will change.

Nevertheless, with the new ASEAN Charter, this situation could change. Non-traditional security — transnational crime, piracy, terrorism, pandemics, human and drug trafficking — require multilateral cooperation.

Moreover, because all states benefit when these scourges are contained, the political support needed to cope effectively with these challenges may be more forthcoming than when states deal with traditional security concerns such as territorial and resource disputes. Over the next several years, if the ASEAN states, as part of their Security Community responsibilities, craft new ways of dealing with non-traditional threats, then genuine multilateral security may come into its own on a track that runs parallel to traditional bi-and trilateral security arrangements.

NOTES

1. ASEAN members are Malaysia, Singapore, Thailand, Indonesia, the Philippines, Brunei, Laos, Cambodia, Vietnam, and Myanmar. East Timor, which seceded from Indonesia in 1999, is not yet a member.
2. Michael Leifer, "The ASEAN Peace Process: A Category Mistake", *Pacific Review* 12, no. 1 (1999): 37.
3. Lorraine Elliott, "ASEAN and Environmental Cooperation: Norms, Interests, and Identity", *Pacific Review* 16, no. 1 (2003): 30–31; and Amitav Acharya, *The Quest for Identity: International Relations of Southeast Asia* (Singapore: Oxford University Press, 2000). For the changes proposed for a new ASEAN Charter, see the ASEAN December 2006 Summit documents.
4. Rajshree Jetly, "Conflict Management Strategies in ASEAN: Perspectives for SAARC", *Pacific Review* 16, no. 1 (2003): 55. Also see Amitav Acharya, "Competing and Congruent Approaches to Security Cooperation in the Asia-Pacific Region: A Concept Paper", unpublished, Singapore 2002.
5. Nayan Chanda, "Southeast Asia After September 11", in *George W. Bush and Asia: A Midterm Assessment*, edited by Robert Hathaway and Wilson Lee (Washington, DC: Woodrow Wilson Center for Scholars, 2003), pp. 118–19.
6. A good review of Southeast Asia's bilateral conflicts can be found in "Southeast Asia — Security," stratfor.com, 12 February 2003.
7. Chanda, "Southeast Asia After September 11", p. 129.
8. Amitav Acharya, *Constructing a Security Community in Southeast Asia: ASEAN and the Problem of Regional Order* (New York: Routledge, 2001), p. 121.
9. Sheldon W. Simon, "Asian Armed Forces: Internal and External Tasks and Capabilities", in *The Many Faces of Asian Security*, edited by Sheldon W. Simon (New York: Rowman and Littlefield, 2001), pp. 49–70. Also see Archarya, *Constructing a Security Community in Southeast Asia*, pp. 150–51.
10. *Straits Times*, 18 May 2002; and Robert Karniol, "A Total Defence", *Jane's Defence Weekly*, 28 August 2002, p. 25.
11. Kumar Ramakrishna, "Applying the U.S. National Security Strategy for Countering Terrorism to Southeast Asia" (paper prepared for the Institute for

National Strategic Studies — U.S. Institute of Peace Workshop on Terrorism's New Front Lines: Adapting U.S. Counter-Terrorism Strategy To Regions of Concern, Washington, DC, 8–9 May 2003, pp. 7–9).

12   Sheldon W. Simon, "Southeast Asia's Defense Needs: Change of Continuity?" in *Strategic Asia 2005–06: Military Modernization in an Era of Uncertainty*, edited by Ashley Tellis and Michael Wills (Seattle: The National Bureau of Asian Research, 2005), p. 277.

13   Author's discussion with a high-ranking U.S. naval officer at the Institute of National Strategic Studies—U.S. Institute of Peace Workshop on Terrorism's New Front Lines, 8 May 2003.

14   See the discussion in Sheldon W. Simon, "Theater Security Cooperation in the U.S. Pacific Command: An Assessment and Projection", *NBR Analysis*, August 2003.

15   "Thailand Set to Join Malacca Patrols", *Bangkok Post*, 20 August 2007; *Antara* (Jakarta), 29 August 2007; "UN-backed Project to boost safety, security in vital Malacca Shipping Lanes", UN News Service, 11 September 2007. "Indonesia and Thai Navies Reach Cooperation Agreement", Antara (Jakarta), 8 April 2008.

16   See "ASEAN Police to Set Up Anti-terrorism Task Force", news release by the ASEAN Secretariat (Jakarta), 22 January 2003.

17   Andrew Tan, "Terrorism in Singapore: Threat and Implications", *Contemporary Security Policy* 23, no, 3 (December 2002): 1–18.

18   For an extended discussion see Sheldon W. Simon, "U.S.-Southeast Asian Relations: Burma Heats Up and the U.S. Blows Hot and Cold", *Comparative Connections: A Quarterly E-Journal of East Asian Bilateral Relations* 9, no. 3 (October 2007): 64–65.

19   Barry Desker, "ASEAN: Time to Suspend Myanmar", *RSIS Commentaries* (Singapore), 4 October 2007.

20   "Burmese Junta Should Be Offered Shared Role", *Antara* (Jakarta), 3 October 2007; *Thai News Agency*, 8 October 2007; *Zhanggao Tongxun She* (Hong Kong), 6 October 2007.

21   *Agence France Presse* (Hong Kong), 10 October 2007; and "UN's Envoy Suggests Incentives for Myanmar", *International Herald-Tribune*, 17 October 2007.

22   This discussion is drawn from Sheldon W. Simon, "U.S. Frustrated as Burmese Junta Obstructs Cyclone Relief", *Comparative Connections* 10, no. 2 (July 2008): 61–72.

23   Ralph Cossa and Brad Glosserman, "Regional Overview: Renewed Hope in the Year of the Golden Pig", *Comparative Connections* 9, no. 1, (April 2007): 5–6.

24   Alistair Miller and Eric Rosand, "Implementing the UN General Assembly's Global Counter-Terrorism Strategy in the Asia-Pacific", *Asian Security* 3,

no. 3 (2007): 189; and Tommy Koh, Walter Woon, Andrew Tan, and Chan Sze-Wei, "The ASEAN Charter", *PacNet 33A* (Honolulu, Pacific Forum), 6 September 2007.

[25] Interview with an ASEAN official conducted by author in Singapore, 18 October 2007.

[26] For additional discussion of the ASEAN Charter, see Sheldon W. Simon, "ASEAN and Multilateralism: The Long Bumpy Road to Community", *Contemporary Southeast Asia* 30, no. 2 (August 2008).

[27] "ASEAN Fails to Reach Human Rights Accord", *Australian Broadcasting System*, 30 July 2007; Kavi Chongkittavorn, "ASEAN Charter: Should We Settle for Second Best?" *The Nation* (Bangkok, online version), 14 August 2007; and Amando Doronila, "Out of Step with ASEAN", Inquirer.net (Manila), 5 August 2007.

[28] This new security agenda is explored in Sheldon W. Simon, ed., *The Many Faces of Asian Security* (Boulder: Rowman and Littlefield, 2001).

[29] Trevor Findlay, "The Regional Security Outlook", in *Asia-Pacific Security: Less Uncertainty, New Opportunities*, edited by Gary Klintworth (New York: St. Martin's Press, 1998), pp. 275–92.

[30] Mely Caballero-Anthony, "Partnership for Peace in Asia: ASEAN, the ARF, and the United Nations", *Contemporary Southeast Asia* 24, no. 3 (December 2002): 536–37.

[31] See Seng Tan et al., *A New Agenda for the ASEAN Regional Forum* (Singapore: Institute for Defence and Strategic Studies, 2002), pp. 14–15.

[32] Ibid., pp. 32, 35.

[33] Ibid., pp. 43, 48, 66.

[34] *ARF Statement Against Terrorist Financing*, 30 July 2002.

[35] Recent assessments of the ARF may be found in Evelyn Goh, "Great Powers and Hierarchical Order in Southeast Asia: Analyzing Regional Security Strategies", *International Security* 32, no. 3 (Winter 2007–08), especially pp. 124, 129–131, 140, 144, and 146; and Etel Solingen, "The Genesis, Design, and Effects of Regional Institutions: Lessons from East Asia and the Middle East", *International Studies Quarterly* 52, no. 2 (June 2008): 276–79.

[36] Mark Manyin et al., *Terrorism in Southeast Asia* (Washington, DC: Congressional Research Service Report for Congress, 26 March 2003), pp. 16–17.

[37] *Agence France Presse* (Hong Kong), 8 April 2003, in *Foreign Broadcast Information Service (FBIS): Daily Report — East Asia*, 9 April 2003.

[38] *Agence France Presse* (Hong Kong), 26 December 2002, in *FBIS: Daily Report — East Asia*, 27 December 2002.

[39] *Agence France Presse* (Hong Kong), 16 January, 28 April, and 16 May 2003, in *FBIS: Daily Report — East Asia*, 19 January, 29 April, and 19 May 2003 respectively, as well as the *Philippine Daily Inquirer*, 10 April 2003, in *FBIS: Daily Report — East Asia*, 11 April 2003.

40 Bernama (Kuala Lumpur), 13 March 2003, in *FBIS: Daily Report — East Asia*, 17 March 2003; and *Agence France Presse* (Hong Kong), 7 May 2003, in *FBIS: Daily Report — East Asia*, 8 May 2003.
41 Neela Banerjee and Keith Bradsher, "A Vulnerable Time to be Moving Oil by Sea", *New York Times*, 19 October 2002.
42 Mark Valencia, "Southeast Asia Piracy Runs Rampant; Coastal States at Loggerheads over Protection", *Washington Times*, 4 June 2001.
43 "Regional Worries Speed Singapore-Malaysia Arms Race", stratfor.com, 23 August 2002.
44 Nick Brown, "Report Reveals Decline in Piracy", *Jane's Defence Weekly*, 31 January 2007. p. 5.
45 Keith Bradsher, "Attacks on Chemical Ships in Southeast Asia Seem to be Piracy, not Terror", *New York Times*, 27 March 2003.
46 John Garfano, "Power, Institutions, and the ASEAN Regional Forum: A Security Community for Asia?" *Asian Survey* 42, no. 3 (May/June, 2002): 520.
47 Sheldon W. Simon, "U.S.-Southeast Asian Relations: U.S. Frustrated as Burmese Junta Obstructs Cyclone Relief", *Comparative Connections: An E-Journal of East Asian Bilateral Relations* (Honolulu: Pacific Forum/CSIS, July 2008).
48 Sheldon W. Simon, "Theater Security Cooperation in the U.S. Pacific Command: An Assessment and Projection", *NBR Analysis* (August 2003).

REFERENCES

Acharya, Amitav. *The Quest for Identity: International Relations of Southeast Asia*. Singapore: Oxford University Press, 2000.

————. *Constructing a Security Community in Southeast Asia: ASEAN and the Problem of Regional Order*. New York: Routledge, 2001.

————. "Competing and Congruent Approaches to Security Cooperation in the Asia-Pacific Region: A Concept Paper", Unpublished paper, Singapore 2002.

Agence France Presse (Hong Kong), 26 December 2002. *Foreign Broadcast Information Service (FBIS): Daily Report — East Asia* (hereafter FBIS: Daily Report — East Asia), 27 December 2002.

————. 16 January 2003. *FBIS: Daily Report — East Asia*, 19 January 2003.

————. 8 April 2003. *FBIS: Daily Report — East Asia*, 9 April 2003.

————. 28 April 2003. *FBIS: Daily Report — East Asia*, 29 April 2003.

————. 7 May 2003. *FBIS: Daily Report — East Asia*, 8 May 2003.

————. 16 May 2003. *FBIS: Daily Report — East Asia*, 19 May 2003.

————. 10 October 2007. *FBIS: Daily Report — East Asia*, 11 October 2007.

ARF. *ARF Statement on Measures Against Terrorist Financing*, 30 July 2002.

"ASEAN Fails to Reach Human Rights Accord". *Australian Broadcasting System*, 30 July 2007.

"ASEAN Police to Set Up Anti-terrorism Task Force". *UN Secretariat* (Jakarta), 22 January 2003.

Banerjee, Neela and Keith Bradsher. "A Vulnerable Time to be Moving Oil by Sea". *The New York Times*, 19 October 2002.

Bernama (Kuala Lumpur), 13 March 2003, in *FBIS: Daily Report — East Asia*, 17 March, 2003.

Bradsher, Keith. "Attacks on Chemical Ships in Southeast Asia Seem to be Piracy, not Terror". *New York Times*, 27 March 2003.

Brown, Nick. "Report Reveals Decline in Piracy". *Jane's Defence Weekly*, 31 January 2007, p. 5.

"Burmese Junta Should Be Offered Shared Role". Antara, 3 October 2007.

Caballero-Anthony, Mely. "Partnership for Peace in Asia: ASEAN, the ARF, and the United Nations". *Contemporary Southeast Asia* 24, no. 3 (2002): 528–49.

Chanda, Nayan. "Southeast Asia After September 11". In *George W. Bush and Asia: A Midterm Assessment*, edited by Robert Hathaway and Wilson Lee. Washington, DC: Woodrow Wilson Center for Scholars, 2003.

Chongkittavorn, Kavi. "ASEAN Charter: Should We Settle for Second Best?" *The Nation*, Bangkok, Internet version, 14 August, 2007.

Cossa, Ralph and Brad Glosserman. "Regional Overview: Renewed Hope in the Year of the Golden Pig". In *Comparative Connections* 9, no. 1, 2007 <http://www.csis.org/media/csis/pubs/0701q_overview.pdf> (accessed 25 February 2009).

Desker, Barry. "ASEAN: Time to Suspend Myanmar". *RSIS Commentaries* (Singapore), 4 October 2007.

Doronila, Amando. "Out of Step with ASEAN". Inquirer.net (Manila), 5 August 2007.

Elliot, Lorraine. "ASEAN and Environmental Cooperation: Norms, Interests, and Identity". *Pacific Review* 16, no. 1 (2003): 29–52.

Findlay, Trevor. "The Regional Security Outlook". In *Asia-Pacific Security: Less Uncertainty, New Opportunities*, edited by Gary Klintworth. New York: St. Martin's Press, 1998.

Garfano, John. "Power, Institutions, and the ASEAN Regional Forum: A Security Community for Asia?" *Asian Survey* 42, no. 3 (May/June, 2002): 502–21.

Goh, Evelyn. "Great Powers and Hierarchical Order in Southeast Asia: Analyzing Regional Security Strategies". *International Security* 32, no. 3 (Winter 2007–8): 113–57.

"Indonesia and Thai Navies Reach Cooperation Agreement". Antara, 8 April 2008.

Jetly, Rajshree. "Conflict Management Strategies in ASEAN: Perspectives for SAARC". *The Pacific Review* 16, no. 1 (2003): 53–76.

Karniol, Robert. "A Total Defence". *Jane's Defence Weekly*, 28 August 2002, p. 25.

Koh, Tommy, Walter Woon, Andrew Tan, and Chan Sze-Wei, "The ASEAN Charter," *PacNet 33A* (Honolulu, Pacific Forum), 6 September 2007.

Leifer, Michael. "The ASEAN Peace Process: A Category Mistake". *Pacific Review* 12, no. 1 (1999): 25–38.

Manyin, Mark, Richard Cronin, Larry Niksch, and Bruce Vaughn. *Terrorism in Southeast Asia*. Washington, DC: Congressional Research Service Report for Congress, 26 March 2003.

Miller, Alistair and Eric Rosand. "Implementing the UN General Assembly's Global Counter-Terrorism Strategy in the Asia-Pacific". *Asian Security* 3, no. 3 (2007): 181–203.

Ramakrishna, Kumar. "Applying the U.S. National Security Strategy for Countering Terrorism to Southeast Asia". Paper prepared for the Institute for National Strategic Studies — U.S. Institute of Peace Workshop on Terrorism's New Front Lines: Adapting U.S. Counter-Terrorism Strategy To Regions of Concern, Washington, DC, 8–9 May 2003.

"Regional Worries Speed Singapore-Malaysia Arms Race". stratfor.com, 23 August 2002.

Simon, Sheldon W. "Asian Armed Forces: Internal and External Tasks and Capabilities". In *The Many Faces of Asian Security*, edited by Sheldon W. Simon. New York: Rowman and Littlefield, 2001.

———. "Theater Security Cooperation in the U.S. Pacific Command: An Assessment and Projection". *NBR Analysis*, August 2003.

———. "Southeast Asia's Defense Needs: Change of Continuity?" In *Strategic Asia 2005–06: Military Modernization in an Era of Uncertainty*, edited by Ashley Tellis and Michael Wills. Seattle: The National Bureau of Asian Research, 2005.

———. "U.S.-Southeast Asian Relations: Burma Heats Up and the U.S. Blows Hot and Cold". *Comparative Connections: A Quarterly E-Journal of East Asian Bilateral Relations* 9, no. 3 (2007): 65–78.

———. "U.S. Frustrated as Burmese Junta Obstructs Cyclone Relief". *Comparative Connections*, July 2008.

———. "ASEAN and Multilateralism: The Long Bumpy Road to Community". *Contemporary Southeast Asia* 30, no. 2 (2008): 264–92.

Solingen, Etel. "The Genesis, Design, and Effects of Regional Institutions: Lessons from East Asia and the Middle East". *International Studies Quarterly* 52, no. 2 (June 2008): 261–94.

"Southeast Asia — Security," stratfor.com, 12 February 2003.

Tan, Andrew. "Terrorism in Singapore: Threat and Implications". *Contemporary Security Policy* 23, no. 3 (2002): 1–18.

Tan, See-Seng, Ralf Emmers, Mely Caballero-Anthony, Amitav Acharya, Barry Desker, and Kwa Chong Guan. *A New Agenda for the ASEAN Regional Forum*. Singapore: Institute for Defence and Strategic Studies, 2002.

"Thailand Set to Join Malacca Patrols". *Bangkok Post* (online version) 20 August 2007.

"UN-backed Project to boost safety, security in vital Malacca Shipping Lanes". UN News Service. 11 September 2007.

"UN's Envoy Suggests Incentives for Myanmar". *International Herald-Tribune*, 17 October 2007.

Valencia, Mark. "Southeast Asia Piracy Runs Rampant: Coastal States at Loggerheads over Protection". *Washington Times*, 4 June 2001.

PART II

Case Studies — Mainland Southeast Asia

3

Vietnam-Thailand Relations after the Cold War

Nguyen Vu Tung

In many respects, Thailand holds a special place in Vietnam's policy toward Southeast Asia. Vietnam and Thailand are major countries of mainland Southeast Asia. The geographical proximity has made Thailand most sensitive to developments in Indochina to which Vietnam attaches a special importance. In addition to this consideration, the relationship between Vietnam and Thailand has always been the barometer of that between Vietnam and ASEAN countries, especially before Vietnam joined the Association. Maisrikrod noted that "regional order in Southeast Asia during most of the 1980s was centred around the Thai-Vietnamese relationship."[1] Soon after the Vietnam War ended, Vietnam and Thailand established diplomatic relations, in August 1976. Relations between the two countries however fell to the state of hostility as Thailand became the

The analyses and arguments presented in this chapter are the author's personal views and might not reflect those held by institutions that the author is affiliated with.

ASEAN front-line state to oppose the so-called "Vietnamese occupation of Cambodia". Since the end of the Cold War, relations between Vietnam and Thailand have reflected the general trend toward greater regional cooperation. In the 1980s the two countries began to rebuild a rounded relationship, which has been described by the Vietnamese side as "friendly and better than ever before",[2] and by the Thais as "mutually productive and beneficial" based on "friendship, trust, and mutual respect".[3]

Many reasons have been provided to explain the positive movement in Vietnamese-Thai relations. This chapter argues that the improvement in relations was a result of a combination of the relaxation of international and regional tensions, a comprehensive course of reforms in Vietnam, and changes in Thailand's foreign policies. Above all, however, the changes in foreign policy priorities in Vietnam helped start a chain reaction that worked toward the betterment of bilateral relations. Furthermore, the regional frameworks in which both countries are involved helped to consolidate this bilateral relationship. Last but not least, increased interactions and greater understanding at the people-to-people level has also contributed to good relations between the two countries. The combination of these factors suggest that the two countries can enjoy conditions for long-lasting friendly relations. Both realist and constructivist approaches should feel comfortable with these factors in providing explanations for the current and future state of relations.

Missed Opportunities: Relations between the Early 1970s and Mid-1980s

A number of observers and scholars have argued that Vietnam and Thailand share many historical, social, and cultural characteristics that could provide a sound basis for bilateral relations to develop. They cite the sympathy and support by the Thai people and authorities for the Vietnamese cause of national independence, from 1944 to 1947.[4] They also cite cultural and religious affiliations as important contributing reasons. Deesrisuk, for example, argued that the establishment of diplomatic relations between Vietnam and Thailand was a "reaffirmation of ties and linkages between two groups of peoples which had existed for centuries, for as two of the ancient civilizations of Southeast Asia, our forefathers had rich and varied historical relationships."[5] Hoang Khac Nam argued that natural, economic, social, and cultural similarities led to similar worldviews, which explains the origin and development of this bilateral relationship.[6] This type of argument seems to suggest that there is no conflict of national interests in Vietnam-Thailand relations, and that there exist between the two countries many favourable conditions for good relations to automatically develop. Therefore, many seem to see the deterioration of relations between Vietnam and Thailand as mainly the result of external factors. Song Tung wrote, "From a historical perspective, we can see that whenever there were foreign intervention and interference, the two countries engaged in a forced confrontation. But when the external forces were removed, sincere friendship was restored and strengthened."[7]

This study, however, argues that differences of worldview and conflicts in national interests did contribute to the state of hostility between the two countries in the 1980s, although efforts to develop bilateral relations were made in the early 1970s and gained momentum soon after Vietnam achieved national independence and unification in April 1975. In other words, the focus on external variables, although plausible and important, cannot fully explain why Vietnam and Thailand failed to improve relations in the late 1970s and 1980s when conditions were good and opportunities were available. In the same vein, the change in worldview and re-ordering of foreign policy priorities in Hanoi, together with the relaxation of international tensions after the Cold War, led to the improvement in Vietnam-Thailand relations from the late 1980s.

It must be noted here that geo-strategic and economic considerations did influence the thinking of Vietnamese policymakers when relations with Southeast Asian states were designed. Arguments for the establishment of diplomatic relations with Thailand as well as other ASEAN countries were made on the grounds of national interest. For example, a Vietnam Ministry of Foreign Affairs (MOFA) report of 1974 stressed that "developing relations with neighbouring countries is a task of primary importance in the foreign affairs of any state, for neighbouring countries are closely linked with the security and economic development of the state concerned."[8]

Indeed, relations between Vietnam and Thailand developed according to this logic. Thailand in 1973 made several initiatives to open contact with Hanoi. In 1974, Foreign Ministers of Vietnam and Thailand exchanged letters about developing bilateral relations. Between May 16 and 29, 1975 — that is two weeks after the fall of Saigon — negotiations on normalization of relations were held between the Thai and PRG/DRV (Provisional Revolutionary Government/Democratic Republic of Vietnam) delegations. In April 1976, Thai Foreign Minister Bhichai Rattakul met Vietnamese Deputy Foreign Minister Phan Hien in Bangkok, and in June led a governmental delegation to visit Hanoi. On 6 August 1976 Vietnam and Thailand signed a joint statement to officially establish diplomatic relations. But until December 1977, no concrete steps were taken to develop the relationship due to changes in Thai politics. On 1 December 1977, Thai and Vietnamese Ambassadors in Vientiane signed the Vientiane Statement to take immediate measures to normalize relations between Vietnam and Thailand. These measures included the official visit by Vietnamese Foreign Minister Nguyen Duy Trinh to Thailand, where the two sides agreed to open embassies as soon as possible, settle remaining issues, and signed Agreements on Trade, Economic and Technological Cooperation and Civil Aviation Transportation. Vietnam opened its embassy in Bangkok in February 1978. In September 1978, Vietnamese Prime Minister Pham Van Dong visited Thailand, beginning his tour of five ASEAN countries. Also in 1978, a joint committee met in Bangkok to discuss issues related to Vietnamese living in Thailand. In the same year the Thai Government granted Vietnam two million baht to help victims of floods.[9] Economic cooperation began to develop. Thailand agreed to provide Vietnam with a loan of a hundred million baht, sold 145,000 tons of rice and 50,000 tons of maize to the country, and bought 27,600 tons of coal.[10] Hanoi in 1978 even cut relations with the Thai Communist Party, partly to convince Bangkok that Vietnam did not have plans to interfere with Thailand's domestic politics, thus hoping to neutralize Thailand in the widening rifts between Vietnam and Kampuchea as well as between Vietnam and China. In this context, Hanoi's policy to enter a new stage of relations with Thailand was clearly influenced by national construction and security considerations. Therefore, when Vietnam and Thailand established diplomatic relations in 1976, the conventional wisdom was that the relationship was put on "a good start".[11]

But this good start did not lead to a substantive change in relations. This was because Hanoi's policy was still influenced by a communist ideology that prevented its leaders from having a good understanding of the changes in Southeast Asia and the world, particularly in respect to relations with the large powers.

There were several implications to Vietnam-Thailand relations of this worldview. First of all, it described Thailand — together with other ASEAN members — as a henchman of the United States. This attitude was a result of the lingering memory of Thailand's involvement in the Vietnam War and the continued existence of U.S. military bases in Thailand, which were believed to be evidence of Bangkok's support of the hostile American policy against Vietnam after 1975. Further, the political and economic system in Thailand was viewed as a product of neo-imperialism that benefited foreign capitalists and their local lackeys at the expense of the working people, and prevented revolution from developing in Thailand at a time Hanoi believed conditions in Southeast Asia were favourable for such radical changes. Taken together, Thailand was seen as anti-communist, reactionary, and above all, a country of opposing ideology. Hanoi, therefore, held back from developing meaningful relations with Bangkok, and even accused the foreign policy of Thailand — as well as other ASEAN countries — of being not "genuinely peaceful, independent, and neutral".[12]

In addition, the hubris of victory in the periods after January 1973 and April 1975 seemed to influence the way Hanoi constructed new relations with Thailand. On the one hand, as mentioned above, Hanoi started to acknowledge the geo-politics and geo-economics of improved relations with Thailand and other ASEAN countries when the war against the United States was ending. Yet, on the other hand, it seems that as the victor in the conflict, Hanoi wanted to impose its own vision of international relations in Southeast Asia according to its perceived stature and preferred objectives. This was evident in Hanoi's reaction to ASEAN initiatives to get Vietnam involved in ASEAN activities, and its announced position with regard to the establishment of relations with ASEAN countries in general and with Thailand in particular.

As early as January 1973, Hanoi believed that it had an enhanced stature in Southeast Asia. A MOFA report written in 1974 stressed the new position of Vietnam with regard to ASEAN countries as follows, "Many states have considered Vietnam as a superpower" and therefore, "activities at the regional level will be meaningless without the participation of Vietnam." It also stressed, "Other Southeast Asian countries have recognized that regional problems cannot be solved without our participation. Therefore, all of them want to have relations with us."[13] The general mood in Hanoi at that time was that initiatives by Thailand — and other ASEAN countries — toward improvement of relations with Vietnam and neutralization of Southeast Asia were the result of their acknowledgement of Vietnam's power and position in the region. The MOFA Report stressed, "They have now come to understand that their policies toward Vietnam in the past were wrong, and therefore want to change and correct these policies, to enhance understanding and proceed to establishing friendly relations." It also suggested, "We should develop relations with Southeast Asian states to show the goodwill of a victorious country."[14]

It seemed that based on this understanding, Hanoi wanted to set the terms for the development of relations with ASEAN countries. Negotiations between Vietnam and Thailand on normalization of relations (from 21 to 29 May 1975) failed due in part to Hanoi's demand for the withdrawal of all U.S. troops and bases from Thailand. The Four-Point Position was another case in point. Hanoi's criticism of ASEAN of not being genuinely peaceful, independent, and neutral was in fact an introduction (and perhaps an imposition) of Hanoi's worldview on regional cooperation. By focusing on genuine peace, independence and neutrality, as it has been argued, Hanoi tried to set the "entry barrier" for ASEAN countries, and this implied that "ASEAN states should reject their own models of political, security and economic development if they wanted to improve relations with Vietnam."[15]

The same approach was applied to Thailand. In March 1976, a commentary in *Nhan Dan* (People's Daily) read:

> The continued presence of US military forces in Thailand and the previous acts of aggressions [during the Vietnam War] perpetrated by the U.S. imperialists from Thailand are both root and immediate causes that obstruct and damage the relations between Vietnam and Thailand. Therefore, completely abolishing the U.S. military presence in every aspect would open a new period of very good, friendly and cooperative relations between the two countries.[16]

In short, the ideology-based worldview, the euphoria of victory, and the memory of Thailand's past involvement in the Vietnam War collectively led to the "missed opportunities"[17] to improve relations between Vietnam and Thailand in the late 1970s. Vietnam was not able to introduce an effective foreign policy to take advantage of the reconciliatory stance by ASEAN in general and Thailand in particular to work collectively on the construction of a new regional order for peaceful coexistence among Southeast Asian states in the aftermath of the Vietnam War.

Conflict of national interests also played an important role in explaining why relations between Vietnam and Thailand became hostile in this period. Vietnam's involvement in Cambodia was a case in point. Traditionally, Vietnam and Thailand are two of the competitors for influence in Cambodia, and to a lesser extent Laos.[18] Thailand therefore, was most sensitive to Vietnam's post-war foreign policy priority toward Southeast Asia in general and Indochina in particular. In this connection, the unified Vietnam caused security concerns in Thailand as Bangkok feared that Hanoi could interfere in Thai domestic politics through its continued relations with the Communist Party of Thailand (CPT) and the existence of Vietnamese living in Thailand. But this fear was more hypothetical than real for a number of reasons. Although Hanoi's rhetoric of "supporting communist parties and progressive forces" in Southeast Asia was more vocal in the post-1975 period, no substantial actions were undertaken because of Hanoi's focus on post-war economic reconstruction. Indeed, no concrete plan for "export of revolution" was detected nor was there any plan to turn the community of Vietnamese living in Thailand into a "fifth column" inside Thai society. Furthermore, Hanoi did not support Thai and other local communist parties because it believed that they were Maoist and pro-PRC in nature. As mentioned above, in 1978 Vietnam cut relations with the CPT. It was not practical for Vietnam to export revolution to Thailand, so fears of this taking place were unfounded.[19]

The only concern was then related to Hanoi's ambition in Indochina. This fear was materialized when Vietnam sent troops to Cambodia. Hanoi's approach to ASEAN and Thailand — criticism of the nature of the association, political and economic regimes, and mode of foreign relations of the member states — had caused a great amount of suspicion and apprehension in ASEAN countries. At the same time, Hanoi's stress on building Indochina into a bloc of countries that followed new principles of international relations suggested that it was ready to lead the grouping of Indochinese states to challenge ASEAN as a bloc. Hanoi's reluctance to enter rapprochement with ASEAN states made ASEAN more watchful for the next moves by Vietnam. As a result, when Vietnam sent troops to Cambodia to put an end to the genocidal regime of the Khmer Rouge, the resultant presence of Vietnamese armed forces and the existence of a pro-Vietnamese government in Cambodia caused ASEAN states, especially Thailand, to believe that Vietnam was trying to put the whole of Indochina under its sphere of influence in a zero-sum fashion. In this case, Thailand sought to firmly confront Vietnam out of considerations of national interest. From as early as the late 1960s, and throughout the Cambodia crisis, Thailand entered into cooperation with Beijing to check Vietnam's regional ambition. The country also provided the Khmer

Rouge and other forces resisting the pro-Vietnamese regime in Phnom Penh with material assistance and sanctuaries. In addition, Bangkok was able to persuade other ASEAN countries to maintain a tough line toward Vietnam at a time when some ASEAN countries, including Indonesia and Malaysia, believed that early rapprochement with Vietnam would help resolve the crisis and that prolonged hostility would invite external powers to interfere with Southeast Asian affairs.[20] As a result, since late 1979, relations with Thailand became tense as Thailand became the ASEAN front line state against Vietnam in all regional and international fora, demanding the withdrawal of Vietnamese troops from Kampuchea and considering this the prerequisite for normalization of relations between Vietnam and Thailand.

During this time, however, limited contacts between the two countries were still maintained. For example, in January 1979, Thailand renewed the civil aviation agreement with Vietnam. In 1985, the Thai Foreign Minister stated that Bangkok "did not encourage nor prevent private enterprises from Thailand to do business with Vietnam"; unofficial trade relations were resumed in the same year. Between April and October 1986 top diplomats of the two countries met to discuss bilateral relations. According to MOFA analyses, these moves were taken to induce Vietnam into a solution of the Cambodian problem that would take Vietnam's interest into consideration and pave the way for Thailand to take the lead in the eventual ASEAN-Vietnam rapprochement.[21]

Improved Relations: From 1986 to the Present

Vietnam's change of foreign policy priorities in the aftermath of the Cold War and its acceptance of the ASEAN mode of regional cooperation are the two main factors that have contributed to the removal of the mutual suspicion and hostility of the 1980s and the improvement in Vietnam-Thailand relations since the 1990s. Facing a state of "socio-economic crisis" at home and diplomatic isolation and economic embargo abroad, Hanoi began from 1986 a course of comprehensive reforms — known as Doi Moi — opening up a process in which a new worldview was introduced and foreign policy objectives were re-prioritized as a result.

A number of aspects of the new thinking in Vietnam's foreign affairs and the resultant new foreign policy, which were conducive to improving Vietnam-Thailand relations, are worthy of mention. Firstly, national interest had emerged as the more important base for formulation and implementation of foreign policy. In the period after 1986, the creation of an external environment for national reconstruction emerged as the number one national interest. In 1988, the Thirteenth Communist Party of Vietnam (CPV) Politburo adopted a resolution which noted, with "a strong economy, just-enough defence capabilities, and expanded external relations, Vietnam can enjoy conditions for protecting the country's security."[22] A closer look at this "order of importance" suggests that diplomacy was to be of greatest utility, for expanded external relations in fact would play a key role in building the external environment for Vietnam to develop a strong economy that allowed the country to seek its niche in the regional and international economies based on its comparative advantages. Friendly and cooperative relations with other countries would also allow Vietnam to reduce military spending and shift more resources to economic development. In other words, seeking good relations with other countries became a policy priority in Vietnamese foreign relations.[23] The Politburo also stressed the new foreign policy guideline "to have more friends and fewer enemies".[24] Basically, befriending foreign countries became a matter of national interest in Vietnamese foreign policy.[25]

Of course, the new thinking in Vietnam's foreign affairs was immediately influenced by changes in the Soviet Union's foreign policy. Due to the more limited capability to provide aid and the need to improve relations with the United States and China, Moscow began to disengage itself from and encouraged political settlements of conflicts in the Third World. As a result, Moscow reduced economic and military assistance to its allies. When the Soviet Union stopped giving aid to Vietnam and bilateral trade in 1990 fell from eighty per cent to fourteen per cent of Vietnam's total foreign trade,[26] Hanoi had to design a new foreign policy to meet its security and development needs (as well as to seek solutions to the Kampuchea issue). In other words, when the reliance on Soviet military and economic aid was no longer feasible, the need to seek alternatives to Soviet assistance became more urgent.

At the same time, however, the decline of the Soviet Union in the late 1980s also indicated that Moscow's constraints on Hanoi's efforts to have greater foreign policy autonomy were lessened. The two processes, namely the change of the leadership's worldview and the reduction of Soviet aid, became mutually reinforcing. As a result, the drive for developing friendly external relations with the non-communist states was in full swing in 1991 when the Soviet Union ceased to exist.[27] In short, the reduction of Soviet aid, the disintegration of the Soviet bloc, and the collapse of the Soviet Union served as catalysts for further policy changes in Hanoi. The withdrawal of troops from Cambodia then represented a first policy step that Hanoi had to take to remove the "greatest obstacle" to improvement of relations with other countries.

Secondly, and related to the point above, Hanoi policymakers have attached special importance to the improvement of Vietnam's relations with neighbouring countries in Southeast Asia. With the Thirty-second Politburo Resolution adopted in July 1986, for the first time, peaceful coexistence became the new principle for Vietnam's relations with ASEAN countries.[28] Further, the Thirteen Politburo Resolution adopted in May 1988 stressed that Vietnam did not want to continue the confrontation between the socialist Indochina bloc against the capitalist ASEAN grouping. In particular, it stressed the need to remove the stalemate in relations with Thailand.[29] Acting in accordance with the Resolution, on 26 May 1988, Vietnam removed troops stationed in the border areas with Thailand. On 26 September 1989, Vietnam completed its unilateral troop withdrawal from Kampuchea without linking it to the political solution of the Cambodia problem.

The withdrawal of Vietnamese troops from Cambodia and acceptance of the UN-led solution to the Cambodia problem then represented the third aspect of the new foreign policy thinking and the direct reason to explain the improvement of relations with Thailand. The absence of Vietnamese troops, first in the Thai-Cambodia border areas, then in the entirety of Cambodia, reduced the direct military threat that Thailand felt from Vietnam. Furthermore, Vietnam's Cambodia policy in essence was Hanoi's policy of disengagement from Cambodia. Hanoi began to accept a coalition government in Phnom Penh, which would be set up following national elections organized and verified by the UN and the new Cambodian Government's foreign policy which would turn Cambodia into a country both friendly and at the same time more independent from Vietnam. Also, Vietnam's troop withdrawal from Kampuchea and the UN-imposed solution to the Cambodia problem helped to clear Thailand's lingering suspicion about Vietnam's ambition in Indochina in general and in Cambodia in particular. It seems that Cambodia had returned to the traditional role of a buffer zone between Vietnam and Thailand, which is acceptable to and in accordance with the national interests of both Vietnam and Thailand. The thorniest issue between Vietnam and Thailand was thus removed. It was not coincidental that when Vietnam announced the phased troop withdrawal from Kampuchea, Thailand introduced the new Indochina policy. On 25 August 1988, Thai Prime Minister Chatichai Choonhavan said he wanted to turn Indochina "from the battlefield into a market place".[30] In January 1989, Thai Foreign Minister Siddhi Savetsila visited Vietnam to "open a new chapter in the relations between Vietnam and Thailand." In February 1990, he confirmed that Thailand's policy toward Vietnam "has moved from confrontation to cooperation".[31] When the Agreement on Cambodia was concluded in Paris on 24 October 1991, Nguyen Manh Cam said, "the last obstacle to the normalization of relations" with ASEAN countries was removed.[32] The Paris Agreement provided the long-held contest of national interest between Thailand and Vietnam with a decent solution. More importantly, it showed the absence of a "bad loser" feelings about Cambodia. To the contrary, Hanoi began in earnest to focus on developing relations with ASEAN countries, including Thailand.

The need to improve relations with Thailand and other ASEAN countries became more urgent for Hanoi as the socialist bloc was quickly disintegrating. In June 1992, the Third Plenum of the CPV Central Committee adopted a resolution regarding a new orientation of Vietnam's foreign policy. Nguyen Manh Cam said that policy with regard to Southeast Asian states was extremely important because of its "geo-strategic nature".[33] The Resolution also argued that good relations with ASEAN countries would on the one hand pave the way for Vietnam to improve relations with big powers. On the other hand, it would serve as a training ground for the country to economically integrate itself with the rest of the world.[34] ASEAN as a whole and Thailand in particular was therefore seen in a new light. Tran Quang Co had earlier made this point: "Vietnam is fully aware that it is a part of Southeast Asia and clearly understands the great importance of the establishment of friendly and cooperative relations with other countries in the region."[35] In the new context of the end of the Cold War, a sense of déjà vu has returned to Vietnam's policy toward Southeast Asia. Similar to the period of the early 1970s, great importance has been attached to the Southeast Asian region for strategic and economic reasons. What is different is that the ideological element now plays a less important role as Vietnam increasingly finds itself belonging to the region and linking its prosperity and security to Southeast Asia. The collapse of the Soviet bloc, as it turned out, was a blessing in disguise, for it made Vietnam more determined to engage in genuine reconciliation and meaningful improvement of relations with ASEAN countries. In this connection, special importance was attached to improving relations with Thailand because Hanoi believed that the improvement of relations between Thailand and Vietnam — "representatives of two groups of opposing ideologies" — would be seen as the litmus test for Vietnam-ASEAN relations.[36] In other words, having good relations with Thailand was in keeping with the new national interest that Hanoi perceived.

The shift in Thai foreign policy orientation after the end of the Cold War also helped to end the political animosity between the two countries and led to an improvement of bilateral relations. As Maisrikrod pointed out, the relaxation of international and regional tensions and the re-emergence of "full democracy" were factors that led to radical changes in Thai foreign policy. The changes included the shift in mentality in Thai foreign policy, namely to depart from seeing "neighbours as enemies" and to present Thailand as a "sincere and compassionate neighbour", as well as adopting a reconciliatory approach toward Vietnam, namely to embark on concrete cooperation measures.[37] The author also quoted Thai analyst Kavi Chongkittavorn who argued in 1992 that "Thailand's biggest challenge is how to work towards a trustful relationship with Vietnam."[38]

The ASEAN factor also contributed greatly to the improvement of Vietnam-Thailand relations. As mentioned earlier, the Thirteenth Politburo Resolution introduced in May 1988 marked the end of the state of Indochina-ASEAN confrontation. Following the withdrawal of Vietnamese troops from Kampuchea in 1989 and the Paris Agreement on Cambodia in 1991, the process to join ASEAN began. In June 1991, Hanoi decided to accede to the Treaty of Amity and Cooperation in Southeast Asia (TAC, or the Bali Treaty). And in October, Prime Minister Vo Van Kiet told the *Bangkok Post*, "Vietnam wants to join ASEAN." In June 1992, Vietnam became an observer in ASEAN. In 1994 it joined the ASEAN Regional Forum (ARF), and in 1995 it joined ASEAN.[39] This process was Vietnam's "implicit acceptance" of the ASEAN mode of international relations for the regional countries in general and the ASEAN mode of conflict management in particular.[40] In addition, as Laos and Cambodia were admitted to ASEAN as new members in 1997, the "ASEAN Way" had thus been accepted in the entirety of Southeast Asia, which in practice put an end to the division of Southeast Asia into two blocs. That was the logic behind the ASEAN expansion in the aftermath of the Cold War, Vietnam's improved relations with ASEAN countries and its eventual membership in ASEAN. In this connection, it is noteworthy that Vietnam's membership in ASEAN helps to consolidate a new state identity for Vietnam, now being a Southeast Asian country. Moreover, a shared identity — supported by more interactions and cooperation as well as conditioned by ASEAN institutional rules and norms — helps to boost cooperation at both regional and bilateral levels. As it has been argued, "The case of ASEAN identity-based cooperation allows us to hope for prolonged regional unity."[41] Writing in 1994, Vu Khoan states:

> The ASEAN countries desire for peace, stability and expanded cooperation is in keeping with our policy that tries to take advantage of the favourable international conditions and the emerging environment of peace and stability to construct and defend our country. The ASEAN foreign policy, therefore, is compatible with the foreign policy of diversification and multilateralization of our external relations in which the primary focus is on cooperation with countries in Southeast Asia.[42]

Against this background, the bilateral relationship between Vietnam and Thailand now rests on a firmer basis of enduring ASEAN peace in the post–Cold War era and develops in many fields.

Building Mutual Trust

Efforts have been made to strengthen bilateral relations. Confidence building measures in some very sensitive areas undertaken to clear mutual suspicion were given first priority. First of all, Vietnam and Thailand quickly solved territorial disputes. After nine rounds of negotiations, the two countries signed on 9 August 1997 an agreement demarcating the overlapping sea zones related to the continental shelf and Exclusive Economic Zone boundaries in the disputed area in the Gulf of Thailand (to the south-west of Vietnam and north-east of Thailand). The document entered into force on 27 February 1998.[43] The agreement, together with bilateral cooperation in solving fishery disputes and restoring order at sea helped to minimize potential causes of future conflicts. In March 1995, the first meeting of the high-level Joint Committee on Fisheries and Marine Order took place; the two sides inked an agreement on cooperation in maintaining order at sea and in the joint development of marine resources.[44]

According to Thayer, "the opening of regional defence contacts, especially in the early 1990s, pre-dated Vietnam's official membership in ASEAN, and marks the real commencement of defence diplomacy by Vietnam. Thailand ranked first among the ASEAN countries with which Vietnam had "relative intensity of high-level defence exchanges."[45] In 1992, General Suchinda Kraprayoon, the then Supreme Commander and Chief of the Army, invited Vietnamese Armed Forces to observe the annual Thai-U.S. joint military exercise, "Cobra Gold". Vietnam has, since 2002, sent observers to this exercise.

In 1995, the two countries agreed in principle to set up joint patrol teams in the Gulf of Thailand.[46] Since 9 February 2001 the Vietnamese and Thai navies have conducted joint sea patrols in the area.[47] This exercise has become institutionalized: apart from regular joint patrols, Thai and Vietnamese navies inform each other of activities conducted in the area and a hotline has been established for the purpose of information sharing and crisis prevention.[48] Vietnam also enlists Thailand's cooperation in checking anti-government activities by Vietnamese living overseas. During his visit to Vietnam in March 2008, Thai Prime Minister Samak Sundaravej stated that the Thai Government followed the policy that "outlaws any groups, organizations, and individuals that use Thailand's territory to sabotage Vietnamese security."[49] In July 2008, the Joint Committee on political and security cooperation met for the third time and exchanged views on a wide range of issues, including non-traditional security threats, energy, and food crises. The two sides also agreed on a cooperative plan between 2008 and 2010.[50]

Last but not least, Thailand relaxed controls over Vietnamese migrating to Thailand in the period from 1945 to 1954.[51] In 1990, Thailand started to grant them Thai citizenship, because it "no longer feared external threat".[52] According to a report by the Vietnamese Embassy in Bangkok, 22,116 people of Vietnamese origin had been provided Thai citizenship by September 2000. The report predicted that by 2002 this issue would have been satisfactorily resolved.[53] Associations of Vietnamese in Thailand have been registered in the four provinces of Sakon Nakhon, Udonthani, Nong Khai, and Mukdahan with the encouragement of the Thai authorities.[54] Thai authorities also paid homage to Ho Chi Minh, naming a village, where he and other Vietnamese revolutionaries had lived, as "Village of the President" (Ban Nazok in Thai) — an act that has won the hearts of many people in Vietnam. In May 2000, the two countries signed a mutual visa-exemption agreement for people holding ordinary passports. These are very effective measures of confidence building that help to consolidate bilateral relations, especially when they are conducted by military and security establishments. In short, after Vietnam became an ASEAN member in 1995, Vietnam and Thailand ceased to see each other as external threats, and Thailand ceased to consider Thais of Vietnamese origin as "the fifth column" in Thailand.

Substantializing the Bilateral Cooperation

Bilateral relations with Thailand developed in other areas as well. As of 2007, the two countries have signed about thirty agreements to support political, economic, social, environmental, and educational cooperation.[55] Contacts, including visits by heads of state and MOFA consultations, have become regular. The Vietnamese and Thai Governments held the first joint Cabinet meeting in February 2004 in which the two countries signed a "Joint Declaration on The Framework of Strategic Cooperation in The First Half of Twenty-first Century". Such a meeting had not been previously conducted in relations between the two countries or with any other ASEAN member state. Apart from the joint ASEAN projects for ASEAN Community building, Vietnam and Thailand also actively cooperate in other projects of a multilateral nature designed for mainland Southeast Asia, such as the Ayeyawady–Chao Phraya–Mekong Economic Cooperation Strategy, a cooperation framework between Cambodia, Laos, Myanmar, Thailand, and Vietnam; the Trans-Asia Highway linking central Vietnam with Laos, Thailand, and Myanmar (East-West Economic Corridor); and the Greater Mekong Sub-region among Vietnam, Thailand, Laos, Myanmar, and China.

According to MOFA statistics, trade between Vietnam and Thailand in 2007 amounted to US$4.8 billion, a 21.3 per cent increase as compared with 2006. Thailand is Vietnam's sixth largest exporter. Trade with Thailand amounted to 20 per cent of Vietnam's total foreign trade. As of October 2007, Thailand had 160 investment projects in Vietnam, with a registered fund worth US$1.56 billion. Thailand is the twelfth largest foreign investor and the second largest ASEAN country investing in Vietnam.[56] In addition, between 1995 and 2000, Thailand provided Vietnam with 300 million baht in the form of official development aid.[57]

Last but not least, people-to-people contacts have increased a great extent. In 2006, over 200,000 Vietnamese tourists visited Thailand, and 120,000 Thais went on to visit Vietnam.[58] According to Vietnam Airlines officials, out of eight foreign airlines operating in Vietnam, five are from Thailand. From October 2007, Thai Airways alone had thirty-one flights to Vietnam every week.[59] The increased level of people-to-people contacts has been one of the most noteworthy aspects in the bilateral relations, as a MOFA report pointed out: "When these contacts and interactions intensify, peoples of the two countries know more about the other nation's history, culture and traditions. This new understanding and a sense of greater commonalities then serves as the "glue" for official diplomatic and economic relations to develop."[60]

Residual Issues

There are, however, complexities and constraints in this relationship. Vietnam continues to suffer from trade deficits with Thailand. According to a MOFA report, bilateral trade in 2007 amounted to US$4.8 billion, a 21.3 per cent increase as compared with 2006. Yet Vietnam suffers from a big trade deficit, with imports amounting to US$3.7 billion, a 23.2 per cent increase compared with 2006. In January 2008 alone, Vietnamese exports to and imports from Thailand were recorded at US$109 million and US$372 million respectively, a 58.0 and 45.2 per cent increase as compared with 2007 figures.[61] Moreover, Vietnam and Thailand seem to compete in some areas such as rice export and attracting foreign direct investment. However, according to some analyses, the two countries may not necessarily engage in fierce economic competition, because Thailand is more developed than Vietnam and some efforts at portraying Vietnam as a potential economic rival is mainly for Thai domestic consumption.[62] In addition, the verdict by the Thai court of justice not to extradite Vo Van Duc and Ly Tong — Americans of Vietnamese origin, who had been accused by Hanoi of committing terrorist acts against Vietnam and who are now imprisoned in Thailand on criminal charges — has soured political relations. Since September 2006, Hanoi has postponed the third round of talks on political and security cooperation and cancelled the Joint Consultative Mechanism at the deputy foreign minister level. It shows that differences in political and legal systems can still cause complications for relations between the two countries. The situation is, however, compounded mainly by ongoing political instability in Thailand. Since the September 2006 coup that removed Prime Minister Thaksin Shinawatra from power, Thailand became less active in conducting political exchanges and both governments have adopted a wait-and-see approach. The second joint Cabinet meeting has not been held as scheduled. In March 2008, and July 2009, Thai

Prime Ministers Samak Sundaravej and Abhisit Vejjajiva visited Hanoi respectively, while the visit to Hanoi by the Thai Foreign Minister in September 2008 was cancelled due to his resignation.

Conclusion

Vietnamese-Thai relations, in the final analysis, is a case study to show how changes in worldview and re-ordering of foreign policy priorities gave rise to changes in the foreign relations of Vietnam after 1986. Without this novel and somewhat revolutionary start, relations between Vietnam and Thailand could not develop to how they are now. As a side note, the realist logic on international relations seems plausible when states can change their relations between friendship and hostility based on their national interests, especially when the external environment changes. But on deeper analysis, Vietnam and Thailand can be seen to have been engaging in a relationship which promises long-lasting cooperation and friendship.

This positive perception can be justified on the following grounds. Firstly, the new worldview and the subsequent re-definition of national interests and re-ordering of foreign policy priorities have led Vietnam to see Thailand in a new light, less influenced by ideological considerations and wartime experiences. A good relationship with Thailand then became a priority to ensure favourable external (strategic and economic) conditions for Vietnam to focus on national construction, in order to pave the way for good relations with other ASEAN countries. In addition, when Vietnam and other Indochinese states joined ASEAN, the multilateral context helped to ensure that relations between Vietnam and Thailand (as well as those between Vietnam and Laos and Cambodia), could be based on the widely recognized principles of peaceful co-existence, good neighbourliness, non-interference, no use of force or threat of force, and the ASEAN Way of consensus building and consultation. In other words, the shared norms and identity, consolidated by increased interactions at all levels among ASEAN countries, have helped standardize behaviour for all the Southeast Asian states. Good relations between Vietnam and Thailand (and other ASEAN nations as well) have helped to consolidate the new identity of Vietnam, being a Southeast Asian nation and a member of ASEAN, which in turn, further promotes Vietnam-Thailand relations. In short, the bilateral and multilateral dynamics have provided a good basis for stable, friendly and cooperative relations between the two countries in the post–Cold War era.

NOTES

[1]   Surin Maisrikrod, "The Peace Dividend in Southeast Asia: The Political Economy of New Thai-Vietnamese Relations", *Contemporary Southeast Asia* 16, no. 1 (June 1994): 47.

[2]   "PM Ends the Tour to Three Neighbouring Countries", Ministry of Foreign Affairs, Vietnam (hereafter cited as MOFA). Hanoi, December 2006 <http://www.mofa.gov.vn/vi/nr040807104143/nr040807105001/ns061222084106> (accessed 25 February 2009).

[3]   Kriengsak Deesrisuk, Thai Ambassador to Vietnam, "Speech at the Conference to Commemorate the 25th Anniversary of Establishment of Thai-Vietnamese Relations" (Hanoi, 8 June 2001), in *Vietnam-Thailand Relations: Forward to the Future* (Hanoi: Institute for International Relations, 2001), p. 26.

[4]   Institute for International Relations, *Chu tich Ho Chi Minh va Cong tac Ngoai giao* [President Ho Chi Minh and diplomatic affairs] (Hanoi: Truth Publishing House, 1991); Le Van Luong, "Vietnam and Thailand: Toward a Stable and Long-Lasting Partnership in the 21st Century", in *Vietnam-Thailand Relations: Forward to the Future* (Hanoi: Institute for International Relations, 2001), pp. 29–30. See also Nguyen Song Tung, "Forced Confrontation and Sincere Friendship", in *Vietnam-Thailand Relations: Forward to the Future*, pp. 43–46.

[5]   Kriengsak Deesrisuk, "Speech at the Conference to commemorate the 25th anniversary of establishment of Thai-Vietnamese relations", p. 23.

[6]   Hoang Khac Nam, "Vietnam-Thailand Relations", in *Vietnam-ASEAN: Bilateral and Multilateral Relations*, edited by Vu Duong Ninh (Hanoi: National Politics Publishing House, 2004), pp. 276–78.

[7]   Nguyen Song Tung, "Forced Confrontation and Sincere Friendship", p. 47.

[8]   The report also stressed that, "Developing relations with ASEAN countries was specially designed to create a security belt around Vietnam consisting of the neighbouring Southeast Asian countries, thus facilitating the task of seeking long-term security and strengthening national defence and serving other revolutionary purposes." Besides, ASEAN countries could "contribute to the healing of the wounds of war, restoring and developing the economy, and enhancing our national defence capability, because we could take advantage of the favourable geographical and natural conditions that ASEAN states could offer." See Nguyen Vu Tung, "The 1973 Paris Agreement and Vietnam-ASEAN Relations", in *The Third Indochina War: Conflict between China, Vietnam and Cambodia, 1972–1979*, edited by Odd Arne Westad and Sophie Quinn-Judge (London, Routledge, 2006), p. 105.

[9]   Le Van Luong, "Vietnam and Thailand: Toward a Stable and Long-Lasting Partnership in the 21st Century," pp. 30–34.

[10] Nguyen Vu Tung, "The 1973 Paris Agreement and Vietnam-ASEAN Relations", p. 108.

[11] Luu Van Loi, *50 Years of Vietnamese Diplomacy, Vol. 2, 1975–1995* (Hanoi: Public Security Publishing House, 1998), p. 247. See also MOFA, *Vietnamese Diplomacy, 1945–2000* (Hanoi: National Politics Publishing House, 2002), p. 300.

[12] See Nguyen Vu Tung, "The 1973 Paris Agreement and Vietnam-ASEAN Relations", pp. 103–20. On 5 July 1976, Vietnamese Foreign Minister Nguyen Duy Trinh announced the Four-Point position with regard to relations with ASEAN countries. He stressed: "The Vietnamese people entirely support the just cause of the Southeast Asian peoples for national independence, peace, democracy, and social progress; we also support the Southeast Asian states to become genuinely independent, peaceful, and neutral, without imperialist military bases and armed forces on their soil."

[13] MOFA Annual Report of 1974. See also Nguyen Vu Tung, "The 1973 Paris Agreement and Vietnam-ASEAN Relations", pp. 104 and 121.

[14] Ibid., p. 104.

[15] Ibid., p. 118.

[16] "The Heated Struggle before the Election Day in Thailand", *Nhan Dan*, 3 March 1976.

[17] Trinh Xuan Lang, "Some Reflections on Our Policies towards ASEAN Countries and the USA from 1975 to 1979", *Proceedings of the Seminar on 50 Years of Vietnamese Diplomacy* (Hanoi: Institute for International Relations, 1995), p. 50. See also Shee Poon Kim, *The ASEAN States' Relations with the Socialist Republic of Vietnam* (Singapore: Chopmen Publisher, 1980).

[18] Hoang Khac Nam, "Vietnam-Thailand Relations," p. 282. See also Maisrikrod, "The Peace Dividend in Southeast Asia", p. 48, and footnote 4, p. 64.

[19] Kavi Chongkittavorn even suggested that the communist threat Thailand perceived in Vietnam never existed. See Maisrikrod, "The Peace Dividend in Southeast Asia", p. 64.

[20] For an account of Thailand's policy toward Vietnam during the Cambodia crisis, see Nayan Chanda, *Brother Enemy: The War after the War* (New York: Macmillan, 1986), pp. 389–96.

[21] MOFA Asian-2 Department Report.

[22] Nguyen Co Thach, "Changes in the World and Our New Thinking", in *Vietnamese Foreign Policy Volume Two*, edited by Nguyen Vu Tung (Hanoi: World Publishing House, 2007), p. 43.

[23] For an analysis of Vietnam's new foreign policy, see Nguyen Vu Tung, "Vietnam's Membership in ASEAN: A Constructive Interpretation", *Contemporary Southeast Asia* 29, no. 3 (December 2007): 489–92.

24 Vu Duong Huan, *Contemporary Vietnamese Diplomacy (1975–2002)* (The Institute of International Relations, 2002), p. 54.
25 In 2003, the 8th Communist Party of Vietnam (CPV) Central Committee Plenum adopted a resolution which said, in part: "maintain[ing] the peaceful and stable external environment for socio-economic development is the highest national interest of our country." See Communist Party of Vietnam, *The 8th Central Committee Plenum Documents* (Hanoi: National Politics Publishing House, 2003), p. 45.
26 Richard Betts et al., *Time for a Critical Decision on Vietnam: It is Time for the US to End its Economic Embargo on Vietnam and Establish Diplomatic Relations* (Columbia University: East Asian Institute, 1992), pp. 6–7.
27 Porter, "The Transformation of Vietnam's Worldview: From Two Camps to Interdependence," p. 1. Discussions of the identity-finding process will be presented later.
28 Vu Duong Huan, *Contemporary Vietnamese Diplomacy (1975–2002)*, p. 65.
29 Ibid., p. 74. The 7th CPV National Congress resolution considered" develop[ing] friendly relations with Southeast Asian states, striving for a Southeast Asia of peace, friendship, and cooperation" as one of the priorities of Vietnam's foreign relations. See Communist Party of Vietnam, *Documents of the 7th National Congress* (Hanoi: National Politics Publishing House, 1991), p. 89.
30 Vu Duong Huan, *Contemporary Vietnamese Diplomacy (1975–2002)*, p. 75. See also Maisrikrod, "The Peace Dividend in Southeast Asia", p. 49.
31 MOFA Asia-2 Department Report.
32 Speech by Foreign Minister Nguyen Manh Cam at the International Conference on Cambodia held in Paris on 23 October 1991, printed in *Nhan Dan*, 24 October 1991.
33 Nguyen Manh Cam, "Tren duong trien khai chinh sach doi ngoai moi" [Towards the Implementation of the New Foreign Policy], in *Hoi nhap quoc te va giu gin ban sac* [International integration and maintaining our identity] (Hanoi: National Politics Publishing House, 1995), p. 161.
34 Ibid., p. 163.
35 Tran Quang Co, "Prospects for Peace and Development in Southeast Asia", in *Hoi nhap quoc te va giu gin ban sac* [International integration and maintaining our identity] (Hanoi: National Politics Publishing House, 1995), p. 28.
36 The author's interviews with senior diplomats in Hanoi in July and August 2008.
37 Maisrikrod, "The Peace Dividend in Southeast Asia", pp. 49, 51 and 63.
38 Ibid., p. 63. In a recent study on Thailand-Vietnam relations, Thananan Boonwanna argued that the Cold War mentality and the military governments in Thailand were the main factors influencing the definition of national interest and security, and, as a result, Thai policy toward Vietnam. See Thananan

Boonwanna, "Thailand-Vietnam Relations: 1976–2004" (Ph.D. dissertation, Vietnam National University, 2008).

[39] For the chronology of Vietnam joining ASEAN, see Nguyen Vu Tung, "Testing the Institutionalist Approach: Cooperation between Vietnam and ASEAN", in *Vietnam's New Order: International Perspectives on the State and Reform in Vietnam*, edited by Stéphanie Balme and Mark Sidel (New York: Palgrave Macmillan, 2007), p. 53.

[40] Luu Doan Huynh at the 3rd Asia-Europe Roundtable, *Peace and Reconciliation: Success Stories and Lessons in Asia and Europe* held in Hanoi on 20–21 October 2003.

[41] Nguyen Vu Tung, "Vietnam's Membership in ASEAN", p. 499.

[42] Vu Khoan, "Vietnam and ASEAN", in *Hoi nhap quoc te va giu gin ban sac* [International integration and maintaining our identity] (Hanoi: National Politics Publishing House, 1995), p. 31.

[43] See Nguyen Hong Thao and Ramses Amer, "Vietnam's Settlement of Border Disputes with Neighbouring Countries: A Contribution to Regional Peace and Security", paper prepared for the panel on "International Relations between Vietnam and Other Regional Countries", at the Third International Conference on Vietnam Studies held in Hanoi, 4–7 December 2008. See also Ramses Amer and Nguyen Hong Thao, "Vietnam's Border Disputes: Assessing the Impact on Its Regional Integration", in *Vietnam's New Order: International Perspectives on the State and Reform in Vietnam*, edited by Stéphanie Balme and Mark Sidel (New York: Palgrave/Macmillan, 2007).

[44] Ramses Amer, "Vietnam and Its Neighbours: The Border Dispute Dimension", *Contemporary Southeast Asia* 17, no. 3, (December 1995): 310.

[45] Carlyle A. Thayer, "Vietnam's Defence Policy and its Impact on Foreign Relations", paper for the 6th Euro-Viet Conference organized by the Asien-Afrika Institut and Universitat Hamburg, held in Hamburg, Germany 6–8 June 2008. According to Thayer, of the 364 high-level exchange visits, Vietnam received 207 delegations and sent 157 delegations abroad. When the frequency of high-level exchanges is calculated (total of delegations received and sent to the period ending in 2004), three countries account for nearly a third of all delegations: Laos (40 exchanges), China (33 exchanges), and Thailand (26 exchanges). The next tier of exchanges included: Cambodia (20); India (16); the Philippines and Russia (13 each); the United States (11); France, Indonesia, and Singapore (10 each); Cuba and Japan (9 each); Australia (8); North Korea, South Korea, and Malaysia (7 each); Italy, Myanmar, and Ukraine (6 each); and Poland and Slovakia (4 exchanges each).

[46] Amer, "Vietnam and Its Neighbours", p. 310.

[47] Naval Commander Decree coded 1836/CT-TL on Viet-Thai joint sea patrol <http://www.quansuvn.net/index.php?topic=60.220> (accessed 21 August

2008). On 2 July 2008, Vietnam's Navy sent two warships to participate in the joint patrol and visit the military port of Sattahip in the south of Thailand <http://www.bbcvietnamese.com> (accessed 8 July 2008).

48 The author's interviews with Vietnamese armed forces officials who wish to remain anonymous (Hanoi, October 2009).

49 Xuan Linh, "Thailand Does Not Allow Anyone to Use its Territory to Plot against Vietnam", VietNamNet <http://vietnamnet.vn/chinhtri/2008/03/77 5005/> (accessed 3 July 2008).

50 See <http://www.bbcvietnamese.com> (accessed 8 July 2008) for more details.

51 For an account on how Thailand solved the "old" Vietnamese refugee problem, see Maisrikrod, "The Peace Dividend in Southeast Asia", pp. 50–51.

52 Comments made in Nong Khai on 29 October 1993 by the Deputy General Secretary of Thailand's National Security Council, Khajadpai Buruspatana, at a seminar on refugees. See also MOFA Asia-2 Department Report 1993.

53 MOFA Asia-2 Department Report.

54 MOFA Asia-2 Department Report, March 2008. See also Xuan Linh, "Thailand Does Not Allow Anyone to Use its Territory to Plot against Vietnam".

55 Thu Van, "31 Years of Viet-Thai Relations", *Tuan bao Quoc te* [International Weekly] no. 16, 17 April 2003.

56 MOFA, "Vietnam-Thailand Relations." <http://www.mofa.gov.vn/vi/cn_vakv/ca_tbd/nr040819104152/ns070801102436> (accessed 15 August 2008). In 2001, Thailand's foreign direct investment to Vietnam accounted for about twelve per cent of total foreign direct investment from ASEAN countries. MOFA Asia-2 Department Report 2001–2002.

57 MOFA Asia-2 Department Report.

58 MOFA, "Vietnam-Thailand Relations". According to statistics of the General Department of Vietnam Tourism, the number of Thai tourists in Vietnam in the first half of 2008 reached 122,415, a thirty-two per cent increase from 2007. <http://www.vietnamtourism.gov.vn/index.php?option=com_content&task=view&id=5190&Itemid=145> (accessed 21 July 2008). Another source reveals that the number of Vietnamese tourists to Thailand reached 300,000 in 2008 while the number of Thai tourists to Vietnam was half this. See Thai Ha, "What Vietnam Should Learn from Thailand's Tourism?" in *Vietnam Economic Review*, 7 November 2008, p. 12.

59 "Thi truong hang khong se tang cao hon du kien" [Unexpected increase in the airlines business] <http://www.giaothongvantai.com.vn/PortletBlank.aspx/B9AE> (accessed 21 July 2008).

60 MOFA Asia-2 Department Report, 2001, p. 64. Indeed, Vietnamese tourists often hold positive feelings about Thailand after their trips. This point has been widely shared by Vietnamese diplomats who the author interviewed in the Vietnamese Embassy in Bangkok in 2005–8.

⁶¹   MOFA Asia-2 Department Report, March, 2008.
⁶²   The author's interview with Vietnamese diplomats in Bangkok in 2007–8.

REFERENCES

Amer, Ramses. "Vietnam and Its Neighbours: the Border Dispute Dimension". *Contemporary Southeast Asia* 17, Number 3 (December 1995): 298–318.
Amer, Ramses and Nguyen Hong Thao. "Vietnam's Border Disputes: Assessing the Impact on Its Regional Integration". In *Vietnam's New Order: International Perspectives on the State and Reform in Vietnam*, edited by Stéphanie Balme and Mark Sidel. New York: Palgrave Macmillan, 2007.
———. "Vietnam's Settlement of Border Disputes with Neighbouring Countries: A Contribution to Regional Peace and Security". Paper prepared for the panel on "International Relations between Vietnam and Other Regional Countries", at the *Third International Conference on Vietnam Studies*, Hanoi, Vietnam, 2008.
Boonwanna, Thananan. "Thailand-Vietnam Relations: 1976–2004". Ph.D. dissertation, Department of History, College of Social Science and Humanities, Vietnam National University, Ho Chi Minh City, 2008.
Chanda, Nayan. *Brother Enemy: The War after the War*. New York: Macmillan, 1986.
Communist Party of Vietnam. *Documents of the 7ᵗʰ National Congress*. Hanoi: National Politics Publishing House, 1991.
———. *The 8ᵗʰ Central Committee Plenum Documents*. Hanoi: National Politics Publishing House, 2003.
Deesrisuk, Kriengsak. "Speech at the Conference to Commemorate the 25ᵗʰ Anniversary of Establishment of Thai-Vietnamese Relations". In *Vietnam-Thailand Relations: Forward to the Future*. Hanoi: Institute for International Relations, 2001.
"Foreign Minister Nguyen Manh Cam's Speech at the International Conference on Cambodia in Paris 23 October 1991". *Nhan Dan*, 24 October 1991.
Hoang Khac Nam. "Vietnam-Thailand Relations". In *Vietnam-ASEAN: Bilateral and Multilateral Relations*, edited by Vu Duong Ninho. Hanoi: National Politics Publishing House, 2004.
Institute for International Relations. *Chu tich Ho Chi Minh va Cong tac Ngoai giao* [President Ho Chi Minh and diplomatic affairs]. Hanoi: Truth Publishing House, 1991.
Le Van Luong. "Vietnam and Thailand: Toward a Stable and Long-Lasting Partnership in the 21ˢᵗ Century". In *Vietnam-Thailand Relations: Forward to the Future*. Hanoi: Institute for International Relations, 2001.
Luu Doan Huynh. "Vietnam and ASEAN Relations in Retrospect". In *Peace and Reconciliation: Success Stories and Lessons in Asia and Europe*, edited by

Bertrand Fort and Norbert von Hofmann. Singapore: Asia-Europe Foundation, 2004.

Luu Van Loi. *50 Years of Vietnamese Diplomacy, Vol. 2, 1975–1995*. Hanoi: Public Security Publishing House, 2002.

Maisrikrod, Surin. "The Peace Dividend in Southeast Asia: The Political Economy of New Thai-Vietnamese Relations". *Contemporary Southeast Asia* 16, no. 1 (June 1994): 46–66.

Ministry of Foreign Affairs (MOFA), Vietnam. "Vietnam-Thailand Relations." Hanoi: Vietnam, 2008 <http://www.mofa.gov.vn/vi/cn_vakv/ca_tbd/nr040819104152/ns070801102436> (accessed 15 August 2008).

MOFA, Vietnam. *Vietnamese Diplomacy, 1945–2000*. Hanoi: National Politics Publishing House, 2002.

————. Annual Reports from 1972–1974.

————. Asia-2 Department Reports from 1974–1975.

————. Asia-2 Department Reports from 1990–1995.

————. Asia-2 Department Reports from 2001–2008.

Nguyen Co Thach. "Changes in the World and Our New Thinking". In *Vietnamese Foreign Policy Volume Two*, edited by Nguyen Vu Tung. Hanoi: World Publishing House, 2007.

Nguyen Manh Cam. "Tren duong trien khai chinh sach doi ngoai moi" [Towards the implementation of the new foreign policy]. In *Hoi nhap quoc te va giu gin ban sac* [International integration and maintaining our identity]. Hanoi: National Politics Publishing House, 1995.

Nguyen Song Tung. "Forced Confrontation and Sincere Friendship". In *Vietnam-Thailand Relations: Forward to the Future*. Hanoi: Institute for International Relations, 2001.

Nguyen Vu Tung. "The 1973 Paris Agreement and Vietnam-ASEAN Relations". In *The Third Indochina War: Conflict between China, Vietnam and Cambodia, 1972–1979*, edited by Odd Arne Westad and Sophie Quinn-Judge. London: Routledge, 2006.

————. "Testing the Institutionalist Approach: Cooperation between Vietnam and ASEAN". In *Vietnam's New Order: International Perspectives on the State and Reform in Vietnam*, edited by Stéphanie Balme and Mark Sidel. New York: Palgrave Macmillan, 2007.

————. "Vietnam's Membership in ASEAN: A Constructive Interpretation". *Contemporary Southeast Asia* 29, no 3, (December 2007): 483–505.

Shee, Poon Kim. *The ASEAN States' Relations with the Socialist Republic of Vietnam*. Singapore: Chopmen Publishers, 1980.

"The Heated Struggle before the Election Day in Thailand". *Nhan Dan*, 3 March 1976.

Thai Ha. "What Vietnam Should Learn from Thailand's Tourism?" *Vietnam Economic Review*, 7 November 2008.

Thayer, Carlyle A. "Vietnam's Defence Policy and its Impact on Foreign Relations". Paper for the 6th Euro-Viet Conference organised by the Asien-Afrika Institut and Universitat Hamburg, held in Hamburg, Germany 6–8 June 2008.

Thu Van. "31 Years of Viet-Thai Relations". *Tuan bao Quoc te* [International weekly], no. 16, 17 April 2003.

Tran Quang Co. "Prospects for Peace and Development in Southeast Asia". In *Hoi nhap quoc te va giu gin ban sac* [International integration and maintaining our identity]. Hanoi: National Politics Publishing House, 1995.

Trinh Xuan Lang. "Some Reflections on Our Policies towards ASEAN Countries and the USA from 1975 to 1979". In *Proceedings of the Seminar on 50 Years of Vietnamese Diplomacy*. Hanoi: The Institute for International Relations, 1995.

Vu Duong Huan. *Contemporary Vietnamese Diplomacy (1975–2002)*. Hanoi: The Institute of International Relations, 2002.

Vu Khoan. "Vietnam and ASEAN". In *Hoi nhap quoc te va giu gin ban sac* [International integration and maintaining our identity]. Hanoi: National Politics Publishing House, 1995.

Xuan Linh. "Thailand Does Not Allow Anyone to Use its Territory to Plot against Vietnam". *VietNamNet*, March 2008 <http://vietnamnet.vn/chinhtri/2008/03/775005/> (accessed 3 July 2008).

4

Cambodia and Vietnam: A Troubled Relationship

Ramses Amer

Purpose and Structure

The purpose of this study is to analyze the relationship between Cambodia and Vietnam through the disputed issues that have, and in some cases still do, affected the bilateral relations.[1] The study deals primarily with the post–1975 period. However, to explain and assess developments and issues of this period, events that took place before 1975 will be referred to. The choice of 1975 is based on the key developments then taking place in the two countries, with communist forces emerging victorious in both Cambodia with the capture of Phnom Penh on 15 April and in the then Republic of Vietnam (South) with the capture of Saigon on 30 April. In order to avoid highlighting some factors, to the detriment of other factors, the empirical developments will be outlined and based on the pattern of interaction. Factors influencing developments will be identified and analyzed. This approach has been tested in earlier research on relations between China and Vietnam and it has contributed to making studies of the relationship more analytical and problem oriented rather than merely descriptive.[2]

The structure of the study is its division into two main parts. First, the empirical part, in which the development of bilateral relations between Cambodia and Vietnam since 1975 is outlined. The second part encompasses two sections, the first is devoted to identifying key factors and issues affecting bilateral relations and discussing their relative importance, while the second a more general concluding analysis.

Cambodia-Vietnam Relations since 1975

Descent into Deep Conflict 1975–78[3]

Following the end of the wars in Vietnam and in Cambodia, border clashes occurred between the two countries during May and June 1975 but were settled in conjunction with a high level meeting in Hanoi in June. A fairly stable situation continued to prevail on the common border throughout 1975 and 1976. In 1976, an attempt was made to settle the dispute over the delimitation of the common land and sea borders by negotiations, but the discussions broke down at a preparatory meeting held in Phnom Penh in May 1976.

In early 1977, Cambodia started to "patrol" disputed border areas, which it regarded as Cambodian territory, but were under Vietnamese control. Vietnam reacted by strengthening its positions along the border. From March 1977, Cambodia escalated its activities to artillery shelling and attacks against Vietnam. The border war had thus started, and during the second half of 1977 it escalated into a full-scale war. In December 1977, Vietnam launched a major attack to which Cambodia reacted by breaking off diplomatic relations on 31 December. The armed conflict continued unabated during 1978. The movement of refugees from Cambodia to Vietnam increased after an attempted rebellion against the Cambodian Government late in the spring and summer of 1978, which led to a purge in the Eastern Zone of Cambodia. The refugees in Vietnam sought to organize themselves in opposition to the government in Cambodia, and on 2 December 1978 a resistance organization was created under the name of the Kampuchean National Front for National Salvation (KNUFNS).

On 25 December 1978 an estimated 100,000 Vietnamese troops backed by some 20,000 KNUFNS troops entered Cambodia. They swiftly overcame the resistance of the Cambodian troops, and on 7 January 1979 Phnom Penh was captured after only two weeks of fighting.

The deterioration of bilateral relations shows that Vietnam gradually became Cambodia's main foreign enemy. There were other indications of the anti-Vietnamese policies of the Cambodian authorities. One example was the treatment of the ethnic Vietnamese who remained in the country in 1975. Following the large-scale exodus in the early 1970s, the ethnic Vietnamese remaining in Cambodia can be estimated to have been about 200,000 by the mid-1970s. Many of them were expelled from Cambodia after the change of government in 1975. In 1978, Vietnam requested assistance from the United Nations High Commissioner for Refugees (UNHCR) to cope with 341,400 refugees who had arrived from Cambodia since 1975. Among these refugees there were 170,300 ethnic Vietnamese. Thus, out of the 450,000 Vietnamese in Cambodia in early 1970, 250,000 left in 1970–71 and 170,300 left after 1975. These two exoduses, involving approximately 420,000 refugees, left only some 30,000 ethnic Vietnamese in Cambodia, many of whom died of starvation, diseases, or executions between 1975 and 1978. This meant that the Vietnamese minority had all but completely disappeared from Cambodia by the end of 1978.

The conflict between Cambodia and Vietnam during the second half of the 1970s did not lead to or deepen peace and cooperation in the regional and international situation. Regionally, the Cambodia-Vietnam relationship was considerably affected by relations between China and Vietnam. In fact, Cambodia became a major factor in Sino-Vietnamese relations. As long-term relations between China and Vietnam were manageable, China opted not to take sides in the brewing conflict between Cambodia and Vietnam, but as relations became strained China gradually began to support Cambodia. And it seems the decision to side with Cambodia was taken in late 1977. During 1978, China's support increased and it became the major source of foreign support to Cambodia.

As the conflict between Vietnam and Cambodia deepened in 1978, Vietnam gradually came to view Cambodia's policy as encouraged by, and later orchestrated by, China. From a security viewpoint, Vietnam perceived that it was facing a two-front struggle against a Chinese-led threat, with one front in the north bordering China and the other in the south-west bordering Cambodia. This triangular conflict situation became known as the "Third Indochina Conflict" or the "Third Indochina War". The international ramifications were primarily the developments that led to the formalization of an alliance between the Soviet Union and Vietnam in November 1978 and the full normalization of relations between China and the United States on 1 January 1979. Thus, two strategic alliances had been created, a Soviet-Vietnamese and a Sino-American, a strategic development that would have considerable impact on the Cambodian Conflict from 1979 onwards.[4]

The Period of the Cambodian Conflict 1979–91

Following the fall of Phnom Penh in early January 1979 a People's Revolutionary Council was set up by the KNUFNS, with the assistance of Vietnam, to act as a provisional government. The new Cambodian administration later gave the country the name of People's Republic of Kampuchea (PRK). The PRK/State of Cambodia (SOC)[5] period lasted de facto until the establishment of the United Nations Transitional Authority in Cambodia (UNTAC) in March 1992.

The PRK/SOC period in modern Cambodian history has been subject to much controversy both in international politics and in the scholarly literature. One of the major issues of dispute is the degree of Vietnamese influence from 1979 to the early 1990s. Vietnam's massive and direct military and political influence was undeniable in the early years of the PRK, but as Vietnam began to withdraw its troops and gradually diminished its direct political tutelage over the new administration during the second half of the 1980s, the picture became more complex. Vietnam officially completed the withdrawal of its troops from Cambodia in September 1989.

Given the relationship between the PRK/SOC and Vietnam, the two countries enjoyed good overall relations. The relations between Vietnam and the Cambodian parties opposing its presence in the country was diametrically opposite, with an armed struggle that pitted the PRK/SOC with Vietnamese troops (up to their final withdrawal in late September 1989) against the forces of the overthrown Democratic Kampuchea (DK, later Party of Democratic Kampuchea [PDK]) and two other groups, the Front Uni National pour un Cambodge Indépendant, Neutre, Pacifique et Coopératif (FUNCINPEC) and the Khmer People's National Liberation Front (KPNLF). These three parties formed the Coalition Government of Democratic Kampuchea (CGDK)[6] on 22 June 1982.

The new order installed in Cambodia came about with extensive Vietnamese assistance, and people who had sought refuge in Vietnam in the 1975–78 period began to return to Cambodia. This process involved not only ethnic Khmers but also ethnic Vietnamese, leading to the re-emergence of a Vietnamese minority in Cambodia, which became the source of widespread international concern. The ethnic Vietnamese coming to Cambodia were all seen as part of a process of "Vietnamization" of the country.[7] Whether they were returnees who had been forced out of Cambodia during the 1970s or new migrants, they were all perceived to be part of a larger Vietnamese scheme to gain influence and even to colonize Cambodia. Evidence of just how far reaching the international concern was is the inclusion of the following paragraph in the adopted resolution on the agenda item, "The situation in Kampuchea", at the 38th session of the General Assembly of the United Nations in 1983: *"Seriously concerned* about reported demographic changes being imposed in Kampuchea by foreign occupation forces"[8]. The resolutions adopted at sessions 39 to 44 (1984–89) also included paragraphs on demographic changes being imposed in Cambodia.[9]

The ethnic Vietnamese settling down in Cambodia became one of the major issues in the discourse of the Cambodian groups opposed to the PRK/SOC and to the Vietnamese influence in the country. As early as 1979 the DK claimed that 300,000 Vietnamese had settled in Cambodia and in 1981 the figure was up 500,000. In 1984, the President of the CGDK, Prince Norodom Sihanouk, put the number at 600,000 and in 1986 the figure was up to 700,000. In 1988 Son Sann, Prime Minister within the CGDK claimed that the number was between 800,000 and one million and that in 1989 there were one million Vietnamese settlers in Cambodia.[10]

The official policies of the PRK towards "Vietnamese residents" were outlined in a publication of September 1983.[11] The PRK estimated that by mid-1983 there were about 56,000 "Vietnamese residents" in Cambodia and that they had returned after the PRK had authorized them to do so.[12] The official policy of the PRK sought to regulate the Vietnamese migration to Cambodia but not to prevent it.

There is a considerable discrepancy between the PRK's claim of 56,000 ethnic Vietnamese in 1983 and the CGDK's claim of 600,000 settlers in 1984.

During the 1980s Vietnam and the PRK signed agreements relating to the common borders. An agreement on "historic waters" was signed on 7 July 1982. These historic waters were defined as being located between the coast of Kien Giang Province, Phu Quoc Island and the Tho Chu islands on the Vietnamese side, and the coast of Kampot Province and the Poulo Wai islands on the Cambodian side. The agreements stipulated that the two countries would hold, "at a suitable time", negotiations to determine the maritime frontier in the historic waters. Pending such a settlement the two countries would continue to regard the Brévié Line drawn in 1939 as the dividing line for the islands within the historic waters, and the exploitation of the zone would be decided by "common agreement".[13] This was followed by the signing of a treaty on the settlement of border problems between Cambodia and Vietnam and an agreement on border regulations on 20 July 1983 in Phnom Penh.

According to the treaty, the two sides agreed to regard as the national border the "present line" between the two countries, defined on a 1/100,000-scale map published by the Geographic Service of Indochina in use before 1954 or at a date very near 1954.[14] The delimitation of the land and sea borders would be undertaken in the spirit of "equality and mutual respect" in the interests of the special relations between the two countries and in conformity with international law and practice.[15] Finally, on 27 December 1985, the "Treaty on the Delimitation of the Vietnam-Kampuchea Frontier" was signed by the two countries.[16] It was ratified by the Council of the State of Vietnam on 30 January 1986 and by the National Assembly of the PRK on 7 February 1986.[17] The principle governing the settlement of the border disputes between the two countries was to be respect for the "present demarcation line", specified as "the line that was in existence at the time" of independence. This line was retained by the two countries, following the principle *uti possidetis* (as you possess). The parties of the CDGK refuted the agreements imposed on Cambodia by the Vietnamese, and thus they should not be accepted as valid.

The Cambodian Conflict was formally resolved through the Paris Agreements on Cambodia of 23 October 1991. The developments between Vietnam's military intervention and settlement of the conflict through the signing of the Paris Agreements on Cambodia can be divided into three phases: First the confrontation phase (1979–86), followed by the dialogue phase (1987–89), and finally the conflict-resolution phase (1990–91).[18]

Peacekeeping Period: 1992 to Mid-1993

Following the Paris Agreements the United Nations carried out an ambitious peacekeeping operation in Cambodia leading up to general elections in May 1993. During the period of UNTAC one issue dominated relations both between Cambodia and Vietnam and between UNTAC and Vietnam; namely the situation of the ethnic Vietnamese in Cambodia and the reoccurring attacks on the ethnic Vietnamese during this period. The former parties to the CGDK/NGC (National Government of Cambodia) attempted to limit the number of ethnic Vietnamese who could take part in the planned general elections. This was most evident in the discussion prior to the adoption of the Electoral Law in 1992. On 5 August 1992, the Supreme National Council adopted an electoral law drafted by UNTAC. The electoral law enfranchised any eighteen-year-old person born in Cambodia with a mother or a father born in the country or, in the case of those born overseas, with a mother or a father born in Cambodia whose mother or father was also born in the country (i.e., one grandparent also born in Cambodia).[19] This constituted a revision of the provisions of the Paris Agreements on Cambodia, which stated that any eighteen-year-old born in Cambodia or the child of a person born in Cambodia would be eligible to vote.[20] The PDK opposed the electoral law primarily because it would allow ethnic Vietnamese in Cambodia to vote.[21] The intention of the law was to disenfranchise new Vietnamese settlers but not ethnic Vietnamese who lived in the country in the pre–1970 period.

Armed attacks leading to deaths among the ethnic Vietnamese were reported in April, May, July, October, November, and December 1992. During the first two months of 1993, no killings of ethnic Vietnamese in Cambodia were reported. The situation would be dramatically reversed during the month of March. It all started with an announcement by UNTAC on 1 March that it had discovered three Vietnamese men who had served with the Vietnamese forces in Cambodia and whom UNTAC therefore regarded as "foreign forces". UNTAC requested Vietnam to take the three persons back as Vietnamese "nationals". All three men were in possession of identity cards issued by SOC and two of them were still serving in the Cambodian People's Armed Forces, i.e. the armed forces of SOC.[22] Vietnam refused to take the three men back, claiming that they were civilians and Cambodian "citizens", married to Cambodian women. Vietnam also publicly rejected UNTAC's stand on the matter and reiterated that it had never sent any troops back to Cambodia after the final withdrawal of Vietnamese troops in September 1989.[23]

The increase in attacks in March forced some 21,000 ethnic Vietnamese to seek refuge in Vietnam. Armed attacks against ethnic Vietnamese continued in April and in May. Even after the general elections held in late May attacks were reported in June.[24]

Developments Since Mid-1993

After the formation of a coalition government in Cambodia following the elections of May 1993 relations reverted to a purely bilateral one again. Up to early 2000, the relationship was dominated by two issues: the territorial issues and the ethnic Vietnamese in Cambodia and the repeated attacks against that minority. Thereafter the main disputed issues have been the territorial ones.

With the exception of the periods January 1995 to April 1996 and July 1997 to March 1998, there were repeated attacks on ethnic Vietnamese in Cambodia, prompting Vietnam to protest and to raise the issue in bilateral talks with Cambodia. In response to several attacks in 1994 the two countries agreed, in connection with a visit by Cambodia's First Prime Minister Prince Norodom Ranariddh to Vietnam in January 1995, to hold a meeting of experts to discuss the issue of ethnic Vietnamese in Cambodia. It can also be noted that Cambodia pledged that the Immigration Law — adopted by the Cambodian National Assembly on 26 August 1994 — would not be aimed at "confining or deporting en masse Vietnamese nationals". Cambodia also stated that it would "try to do everything", in conformity with Cambodian regulations and "within its capacity", to ensure the safety of the "Vietnamese nationals" in Cambodia.[25]

The first meeting of the expert-level working groups on the issue of the ethnic Vietnamese in Cambodia was held in Phnom Penh on 29–30 March. The two sides had "frank, friendly discussions" and they achieved "some results".[26] The second meeting was held in Hanoi on 28–29 July and an agreement was reached on measures to "settle the number of Vietnamese refugees" in Chrey Thom in Kandal Province. It was also decided to continue the discussions on other issues.[27]

The first of the renewed attacks in May 1996 came during a period of increased bilateral tensions relating to the border issues. Already in January, Cambodia's First Prime Minister, Prince Ranariddh, claimed that Vietnamese farmers backed by troops had encroached on Cambodian territory in three of Cambodia's border provinces — Svay Rieng, Prey Veng, and Kompong Chang — since the beginning of the year.[28] Another indication of the level of accusation came on 14 March when the *National Voice of Cambodia* broadcasted a speech made by First Prime Minister Ranariddh in Svay Rieng Province in which he elaborated on the border problems and discussed the historical loss of land to Vietnam and to Thailand. He reiterated the accusations that Vietnam was encroaching on Cambodian territory. He referred to the situation as one of Vietnamese "annexation" of land in Svay Rieng and other Cambodian provinces. He repeated his displeasure with the fact that a meeting with his Vietnamese counterpart had yet to take place and stated that he favoured a process of peaceful resolution of the border problems in order to avoid an armed clash. However, he also stressed that the Khmer Royal Armed Forces had the duty and obligation, if needed, to defend the Cambodian territory. Finally, he emphasized that the Cambodian side would not retreat because if it did the "incidents" along the border would continue "forever".[29]

Vietnam denied the accusations and in early April Vietnam's Prime Minister Vo Van Kiet made an official visit to Cambodia to discuss the border issue and other matters.[30] This trip helped to defuse the crisis and the first meeting of the working groups of experts on border issues from the two countries was held in Ho Chi Minh City on 20–23 May 1996.[31]

Interestingly enough, the defeat of Prince Norodom Ranariddh in July 1997 and the election of Ung Huot to the post of First Prime Minister led to a period of improved bilateral relations. During the second half of 1997 and the first quarter of 1998, there was no Vietnamese reaction to attacks on ethnic Vietnamese in Cambodia, thus indicating that anti-Vietnamese activities in Cambodia were on the decline during this period. On border issues, the improved relations were displayed by the initiation of talks on the maritime disputes following Cambodian complaints that the Thai-Vietnamese boundary agreement of August 1997 encroached on Cambodian waters. During high-level discussions in connection with Huot's visit to Vietnam in late May and early June 1998, both parties agreed that they would strengthen coordination to resolve the "remaining" bilateral problems "before" the year 2000.[32] This was followed by expert-level talks in Phnom Penh on 18–20 June 1998 which resulted in an agreement to set up a joint border commission to handle the border disputes. This prompted Huot to state that he was confident that the border issues could be resolved "before" the year 2000.[33]

Attacks against ethnic Vietnamese in Cambodia reoccurred in April 1998. Further evidence of the precarious situation of the ethnic Vietnamese were anti-Vietnamese statements made by the opposition during the election campaign ahead of the general elections held on 26 July 1998.[34] The political tensions between the leading Cambodian parties following the elections and the difficult process in forming a coalition government — an agreement was reached on 25 November — was marked by anti-Vietnamese actions.

The bilateral dialogue on border issues was resumed after a new coalition government had been formed in late 1998. The bilateral talks did progress into the year 2000 with expectation that an agreement would be reached by the end of that year. However, this did not materialize, and for a few years talks were more sporadic. Eventually the two countries managed to make progress in the talks on the land border disputes, resulting in the agreement on a Supplementary Treaty on 10 October 2005. Following the completion of the ratification process in both countries, the exchange ratification documents for the Supplementary Treaty took place on 6 December 2005 and thus it entered into force.[35]

This border agreement coupled with a number of high-level visits display a more cooperative phase in bilateral relations between Cambodia and Vietnam. This can be seen from the Joint Statement issued in connection with Cambodian Prime Minister Hun Sen's visit to Vietnam on 6–7 March 2006[36] and from the joint press release issued in connection with the visit by Vietnam's President Nguyen Minh Triet to Cambodia on 27 February–1 March 2007.[37] More recently, Cambodia's King Norodom Sihamoni made an official Visit to Vietnam on 24–26 June 2008.[38] The high-level talks between the two countries aim at promoting overall collaboration. This can also be seen through the strengthening of collaboration between the national assemblies of the two countries.[39] Cooperation in the economic field is a priority and efforts are being made to expand trade relations.[40] Another area of priority is border security and stability, which involves collaboration between provinces and localities, as well as demarcation of the land border. The demarcation of the land border is expected to be completed by 2012.[41] In the context of the land border a notable agreement was reached on 26 August 2008 between Cambodia, Laos, and Vietnam relating to the point of intersection where the borders of the three countries meet.[42] The two countries are also working together within sub-regional and regional frameworks, e.g. ASEAN, the Mekong River Commission, the Greater Mekong Sub-region, and the "Cambodia-Laos-Vietnam development triangle".[43]

Contentious Issues in Cambodia-Vietnam Relations

Key Issues

The key issues in the relationship between Cambodia and Vietnam encompass issues of disputes as well as broader factors such as perceptions of the other. The latter will be addressed first since it can help explain the course of action of the two countries in relation to other factors and disputed issues. In the context of this study and based on the empirical overview above, the following issues/factors will be analyzed: perceptions of history, territorial disputes, ethnic Vietnamese in Cambodia, and ethnic Khmer in Vietnam. The issues are not ranked in order of importance.

Perceptions of the Other

The perceptions of the other are of considerable importance to understand the patterns of development of the relations between Cambodia and Vietnam in the post-1975 period. It can help explain the behaviour of Cambodia both directly through the influence on government policies towards Vietnam and also indirectly through the pressure put on the Cambodian authorities in dealing with and pursuing their policies towards Vietnam. The issue of perception of Vietnam and the Vietnamese, i.e. the majority ethnic group in Vietnam, the Kinh, is a question of elite perceptions in Cambodian society and not one of small politically-isolated groups pursuing anti-immigrant views and policies. The rhetoric relating to the "youn", a pejorative relating to all Vietnamese,[44] as a source of most problems and shortcomings in Cambodia was in evidence in the campaign leading up to the general elections in 1998,[45] but can also be seen in Cambodian politics and government policies in all periods since independence from France in 1953, with the exception of the PRK/SOC era. Of course, during the latter period, the parties loyal to the CGDK/NGC were vehemently opposed to Vietnam. In other words, the anti-Vietnamese stand displayed by generations of Cambodian politicians seems to transcend ideological differences since royalists, conservatives, liberals, and communists have either been or are currently displaying anti-Vietnamese sentiments.[46] The anti-Vietnamese rhetoric in Cambodian politics is linked to the historical fact that it was the pro-Thai (Siam) part of the Khmer Royalty that emerged victorious from the internal struggles with strong external involvement by the then Siam and Vietnam in the first half of the 19th century. The historical and modern factors have combined to create an elite-driven perception of Vietnam as an enemy and of the ethnic Vietnamese as a persistent problem in Cambodian society. The perception of Vietnam as an explicit, implicit, or potential enemy complicates bilateral relations and influences the overall relationship between the two countries as well as the management of specific bilateral issues.

The existence of a negative perception of another country is not unique to Cambodia, as displayed by Vietnamese perception of China's behaviour towards Vietnam during their conflict in the late 1970s and into the 1980s.[47] However, with the normalization of relations with China the propagation of such views were abandoned by Vietnam. This has not been the case in Cambodia. The persistence of the negative attitude and the prominent role it has played in domestic Cambodian politics is also notable as it affects not only the country's foreign policy but also its domestic policies. Also, the fact that the negative perception is directed at the Vietnamese minority is problematic and has had very negative repercussions for that minority.

Perceptions of History

Cambodia and Vietnam have very different perceptions of the historical relations that they share. Broadly speaking, Cambodia's perception is that Vietnam has expanded its territory at the expense of Cambodia, in particular in the Mekong Delta area. In Vietnam, the so-called march to the South is perceived as a gradual migration movement, not as an expansion at the expense of Cambodia. Also, in the pre-colonial period the Cambodian side identifies repeated Vietnamese interventions in Cambodia's internal affairs. The issue of territorial changes continued into the colonial period during which Cambodia perceives that the French adjusted the borders between the French colony of Cochinchina and the French protectorate of Cambodia to the advantage of the colony. As seen from the perspective of French colonial policies the logic was to maximize its own benefits through its colony and the adjustments were not made for the sake of the Vietnamese.

In more modern times, the outcome of the Geneva Conference in 1954 that ended the First Indochina War created varying interpretations by the two countries. This was most evidently displayed after 1975 when the DK interpreted the outcome of the Geneva Conference as evidence that the Vietnamese, i.e. the Vietminh, had failed to look after the interests of the Khmer Issarak in Cambodia. Vietnam was more concerned about the fact the both the Soviet Union and China agreed to the "temporary" division of Vietnam along the 17th parallel. The interpretation of the DK may appear strange since the Vietminh was not even in a position to influence the negotiated outcome of the Geneva Conference relating to the situation in Vietnam and was compelled to accept the temporary division of the country. Also of importance was the fact that Cambodia had been granted full independence in 1953, the year before the Geneva Conference, and thus the situation in the country was not part of the deliberation in Geneva.[48]

In addition, the DK resented the Democratic Republic of Vietnam (North-Vietnam) and the latter's policies of support to Prince Sihanouk in the late 1960s when armed struggle had been launched against his rule by Communist forces in Cambodia. Although the expansion of the war in Vietnam into Cambodia in 1970 and the overthrow of Prince Sihanouk brought about a formal alliance between the Cambodian communists and the Vietnamese, relations were often strained and Khmer cadres returning from the Democratic Republic of Vietnam were executed.[49] The DK also rejected any ceasefire in Cambodia following the Paris Peace Accords of 1973, thus displaying deep differences in policies as compared to its Vietnamese counterparts.[50]

Territorial Disputes

Territorial issues have been on the bilateral agenda since the end of the First Indochina War. In the post–1975 era, the issues have led to periods of serious tension and even to military clashes in the late 1970s. The negotiations have resulted in the agreements of the 1980s and more recently, in 2005, in the Supplementary Treaty relating to the land border. The land border is currently being demarcated, a process that is expected to be completed by 2012. The remaining challenge is how to manage the maritime disputes between the two countries.

The territorial issues are politically sensitive, in particular in Cambodia, since there is a strong established perception that Cambodia has historically lost territory to Vietnam. The broader perception that Vietnam is the cause of most problems that Cambodia is facing reinforces the presupposition that Vietnam wants to take control of Cambodian territory. The fact that the political opposition and parts of the civil society in Cambodia have been very vocal in criticizing any move by the Cambodian Government aimed at resolving the territorial issues has complicated the negotiations between the two countries. The difficulties involved in negotiating the land border issue were displayed when Vietnamese officials announced that the two sides would sign an agreement by the end of 2000 and this did not materialize. The agreement was only signed in October 2005.

The deep crisis that occurred in 1996 when the then First Prime Minister Prince Ranariddh pursued a campaign of openly accusing

Vietnam of violating Cambodia's territorial integrity and of nibbling away at Cambodian land along the common border caused serious tension in bilateral relations. Empirical evidence did not support the claims made by Prince Ranariddh and it appears that his campaign was motivated more by domestic Cambodian politics and his power struggle with the then Second Prime Minister Hun Sen than by actions carried out by Vietnam in the border areas. In other words, Ranariddh was trying to gain nationalistic credentials by talking tough to Vietnam and by playing on anti-Vietnamese sentiments in Cambodia.

Territorial issues are difficult to handle even when the countries involved enjoy very good relations. Thus, the task of managing the territorial issues between Cambodia and Vietnam has not been facilitated by the politicization of the issues in the context of domestic politics in Cambodia in the 1990s. This has complicated the task of the Cambodian negotiators in particular at times when the co–Prime Ministers pursued different policies on the issue. It has of course also made it more difficult for Cambodia to pursue a consistent policy and negotiating strategy. From the Vietnamese perspective, the problem has been how to handle changes and contradictions in the Cambodian approach and also to assess the possible impact on domestic political developments in Cambodia on the negotiations.

Ethnic Vietnamese in Cambodia

The ethnic Vietnamese in Cambodia has been an issue in bilateral relations since 1954. The ousting of Prince Sihanouk in 1970 led to an acute crisis where attacks on ethnic Vietnamese were carried out. This resulted in several thousand casualties and some 250,000 ethnic Vietnamese fleeing Cambodia for Vietnam. Most of the remaining ethnic Vietnamese were expelled in 1975 by the DK authorities, while many of the remaining Vietnamese died from disease or starvation during the DK years. Through the 1980s, the situation was better for the ethnic Vietnamese and the community re-emerged. The 1990s saw repeated attacks on the ethnic Vietnamese both during the UNTAC period and afterwards. It was not until the early 2000s that open attacks ceased. The attitude of Vietnam is interesting to analyze, in particular during the 1990s, i.e. from the UNTAC period, and onwards. Vietnam consistently made official protests against attacks on the ethnic Vietnamese in Cambodia and called on the Cambodian authorities to protect the ethnic Vietnamese and ensure they were not discriminated against. This put the issue of the ethnic

Vietnamese firmly on the agenda between the two countries up to the early 2000s.

Ethnic Khmers in Vietnam

This issue has consistently been a concern and a theme in Cambodian official policy and relations with Vietnam and in the internal political debate in Cambodia, under the banner of defending the rights of the "Khmer Krom", i.e. ethnic Khmers in Vietnam. It is at times linked to claims to the so-called "Kampuchea Krom", i.e. the areas of Vietnam located in the Mekong Delta including Ho Chi Minh City. During the 1950s and 1960s, it was linked to what was perceived to be discriminatory policies in the then Republic of Vietnam. Against the unified Vietnam it is more part of a general anti-Vietnamese stand that includes other elements such as territorial issues. It can be noted that some of the cross-border attacks in 1977 and 1978 were directed at Khmer villages in southern Vietnam, causing a number of civilian casualties among the inhabitants.

In view of the sensitiveness of the situation and the fact that a number of Cambodian groups keep a vigilant eye on the situation of the ethnic Khmer in Vietnam, the Vietnamese authorities are keen to display that ethnic Khmers are not discriminated against. The demographic developments relating to the ethnic Khmer in Vietnam display a continuous growth in the post–1975 period as seen in the data of the official censuses. Thus, contrary to the situation of the ethnic Chinese in Vietnam, there has been no decline in the number of ethnic Khmer and consequently no major migration out of Vietnam.

It can also be noted that there has been no large-scale migration or expulsion of ethnic Khmers from Vietnam comparable to the fate of the ethnic Vietnamese in Cambodia in the 1970s.

Concluding Analysis

The relationship between Cambodia and Vietnam has been plagued by two core disputed issues: the territorial disputes and the situation of the ethnic Vietnamese in Cambodia. The efforts by the two countries to address these core disputed issues have been complicated by the legacy of interpretations of history as well as by deep-rooted negative perceptions of the other. The latter is most obvious in Cambodian elite perceptions of Vietnam and the Vietnamese. The anti-Vietnamese perceptions transcend ideological differences in Cambodia as illustrated by the fact that the administrations of the Lon Nol and the DK periods — despite their diametrically opposing ideological systems — displayed and implemented anti-Vietnamese policies. Also alarming is that the greater political pluralism ushered in through the United Nations' peace-keeping operation, with multi-party elections and a considerable growth in the number of NGOs in Cambodia, has not led to the disappearance of the anti-Vietnamese discourse. On the contrary, a section of Cambodian civil society criticizes the government for pursuing negotiations and for reaching agreements with Vietnam. The reaction to the 2005 supplementary border treaty was scepticism and even overt criticism by some groups, thus assuming that such an agreement would by definition be negative for Cambodia.

Since collaboration between the two countries would be mutually beneficial through increased trade and through coordination of policies in fields where the interests of the two countries converge — e.g. on the utilization of the waters of the Mekong River — domestic support in Cambodia for a collaborative foreign policy towards and with Vietnam would be a positive development. It would create more conducive conditions for negotiations on maritime disputes between the two countries. A unified Cambodian approach would also better serve Cambodia's long-term interests. It would facilitate the task of its negotiators and even possibly strengthen their bargaining position in such negotiations.

Bilateral relations in recent years have shown that the two countries are making efforts to improve and expand relations. The progress in managing border disputes, in particular the land border, is evidence of this collaboration. The high-level talks in recent year have demonstrated that the current leadership in the two countries are willing to move relations forward so as to achieve deepened collaboration and expanded cooperation (in for example the economic field). The main ambition of both Vietnam and Cambodia is to expand economic relations. If the efforts can be sustained and the remaining disputed issues, i.e. the maritime disputes, can be managed peacefully, the relationship between Cambodia and Vietnam will substantially develop from being troubled to cooperative.

It is notable that the two countries officially claim to be working closely in both regional and sub-regional frameworks, most notably within ASEAN as well as in both the Mekong River Commission and the Greater Mekong Sub-region, as well as within the context of the Cambodia-Laos-Vietnam development triangle.

It can be concluded that the relationship between Cambodia and Vietnam is essentially a bilateral one that has been considerably influenced by both global and regional developments.

NOTES

[1] This study draws on earlier research focused on two core dimensions and issues in Cambodian-Vietnamese relations, namely the ethnic Vietnamese minority in Cambodia and the border disputes between the two countries. For the ethnic Vietnamese minority in Cambodia see Ramses Amer, "Cambodia's Ethnic Vietnamese — Minority Rights and Domestic Politics", *Asian Journal of Social Science* 34, no. 3 (2006): 388–409 (hereafter Amer, "Cambodia's Ethnic Vietnamese"); and Ramses Amer, "The Ethnic Vietnamese in Cambodia — A Minority at Risk?" *Contemporary Southeast Asia* 16, no. 2 (September 1994): 210–38 (hereafter Amer, "The Ethnic Vietnamese"). On the border disputes between the two countries see Ramses Amer, "The Border Conflicts between Cambodia and Vietnam", *Boundary and Security Bulletin* 5, no. 2 (Summer 1997): 80–91 (hereafter Amer, "The Border Conflicts"); and Ramses Amer, "Managing Border Disputes in Southeast Asia", *Kajian Malaysia: Journal of Malaysian Studies* XVIII (Special Issue on Conflict and Conflict Management in Southeast Asia), nos. 1–2 (June–December 2000): 40–42 (hereafter Amer, "Managing Border"). For research pertaining to the Vietnamese intervention in Cambodia launched in late December 1978, see Ramses Amer, *The United Nations and Foreign Military Interventions. A Comparative Study of the Application of the Charter. Second Edition*, Report, No. 33 (Uppsala: Department of Peace and Conflict Research, Uppsala University, 1994) (hereafter Amer, *The United Nations*).

[2] This approach has been used in Ramses Amer, "Sino-Vietnamese Normalization in the Light of the Crisis of the Late 1970s", *Pacific Affairs* 67, no. 3 (Fall 1994): 357–83; Ramses Amer, "Sino-Vietnamese Relations: Past, Present and Future", in *Vietnamese Foreign Policy in Transition*, edited by Carlyle A. Thayer and Ramses Amer (Singapore: Institute for Southeast Asian Studies; New York: St Martin's Press, 1999), pp. 68–130; and Ramses Amer, "Assessing Sino-Vietnamese Relations through the Management of Contentious Issues", *Contemporary Southeast Asia* 26, no. 2 (August 2004): 320–45.

[3] The parts of this section dealing with the relations between Cambodia and Vietnam are derived from Amer, *The United Nations*, pp. 38–40. For an overview of the accusations put forward by the two countries against each other vis-à-vis the attacks along the border see ibid., pp. 195–201. The information relating to the situation of the ethnic Vietnamese in Cambodia

and their resultant exodus is derived from Amer, "The Ethnic Vietnamese", pp. 216–19, and Amer, "Cambodia's Ethnic Vietnamese", pp. 389–90.

⁴ Studies dealing with the Third Indochina Conflict or Third Indochina War include: Steven J. Hood, *Dragons Entangled. Indochina and the China-Vietnam War* (Armonk and London: Sharpe, East Gate Books, 1992); Edward C. O'Dowd, *Chinese Military Strategy in the Third Indochina War: The Last Maoist War* (London and New York: Routledge, 2007); Robert S. Ross, *The Indochina Tangle: China's Vietnam Policy 1975–1979* (New York: The East Asian Institute, Columbia University, Columbia University Press, 1988); *The Third Indochina Conflict*, edited by David W.P. Elliot (Boulder: Westview Press, 1982); and, *The Third Indochina War: Conflict between China, Vietnam and Cambodia, 1972–79*, edited by Odd Arne Westad and Sophie Quinn-Judge (London and New York: Routledge, 2006).

⁵ On 30 April 1989 the PRK officially changed its name to the State of Cambodia.

⁶ The CGDK officially changed its name to National Government of Cambodia in February 1990.

⁷ For details pertaining to the alleged "Vietnamization" of Cambodia during the PRK/SOC period see, for example, Marie Alexandrine Martin, "Le processus de vietnamisation au Cambodge" [The process of vietnamization in Cambodia], *Politique Internationale*, no. 24 (Été 1984): 177–91 (hereafter Martin, "Le processus"); Marie Alexandrine Martin, *Le mal Cambodgien: Histoire d'une société traditionelle face à ses leaders politiques 1946–1987* [The bad state of Cambodia: History of a society facing its political leaders 1946–1987] (Paris: Hachette, 1989), pp. 206–27; J.R. Pouvatchy, *The Vietnamisation of Cambodia*, ISIS Seminar Paper (Kuala Lumpur, Institute of Strategic and International Studies, Malaysia, 1986); and, "The Vietnamisation of Kampuchea: A New Model of Colonialism", *Indochina Report*, pre-publication issue (October 1984) (hereafter "The Vietnamisation of Kampuchea").

⁸ General Assembly Resolution 38/3 (27 October 1983).

⁹ General Assembly Resolutions: 39/5 (30 October 1984); 40/7 (5 November 1985); 41/6 (21 October 1988), 42/3 (14 October 1987); 43/19 (3 November 1988); and, 44/22 (16 November 1989). Emphasis added by author. In resolution 44/22, the wording had been changed to "as a result of foreign occupation".

¹⁰ Figures derived from Amer, "The Ethnic Vietnamese", p. 220.

¹¹ *Policy of the People's Republic of Kampuchea with regard to Vietnamese Residents* (Phnom Penh: Press Department, Ministry of Foreign Affairs, 1983).

¹² Ibid., p. 7

¹³ For the full text of the agreement of 7 July 1982 see *British Broadcasting Corporation, Summary of World Broadcasts, Part Three, Far East*, 7074/A3/7–8 (10 July 1982) (hereafter *BBC/FE*). The text of the agreement has also been reproduced in an English language version as "Appendix 2" in Kriangsak

Kittichaisaree, *The Law of the Sea and Maritime Boundary Delimitation in South-East Asia* (Singapore: Oxford University Press, 1987), pp. 180–81.

[14] *BBC/FE/8143/A3/1*; and, Quang, "Vietnam-Kampuchea Border Issue Settled", p. 9.

[15] *BBC/FE/7393/A3/1* (23 July 1983). See also Quang Nghia, "Vietnam-Kampuchea Border Issue Settled", *Vietnam Courier*, no. 4 (1986), pp. 8–9.

[16] For reports from Vietnam and the PRK announcing the signing of the Treaty see *BBC/FE/8143/A3/1–3* (30 December 1985). See also Quang, "Vietnam-Kampuchea", pp. 8–9.

[17] Ibid., pp. 8–9. These agreements are also discussed in Epsey Cooke Farell, "The Socialist Republic of Vietnam and the Law of the Sea: An analysis of Vietnam's behavior within the emerging international ocean regime" (Ph.D. dissertation, University of South Carolina 1992), pp. 327–36; and in Pierre-Lucien Lamant, "La frontière entre le Cambodge et le Viêtnam du milieu du XIXe siècle à nos jours" [The border between Cambodia and Vietnam from the middle of the 19th century to our days], in *Les frontières du Vietnam. Histoire des frontières de la Péninsule Indochinoise* [The borders of Vietnam. History of the borders of the Indochina Peninsula], Travaux du Centre d'Histoire et Civilisations de la Péninsule Indochinoise publiés sous la direction de P.B. Lafont, Collection Recherches Asiatiques, dirigé par Alain Forest (Paris: Éditions L'Harmattan, 1989), pp. 180–81.

[18] For a more detailed analysis on the basis of this periodization see Ramses Amer, "Resolving the Cambodian Conflict", in *The Cambodian Conflict 1979–1991: From Intervention to Resolution*, by Ramses Amer, Johan Saravanamuttu and Peter Wallensteen (Penang: Research and Education for Peace, School of Social Sciences, Universiti Sains Malaysia, and Department of Peace and Conflict Research, Uppsala University, 1996), pp. 12–36.

[19] *BBC/FE/1464/B/1* (20 August 1992).

[20] A/46/608-S/23177 (30 October 1991).

[21] *BBC/FE/1460/B/2* (15 August 1992).

[22] S/25719 (3 May 1993); and *BBC/FE/1626/i* (2 March 1993). A further four Vietnamese men were later identified as "foreign forces" by UNTAC (S/25719).

[23] *BBC/FE/1630/A1/2* (6 March 1993).

[24] For details on the attacks on the Vietnamese during the peacekeeping period see Amer, "The Ethnic Vietnamese", pp. 222–28.

[25] *BBC/FE/2204 B/2–3* (18 January 1995); and, 2205 B/1-3 (19 January 1995).

[26] Ibid., 2269 B/4 (4 April 1995).

[27] Ibid., 2371 B/1 (2 August 1995).

[28] The report on this statement was carried by Radio Australia on 17 January 1996 (Ibid., 2512 B/1 [18 January 1996]). The names of the provinces were listed in the first Vietnamese reaction (Ibid., 2513 B/3 [9 January 1996]).

29　Ibid., 2562 B/1–2 (16 March 1996).

30　Ibid., 2584/B/2 (12 April 1996).

31　Ibid., 2628 B/4 (3 June 1996).

32　For Cambodia's complaints about the Thai-Vietnamese agreement see ibid. 3223 B/2–3 (11 May 1998); and 3228 B/14 (16 May 1998). For the Vietnamese response see ibid. 3228 B/14. For reports about the visit to Vietnam see ibid. 3241 B/1 (1 June 1998); 3242 B/5–6 (2 June 1998); 3243 B/6 (3 June 1998); and 3245 B/1–2 (5 June 1998).

33　Ibid., 3260 B/2 (23 June 1998); and 3264 B/1 (27 June 1998).

34　For anti-Vietnamese statements by Prince Ranariddh during the election campaign see for example ibid., 3251 B/6 (12 June 1998); and 3282 B/6–7 (18 July 1998).

35　For details on negotiations up to 2000, see Amer, "Managing Border", pp. 40–41. For details up to early 1997 see Amer, "The Border Conflicts", pp. 82–87. For the 2005 agreement, see Ramses Amer and Nguyen Hong Thao, "Vietnam's Border Disputes — Assessing the Impact on Its Regional Integration", in *Vietnam's New Order: International Perspectives on the State and Reform in Vietnam*, edited By Stéphanie Balme and Mark Sidel (New York and Houndmills, Basingstoke, Hampshire: Palgrave Macmillan, 2007), pp. 72 and 78–79; and Ramses Amer and Nguyen Hong Thao, "Vietnam's Border Disputes: Legal and Conflict Management Dimensions", in *The Asian Yearbook of International Law, Vol. 12 (2005–2006)*, edited by B.S. Chimni, Miyoshi Masahiro, and Thio Li-ann (Leiden and Boston: Martinus Nijhoff Publishers, 2007), pp. 123–25.

36　"Vietnam-Cambodia Joint Statement", *Nhan Dan*, 8 March 2006 <http://www. nhandan.com.vn/english/news/080306/domestic_statement.htm> (accessed 26 September 2007); and "Prime Minister of the Socialist Republic of Vietnam visited Cambodia", *Cambodia News*, Vol. 1, March 2006 <http://www. un.int/cambodia/Bulletin_Files/March06/VN_visits_cambo.pdf> (accessed 11 September 2009).

37　"Joint Statement between the Kingdom of Cambodia and the Socialist Republic of Vietnam", *Cambodia News*, Vol. 11, March 2007 <http://www. un.int/cambodia/Bulletin_Files/March07/JOINT_PRESS_STATEMENT_ Cambo_VN.pdf> (accessed 11 September 2009); and "Vietnam and Cambodia issue press release", *Nhan Dan*, 2 March 2007 <http://www.nhandan.com.vn/ english/news/020307/domestic_pre.htm> (accessed 26 September 2007).

38　"Promoting Vietnamese-Cambodian Friendship and co-operation", *Nhan Dan*, 24 June 2008 <http://www.nhandan.com.vn/english/news/240608/ editorial_pre.htm> (accessed 26 June 2008).

39　"Vietnam's National Assembly President Paid Official Visit to Cambodia", *Cambodia News*, Vol. 13, May 2007 <http://www.un.int/cambodia/Bulletin_ Files/May07/Vietnam_visit_Cambodia.pdf> (accessed 11 September 2009); and

"Cambodian, Vietnamese National Assembly Promote Cooperation", *Cambodia News*, Vol. 31, January 2009 <http://www.un.int/cambodia/Bulletin_Files/ Jan09/Cambodian_Vietnamese.pdf> (accessed 11 September 2009).

40   "Cambodia, Vietnam Vow to Reach Two-way Trade of US$2 Billion in 2010", *Cambodia News*, Vol. 38, August 2009 <http://www.un.int/cambodia/Bulletin_ Files/Aug09/Cambodia_Vietnam.pdf> (accessed 11 September 2009).

41   "Promoting Vietnamese-Cambodian Friendship and co-operation", *Nhan Dan*, 24 June 2008 <http://www.nhandan.com.vn/english/news/240608/ editorial_pre.htm> (accessed 26 June 2008); and "Vietnam, Cambodia push for border security", *Ministry of Foreign Affairs of the Socialist Republic of Vietnam* (http://www.mofa.gov.vn/en/nr040807104143/nr040807105001/ ns090818082848) (accessed 15 September 2009).

42   "Cambodia, Laos and Vietnam sign border crossing agreement", *Cambodia News*, Vol. 27, September 2008 <http://www.un.int/cambodia/Bulletin_Files/ Sept08/Cambodia_Laos_Vietnam_sign_border_agreement.pdf> (accessed 11 September 2009); and "Vietnam, Cambodia, Laos sign border crossing agreement", *Ministry of Foreign Affairs of the Socialist Republic of Vietnam*, 27 August 2008 <http://www.mofa.gov.vn/en/nr040807104143/ nr040807105001/ns080827084657> (accessed 19 February 2009).

43   See notes 35 and 36.

44   The argument here is not that the term "Youn" in itself is discriminatory, but rather the way it is used in the political rhetoric and the fact that the ethnic Vietnamese in Cambodia have suffered repeated attacks since 1953.

45   For a detailed analysis of how prominently anti-Vietnam and anti-Vietnamese views were propagated by the two main opposition parties in the campaign leading up to the 1998 general elections, see Caroline Hughes, "International Intervention and the People's Will: The Demoralization of Democracy in Cambodia", in *Conflict and Change in Cambodia*, edited with an introduction by Ben Kiernan and consulting editor Caroline Hughes (London: Routledge, 2007), pp. 45–68.

46   Didier Bertrand makes a similar observation relating to the use of anti-Vietnamese rhetoric for political purposes by Cambodian politicians across the political spectrum, i.e. "royalistes, républicains et les Khmers Rouge" [royalists, republicans and the Khmer Rouge] (Didier Bertrand, "Les Vietnamiens au Cambodge analyse des représentations et des conditions d'une integration" [The Vietnamese in Cambodia analysis of the representations and the conditions for an integration], *Aséanie*, Vol. 2, 1998, p. 39).

47   The most evident display of these Vietnamese views and accusations against China appears in the following Vietnamese publication: *The Truth About Viet Nam–China Relations Over the Last 30 Years* (Hanoi: Ministry of Foreign Affairs, Socialist Republic of Vietnam, 1979).

48   For a detailed analysis of the Geneva Conference of 1954 with a focus on the role played by China, see François Joyaux, *La China et le règlement du premier conflict d'Indochine* (Genève 1954) [China and the Settlement of the First Indochina Conflict (Geneva 1954)], Série internationale — 9, Université de Paris-I Panthéon-Sorbonne, Institut d'histoire des relations internationals contemporaines (IHRIC) (Paris: Publication de la Sorbonne, 1979).

49   Ben Kiernan, "Introduction: Conflict in Cambodia, 1945–2006", in *Conflict and Change in Cambodia*, edited with an introduction by Ben Kiernan and consulting editor Caroline Hughes (London and New York: Routledge, 2007), p. ix.

50   For details on the strained relations see ibid., p. ix; and Christopher E. Goscha, "Vietnam, the Third Indochina War and the meltdown of Asian internationalism", in *The Third Indochina War: Conflict between China, Vietnam and Cambodia, 1972–79*, edited by Odd Arne Westad and Sophie Quinn-Judge (London and New York: Routledge, 2006), pp. 164–73.

REFERENCES

Amer, Ramses. "Sino-Vietnamese Normalization in the Light of the Crisis of the Late 1970s". *Pacific Affairs* 67, no. 3 (Fall 1994): 357–83.

———. "The Ethnic Vietnamese in Cambodia — A Minority at Risk?" *Contemporary Southeast Asia* 16, no. 2 (September 1994): 210–38.

———. *The United Nations and Foreign Military Interventions. A Comparative Study of the Application of the Charter. Second Edition*, Report, no. 33. Uppsala: Department of Peace and Conflict Research, Uppsala University, 1994.

———. "Resolving the Cambodian Conflict". In Ramses Amer, Johan Saravana-muttu and Peter Wallensteen, *The Cambodian Conflict 1979–1991: From Intervention to Resolution*. Penang: Research and Education for Peace, School of Social Sciences, Universiti Sains Malaysia: Department of Peace and Conflict Research, Uppsala University, 1996, pp. 12–36.

———. "The Border Conflicts between Cambodia and Vietnam". *Boundary and Security Bulletin* 5, no. 2 (Summer 1997): 80–91.

———. "Sino-Vietnamese Relations: Past, Present and Future". In *Vietnamese Foreign Policy in Transition*, edited by Carlyle A. Thayer and Ramses Amer. Singapore: Institute of Southeast Asian Studies; New York: St Martin's Press, 1999: 68–130.

———. "Managing Border Disputes in Southeast Asia". *Kajian Malaysia: Journal of Malaysian Studies* XVIII (Special Issue on Conflict and Conflict Management in Southeast Asia), nos. 1–2 (June–December 2000): 40–42.

———. "Assessing Sino-Vietnamese Relations through the Management of Contentious Issues". *Contemporary Southeast Asia* 26, no. 2 (August 2004): 320–45.

————. "Cambodia's Ethnic Vietnamese — Minority Rights and Domestic Politics". *Asian Journal of Social Science* 34, no. 3 (2006): 388–409.

Amer, Ramses and Nguyen Hong Thao. "Vietnam's Border Disputes — Assessing the Impact on Its Regional Integration". In *Vietnam's New Order: International Perspectives on the State and Reform in Vietnam*, edited By Stéphanie Balme and Mark Sidel. New York and Houndmills, Basingstoke, Hampshire: Palgrave Macmillan, 2007, pp. 71–87.

————. "Vietnam's Border Disputes: Legal and Conflict Management Dimensions". In *The Asian Yearbook of International Law, Vol. 12 (2005–2006)*, edited by B.S. Chimni, Miyoshi Masahiro, and Thio Li-ann. Leiden and Boston: Martinus Nijhoff, 2007, pp. 111–27.

Bertrand, Didier. "Les Vietnamiens au Cambodge analyse des représentations et des conditions d'une integration" [The Vietnamese in Cambodia analysis of the representations and the conditions for an integration], *Aséanie*, Vol. 2, 1998, pp. 24–46.

British Broadcasting Corporation, Summary of World Broadcasts, Part Three, Far East, 7074/A3/7–8 (10 July 1982); 7393/A3/1 (23 July 1983); 8143/A3/1–3 (30 December 1985); 1464/B/1 (20 August 1992); 1460/B/2 (15 August 1992); 1626/i (2 March 1993); 1630/A1/2 (6 March 1993); 2204 B/2–3 (18 January 1995); 2205 B/1–3 (19 January 1995); 2269 B/4 (4 April 1995); 2371 B/1 (2 August 1995); 2512 B/1 (18 January 1996); 2513 B/3 (9 January 1996); 2562 B/1–2 (16 March 1996); 2584 B/2 (12 April 1996); 2628 B/4 (3 June 1996); 3223 B/2–3 (11 May 1998); 3228 B/14 (16 May 1998); 3241 B/1 (1 June 1998); 3242 B/5–6 (2 June 1998); 3243 B/6 (3 June 1998); 3245 B/1–2 (5 June 1998); 3251 B/6 (12 June 1998); 3260 B/2 (23 June 1998); 3264 B/1 (27 June 1998); and, 3282 B/6–7 (18 July 1998).

"Cambodia, Laos and Vietnam sign border crossing agreement". *Cambodia News*, Vol. 27, September 2008 <http://www.un.int/cambodia/Bulletin_Files/Sept08/Cambodia_Laos_Vietnam_sign_border_agreement.pdf> (accessed 11 September 2009).

"Cambodia, Vietnam Vow to Reach Two-way Trade of US$2 Billion in 2010", *Cambodia News*, Vol. 38, August 2009 <http://www.un.int/cambodia/Bulletin_Files/Aug09/Cambodia_Vietnam.pdf> (accessed 11 September 2009).

"Cambodian, Vietnamese National Assembly Promote Cooperation", *Cambodia News*, Vol. 31, January 2009 <http://www.un.int/cambodia/Bulletin_Files/Jan09/Cambodian_Vietnamese.pdf> (accessed 11 September 2009).

Elliot, David W.P., ed. *The Third Indochina Conflict*. Boulder: Westview Press, 1982.

Farell, Espey Cooke. *The Socialist Republic of Vietnam and the Law of the Sea: An analysis of Vietnam's behavior within the emerging international ocean regime*. Ph.D. Thesis, University of South Carolina. Ann Arbor: University Microfilms International, 1992.

Goscha, Christopher E. "Vietnam, the Third Indochina War and the Meltdown of Asian Internationalism". In *The Third Indochina War: Conflict between China, Vietnam and Cambodia, 1972–79*, edited by Odd Arne Westad and Sophie Quinn-Judge. London and New York: Routledge, 2006, pp. 152–86.

Hood, Steven J. *Dragons Entangled: Indochina and the China-Vietnam War*. Armonk and London: Sharpe, East Gate Books, 1992.

Hughes, Caroline, "International Intervention and the People's Will: The Demoralization of Democracy in Cambodia". In *Conflict and Change in Cambodia*, edited with an introduction by Ben Kiernan and consulting editor Caroline Hughes. London and New York: Routledge, 2007, pp. 45–68.

"Joint Statement between the Kingdom of Cambodia and the Socialist Republic of Vietnam", *Cambodia News*, Vol. 11, March 2007 <http://www.un.int/cambodia/Bulletin_Files/March07/JOINT_PRESS_STATEMENT_Cambo_VN.pdf> (accessed 11 September 2009).

Joyaux, François. *La China et le règlement du premier conflict d'Indochine*. Genève 1954 [China and the Settlement of the First Indochina Conflict. Geneva 1954]. Série internationale — 9, Université de Paris-I Panthéon-Sorbonne, Institut d'histoire des relations internationals contemporaines (IHRIC). Paris: Publication de la Sorbonne, 1979.

Kiernan, Ben. "Introduction: Conflict in Cambodia, 1945–2006". In *Conflict and Change in Cambodia*, edited by Caroline Hughes. London and New York: Routledge, 2007, pp. vii–xix.

Kittichaisaree, Kriangsak. *The Law of the Sea and Maritime Boundary Delimitation in South-East Asia*. Singapore, Oxford and New York: Oxford University Press, 1987.

Lamant, Pierre-Lucien. "La frontière entre le Cambodge et le Viêtnam du milieu du XIXe siècle à nos jours" [The border between Cambodia and Vietnam from the middle of the 19th century to our days]. In *Les frontières du Vietnam. Histoire des frontières de la Péninsule Indochinoise* [The borders of Vietnam. History of the borders of the Indochina Peninsula], edited by Pierre-Bernard Lafont. Paris: Éditions L'Harmattan, 1989, pp. 156–81.

Martin, Marie Alexandrine. "Le processus de vietnamisation au Cambodge" [The process of vietnamisation in Cambodia]. *Politique Internationale*, no. 24 (Été [Summer] 1984), pp. 177–91.

————. *Le mal Cambodgien. Histoire d'une société traditionelle face à ses leaders politiques 1946–1987* [The bad state of Cambodia. History of a society facing its political leaders 1946–1987]. Paris: Hachette, 1989.

Ministry of Foreign Affairs, Cambodia. *Policy of the People's Republic of Kampuchea with regard to Vietnamese Residents*. Phnom Penh: Press Department, Ministry of Foreign Affairs, 1983.

Ministry of Foreign Affairs, Vietnam. *The Truth About Viet Nam–China Relations Over the Last 30 Years*. Hanoi: Ministry of Foreign Affairs, Socialist Republic of Vietnam, 1979.

O'Dowd, Edward C. *Chinese Military Strategy in the Third Indochina War: The Last Maoist War*. London and New York: Routledge, 2007.

Pouvatchy, J.R. *The Vietnamisation of Cambodia*, ISIS Seminar Paper. Kuala Lumpur, Institute of Strategic and International Studies (ISIS), Malaysia, 1986.

"Prime Minister of the Socialist Republic of Vietnam visited Cambodia", *Cambodia News*, Vol. 1, March 2006 <http://www.un.int/cambodia/Bulletin_Files/March06/VN_visits_cambo.pdf> (accessed 11 September 2009).

"Promoting Vietnamese-Cambodian Friendship and co-operation", *Nhan Dan* [People's Daily] (Vietnam), 24 June 2008 <http://www.nhandan.com.vn/english/news/240608/editorial_pre.htm> (accessed 26 June 2008).

Quang Nghia. "Vietnam-Kampuchea Border Issue Settled". *Vietnam Courier*, no. 4, 1986, pp. 8–9.

Ross, Robert S. *The Indochina Tangle. China's Vietnam Policy 1975–1979*. New York: The East Asian Institute, Columbia University, Columbia University Press, 1988.

UN General Assembly and Security Council A/46/608-S/23177 (30 October 1991).

UN General Assembly Resolutions 38/3 (27 October 1983); 39/5 (30 October 1984); 40/7 (5 November 1985); 41/6 (21 October 1988), 42/3 (14 October 1987); 43/19 (3 November 1988); and 44/22 (16 November 1989).

UN Security Council S/25719 (3 May 1993).

"The Vietnamisation of Kampuchea. A New Model of Colonialism". *Indochina Report*, Pre-Publication Issue. October 1984.

"Vietnam and Cambodia issue press release". *Nhan Dan* [People's Daily] (Vietnam), 2 March 2007 <http://www.nhandan.com.vn/english/news/020307/domestic_pre.htm> (accessed 26 September 2007).

"Vietnam-Cambodia Joint Statement". *Nhan Dan* [People's Daily] (Vietnam), 8 March 2006 <http://www.nhandan.com.vn/english/news/080306/domestic_statement.htm> (accessed 26 September 2007).

"Vietnam, Cambodia, Laos sign border crossing agreement". *Ministry of Foreign Affairs of the Socialist Republic of Vietnam*, 27 August 2008 <http://www.mofa.gov.vn/en/nr040807104143/nr040807105001/ns080827084657> (accessed 19 February 2009).

"Vietnam, Cambodia push for border security". *Ministry of Foreign Affairs of the Socialist Republic of Vietnam* (http://www.mofa.gov.vn/en/nr040807104143/nr040807105001/ns090818082848) (accessed 15 September 2009).

"Vietnam's National Assembly President Paid Official Visit to Cambodia". *Cambodia News*, Vol. 13, May 2007 <http://www.un.int/cambodia/Bulletin_Files/May07/Vietnam_visit_Cambodia.pdf> (accessed 11 September 2009).

Westad, Odd Arne and Sophie Quinn-Judge, eds. *The Third Indochina War:Conflict between China, Vietnam and Cambodia, 1972–79*. London: Routledge, 2006.

5

Thailand-Myanmar Relations: Old Animosity in a New Bilateral Setting

Pavin Chachavalpongpun

Myanmar always has a special place in Thai political memory, albeit not necessarily for the right reasons. It has been made a main pillar for Thai nation-building and has provided a canvas on which the Thai state could paint its version of history based on their acrimonious past. In assessing today's bilateral relationship between Thailand and Myanmar, it is necessary to take historical factors into account. This is because history plays a fundamental role in the formulation of Thai policy towards Myanmar, and more contemporarily, as a justification to antagonize the Myanmar regime whenever bilateral problems arise. For the latter purpose, Myanmar's image as Thailand's number-one enemy would automatically be projected. The exception to this was during the periods of Chatichai Choonhavan (1988–91), Chavalit Yongchaiyudh (1996–97), Thaksin Shinawatra (2001–6), Samak Sundaravej (2008), and Somchai Wongsawat (2008) when Myanmar was reinvented as Thailand's new best friend, purely on the basis of commercial interests. These many faces of Myanmar crafted for political and economic consumption of the Thai elites have a powerful impact on the Thai solutions to problems with Myanmar.

The cordial relations between Thailand and Myanmar do not necessarily contribute positively to a solution of their existing contentious issues. Thailand-Myanmar conflicts have strictly been dealt with in a bilateral context even when both are members of ASEAN, and when ASEAN was ready to step in to help resolve those issues through its disputes settlement mechanism. This chapter argues that there are a number of fundamental reasons behind the reluctance and the unwillingness of both parties to make use of regional mechanisms, including the low level of confidence in regional bodies, the politics of interest that has prevented them from genuinely seeking solutions, and the state perception of sovereignty which has seemed to overpower the need to work at a supra-national level. This study looks more specifically into the case of Thailand-Myanmar conflicts and how they have been managed both bilaterally and regionally. More importantly, it discusses the issues from a Thai perspective; particularly how the shifting Thai policy toward Myanmar has shaped the way the two countries have solved their problems.

The Perpetual Enemy

The story of Thailand-Myanmar relations typically begins with Burma (former name of Myanmar) starring as an aggressive neighbour that invaded Ayutthaya, the old kingdom of Siam (former name of Thailand) — not once, but twice.[1] The collapse of Ayutthaya provided an excellent historical backdrop for subsequent Thai elites to point fingers at Burma for occasional tensions that have erupted in bilateral relations. Even when Burma fell under British colonialism and hardly posed any threat to Thai security, the role of Burma as historical foe lived on, partly because the Thai elites, either under absolute monarchy or military rule, continued to protect their political legitimacy with the depiction of foreigners as enemies. Burma was conveniently nominated as one of them.

During the height of the Cold War, and while Burma was preoccupied with strengthening socialism at home, Thailand emerged as a proxy of the Western-led democratic world. The government of Field Marshal Phibun Songkhram proclaimed an anti-communist policy, while cloaking itself in a democratic veneer even when the regime was highly despotic. The pretension was possible under an international condition of ideological differences in which authoritarian Thailand sided with the democratic camp. Thailand swiftly combined Burma's socialist threat with the historical past. Burma was thus reassigned as the national enemy since it repudiated to align itself with the United States.

Mutual distrust led to armed clashes between the Thai and Burmese armies. To counter the Burmese threat, Thailand supplied arms and other assistance to potential ethnic rebels in Burma through its northern territory.[2] This marked the commencement of the Thai policy of the buffer state, which supported the anti-Rangoon, anti-communist ethnic minorities along the borders with Burma. They represented bulwarks for Thailand against any foreseeable Burmese menace in the form of physical and ideological intrusions.[3] Burma protested to the Thai Government about the flow of weapons,[4] and alleged that ethnic minorities were exchanging some valuable natural resources from areas of their occupancy for weapons from Thailand. The Thai buffer policy and the support given to ethnic minorities in Burma intensified the scale of bilateral conflicts and further augmented a level of mutual hatred that was deeply rooted in their embittered history.[5] Today, although the majority of the ethnic minorities have concluded ceasefire agreements with the Myanmar Government, lingering distrust has prevented the two countries from genuine reconciliation. The porous borders and the ongoing battle between the Myanmar army, or Tatmadaw, and the ethnic rebels, with the Thai involvement, have instigated a series of bilateral contentious issues such as the tide of refugees, illegal labour and migrants from Myanmar, human trafficking, spread of infectious diseases, environmental issues, transnational crime, and most precariously, an influx of deadly drugs into Thailand. These issues continue to pose as critical hurdles in the Thailand-Myanmar relationship.

Thailand has been on the receiving end of narcotic smuggling from the areas controlled by the pro-junta ethnic minorities. The October 2007 report of the United Nations Office on Drugs and Crime showed that Myanmar was now the world's second largest heroin exporter after Afghanistan and that the illicit trade could grow even faster if the government's control over far-flung provinces weakened.[6] Although Myanmar's potential opium production slightly decreased in 2008[7], it as of now remains the second largest exporter of heroin in the world.[8] Thailand is currently the country most affected by narcotic exports from Myanmar, mostly in the form of methamphetamines, known locally as *yaa baa*, with between 700–900 million pills pouring into the country every year. It also ranks first among the highest consumers of methamphetamines in the world.[9]

The Democrat Party, renowned for its anti-junta stance, took advantage of Myanmar's demonic image and a long list of contentious bilateral issues to raise its political score by asserting itself as a champion of democracy against Myanmar's authoritarianism. When the Democrat Party formed the government in 1997, the bilateral relationship turned sour. Thailand consequently resurrected its buffer policy in order to aid Myanmar's pro-democracy activists and anti-junta ethnic insurgents — all this was done in the name of defending democracy. The shift in Thailand's policy toward Myanmar was a direct result of the shifting legitimacy of the Thai leadership. Democracy, not economic interests, was defined as a component of Thai foreign policy. For the Democrat Party, the trait of democracy must therefore be enshrined in the country's perspective toward Myanmar. The Myanmar Government retaliated against Thailand's frigid attitude by closing channels of communication and launching military attacks across the border.[10] During the Democrat administration, Thailand-Myanmar relations worsened. Skirmishes along the border, as a consequence of Thailand's buffer policy, were evidence of deterioration in this bilateral relationship.

This antagonistic view was not one-sided. Elites in Yangon also adopted an anti-Thai attitude, particularly during the culmination of the Cold War. This attitude was a product of their response to the geopolitical reality at the time. After General Ne Win staged the military coup in 1962 against the U Nu government, Thailand-Myanmar relations faced new challenges and gradually deteriorated. Ne Win harboured greater suspicion about Thailand's intention and its support for the minorities sheltering along the border areas, especially the Karen rebels, whom he considered arch-enemies.[11] Ne Win condemned Thailand for setting up a border buffer zone where opposition groups were tolerated as a barrier against the Burmese armed forces and communist insurgents. He once referred to times of mutual conflict, "Our forefathers had fought against one another for no other purpose than to enhance their prestige through military conquest."[12]

Myanmar's suspicion of Thailand has lasted into the present day and helped prolong bilateral conflicts despite efforts of successive governments in both countries to find a long-term solution. For example, Myanmar imposed economic sanctions on Thailand in November 1999 as a result of the Thai Government's decision to release Myanmar's political dissidents who, armed with guns and grenades, took hostages when they commandeered Myanmar's Embassy in Bangkok. Myanmar also supported the Wa soldiers to intrude into Thai territories, leading to serious intermittent skirmishes in 2001, purportedly because the Thai leaders accused Myanmar of being the main source of drugs smuggled into Thailand.

However, the perception of the Thais among the people of Myanmar has been rather different. First, the image of Thailand as Burma's historical enemy is not as stark as that of Burma in the Thai historiography. Burmese historians never treated their kingdom's wars with Siam any more significantly that those with other kingdoms. Second, the people of Myanmar do not "dislike" Thais for a variety of reasons. For example, in the aftermath of Cyclone Nargis in early May 2008, Thailand was one of the first few countries to dispatch urgent humanitarian aid to the affected Myanmar. Although the Thai Government played an important part in the humanitarian assistance offered to the Myanmar people, the Thais' compassion was evident through their generous donation of money, food, medical supplies, and clothes. It is therefore important to justify the state of Thailand-Myanmar relationship through the different perspectives of the state and the people.

The Reinvention of Myanmar

There have been positive aspects in Thailand-Myanmar relations despite the existence of contentious issues. Détente during tensions was achievable when the Thai regime embraced a friendly approach toward Myanmar based on the promotion of commercial benefits. The first wave of détente took place when General Chatichai assumed the premiership in 1988 with an innovative policy of turning the battlefield into a marketplace.[13] Myanmar was overnight reconstructed as Thailand's business partner. To facilitate this new business thrust, Thailand announced a "Constructive Engagement" policy, claiming to help acclimatize Myanmar with regional realities. The reinvention process was re-emphasized following General Chavalit's succession to power in 1996. Under both governments, Thai investment in Myanmar was enthusiastically encouraged, either in the name of national or individual interests. Timber, minerals, fish, gemstones, and even drugs and cheap labour from Myanmar were in high demand in the Thai market. The Thai elites claimed Myanmar might be backward and underdeveloped, but it needed Thai understanding and investments. To appease Myanmar for the sake of economic benefits, Thailand gave full support for the Myanmar admission into ASEAN in 1997 despite international criticism. On the part of Myanmar, the military junta was also eager to trade with Thailand and to partake in regional organization in order to gain cash to sustain its fragile economy as well as political legitimacy once it became a member of ASEAN.[14] Strategic considerations also played their part here. Thailand and other members of ASEAN believed that bringing Myanmar into ASEAN would automatically mean "pulling the country out of the Chinese sphere of influence".[15] ASEAN members also hoped that integrating all countries in Southeast Asia into one regional body would help increase the group's influence and voice, and showcase its solidarity in the international community. Of course, ASEAN was subsequently let down by Myanmar refusing to seriously commence the democratic reforms it had promised prior to its admission into the organization.

The Thailand-Myanmar golden period culminated during the Thaksin administration, again based on excessive commercial interests Thailand was hoping to exploit in resource-rich Myanmar. A Thai scholar summarized that Thailand's Myanmar policy under Thaksin was characterized by accommodation and appeasement, at times bordering on flattery. It was rendered "constructive engagement" completely elastic in accordance with the preferences of Myanmar.[16] Thaksin cultivated a cosy relationship with the Myanmar generals, while pledging to put economic interests before political correctness. The economic outcomes were evident as a result of the friendly relationship. In 2005, the year Thaksin won the second landslide election, Thailand was Myanmar's top trading partner, with total bilateral trade amounting to US$2.5 billion, increasing 27.2 per cent from the previous year. During the Thaksin years, Thai private businesses invested in 56 projects in Myanmar — totalling more than US$1.3 billion, or equivalent to 17.28 per cent of Myanmar's total foreign direct investments.[17] On top of this, Thailand's exports to Myanmar amounted to around US$1.26 billion annually. The total border trade stood at US$2.2 billion in 2005. This flourishing border trade has reaped direct benefits from Thailand's open-border policy as well as the increasingly vibrant trade in the Mekong Region, as reflected in the aspiration behind ACMECS (Ayeyawady–Chao Phraya–Mekong Economic Cooperation Strategy), in which Thailand hoped to bridge the economic gap with its immediate neighbours, including Myanmar.

Smooth relations effectively guaranteed Thaksin's access to the Myanmar economy. Thaksin himself possessed a variety of businesses in this neighbouring country, most predominantly in the telecom industry through the provision of broadband satellite "IPSTAR", a project that was linked with the controversial US$100 million loan from the Export-Import Bank of Thailand to the Myanmar Foreign Trade Bank in June 2004.[18] Thaksin was accused of endorsing widespread suppression of Myanmar dissidents and activists residing in Thailand in order to ensure long-term economic interests in Myanmar. The 2004 Human Rights Watch report reprimanded his government's repatriation programme of placing Myanmar refugees and undocumented asylum-seekers in danger of persecution, arrest, economic sanctions, or other reprisals from the Myanmar authorities upon their return to Myanmar.[19] Myanmar Economic Watch of 2006 also gave a similar account of the rising hardship of Myanmar workers in Thailand and the untold fate of Myanmar migrants who left their country due to human rights violations and civil war to search for shelter on Thai soil.[20] Cosy bilateral ties engendered a devastating impact on Myanmar exiles, refugees, and migrants, especially those who were visibly and vocally opposed to the military government, through various means such as arrests, intimidation, harassment, and deportation.[21]

The military staged a coup that removed Thaksin from power on 19 September 2006. The leader of the coup-makers, General Sonthi Boonyaratglin, nominated General Surayud Chulanont as Prime Minister. During the Surayud government, it can be said that Thailand had no specific policy toward Myanmar. The government repeatedly claimed that it lacked moral authority to preach to its Myanmar counterpart to respect democracy. Furthermore, it was preoccupied with having to clarify itself before the West the reasons behind the power seizure and its intention to reinstall democracy. Old contentious issues in bilateral ties remained frozen in aspic. Retention of the status quo appeared to be the preferred choice for both countries, understandably since Thailand has been heavily reliant on gas imports from Myanmar. Thailand is today the biggest single buyer of Myanmar gas, which makes up about fifty per cent of the country's supply.[22]

When Samak became Prime Minister in February 2008, Thailand-Myanmar relations drastically improved. Economic interests were once again made a determining factor in bilateral relations. Samak visited Naypyidaw in March as part of his introductory tour of ASEAN countries as Thailand's new leader. While in the Myanmar capital, Samak announced the new Thai policy toward Myanmar. First, Thailand would oppose Western sanctions on Myanmar. Second, Thailand hoped to reinforce its economic ties with Myanmar, especially in the production and exploitation of natural gas as well as in hydropower projects. It was obvious that there was no attempt on the Thai part to pressure Myanmar to move towards democracy. The Samak government thought that such pressure would be interpreted as interference in Myanmar's internal affairs. In order to secure its lucrative economic interests, his government also approved the continued house arrest of Aung San Suu Kyi, leader of the National League for Democracy. During the visit of Myanmar's Prime Minister Lieutenant-General Thein Sein to Bangkok in May 2008, Samak said, "They are not releasing her, but they will not interfere with her. They will put her on the shelf and not bother with her which is unacceptable to foreigners." Samak added, "We think it is okay if she is put on the shelf, but others admire her because of it."[23] Foreign governments and the media criticized the Samak government's role in Myanmar's affairs, arguing that its support could only worsen the situation, giving the military junta confidence in its ability to overcome international sanctions.

Power Interests at Play

What and who should be responsible for the current state of Thailand-Myanmar relations? This study argues that it is a combination of structural reasons and the role of the Thai elites that trigger the fluctuations in this bilateral relationship.

The Thai state has long claimed to be the sole player in the domain of foreign policy decision making. The claim was nonetheless questionable considering that domestic and foreign affairs are usually contested by multiple actors for what is believed to be the protection of their own interests. Thailand's relations with Myanmar exemplify how multiple actors could add confusion and complication to the conduct of diplomacy. The Thai elites wanted to deal with the Myanmar Government for numerous purposes, be they for national or personal interests, whereas the military has been more concerned about security issues along the borders. Other political factions and civil society organizations requested that attention be paid to critical social issues, such as the flow of illegal workers and refugees from Myanmar. These represent conflicting policies toward Myanmar.

There appears to be a structural shortcoming in the Thai approach vis-à-vis Myanmar that has proven harmful to the bilateral relationship. It is observable that the Thai military has had a less favourable view of Myanmar than the government in Bangkok whose leaders were evidently more interested in strengthening economic ties. Many army officers have become very judgmental of the state approach toward the Myanmar regime.[24] The lack of a unified approach results in the lack of policy transparency and the gap in perceptions among Thai authorities regarding their understanding of the real problems in Thailand-Myanmar relations. Such a prevailing gap in turn dictates different solutions.

It is also important to elucidate the local conditions that influence the Thai attitude toward resolving bilateral problems with Myanmar. The ghost of the past policy — turning the enemy lands into a marketplace for investors — still casts a long shadow over the public's attitude towards this bilateral relationship. Since Myanmar has been remade into a lucrative market for hungry Thai businesses, public concerns over democracy, human rights, and justice while implementing Thai foreign policy have diminished.[25] It is questionable whether what has been happening in Myanmar is of much concern to most Thai people, except of course the 2007 "Saffron Revolution" which effectively instigated global discontent against the regime,[26] and the devastating impact caused by Cyclone Nargis which hit the Ayeyawady Delta in May 2008.

One needs to look at Thai support for Thaksin's war on drugs in 2003, which ended with the massive extra-judicial killing of over 2,000 suspects, to realize that the Thais' understanding of human rights, democracy, and justice is somewhat at odds with that of the West. Moreover, Myanmar's business opportunities are huge, regardless of whether they are responsible, moral, or legitimate. Every Thai businessman, from the smallest trader all the way to top elites, knows that Myanmar is replete with natural resources. Against this background, it is not surprising that the Thai public at large have failed to question or oppose certain Thai policies towards Myanmar.[27]

When Thaksin rose to power in 2001, the multiple facets of Thai foreign policy, traditionally shaped by the Foreign Ministry ceased to function. Thaksin designed and decided what would be the features of Thai foreign policy; in fact, this was very much driven by his own agenda of advancing personal business interests. He was capable of doing so since his party, the now-defunct Thai Rak Thai Party, held a solid majority in Parliament. What followed was a centralized foreign policy, commanded by Government House. Thaksin sidelined the Foreign Ministry, while encompassing all relevant agencies under his direct control, with intent to craft a more coherent foreign policy.[28] Thaksin shifted the foreign policy focus from democracy, to a more tangible outlook, as reflected in his business-oriented diplomacy.[29] His handling of foreign policy may appear pragmatic. Yet, did it generate any impact on the direction of Thai policy toward Myanmar? Thaksin's own interests in Myanmar, through profitable telecommunication investments, to a certain extent belittled the nation's real interests, as well as putting the already vulnerable relationship at risk since they were solely beneficial to certain power-holders in the Myanmar regime. This explained why the downfall in 2004 of General Khin Nyunt, former Prime Minister and Thaksin's close friend, almost bankrupted Bangkok's relationship with Myanmar. This pattern of building up cosy relations with the Myanmar regime also spilled over into the short-lived period of People's Power Party rule led by two Thaksin-backed proxies, Samak and Somchai. Somchai, remaining in premiership for a little over two months, is Thaksin's brother-in-law.

The current regime of Abhisit Vejjajiva, who is also leader of the Democrat Party, has readjusted the Thai policy toward Myanmar, which is apparently more assertive and less commercialized than that under the Thaksin administration. His Democrat Party has suffered a legitimacy problem since it did not receive the majority vote but was only able to form a coalition government following the dissolution of the People's Power Party. To cloak his government's vulnerability, Abhisit constructed his own legitimacy by appearing to advocate the democratic principle both in his domestic and foreign policies. His strategy was supposed to serve Thailand well as it was the Chair of the ASEAN Standing Committee from July 2008 to December 2009. Moreover, Surin Pitsuwan, Foreign Minister under the Chuan government who initiated the flexible engagement policy in 1999, now heads the ASEAN Secretariat. Regional observers have anticipated a tougher Myanmar policy from Thailand. The Abhisit government, on behalf of ASEAN, released, on 19 May 2009, a statement voicing its "grave concern" over the political situation in Myanmar following the government's decision to press charges against Suu Kyi over the bizarre case of her allowing American John Yettaw into her lakeside residence.[30] The Myanmar Government immediately criticized Thailand for "interfering" in its domestic affairs. The war of words signified the deteriorating state of their bilateral relationship.

Thai politics is the politics of power interests, both in domestic and international domains.[31] Such politics pursued by charismatic leaders largely contributes to the inconsistency of Thai policy toward Myanmar. What has been consistent is only the drive for power interests, either in the form of legitimacy or money. The prioritization of personal interests, albeit highly unsustainable, has the potential of overshadowing the real bilateral issues. Thaksin and some of his predecessors did not even hide the intention to obscure the line between national and personal interests in the conduct of bilateral relations with Myanmar. The ambiguity that has existed in Thai policy represents one fundamental obstacle in the alleviation of the present contentious issues between them.

Dealing with the Problems

It can be argued that the business side of Thailand-Myanmar relations is illusive, even when it generates a substantial income for the Myanmar junta through the sale of its energy resources and other precious commodities, including natural products, to Thailand. The economic gains they have enjoyed over the years, particularly during the Thaksin administration, are insufficient to be used as a parameter for the state of bilateral relations. In fact, the economic aspect symbolizes one of the main reasons why bilateral conflicts remain unrelenting. Elites chose to push contentious issues into the ground and celebrate at the forefront the success of their economic partnership. The Myanmar leaders, having already been heavily reproached by the world community for their vicious regime, would rather want to concentrate on economic interests to shore up their political strength. Likewise, the Thai elites, who were more concerned about their own interests in Myanmar, were also content to brush aside touchy issues and prepared to comply with the junta's demands.

The remaining contentious issues that have plagued the two governments include:

- Ethnic minorities on the border: Thailand was accused of lending its support to the Karen rebels (The Karen National Union) and the Shan State Army (South) against the Myanmar Government.
- Myanmar border troops: The stationing of Myanmar troops and artillery along the border has long become Thailand's security concern.

- Thai illegal fishing within Myanmar maritime territory: Myanmar suspended the sale of trawling licences to Thailand in 2000 after repeated abuses by the Thai trawling fleet.
- Illegal logging inside Myanmar: The Thai exploitation is normally seen in areas beyond the control of the Myanmar military government.
- Illegal Myanmar workers and migrants: They include Myanmar illegal workers, refugees and displaced persons from various ethnic backgrounds, as well as students-in-exile.
- Flow of illegal drugs to Thailand from Myanmar.[32]

More recently, political circumstances in Thailand emerged as another potential hindrance in the management of the real problems with Myanmar. The current political deadlock in Thailand, characterized by a power struggle between Thaksin's remnants and the old establishment, represented by the People's Alliance for Democracy, is holding the country hostage. As a result, the country has failed to pay attention to foreign affairs, including its relations with Myanmar. Domestic and bilateral conditions therefore compel Thailand and Myanmar to keep postponing attempts to resolve bilateral conflicts. The postponement has aggravated the flame of contentious issues, which have never been really solved, just avoided. As much as the problems seem to await a permanent solution, such resolution seems unlikely since both countries' strategic interests and cultural perspectives have been warped by non-rational worldviews and the economic benefit of the leaders. Both sides have still been vying for long-term advantage. Although bilateral issues are usually discussed during regular meetings between Thailand and Myanmar military officers, the impression is that neither side fully trusts the other.[33] Distortions of history and nationalism still command certain negative sentiments towards each other. Therefore, it could take a long time before Thailand and Myanmar could reach an entente cordial. Indubitably, bilateral relations will not become "normal" until democracy is established in both states. Given that Thailand and Myanmar have been undergoing transition towards democracy for decades, there is little sign that such a project will be completed any time soon. Neither side appears ready to finally settle issues because they have been too preoccupied with whipping up domestic frenzy at the expense of normalizing bilateral tensions.

In Thailand, there is some room for the role of civil society groups and non-governmental organizations (NGOs). They moderately thrive amidst the imperfect nature of Thai democracy. While strategic and economic issues in Thailand-Myanmar relations have been rather ambiguous, yet highly protected by the leaders, civil society groups and the NGOs have chosen to voice their concerns over the issues that would stimulate wider societal impact, such as the environment and the threat to human security. For example, the dam project on the Salween River was harshly criticized by NGOs for its environmental repercussions vis-à-vis those who live in the area, which eventually resulted in the reconsideration of the current development. The Living River Siam–Southeast Asia Rivers Network was at the forefront of the opposition to the state's plan to construct five dams on the river to produce cheap hydroelectric energy. The Network reasoned that the dam projects would destroy enormous tracts of invaluable natural resources and, critically, would cause the inevitable influx of refugees from Myanmar into Thailand.[34] At present, the country already hosts at least 140,000 refugees registered in temporary shelters along the border, plus more than one million migrant workers from Myanmar.[35] However, NGOs in Thailand, as elsewhere, have an extremely limited circle of influence, which does not extend to the Myanmar Government at all. They have to find ways of working through other bodies, be they companies or United Nations' agencies, to try and effect change by the military. It is therefore doubtful whether their campaign would have any impact at all on the primary objective; that is, change in Myanmar.[36]

In general, however, civil society groups and NGOs are still treated lightly, since the Thai political structure continues to disapprove of differences of opinion from the bottom-up. The vicious crackdowns on Thai democratic forces in so many political crises — 1973, 1976, and 1992 — are testimony to the state mentality toward public thought and actions. Some Thai quarters are unfamiliar with the nature and purposes of the NGOs, and have begun to question their rationales and activities. In turn, the government has quickly taken advantage of any misperception toward the NGOs by treating them as if they are terrorist groups who need international publicity to guarantee continued foreign funding.[37]

In Myanmar, of course, there are no real civil society groups or NGOs. In fact, the military government was successful in curbing public activities by switching off the educational system, believing that students represented the sources of social dissidence, as well as tearing down the networks among groups of activists. Existing NGOs in Myanmar have been accused by the government of having links with Western powers and have been operating under a climate of fear. Most aggressive Myanmar NGOs and civil society groups are located outside the country and, to some extent, manage to call global awareness to the situations in Myanmar. Yet, the ineffectiveness of the Myanmar NGOs overseas largely stems from the lack of a unified strategy regarding the preferred solution to the political stalemate in the country, as well as its bilateral conflicts with Thailand.

Searching for the Right Mechanisms

A number of mechanisms were set up to oversee bilateral relations on a wide range of aspects. The Thailand-Myanmar Joint Commission on Bilateral Relations was established with an objective to promote overall ties. Co-chaired by Ministers of Foreign Affairs of Thailand and Myanmar, the last meeting, the sixth, was held in Phuket, Thailand, from 6 to 9 January 2002. In areas of economic activities, a Joint Trade Commission was initiated to give a boost to two-way trade. The Joint Trade Commission is co-chaired by Ministers of Commerce, with its fourth meeting organized in Yangon on 26 January 2005. Presently, the trade deficit is in Myanmar's favour, both at the national and border levels. The Thai Government has come to terms with the prevailing trade imbalance amounting to around US$3 billion due to its purchase of gas from Myanmar.[38] The outbreak of the seemingly economic tensions does not therefore normally derive from the existing trade distortion, but rather from the security and political fallout. Myanmar, understanding the power of its economic significance in Thailand's development, has occasionally exploited it as a bargaining chip to demand Thai compliance on other fronts, be they political or military. The retribution for Thai non-compliance typically includes a temporary closing of the border, the creation of instability at the borderlands, and foot-dragging on investments from Thailand. The Joint Commission on Bilateral Relations and Joint Trade Commission often find themselves incompetent and irrelevant in the search for the right solutions since they were never given the real authority to do so. Ultimately, political leaders have preferred to ease bilateral tensions at a personal level instead of making use of the available frameworks.

As for strategic cooperation, three mechanisms were put in place to reinforce military ties between the two states. First, the Joint Boundary Committee (JBC), co-hosted by Deputy Foreign Ministers of Thailand

and Myanmar, was first established in 1967 to serve as a forum to discuss and settle border-related problems, and which has become more complex due to the vast goods, arms, and drug smuggling networks that have developed.[39] The last meeting, its sixth, was held from 30 November to 1 December 2005. Second, the Regional Border Committee (RBC), chaired by the Thai Army Third Division and the Myanmar Army Southeast Division, is in charge of promoting close cooperation and ensuring security along the border. Its latest (twenty-first) meeting was organized from 29 April to 1 May 2005 in Myanmar's Shan State. Third, the Township Border Committee (TBC) has been set up as a forum for leaders at the township level to handle border issues. These mechanisms are considered more effective instruments because of the enthusiastic commitment on the part of military leaders of the two sides who meet regularly once every two years. From the perspective of the Thai army officers, especially in the north of Thailand, peace and security is regarded as the most important aspect in the bilateral relations with Myanmar. To them, the incursions of the Myanmar soldiers in hot pursuit of ethnic rebels frequently sparked tensions and incurred a Thai response with armed troops. The Thai military, in its endeavour to avoid armed clashes, hoped that cooperative frameworks — like the JBC, RBC, and TBC — would be encouraged in order to secure peace in the border areas.

JBC, RBC and TBC are primarily designed to serve as networks for military officers from Thailand and Myanmar to get to know each other and to promote better understanding and mutual trust. Recommendations were made for the Thai provincial governors, army commanders, and military officers to keep up good liaisons with their Myanmar counterparts. On top of this, the Thai security authorities could take advantage of the Thai-Myanmar Association, founded on the urgency of reinforcing cultural ties between the smaller administrative units in Thailand and Myanmar, and between the peoples of the two countries.

The two security mechanisms have however functioned with great difficulties. At times, Myanmar's troops would not hesitate to disparage the JBC, RBC, and TBC and resort to unilateral actions, especially in the ongoing fight with the ethnic minorities, and more so when Myanmar was suspicious of Thai support for ethnic rebels. In the Thai case, different approaches could also derail the efforts of the TBC and RBC. In 2001, for example, the incursion into Thai territory by the Tatmadaw prompted the army to review its security towards Myanmar, while opening up the possibility of a military counterstrike. The Directorate of Joint Civil Affairs of Thailand announced that such a revision must be done without having to wait for the next JBC, RBC, and TBC meetings. The Armed Forces, in contrast, still wished to see the problem handled through the TBC meeting. Once this failed, the talks would then be upgraded to the regional level or higher — this would also help develop relationships with local-level Myanmar officers.[40]

In either approach, the JBC, RBC, and TBC have limited authority to make a decision. Myanmar's local military authorities had to seek permission from the State Peace and Development Council before the two meetings could be convened and produce any tangible results. Myanmar, in particular, turned down Thai proposals for an ad hoc TBC meeting to solve the ongoing security crisis despite the fact that it could potentially develop into a full-scale war. Myanmar was worried that the JBC, RBC, and TBC could be taken up as a political device for Thailand to request the settlement of other security issues, such as territorial demarcation, parts of which have been left undone since the end of World War II.

Moreover, the concept of "security" as understood under the umbrella of JBC, RBC, and TBC is somewhat restricted. Security is defined as strictly military-related issues, such as armed conflicts and ethnic insurgencies. Problems without such military tone are therefore cast out of these security fora. In reality, non-traditional security-based issues increasingly play a significant role in the Thai-Myanmar relations. But the attention to such issues remains deficient as a result of the lack of an appropriate mechanism or perhaps ignorance on the part of both states. From the maltreatment of the Myanmar refugees and illegal workers along the borders, the continuation of the nefarious drugs trade, human trafficking, to the spread of HIV/AIDS — all have been left out of the discussion within the JBC, RBC, and TBC. In one atrocious account, the ethnic minorities, living in a buffer zone between Thailand and Myanmar, while being officially identified as stateless and deliberately marginalized and discriminated against by both governments, have no access to subsidized treatment of HIV/AIDS. The absence of an appropriate venue to address such issues could be seen as the root cause of the problems.[41]

Personal interests and relationships between the Thai and Myanmar elites play an essential role in managing contentious issues, whether between local civilian and military authorities across the border or at the national government level. Domestically and especially since the Thaksin days, the Thai state has remained dominant when it comes to formulating foreign policy, especially with regards to the country's relations with Myanmar. This practice can be justified by the following reasons, namely, the sensitivity of the issues, the lack of a clear policy, the involvement of leaders' private interests, and perhaps, as political observers put it, the compelling ASEAN norms.

The ASEAN Connection

Thailand and Myanmar are both members of ASEAN. Although ASEAN has over the decades achieved a measure of regional coordination, bilateral conflicts between member states have remained persistent, including those between Thailand and Myanmar. And despite the severity of conflicts in specific bilateral relations between ASEAN members, the conflicts themselves have never been brought into discussion within the grouping. Rodolfo Severino, former ASEAN Secretary-General and currently Head of the ASEAN Studies Centre at Singapore's Institute of Southeast Asian Studies, offered his insights when asked about the role of ASEAN in conflict resolution. Severino said that ASEAN had no formal norms governing the internal arrangements in or the domestic behaviour of member states, which explained why solutions in the bilateral context seemed to have been left as the only choice. The solutions then depend on the type and level of severity of a given bilateral problem. Some member states preferred their dispute handled through a legal framework. Some disputes were not so amenable to legal procedures; for example, tensions between Singapore and Indonesia in which the latter refused to ratify defence treaties due to immense pressure from its Parliament. Yet, there were common elements even in the presence of different kinds of bilateral conflicts. ASEAN members have more or less abided by a certain willingness to solve their disputes peacefully and quietly either via diplomatic or jurisdictional channels, Severino reiterated.[42]

Severino emphasized that ASEAN did not have its own court of justice, and there would be no immediate necessity for it to establish its own judicial institution since the International Court of Justice (ICJ) has been available to settle international disputes (Thailand and Cambodia took their dispute over the territorial claims of the Preah Vihear Temple to the ICJ in 1962 in which it ruled in Cambodia's favour). What

ASEAN could do at best in the field of conflict resolution appears to be the provision of venues and the proper atmosphere for discussion and consultation through its many meetings and fora. ASEAN could also offer networks of contacts for members to lessen bilateral tensions through social gatherings. Severino opined that the ASEAN Secretary-General and even the Chairman of the ASEAN Standing Committee had no mandate to bring bilateral conflicts to the discussion table — all had traditionally been conducted informally. Conflict resolution on a bilateral basis is accordingly not included in the ASEAN Charter.[43] Surin said that ASEAN was committed to promoting good relations, not delving into complicated bilateral conflicts among members.[44]

The former ASEAN Secretary-General held the view that the lack of proper mechanisms to deal with bilateral conflicts did not discourage the grouping from lending a helping hand if mediation was needed. ASEAN stood ready to intervene in any bilateral disputes if invited by the parties involved. It could have interfered in the aftermath of the Royal Thai Embassy in Phnom Penh being burned down in 2003 — the first ever attack between members of ASEAN. But Thailand did not invite ASEAN, as was the case in the instance of the temple dispute. In the case of Thailand-Myanmar conflicts, as Severino puts it:

> If ASEAN were to intervene in Myanmar, it would be on account of situations that have to do with illicit drugs from Myanmar to other Southeast Asian countries. Another might be the burden of refugees fuelling pressures in Myanmar. In either case, ASEAN would have to take its signals from Thailand, the country that bears the brunt of Myanmar-related drugs and refugee flows. So far, Thailand has sent no such signals and seems inclined to deal with Myanmar bilaterally on both issues and to keep the rest of ASEAN out of them.[45]

Such a viewpoint may seem to vindicate ASEAN's rigid principle of non-intervention. However, ASEAN could have done more in conflict resolution, such as making use of the ASEAN Troika, proposed by then Prime Minister Chuan Leekpai of Thailand in 1999, which was constituted as an ad hoc body at the ministerial level in order that ASEAN could address more effectively and cooperate more closely on issues affecting regional peace and stability.[46] The initiative behind the ASEAN Troika originated in the regional attempt to ease internal conflicts among political players in Cambodia so as to pave the way for its admission into ASEAN, which succeeded in 1999. After the Cambodian conflicts died down, so did the ASEAN Troika. Many hope that with the ASEAN

Charter being implemented, member countries will from now on make use of the disputes settlement mechanism to solve bilateral conflicts, rather than to tackle them by themselves. The willingness of member states to rely on the regional disputes settlement mechanism will prove the effectiveness of the Charter.

In the context of the contentious issues regarding Thailand and Myanmar, three factors must be taken into account to comprehend why regional approaches were undesired. First, the confidence in regional institutions, both on Thailand's and Myanmar's part, has remained at a low level, owing to their sense of political fragility and lingering suspicions towards each other. With ASEAN adopting a stronger position towards Myanmar now (ASEAN reproached the junta's crackdown on the pro-democracy movement describing its reaction as one of "revulsion"), the junta is increasingly wary of a regional approach. ASEAN's latest intervention in the Suu Kyi trial has intensified the junta's lackadaisical attitude toward regionalism. Myanmar instead chooses to forge its alliances with China and India when it suits its interests.[47] It now even seems to court the United States following the shift of the U.S. policy toward Myanmar.

Second, leaders prefer to manage contentious issues strictly within the bilateral framework away from the public glare and on the basis of compromise, but not necessarily for the interests of their respective countries. Since private economic interests compose the majority part of relationships, contentious issues are quite often dealt with in a manner that would satisfy the power holders who have access to those interests. In the past, Thailand's suppression of the Myanmar dissidents on its soil was carried out in the name of enhancing Thailand-Myanmar's security relations, when in fact by doing so the Thai leaders expected to get in return Myanmar's economic rewards. The visit to Naypyidaw of then Prime Minister Thaksin on 2 August 2006, whose objective was never clarified to the public, was perceived as an achievement amid sporadic military clashes along the border.[48] The lack of political transparency and the struggle for democracy in the two countries greatly contribute to the continued practice of keeping the outsiders out and the do-not-disturb mentality. The management of controversial issues is intimately contingent on considerations of regime types and political conditions.

Third, bilateralism is complexly intertwined with the states' perception of sovereignty, no matter if that perception is real or hollow. Myanmar had long been suppressed under British colonialism while Thailand was technically colonized by its own military despots. Leaders of later generations keep on exploiting historical vulnerability to shore up their power by stressing the need to defend sovereignty against foreign intervention. They have constantly employed historical and political tactics to guard against the outsiders' involvement, while retaining their authority in dealing with their own issues. In fact, the arbitrary employment of sovereignty has little to do with the anxiety of being interfered with by outsiders, but more to do with the state's attempt to sustain its legitimacy and interests in the face of surrounding challenges.

Conclusion

This chapter commenced with the enigma of the shared history between Thailand and Myanmar, which, for much of their bilateral interactions, has served as an obstacle to the rebuilding of mutual trust. The downplaying of historical bitterness could only be made possible when economic interests, public or private, were prioritized in the relationship. When bilateral relations were relatively smooth, as a consequence of good business ties, leaders tended to put contentious issues back in the closet. Considering its economic dependency on Myanmar, especially the huge import of Myanmar gas to light up the whole of Bangkok, Thailand has treaded a cautious path in its conduct of diplomacy vis-à-vis Myanmar. In ASEAN, Thailand has traditionally preferred to let others handle the Myanmar issue, with the exception of the period of governance under the Democrat Party. As a neighbour, Thailand claimed that the Myanmar issue was just too delicate and sensitive, and therefore did not wish to provoke the regime. On the other hand, Myanmar never hesitated to blast Thailand as their relations became thorny, even to the extent of insulting members of the Thai royal family.[49]

Different regimes with different outlooks on foreign relations can certainly produce different thoughts on conflict resolution. It is apparent that when contentious issues erupt, which seemingly suggests management failure, bilateral relations sour. If cosy personal relations are evident between leaders of the two countries, it might then be inferred that contentious issues will be kept in check and that commercial interests will be well served resulting in the impression of warmer bilateral relations. Have contentious issues ever been solved even at the height of the amicable relationship? The answer is *no*. There are certain interests on both sides to keep contentious issues unsettled. They need some kind of bargaining power to get them through such an extremely fragile relationship.

Since the world has become increasingly globalized with new issues emerging on a daily basis, conducting diplomacy in a completely bilateral manner is getting more elusive. Because of the huge commercial competition now taking place in Myanmar, especially between the three bordering powers — China, India, and Thailand — Thai relations with Myanmar will never be so simple as purely bilateral as they have been in the previous decades. While Thailand covets energy and commercial opportunities in Myanmar, the multilateral picture will always factor into the bilateral relations.

NOTES

[1] During the administration of Field Marshal Phibun Songkhram (1938–44), he changed the name of the country from Siam to anglicized Thailand in 1939, claiming that the new name would portray better the sense of nationhood within, and convey a message that the Thai races for the first time were integrated under his rule. Of course, the change of the country's name was part of Phibun's attempt to legitimize his rule through the plotted nationalism.

[2] In John W. Garver, *The Sino-American Alliance* (New York and London: East Gate Books, 1997), pp. 149–50.

[3] Despite the fact that the ethnic minorities were de facto allies of the Burmese Communist Party, the Thai government ensured that the military and financial assistance offered to the ethnic groups would keep the Burmese Communist Party inactive in the areas under the Thai occupation. See, Charles B. Smith, *The Burmese Communist Party in the 1980s* (Singapore: Institute of Southeast Asian Studies, 1984).

[4] Robert H. Taylor, *Foreign and Domestic Consequences of the KMT Intervention in Burma*, Data Paper No. 93 (Ithaca: Department of Asian Studies, Cornell University, 1973), p. 20.

[5] In this period, Myanmar made several requests to Thailand in connection with ethnic insurgents along the border. It reportedly asked the Thai Government to prevent foreigners from gaining access to ethnic armies; to stem the supply of arms and ammunition reaching the border; to disarm and detain insurgents who retreat from battle, and if possible, turn them over to the Myanmar authorities; and to understand that Myanmar's armed forces had no intention of occupying Thai territory. See, Maung Aung Myoe, *Neither Friend Nor Foe: Myanmar's Relations with Thailand Since 1988: A View From Yangon*, Monograph No. 1 (Singapore: Institute of Defence and Strategic Studies, 2007.

[6]   Betsy Pisik, "Myanmar Now 2nd Largest Heroin Exporter", *Straits Times*, 12 October 2007, p. 20.

[7]   United Nations Office on Drugs and Crime, Narcotic Production in 2008 <http://www.unodc.org/documents/wdr/WDR_2009/WDR2009_Statistical_annex_production.pdf> (accessed 23 September 2009).

[8]   Ng Han Guan, "Myanmar Refugees Leave China as Battle Ending", Associated Press, 31 August 2009 <http://www.realclearworld.com/news/ap/international/2009/Aug/31/myanmar_refugees_leave_china_as_battles_ending.html > (accessed 23 September 2009).

[9]   "A Failing Grade: Burma's Drug Eradication Efforts", *ALTSEAN Burma*, Special Report (November 2004), p. 142.

[10] During the Democrat government, two incidents indicated a deteriorating relationship with Burma: One was the seizure of the Myanmar Embassy in Bangkok by the "Vigorous Burmese Student Warriors" (VBSW) on 1 October 1999, and the other was the episode in which 20 armed rebels of the "God's Army" raided a hospital in Rachaburi Province and took up to 800 patients hostage on 24 January 2000.

[11] Kavi Chongkittavorn, "Thai-Burma Relations", in *Challenge to Democratisation in Myanmar: Perspectives in Multilateral and Bilateral Response* (Stockholm: International Institute for Democratic and Electoral Assistance, 2001), p. 119.

[12] See S.C. Banerji, "Burma Meets Thailand", in *The King of Thailand in World Focus*, edited by Denis D. Gray (Bangkok: The Foreign Correspondent's Club of Thailand, 2007), quoted in Yeni, "King of Heart", *The Irrawaddy* 15, no. 12 (December 2007).

[13] The original marketplace policy was implemented in turning war-torn Cambodia into an investment-friendly market for Thai businesses toward the end of the 1980s. Its success provided consideration for the Chatichai government to also turn Burma into a potential market place for Thailand.

[14] See, Pavin Chachavalpongpun, *A Plastic Nation: The Curse of Thainess in Thai-Burmese Relations* (Lanham: University Press of America, 2005), Chapter 6.

[15] Aung Zaw, "ASEAN-Burma Relations", in *Challenge to Democratisation in Myanmar: Perspectives in Multilateral and Bilateral Response* (Stockholm: International Institute for Democratic and Electoral Assistance, 2001), p. 56.

[16] Thitinan Pongsudhirak, "A Win-Win-Win Proposition for Thaksin", *The Irrawaddy*, August 2005 <http://www.irrawaddy.org> (accessed 1 October 2008).

[17] Ministry of Foreign Affairs of Thailand <http://www.mfa.go.th> (accessed 25 August 2008).

[18] Apichai Boontherawara, President of the EXIM Bank, told the media of this information. In "Bt4-bn Burma Loan Fine: EXIM", *The Nation*, 4 October 2006.

19   "Out of Sight, Out of Mind: Thai Policy toward Burmese Refugees", *Human Rights Watch* 16, no. 2 (February 2004): 35.

20   Alison Vicary, "Employment and Poverty in Mae Hong Son Province Thailand: 'Burmese Refugees in the Labour Market'", in *Burma Economic Watch*, Economic Department of Macquarie University, Australia, No. 1 (2006), p. 51. Also see, Dennis Arnold, *The Situation of Burmese Migrant Workers in Mae Sot, Thailand*, published online by the City University of Hong Kong Southeast Asia Research Centre Working Papers Series <http://www.cityu.edu.hk/searc> (accessed 25 August 2008).

21   "Out of Sight, Out of Mind: Thai Policy toward Burmese Refugees", p. 3.

22   Through concessions granted to the PTT Exploration and Production Co. Ltd. in the Yadana and Yetagun fields in the Bay of Bengal, Thailand is at present importing about nine billion standard cubic feet a day, and wishes to buy an additional hundred million cubic feet of gas per day to match its rising domestic demand.

23   Pavin Chachavalpongpun, "Economics Trumps Politics", *Straits Times*, 5 May 2008.

24   In an email interview with Bertil Lintner, the author of *Burma in Revolt: Opium and Insurgency Since 1948* (1999).

25   In a conversation with David Fullbrook, independent political analyst, Bangkok, March 2007.

26   Indeed, those who staged demonstrations against the brutal regime on the streets of Bangkok were mostly Myanmar and international activists, with only a handful of Thai participants. See "Activists Protest Outside Embassy", *The Nation*, 27 August 2007.

27   In a conversation with Fullbrook.

28   For further discussion on the structural weakening of Thai democracy as a result of the centralized policy of Thaksin, see N. Ganesan, "Appraising Democratic Consolidation in Thailand under Thaksin's Thai Rak Thai Government", *Japanese Journal of Political Science* 7, no. 2 (2006): 10–16.

29   McCargo and Ukrist call this policy an "Asia-centred regionalist policy". Such policy bore fruits as Thaksin, in his capacity as Prime Minister, paid an official visit to Myanmar (19–20 June 2001), reciprocated by Lieutenant-General Khin Nyunt's visit to Thailand from 3–5 September 2001. Khin Nyunt is former Prime Minister of Myanmar. See Duncan McCargo and Ukrist Pathmanand, *The Thaksinisation of Thailand* (Copenhagen: Nordic Institute of Asian Studies, 2005), p. 53.

30   <http://www.aseansec.org/PR-ASEANChairmanStatementonMyanmar.pdf> (accessed 25 June 2009).

31   Suchit Bunbongkarn, *State of the Nation: Thailand* (Singapore: Institute of Southeast Asian Studies, 1996), p. 78.

32   Kavi, "Thai-Burma Relations", pp. 117–30.

[33] In an email interview with Lintner.

[34] Pianporn Deetes, "The Invisible Costs of the Salween Dam Projects", *The Nation*, 28 February 2007.

[35] In the International Conference of Japanese Diet Members and ASEAN Parliamentarian Members / Burma: The Way to Democratise, Buranaj Smutharaks, former Secretary to Prime Minister Chuan Leekpai (1997–2001) echoed his concern over the influx of Myanmar refugees and illegal workers, and thus proposed the founding of the "programme of action" that could be led by Japan together with other stakeholders in the region to solve the human security crisis in Myanmar. The conference was held in Tokyo, Japan, on 22 May 2007.

[36] "NGOs and the Exile Opposition", in *Challenge to Democratisation in Myanmar: Perspectives in Multilateral and Bilateral Response* (Stockholm: International Institute for Democratic and Electoral Assistance, 2001), p. 30.

[37] William A. Callahan, *Imagining Democracy: Reading the Events of May in Thailand* (Singapore: Institute of Southeast Asian Studies, 1998), p. 130.

[38] The Ministry of Foreign Affairs of Thailand <http://www.mfa.go.th> (accessed 10 June 2008).

[39] Kavi, "Thai-Burma Relations", p. 120.

[40] Wassana Nanuam, "Reviews of Security Policy Sought", *Bangkok Post*, 28 February 2001.

[41] Tamarat Chumpon, "Burma and Thailand Should Settle Stateless Issue", *The Irrawaddy*, 28 July 2006 <http://www.irrawaddy.org> (accessed 30 July 2006).

[42] In an interview with Rodolfo Severino, Singapore, 31 October 2007.

[43] In an interview with Severino.

[44] Interview with Surin Pitsuwan, former Foreign Minister of Thailand and incoming ASEAN Secretary-General, Singapore, 21 October 2007.

[45] Rodolfo C. Severino, *Southeast Asia in Search of an ASEAN Community: Insights from the Former ASEAN Secretary-General* (Singapore: Institute of Southeast Asian Studies, 2006), p. 148.

[46] For details on the ASEAN Troika terms of reference, see <http://www.aseansec.org/3701.htm> (accessed 12 September 2008).

[47] "China, Russia: No to Burma Sanctions", 26 October 2007 <http://www.intellasia.net/news/articles/regional/111236091.stml> (accessed 27 October 2007).

[48] Thaksin's one-day visit to Myanmar on 2 August 2006 took place just six weeks before his regime was overthrown by the military. The visit was significant for a number of reasons. Of greatest importance was the fact that Thaksin became the first ASEAN leader to pay an official visit to Myanmar's new capital — Naypyidaw. It was widely reported that Thaksin was trying to a great extent to reconnect with General Than Shwe, Myanmar's President and

Chairman of the State Peace and Development Council since the fall of Khin Nyunt seriously damaged his personal relationship with Myanmar and his business empire in the country. Therefore, the visit was believed to be very much a private business even though Thaksin was accompanied by a large delegation comprising ministers and the Thai army commander.
49 In an email interview with Lintner.

REFERENCES

ALTSEAN Burma, "A Failing Grade: Burma's Drug Eradication Efforts". Special Report, November 2004.

Arnold, Dennis. "The Situation of Burmese Migrant Workers in Mae Sot, Thailand". The City University of Hong Kong Southeast Asia Research Centre Working Papers Series <http://www.cityu.edu.hk/searc> (accessed 25 August 2008).

Banerji, S.C. "Burma Meets Thailand". In The King of Thailand in World Focus, edited by Denis D. Gray. Bangkok: The Foreign Correspondent's Club of Thailand, 2007.

Bunbongkarn, Suchit. State of the Nation: Thailand. Singapore: Institute of Southeast Asian Studies, 1996.

Callahan, William A. Imagining Democracy: Reading the Events of May in Thailand. Singapore: Institute of Southeast Asian Studies, 1998.

Chachavalpongpun, Pavin. A Plastic Nation: The Curse of Thainess in Thai-Burmese Relations. Lanham: University Press of America, 2005.

———. "Economics Trumps Politics". Straits Times, 5 May 2008.

Chongkittavorn, Kavi. "Thai-Burma Relations". In Challenge to Democratisation in Myanmar: Perspectives in Multilateral and Bilateral Response. Stockholm: International Institute for Democratic and Electoral Assistance, 2001.

Chumpon, Tamarat. "Burma and Thailand Should Settle Stateless Issue". The Irrawaddy, 28 July 2006.

Deetes, Pianporn. "The Invisible Costs of the Salween Dam Projects". The Nation (Thailand), 28 February 2007.

Ganesan, N. "Appraising Democratic Consolidation in Thailand under Thaksin's Thai Rak Thai Government". Japanese Journal of Political Science 7, no. 2 (2006): 10–16.

Garver, John W. The Sino-American Alliance. New York and London: East Gate Books, 1997.

Ghosh, Nirmal. "Thailand Treads Cautiously over Myanmar Issue". Straits Times, 15 October 2007.

Human Rights Watch. "Out of Sight, Out of Mind: Thai Policy toward Burmese Refugees". Human Rights Watch 16, no. 2 (February 2004).

Lintner, Bertil. "Burma in Revolt: Opium and Insurgency since 1948". Chiangmai: Silkworm Books, 1999.

McCargo, Duncan and Ukrist Pathmanand. *The Thaksinisation of Thailand*. Copenhagen: Nordic Institute of Asian Studies, 2005.

Myoe, Maung. *Neither Friend Nor Foe: Myanmar's Relations with Thailand since 1988: A View from Yangon*, Monograph No. 1. Singapore: Institute of Defence and Strategic Studies, 2001.

Nanuam, Wassana. "Reviews of Security Policy Sought". *Bangkok Post*, 28 February 2001.

Pisik, Betsy. "Myanmar Now 2nd Largest Heroin Exporter". *Straits Times*, 12 October 2007.

Pongsudhirak, Thitinan. "A Win-Win-Win Proposition for Thaksin". *The Irrawaddy*, August 2005 <http://www.irrawaddy.org> (accessed 1 October 2008).

Severino, Rodolfo C. *Southeast Asia in Search of an ASEAN Community: Insights from the Former ASEAN Secretary-General*. Singapore: Institute of Southeast Asian Studies, 2006.

Smith, Charles B. *The Burmese Communist Party in the 1980s*. Singapore: Institute of Southeast Asian Studies, 1984.

Taylor, Robert H. *Foreign and Domestic Consequences of the KMT Intervention in Burma*, Data Paper No. 93. Ithaca: Cornell University, 1973.

Vicary, Alison. "Employment and Poverty in Mae Hong Son Province Thailand: Burmese Refugees in the Labour Market". In *Burma Economic Watch*, No. 1. Economic Department of Macquarie University, Australia (2006).

Yeni. "King of Heart". *The Irrawaddy* 15, no. 12, December 2007.

Zaw, Aung. "ASEAN-Burma Relations". In *Challenge to Democratisation in Myanmar: Perspectives in Multilateral and Bilateral Response*. Stockholm: International Institute for Democratic and Electoral Assistance, 2001.

6

Thailand-Malaysia Bilateral Relations

N. Ganesan

Thai-Malaysian bilateral relations have undergone some turbulence since the 1990s up until now. Prior to that and especially during the Cold War both countries had broadly convergent foreign and defence policies that were essentially anti-communist and pro-Western. Apart from such broad strategic convergence, both countries had common security threats that necessitated coordinated security cooperation. Such threats included an active communist insurgency, banditry, and transnational criminal activities. At the elite interpersonal level, Malaysia's first Prime Minister, Tunku Abdul Rahman, had Thai ancestry and maintained very cordial relations during his term in office from 1957 to 1969. Reciprocally, Thai elite also treated Malaysia as a special case and maintained friendly bilateral relations. From 1967 onwards, the Association of Southeast Asian Nations (ASEAN) provided similar structural coherence at the broader regional level. After the communist victory at the conclusion of the Second Indochina War in 1975, ASEAN became galvanized to deal with what was perceived as threats to Thai sovereignty and security. Hence, between 1975 and 1988, ASEAN provided structural cohesion and support to the bilateral relationship. However, the fall of the Prem government in Thailand in April 1988 led in turn to a new policy initiative under the Chatichai government that downgraded Vietnam as a source of threat to Thai security.

This new Indochina Initiative disengaged Thailand from previous ASEAN policies toward Vietnam and resulted in closer Thai collaboration with the countries of mainland Southeast Asia. Almost simultaneously, Thailand-Malaysian bilateral relations deteriorated rapidly. Since then and into the post–Cold War period, Thailand-Malaysian bilateral relations have been subject to more turbulence than before. The issues that have led to a deteriorated relationship include an admixture of traditional and non-traditional security concerns. More recently, the ongoing political violence in southern Thailand has been a serious source of bilateral tensions.

This chapter examines Thai-Malaysian relations from a historical and structural perspective. It identifies the issues that at different times have troubled the relationship and how well they have been dealt with by both countries. There is also an attempt to ascertain the impact of idiosyncratic factors on the general state of the relationship. The chapter is divided into a total of five sections. The first of these identifies the historical patterns of interaction between the countries while the second periodizes the bilateral relationship. The third section then goes on to identify contentious issues in the bilateral relationship and the fourth examines how such issues are traditionally resolved between both countries. The fifth section looks at the correlation between structural and agency relations in dispute management and identifies how political leadership generally performs the function of an important intervening variable in the bilateral relationship. This observation was certainly the case with both Prime Minister Mahathir of Malaysia and Thaksin Shinawatra of Thailand. Whereas strong and charismatic leaders have been able to steer the relationship better and place it on a more even keel, they are equally prone to nationalistic rhetoric that damages the relationship as well.

Historical Patterns of Interaction between Thailand and Malaysia

The bilateral relationship between Thailand and Malaysia has traditionally been reasonably dense although much of the regular interaction between the two countries is concentrated between northern peninsular Malaysia and southern Thailand. The primary reason for this geographic concentration is both a function of historical factors and geographical proximity. Both countries share a long common border between them at this narrow bottleneck that separates mainland Southeast Asia from the maritimes. If geography naturally facilitated this transactionalism, historical developments, and in particular the transfer of sovereignty between the four northern Malaysian states and the four southern Thai provinces, have complicated matters.[1] There is also an important economic dimension to the bilateral relationship. Thailand has publicly articulated a Joint Development Strategy with Malaysia through the coordinated development of education, employment, and entrepreneurship. In 2008 total bilateral trade was valued at US$19 billion out of which border trade alone accounted for US$13.3 billion. This was a 20 per cent increase over the previous year.[2] Malaysia-Thailand joint investment projects also receive promotional privileges in Thailand. The Indonesia-Malaysia-Thailand Growth Triangle, an ASEAN sub-regional economic initiative, is also closer to fruition after the political settlement in Aceh, Indonesia. Finally, Malaysians typically comprise the largest group of foreign tourists to Thailand.

Strictly speaking, it would be accurate to note that Thailand has had greater interaction with the countries of mainland Southeast Asia like Cambodia, Laos, Myanmar, and Vietnam. This sphere of interaction and influence was informed by Thailand's location, its ethno-linguistic and religious calibration and, after World War II, dynamics associated with the Cold War. Thailand's central role as an ally of the United States and member of the Southeast Asia Treaty Organization (SEATO) made it a lynchpin of the U.S. effort to contain communism in the region.[3] Consequently, Thailand became deeply involved in the Second and Third Indochina Wars that collectively lasted till 1989. Structural and ideological considerations, whether derived from the Cold War or the subsequent Sino-Soviet rivalry, invariably involved Vietnam and through it the Indochina security complex that encompassed Thailand.[4]

Similarly, it is arguable that Malaysia was traditionally much more predisposed to dealing with maritime Southeast Asia. Early empires in the maritimes often spanned areas between Malaysia and Indonesia. Similarly, principalities and kingdoms between these two countries often competed for control of peoples and trade. Geographical proximity was layered by common bonds of ethnicity and religion. British colonization also brought the territories of peninsular Malaya into much greater interaction with the Straits Settlements, and the North Borneo territories of Sabah, Sarawak, and Brunei. Countries in the maritimes were also subjected to the Malay Archipelago complex that was centred on Indonesia during the Cold War.[5] The elevation in importance of the Indochina security complex after the communist victory and reunification of Vietnam in 1975 meant the decompression of the Indochina security complex in turn.

Yet, the structures spawned by the Cold War in Southeast Asia did not entirely isolate Malaysia and Thailand. Communist insurgency that was a problem in both countries from the 1950s constituted a common security threat that in turn led to greater security cooperation between the two. Since the two insurgent movements, the Communist Party of Malaya (CPM) and the Communist Party of Thailand (CPT), shared a common sanctuary in Yala in southern Thailand, there was good reason for joint operations. In fact, at the height of the counter-insurgency operations, security forces from Thailand and Malaysia evolved protocol for cross-border patrols and hot pursuit of insurgents. Similarly, although Malaysia's external defence in the post-independence period was inspired and anchored by the United Kingdom through the Anglo-Malayan Defence Agreement (1957–71) and the Five Power Defence Arrangements (1972–the present), it was part of a larger web of Western security architecture. Consequently, similar external predispositions and priorities prevailed. In fact, it was against this backdrop that the inauguration of the pro-Western and developmentalist Suharto government in Indonesia led to the formation of the Association of Southeast Asian Nations (ASEAN) in 1967 that included both Malaysia and Thailand. Structurally and ideologically, Thailand was much more a part of maritime Southeast Asia that formed the core of ASEAN than the mainland up until the late 1980s.

The ASEAN decision to recognize Thailand's "frontline" status against the spread of communism following the Vietnamese occupation of Cambodia from 1979 also provided greater coherence and convergence between the foreign and defence policies of both countries. In this regard, it is arguable that Malaysia and Thailand had many common domestic and foreign policy issues that led to implicit bilateral cooperation and coordination. The post–Cold War period that led to the unravelling of such convergent issues in turn heralded a more turbulent bilateral relationship.[6] The rise to the fore of unconventional security threats like illegal migration, illegal fishing, religious extremism and related violence worsened the structural decompression. And the strong leadership style that drew on nationalism exerted by the likes of

Prime Minister Mahathir Mohamad and Thai Prime Minister Thaksin Shinawatra further worsened matters. Fortunately and perhaps oddly enough, the situation has been much more stable under the Thai military government since 2006. Leadership transition in Malaysia in 2004 was also helpful in soothing the relationship. It is now on a reasonably even keel.

Periodization of Thai-Malaysian Relations

Historians typically tend to examine Thai-Malaysian bilateral relations in three phases. The first or pre-colonial period is often referred to as the *bunga mas* (gold flowers) and *bunga perak* (silver flowers) or traditional phase. During this period, the states of northern peninsular Malaysia had a tributary relationship with the Siamese monarchy and presented gifts as part of a subordinate relationship with Siam. Afterwards came the colonial or semi-modern phase where the British and the Japanese tended to decide on the nature of Thai-Malaysian relations as colonizers or occupiers. And finally, the post-independence or modern phase of Thai-Malaysian bilateral relations began after Malaya first achieved independence in 1957.[7] It is often noted that from as early as the thirteenth century, Thai rulers have realized the importance of having friendly cooperation with the southern states in order to retain Thailand's importance and dominance in the mainland. In all fairness, however, a proper study of bilateral relations should probably begin after the conclusion of World War II in 1945. The reason for this statement is simply the fact that the four north Malaysian states of Perak, Perlis, Kedah, and Kelantan, that were ceded to Thailand by Japan in exchange for Thai cooperation in allowing Japanese troops to transit through Thailand in their aggression against Malaya and Myanmar, were returned. Yet, in international relations, it makes little sense to talk about foreign policy and foreign relations prior to the onset of statehood. In this regard, the earliest starting point will be 1957 when peninsula Malaya first obtained its independence from the British.[8] The first phase can logically be extended from 1957 to 1975. This demarcation suitably takes into account broader structural changes in Indochina as well as the end of military authoritarianism in Thailand. In Malaysia, it coincided with the end of the Razak administration (1970–75). Additionally, both countries were involved in the suppression of armed communist insurgency movements during this period. The CPM and the CPT also shared a common sanctuary close to the Thai-Malaysian border in Yala province.

The second phase that was characterized by the ideological and strategic convergence that obtained from the first phase essentially involved the strengthening of ASEAN and ASEAN initiatives in support of Thailand's status as the "frontline" state, as described earlier. By this time, however, the United States and Soviet Union had achieved détente and Vietnam was really caught in the middle of the Sino-Soviet strategic tension. Nonetheless, to the extent that the changed situation, to all intents and purposes, furthered the cause of revolutionary communism in mainland Southeast Asia, the threat posed to Thailand was regarded as grave. Thailand had traditionally sought a policy of maintaining buffers against potential threats in order to obtain security. Cambodia and Laos were regarded as the equivalent of such buffers against a significantly more powerful Vietnam. The Vietnamese occupation of Cambodia sealed the legitimacy of this perception and galvanized ASEAN into collective action, notwithstanding the Khmer Rouge genocide and its intentional harassment of Vietnam and those of Vietnamese ethnicity. Through ASEAN-led initiatives to deny Vietnam legitimacy for its occupation of Cambodia, Thai and Malaysian foreign policy output were broadly philosophically convergent.[9] This common purpose and coordinated actions within the framework of regionalism also secured Thai-Malaysian bilateral relations.

The third phase essentially spanned the period from 1989 to 2005. During this third period, bilateral relations deteriorated significantly. The structural factors that allowed for external policy convergence between the two countries dissipated rapidly. Domestic political developments in Thailand unseated Prem Tinsulanonda as Prime Minister. His replacement, Chatichai Choonhavan, unveiled a new Indochina initiative in August 1988 that sought to transform the battle fields of Indochina into market places. This policy pronouncement that downgraded Vietnam as a threat to Thai security unravelled the Indochina security complex and pre-empted a regional solution to the Cambodian impasse. Hence, Thai-Malaysian relations lost the comfort of ASEAN's structural accommodation of national differences. This period also witnessed the Vietnamese withdrawal from Cambodia in September 1989 and the disbandment of the CPM and CPT in December 1989. Clearly, both Vietnam and China were competing for ASEAN's favour. However, such courting occurred when the members of ASEAN themselves were losing their cohesiveness and internal tensions reached a high point.[10] The changed external structural circumstances clearly took a toll on ASEAN, and Thai-Malaysian relations were not exempted from this turbulence. The emergence of a number of unconventional security threats also exacerbated the situation.

Whereas the third phase was marked by a measure of stability in Thai-Malaysian relations from the mid-1990s, the outbreak of the Asian financial crisis and its fallout in 1997 generally led to high levels of national stress for most governments. The Malaysian Government under Mahathir that chose an unorthodox remedy to the malaise sought closure and internal economic consolidation. This period of difficulty was then followed by the outbreak of political violence in southern Thailand that was partly related to ethno-religious extremism. The highly provocative pronouncements of Prime Minister Thaksin alleging Malaysian complicity in and assistance for the violence in the south significantly deteriorated bilateral relations. Thai authorities were also accused of widespread abuse and torture of Malay-Muslims during their security operations. The cross-border flow of persons displaced by the violence and the implication of a separatist movement whose leaders were Malaysian also complicated matters. The Malaysian Government offered to cooperate on security issues while stoutly denying any involvement in the violence.

The September 2006 military coup in Thailand that ousted the Thaksin government helped to bring some normality to the bilateral relationship. General Sonthi Boonyaratglin who led the coup is a southern Thai-Muslim with a better feel for the issues at hand. Despite being from the military, he advocated a much more balanced approach in dealing with the violence rather than simply suppressing it militarily — Thaksin's preferred approach. There was also a greater attempt on the part of Thai and Malaysian authorities to document their nationals with dual citizenships and provide security guarantees for displaced persons. And Abdullah Badawi who had earlier succeeded Mahathir in 2004 was also much more amenable to peaceful dialogue and reconciliation. Structurally, ASEAN was moving in the direction of enhancing security in the Strait of Malacca through coordinated patrols among the littoral states and crafting a charter with common norms and aspirations. Consequently, it is arguable that from 2006 both structural and agency reasons were favourable for a return of the bilateral relationship to a modicum of normalcy.

Contentious Issues in the Bilateral Relationship

As mentioned at the outset, there is a significant overhang informing the Thai-Malaysian bilateral relationship. Much of this overhang, as is typically the case, is rooted in historical developments and the transfer of sovereignty of the territories of both countries back and forth.[11] The presence of a sizeable Malay-Muslim minority of approximately seven per cent of the total population in the four Thai southern provinces significantly complicates the situation since this group is also the dominant majority in Malaysia. Consequently, there are extensive transnational linkages and Malaysian sympathies for the seeming political and economic plight of their marginalized brethren across the border in Thailand. It is also not uncommon to have kinship linkages across borders and the volume of trade across the border is certainly significant. If a number of issues may be isolated as sufficiently contentious to trigger bilateral tensions, these would include overlapping territorial claims, ethno-religious extremism and violence, illegal fishing, illegal migration, and smuggling. The importance of these issues at any point varies on general external and internal structural and economic conditions, overall state of bilateral relations, and elite dispositions and anxieties. Additionally, it is not uncommon for problematic issues to be conflated with one another. So, for example, ethno-religious extremism and violence may result in illegal migration. Alternatively, trawlers engaged in illegal fishing may also be involved in smuggling activities.

Overlapping territorial claims have traditionally not been a serious issue in the bilateral relationship. The reason for this observation is that the southern Thai and northern Malaysian borders are reasonably well marked and observed and rarely contested. Additionally, both countries have undertaken measures to resolve overlapping claims. The first of these was a memorandum of understanding in February 1979 on the delimitation of their continental shelf boundary in the Gulf of Thailand. Resources in disputed areas of adjacent sea beds were then resolved through mutual cooperation. It was in this spirit that both countries then established the Malaysia-Thailand Joint Authority. In October 1979, both countries also signed a treaty regarding their territorial sea delimitations in the Gulf of Thailand and the Strait of Malacca. And finally in May 1990, both countries reached agreement on the constitution and other matters pertaining to the Malaysia-Thailand Joint Authority.[12]

Nonetheless, there have been occasions in the past when the Malaysian Government accused the Thai Border Patrol Police of crossing the border into Padang Besar in 1991. This intrusion was in return correlated to cross-border detentions of trawlers and forestry officials and seems to have been a tit-for-tat misadventure rather than any attempt to recover or hold territory. Nonetheless, the Malaysian Government was sufficiently agitated by the incident to reinforce its troop presence in the border area. Additionally there were calls to renegotiate the 1922 Anglo-Thai Border Treaty and Malaysia unilaterally undertook the construction of a retaining wall to enforce previous demarcations and prevent further intrusions. Thailand simply responded by noting that friends do not build walls between themselves.[13] It is also not uncommon for Malaysian soldiers patrolling the joint border areas to occasionally stray into Thai territory and then be repatriated later. In recent developments, the Malaysian Government has moved to streamline border operations by disbanding the Territorial Army 300 series and replacing it with a new Border Regiment.[14] This development makes the present military deployment similar to that of Thailand which utilizes its Border Patrol Police for the same function. However, there is an overlapping claim on an area off the coast of Narathiwat Province in southern Thailand and the state of Kelantan in Malaysia that has oil and gas deposits. Both countries have resolved to jointly explore the resources and share the profits rather than irritate bilateral relations through unilateral actions. This agreement was concluded by the Chuan Leekpai–led government in Thailand and the Mahathir government in Malaysia in 1994.[15]

Ethno-religious extremism and violence is a fairly recent phenomenon in Thai-Malaysian bilateral relations, notwithstanding Thailand's earlier experience with Malay-Muslim armed separatism. This issue has gained importance rapidly despite its recent vintage. The violence, which has been perpetrated on an almost daily basis in the last few years, is usually traced to an arms heist in January 2004 that resulted in the theft of a large number of automatic weapons. However, the preliminary evidence from the field was that the security situation had deteriorated in the face of competition between the police and the military. Additionally, there were widespread allegations of police and military involvement in torture and abuse of local Muslim villagers.[16] What began initially as sporadic and uncoordinated violence rapidly deteriorated into large scale and serious attacks on public officials, Buddhist monks, teachers, and innocent passers by. There have also been regular and spectacularly coordinated bombing campaigns. Most observers agree that the intensity of the violence has become significantly exaggerated after a botched attempt by the Thaksin government to break up a demonstration that led to the death of seventy-eight people. Thaksin remained unrepentant and a previous attack on a historic mosque also enraged the sentiments of the predominantly Malay-Muslim southern population.[17] Widespread charges of government complicity in random violence and disappearances of people led to an extremely charged atmosphere. Citing a major national security threat, the Thai Government declared martial law in the four southern provinces and periodically extended it. More than 4,000 people have now been killed as a result of the ongoing violence since 2004, and some analysts think that the violence is deteriorating into a protracted civil war.[18]

The outbreak of violence in the Thai southern provinces led in turn to a steady stream of refugees across the border into Malaysia. There had always been cross border economic migrants before but new migrants alerted the Malaysian authorities and general public to the deep sense of insecurity and fear for their lives in Thailand. Consequently, when a large group of some 130 Malay-Muslims from Thailand sought sanctuary in Malaysia, the Thai Government was visibly upset and called for their repatriation. Malaysia, in sympathy with the "refugees", decided to offer them sanctuary. The entire episode led to heightened tensions between the two countries.[19] Additionally, when Thaksin was Prime Minister, both he and senior officials from Thailand accused Malaysia of supporting the simmering insurgency in Thailand. These pronouncements naturally led to tit-for-tat accusations of improper conduct and mismanagement of a mutual problem.[20] Since 2006, the situation between the two countries has become much better, at least in part owing to much less aggressive posturing and pronouncements from Thai authorities. On the other hand, there have been mutual agreements to document and deal with those having dual citizenship.[21] In fact, in the most recent pronouncements, senior Thai officials have actually asked for Malaysian assistance to help deal with the violence which has gone on unabated.

The issue of illegal fishing has become rather serious in Southeast Asian waters since the 1990s. This is not to suggest that such activities were previously absent. Rather, it has become significantly exaggerated in recent times. Whereas this development is partly a function of the depletion of fish stocks, particularly in the Gulf of Thailand, it is equally attributable to the cessation of conflict in Indochina and far greater enforcement of maritime boundaries and related resources. In particular, the 1982 United Nations Law of the Sea Conference (UNCLOS) declaration of the 200-kilometre exclusive economic zone as comprising part of a country's sovereign territory has led to far greater regional maritime enforcement. This assertion is particularly true of archipelagic states like Indonesia and the Philippines. Within the parameters of the Thai-Malaysian bilateral relationship, illegal fishing has certainly escalated in terms of importance and it is a significant issue that in the past has strained bilateral relations, although it should be noted that as an issue it had a far greater impact on Thai-Myanmar relations. In the latter relationship, the Myanmar government's previous sale of commercial fishing licences to Thai trawler operators and their abuse of the system significantly complicated the situation. Eventually the Myanmar Government suspended the sale of trawling permits to Thailand in 2000.

Most of the illegal fishing by Thai trawlers in Malaysian waters has occurred off the coast of the Malaysian state of Terengganu. Since 1988 such seizures have become much more frequent, and in 1989 the Royal Malaysian Navy, on routine patrol, detained a large number of trawlers for illegal fishing. The second major incident occurred in 1995 when a Malaysian naval gunboat opened fire on Thai trawlers, which were illegally fishing off Terengganu, after they refused to surrender. As a result of the firefight, two Thai fishermen were killed and the trawler was subsequently seized and towed into port by the Malaysian authorities.

Conflicting reports emerged over the circumstances under which the trawler crew had been shot.[22] Thai trawler operators stationed in southern Thailand decided to take matters into their own hands to resolve the issue. Accordingly, the Malaysian authorities were notified that a flotilla of up to 2,000 trawlers would set sail to block off the entire coast of Terengganu to avenge the deaths of their colleagues. Swift mobilization by the Thai Ministry of Foreign Affairs and Fisheries Department averted what would probably have been a tense standoff, and the trawler operators were dissuaded from fulfilling their threat. Since then, the situation has been much better managed. The most recent seizure of a Thai fishing vessel and crew in Malaysian waters occurred in April 2007.[23]

Apart from these peaks in the tensions, Malaysian authorities have reported illegal-fishing sightings of some 2,000 Thai trawlers annually. However, it is estimated that only ten per cent of such sightings actually led to the seizures of vessels and the arrests of crews. Part of the reason for the low detention rate is the regular intelligence provided over the radio to the trawlers. When alerted to maritime patrols in the vicinity, the trawlers simply sail away and evade capture. Since 2008, as a result of soaring global fuel prices, many trawler operators no longer regard it feasible to operate their boats and many of them are now idly moored along the Thai coast. However, the significant differential in the price of marine fuel, in particular diesel, has in turn led to a marked rise in smuggling activities since the Malaysian Government used to highly subsidize the price of fuel until recently.

Illegal immigration is in fact a major security threat in the case of Malaysia. Most illegal migrants in Malaysia are actually from Indonesia where they blend in easily given ethno-linguistic and religious similarities. This pool alone is thought to number well over a million persons. The tight labour situation in Malaysia in the 1990s and stellar economic performance created ample job opportunities in the construction, plantation, and agricultural sectors of the economy. Relatively high wages, a favourable exchange rate and a secure environment were all factors that worked in Malaysia's disfavour as a preferred destination for illegal migration in Southeast Asia. Although the 1997 Asian financial crisis and subsequent structural weakness of the economy temporarily led to the deportation of large numbers of illegal migrants, the prosperity and opportunities returned a few years afterwards.

Malaysian tensions with Thailand over the issue of illegal immigrants have less to do with the nationality of the migrants than the manner in which they enter the country. Whereas Indonesian migrants enter Malaysia from the sea, those from countries like Bangladesh, Cambodia, Myanmar, and increasingly Nepal, cross over the land border from Thailand. The border between the two countries was traditionally demarcated by the Golok River. Parts of the border are poorly secured and the shallow river provides easy opportunities for cross-border intrusions. The land border has also previously been the staging point for smuggling and banditry, leading to tit-for-tat accusations of poor security arrangements.[24] As for cross-border smuggling, it has always existed between Malaysia and Thailand. Items that are regularly smuggled across borders include rice, rubber, tin, cooking oil, fuel, sugar, and flour.[25] With the exception of rice, most commodities are smuggled from Malaysia into Thailand since the former subsidizes essential foodstuffs. Reverse smuggling typically happens when Thai produce fetches a better price in Malaysia owing to exchange rate differences. Additionally smuggling tends to peak during festive seasons when there tends to be a greater demand for household consumer items.

Resolution of Contentious Issues

For most of the issues examined, both Thailand and Malaysia have generally resorted to enforcement measures to resolve the situation. In other words, most mutual problems that have the potential to lead to deteriorated bilateral ties are securitized and then dealt with by enforcement agencies. To the extent that territoriality and its enforcement are involved even in non-traditional threats like illegal fishing and migration, it is arguable that both states have utilized traditional instruments. The treatment of bilateral problems within a traditional state-centric framework allows both countries to convert a problematic issue into a much more discrete and therefore manageable one. However, such attempts at circumscribing problems are not always successful or may lead to an escalation of tensions, as was the case with the Malaysian acceptance and provision of sanctuary to a large number of Thai Muslims fleeing a difficult situation. And greater surveillance and enforcement often unintentionally leads to the exaggeration of an issue as well. In this regard, both the securitization of issues and their subsequent monitoring raises the awareness of enforcement agencies and their subsequent willingness to get involved in dealing with perceived problematic situations.

Generally Thailand and Malaysia utilize joint border committees to resolve territorial and demarcation disputes. These committees meet regularly to resolve problems and can schedule ad hoc meetings to deal with emergency situations. The committees can also have matters referred to them for resolution by political executive as part of an established method of conflict resolution. Drawing on joint cooperation against communist insurgency and criminal activities in the past, these committees form the bedrock of bilateral conflict resolution. However, resorting to such a resolution is not always easy since proper identification and documentation of individuals and trawlers in the case of illegal migration and illegal fishing respectively is often absent.[26] In the case of illegal fishing, for example, the Thai Overseas Fisheries Association often acts independently of the government's Fisheries Department, representing and negotiating its corporate and members' interests. Additionally, in order to conceal illegal activities involving fishing and smuggling, ingenious methods have been devised to escape detention, including the offloading and transhipment of products at unauthorized destinations.[27] In this regard, the relative mobility of trawlers, for example, makes detection and enforcement of rules rather difficult. Trawler operators are also known to possess sufficient weapons to engage lightly armed enforcement patrols and prevail in a firefight.

The relative independence of the Thai Overseas Fisheries Association, coupled with the ability of large operators to evade registration and enforcement, makes the situation extremely complex. The association is able to circumvent and bypass government regulations and does not always represent the entire trawling community. Since the association is unable to represent and arbitrate membership interests in international disputes, the task typically falls on the Ministry of Foreign Affairs, which appears unprepared to deal with the situation.[28] Alternative regional multilateral channels that can be utilized to resolve fishing disputes include the Marine Science Sub-Committee of the ASEAN Committee on Science and Technology, the ASEAN Fisheries Forum, and the Southeast Asia Program on Ocean Law, Policy and Management.[29]

Illegal immigrants, refugees, and smuggling are similarly dealt with by joint border committees. Occasionally, regional border committees that are subordinate to national committees are utilized. If such committees are unable to resolve a situation or the stakes are too high and conflated with other issues, they are normally resolved bilaterally at the ministerial level. Such representations have been made in the past, although they have not always been successful. Additionally, such negotiations usually involve a bundle of issues, in order that a resolution is mutually beneficial and has a longer shelf life.

As for enforcement agencies that encounter such activities, coordination is an equally difficult problem for the simple reason that detection and detention are undertaken by a wide number of agencies, from fisheries departments, customs and immigration, to the police and navy. Procedures and protocol involved in the documentation of such activities are not always uniform, and there are many instances of unscrupulous agencies resolving a situation within their jurisdiction for monetary gain. These have included in the past the seizure of valuables and equipment, including vehicles and vessels, commodities, and catches.

In view of these problems, all monitoring and enforcement agencies dealing with issues of a bilateral interest or nature should standardize procedures. There should also be a national coordinating agency that can deal with input from multiple channels and act accordingly. To allow for the speedy resolution of issues, involved countries should be notified immediately. Additionally, such agencies should meet regularly and devise efficient and effective measures to deal with abnormal or extraordinary situations. Such measures however involve a measure of devolution of power and authority that may not be easily forthcoming in both countries.

Correlation between Structural and Agency Relations in Dispute Resolution

As is the case with most Southeast Asian countries, both structural and agency reasons can be brought to bear on dispute resolution. In the case of Thai-Malaysian relations, there has been a long tradition of dispute resolution at the structural level. And in fact, the problem sometimes appears to be a case of multiple and overwhelming structures rather than an absence of them. In this regard, as noted earlier, there are problems of coordination between agencies rather than an absence of avenues for dispute resolution. It has also been noted how issues requiring attention can be resolved at the ministerial level or prime ministerial level. Such meetings are sometimes also scheduled on an ad hoc basis on the sidelines of major regional meetings like those of ASEAN, ASEAN Regional Forum (ARF), ASEAN Plus Three, the Asia-Pacific Economic Cooperation forum (APEC) or the East Asian Community meeting.

Agency reasons play an important part in the state of bilateral relations between Thailand and Malaysia. On the one hand, it is arguable that this bilateral relationship has generally been insulated from the turbulence that has characterized Thailand-Myanmar or Malaysia-Singapore relations. A good measure of the reasons for the structural stability of the relationship was the shared ideological outlook that in turn translated into convergent defence and foreign policies. The regional attempt to contain Vietnam's seeming hegemonic behaviour from 1975 also sheltered the relationship within the structural confines of ASEAN under Indonesian leadership that took into account Thai security considerations. However, in the post–Cold War period, much of this seeming strategic convergence dissipated rapidly. Hence, if structural considerations insulated the bilateral relationship from the 1950s to the 1980s, the unravelling of the structures created opportunities for tension. Consequently, it should come as little surprise that the post–Cold War period has led to a rearrangement of policy priorities and relationships. Additionally, it may be remembered that bilateral relations also tended to be cordial early on owing to the Tunku's ancestry and Thai acknowledgement of a special relationship with Malaysia. Both countries also tended to be less nationalistic during the early period and, as a result, elites were easily able to dissipate tensions to avoid them percolating downwards.

The weakness of structural conditions in maintaining Thai-Malaysian relations on an even keel has, unsurprisingly, raised the importance of agency considerations. Nonetheless, both countries, owing to their location and traditional dispositions and trajectories, have looked in different directions; Malaysia towards the maritimes and Thailand towards the mainland. Yet, issues that dominated their bilateral relations multiplied from the 1990s and many of them had a security dimension. Both countries also had Prime Ministers who were highly nationalistic and sometimes made careless foreign policy pronouncements. Mahathir (1981–2004) generally tended to be more considerate in dealing with Asian countries, perhaps with the exception of Singapore and occasionally Indonesia.[30] Thaksin (2001–6), on the other hand, typically tended to be more assertive and nationalistic towards Asian states. Both were strong leaders with high levels of political legitimacy who exercised power when it was needed. Given their charismatic personalities and leadership styles, they also had a disproportionate impact on local structural conditions. In other words, their attitudes and pronouncements on issues tended to have a cascading and reverberating effect on bureaucratic agencies, including joint border committees. Hence, strong leaders generally tended to exercise disproportionate influence on structures.

Nonetheless, not all of such agency influence is always negative. After all, Thaksin did attempt a measure of Asian regionalism and Mahathir equally championed East Asian regionalism.[31] The December 2005 Summit Meeting of the East Asian Community that was held in Kuala Lumpur owed its fruition to the determined lobbying of the Mahathir government to draw Southeast and Northeast Asia closer together. It was the outbreak of the Asian financial crisis in 1997 and its aftermath that served as the catalyst to the eventual formation of the East Asian Community. And during times of good bilateral relations between both countries, both leaders have articulated common preferences and a determination to jointly resolve outstanding issues.[32] In fact Thaksin and

Mahathir hosted the first joint parliamentary meeting between the two countries and Thaksin was also known to admire Mahathir's leadership style.[33] Similarly, Abdullah Badawi and Surayud Cholanont both paid courtesy calls to each other to raise the level of bilateral cooperation and resolve outstanding issues.[34] Following the election of a new civilian government in Thailand, the country's then Prime Minister Samak Sundaravej paid a courtesy call to Malaysia. Both Samak and Badawi also reaffirmed their mutual commitment to maintaining a positive bilateral relationship and encouraged much more cross-border investments to enhance trade.[35] Samak has also expressed his appreciation to Malaysia for developmental assistance and training for Thai Malay-Muslims.[36] Badawi's successor, Najib Tun Razak and current Thai Prime Minister Abhisit Vejjajiva have also pledged to cooperate with each other to promote trade and resolve common problems. In this regard, leadership transition in both countries has led to much less political posturing and much more quiet and contained diplomacy. Yet, the violence and security threat associated with the southern Thai insurgency has tested the bilateral relationship.[37] Notwithstanding this issue as a source of great irritation at the bilateral level, Thailand and Malaysia generally enjoy cordial bilateral ties.

Conclusion

Thai-Malaysian bilateral relations have generally weathered the test of time over the last fifty years. Interestingly, notwithstanding overhangs from the colonial period in the nineteenth and twentieth centuries when territories between the two countries were traded against their will, the structural dictates of the Cold War allowed Thailand and Malaysia to evolve a mutually beneficial bilateral relationship. Much of this benefit was derived from an anti-communist and pro-Western outlook in domestic politics and foreign policy. The joint suppression of the communist insurgency, the formation of ASEAN, and the communist victory in Vietnam provided additional structural factors to weld the relationship up to and through most of the 1980s. Thailand's acknowledgement of maintaining cordial relations with Malaysia in order to buttress its dominance in mainland Southeast Asia and the Tunku's part-Thai ancestry provided additional support to the relationship.

Beginning in the late 1980s and continuing on into the 1990s, the bilateral relationship has been subjected to far greater turbulence than in the past. The dissipation of the Indochinese security complex and the emergence of a number of unconventional security threats significantly complicated the relationship between the two countries. Cross-border intrusions, illegal migration, and illegal fishing have been irritants in the bilateral relationship in the past. Both issues are likely to continue for some time. Increased monitoring of such activities has also resulted in far greater number of such issues being brought to the fore. Since 2004, the political violence related at least in part to Islamic extremism, and Thai police and military repression has severely tested bilateral ties between the two countries. Nonetheless, following leadership transition in Malaysia and Thailand in 2004 and 2006 respectively, the bilateral relationship has been brought to a much more even keel. In this regard, it should be noted that agency factors have the potential to and can indeed exert a powerful influence on the bilateral relationship, notwithstanding the previous importance of structural dictates.

Both countries have generally resorted to joint border committees to resolve bilateral problems that arise between them. These committees are constituted at the national as well as regional levels. Additionally important and/or urgent issues can also be dealt with at the ministerial level. This approach to conflict resolution has generally been successful in the past and, judging from recent pledges and pronouncements from both countries, there is clearly the political will to amicably resolve outstanding issues. In this regard, it may be noted that although the Thailand-Malaysian bilateral relationship is occasionally subjected to turbulence, the situation has never really deteriorated into the possibility of open armed conflict. Thailand's bilateral relationship with Myanmar and Malaysia's bilateral relationship with Indonesia and Singapore have certainly been subjected to far higher levels of turbulence, by contrast.

NOTES

[1]   In 1896, under the terms of the Anglo-French Treaty, Thailand ceded the four southern provinces of Yala, Satun, Narathiwat, and Pattani to the British who controlled Malaya to the south and Burma to the west. Similarly, Siemreap, Battambang, and the east bank of the Mekong delta was ceded to the French Indochinese Union. Then, in 1909, the four southern provinces were reintegrated with Thailand as part of the Anglo-Thai Border Agreements. In 1942, during World War II, the Japanese gave control of the four northern Malay province of Kedah, Perlis, Perak, and Kelantan to Thailand as a gesture

of appreciation for the two landing sites in the east and the south from which they attacked Burma and Malaya. These four provinces were returned to British Malaya after the Japanese surrender in 1945.

2   See text of speech delivered by Thai Prime Minister Abhisit Vejjajiva at the dinner hosted by Malaysian Prime Minister Najib Tun Razak during his visit to Malaysia on 8 June 2009.

3   For a discussion of Thailand-U.S. security relations see Randolph R. Sean, *The United States and Thailand: Alliance Dynamics, 1950–1958* (Berkeley, CA: University of California Press, 1986), and Daniel Fineman, *A Special Relationship: The United States and Military Government in Thailand* (Honolulu: University of Hawai'i Press, 1997).

4   A security complex refers to the dense web of relations between geographically proximate countries. Informed by historical interactions, the complex is relatively self-contained and provides a rank-ordering of states in terms of power. The dominant or hegemonic power seeks to enlarge its influence whereas the lesser powers resist such efforts. In the Indochina security complex, Vietnam performed the function of the hegemon while Thailand resisted the perceived hegemony emanating from revolutionary communism. Cambodia and Laos were unable to retain their neutrality after independence in 1953 and gradually came under the dominance of Vietnam. See Barry Buzan, "The Southeast Asian Security Complex", *Contemporary Southeast Asia* 10, no. 1 (June 1988): 1–16. A refinement of the concept can be found in Muthiah Alagappa, "The Dynamics of International Security in Southeast Asia: Change and Continuity", *Australian Journal of International Affairs* 45, no. 1 (May 1991): 1–37.

5   The Malay Archipelago complex grouped the countries of Indonesia, Malaysia, Singapore, and Brunei. Most of Indonesian hegemonic behaviour in the 1960s was directed towards Malaysia and Singapore while the Borneo states of Sabah, Sarawak, and Brunei were subjected to harassment as part of an Indonesian-inspired North Kalimantan federation in the 1950s. Sukarno's anti-Western and anti-imperialist rhetoric found an easy vent for hegemonic behaviour through the Indonesian military confrontation from 1963 to 1966.

6   See N. Ganesan, "Thailand's Relations with Malaysia and Myanmar in Post–Cold War Southeast Asia", *Japanese Journal of Political Science* 2, no. 1 (May 2001): 127–46.

7   See Kobkhua Suwanathat-Pian, "Special-Thai Malaysian Relations", *Journal of the Malaysian Branch of the Royal Asiatic Society* 75, no. 282 (June 2002): 1–22.

8   Malaysian political independence came in two phases. In the first instance, the nine states of peninsula Malaysia and the two straits territories of Malacca and Penang formed the Federation of Malaya. This federation was subsequently

extended to include the North Borneo states of Sabah and Sarawak and Singapore and renamed the Federation of Malaysia.

[9]   Notwithstanding this broad convergence, both Indonesia and Malaysia generally regarded China as a greater threat to regional stability than Vietnam. Hence, in 1981, both countries announced the "Kuantan Declaration" that sought to accommodate legitimate Vietnamese security interests in the mainland and restrain Chinese hegemonic behaviour in turn, not unlike the Soviet attempt to transform Vietnam into a "third power" and security hedge against China that in turn led to increased Chinese support for the Khmer Rouge in Cambodia to hedge against Vietnam. See Justus M. van der Kroef, "ASEAN, Hanoi, and the Kampuchean Conflict: Between 'Kuantan' and a 'Third Alternative'", *Asian Survey* 21, no. 5 (May 1981): 515–35.

[10] See N. Ganesan, "Taking Stock of Post-Cold war Developments in ASEAN", *Security Dialogue* 25, no. 4 (December 1994): 457–68, and *Bilateral Tensions in Post-Cold War ASEAN* (Singapore: Institute of Southeast Asian Studies, 1999).

[11] For a discussion of the historical overhang and in particular the attempt at separatism see Omar Farouk, "The historical and transnational dimensions of Malay-Muslim separatism in Southern Thailand", in *Armed Separatism in Southeast Asia*, edited by Lim Joo Jock and S. Vani (Singapore: Institute of Southeast Asian Studies, 1984), pp. 234–60.

[12] See Ramses Amer, "Expanding ASEAN's Conflict Management Framework in Southeast Asia: The Border Dispute Dimension", *Asian Journal of Political Science* 6, no. 2 (December 1998): 41–42 and notes 39–41 on page 52; and "The Association of South-East Asian Nations and the Management of Territorial Disputes", *Boundary and Security Bulletin* 9, no. 4 (Winter 2001–2): 81–82 and notes 7–9 on page 92.

[13] Michael Vatikiotis, "Back-yard bickering", *Far Eastern Economic Review* 157: 16 (7 March 1996), p. 22.

[14] "Border Regiment to Monitor Security", *New Straits Times*, 30 January 2008.

[15] Michael Vatikiotis, "Sea worthy", *Far Eastern Economic Review* 157, no. 16 (21 April 1994): 80.

[16] Interview with Dr Panitan Wattanayagorn, October 2004. Also see "Military Abused Us, Say Fleeing Muslims", *Nation*, 19 March 2007, and "Army Admits Southern Killings", *Bangkok Post*, 11 April 2007.

[17] "78 Perish in Custody", *Nation*, 27 October 2004 and "Tak Bai Crackdown: Global Outrage as Grim Details Emerge: PM Shows No Remorse", Ibid., 28 October 2004.

[18] See for example, Duncan McCargo, "Thailand: A State of Anxiety", in *Southeast Asian Affairs 2008*, edited by Daljit Singh and Tin Maung Maung Than (Singapore: Institute of Southeast Asian Studies), pp. 351–52.

19 See "Diplomatic Stalemate: KL Says It Won't Release Refugees", *New Straits Times*, 29 September 2005; "Thailand Must Stop 'Overflow' into Malaysia", Ibid., 20 October 2005; and "Thai Foreign Minister Cuts Off Contact with Malaysia", *ChannelNewsAsia*, 19 October 2005.

20 See "Allegations on Funds For Separatist Groups: We Don't Support Such Groups", *New Straits Times*, 10 December 2004; "Surayud: Malaysia Net Funds Violence", *Bangkok Post*, 22 November 2006; "Prove Separatists Get Tom Yum Money", *New Straits Times*, 22 November 2006.

21 "Thai-Malaysian Ties On the Mend", *Nation*, 24 February 2006; "KL Willing to Join Insurgent Peace Talks", *Bangkok Post*, 17 October 2006; "Malaysia, Thailand Plan Measures to End Southern Strife", ChannelNewsAsia, 23 March 2007; "It's War against Smugglers", *New Straits Times*, 11 April 2007; "Govts to Share ID Data on Citizens", *Bangkok Post*, 2 May 2007; "Malaysia Asked to Help Track Militants", ibid., 17 August 2007; and "Thailand, Malaysia Cooperate against Insurgency", ibid., 22 August 2007. In the most recent development, travellers from Wang Kelian in Perlis and Wang Prachan from Thailand are now required to carry border passes during cross-border travels during weekends. This requirement was previously observed only during weekdays. See "Border Pass Now a Must for Weekend Travel", *New Straits Times*, 21 January 2008.

22 A Thai academic confided in December 1995 that the Thai version of the incident was that the two fishermen had been shot at point-blank range.

23 "Thai Fishing Vessel Seized", *New Straits Times*, 27 April 2007.

24 See "Malaysia to form patrol regiment to guard border with Thailand", *The Nation*, 3 August 2005; and "Thailand to extend security wall on Malaysian border", ibid., 2 May 2007.

25 See for example, "Subsidised Diesel Sold by Fishermen to Thais", *New Straits Times*, 15 April 2008; and "Sugar trail to Thailand", ibid., 23 January 2008.

26 So, for example, the "Fisheries Department [in Thailand] has the responsibility for issuing fishing licences, while it is the Harbours Department that licenses fishing boats, while neither department appears to have the means to enforce fishing laws". See John G. Butcher, "Why Do Thai Trawlers Get into So Much Trouble?", unpublished manuscript, Western Australian Maritime Museum, November 1999.

27 In 1995, the Thai Director General of Fisheries lamented lax law enforcement in the industry by noting that "Fishermen can catch any number of fish, have any number of vessels and use any kind of gear", *Bangkok Post*, 20 December 1995, quoted in Butcher, "Why Do Thai Trawlers Get into So Much Trouble?", p. 11.

28 Typically, it is the Thai Office of Protection that provides the Ministry of Foreign Affairs with information on detention of vessels and crew by other countries for illegal fishing. Since trawler operators are often unprepared to

face the consequences of illegal fishing, many such detentions and seizures are typically left unreported.

[29] See Aprilani Soegiarto, "Sustainable Fisheries, Environment and the Prospects of Regional Cooperation in Southeast Asia", paper presented at the Nautilus Institute Workshop in East-West Centre, Honolulu, on 23–25 September 1994.

[30] Mahathir established quite a reputation for himself as a champion of Third World causes, from deforestation to carbon dioxide emissions. He always argued that the West was hypocritical in demanding concessions that it did not itself observe. During his tenure, Mahathir had a number of high profile disagreements with Australia, the United Kingdom, and the United States. He was especially critical of Indonesia's seeming unwillingness in dealing with forest fires whose smoke blanketed Malaysia. In the case of Singapore, major sources of disagreement included marine reclamation and the sale of sand for it, the sale price of water, replacement of the existing causeway between the two countries with a bridge, the development of Malaysian Railway Land in Singapore, and low flight over-space for Singapore fighter aircraft. As for Thaksin, he tended to be especially nationalistic towards Malaysia on the issue of the southern Thai violence and towards Myanmar at a general level.

[31] See N. Ganesan, "Malaysia in 2003: Leadership Transition with a Tall Shadow", *Asian Survey* 44, no. 1 (January/February 2004): 70–77 and "Thaksin and the Politics of Domestic and Regional Political Consolidation in Thailand", *Contemporary Southeast Asia* 26, no. 1 (April 2004): 26–44.

[32] The most recent such arrangement was an agreement "to strengthen their cooperation regarding security in coastal waters and on the high seas, intelligence sharing and the containment of insurgence". See "Thailand, Malaysia Step Up Naval Accord", *Bangkok Post*, 14 July 2006. Also see "New Scanners At Border Checkpoints", *New Straits Times*, 1 November 2007.

[33] "Joint Cabinet Meeting an Historic First", *Bangkok Post*, 12 December 2002. Also see the Malaysian interview with Thaksin entitled "Thaksin Outlines Thai Vision", *New Straits Times*, 11 July 2003; and "Ties with KL Have Improved, Says Surakiat", *Bangkok Post*, 12 August 2005.

[34] See "KL Sees Light at the End of South Tunnel", *Bangkok Post*, 14 February 2007; "PM: More Trade Will Boost KL-Bangkok Ties", *New Straits Times*, 22 August 2007; "Thailand-Malaysia Bridge to Open in Dec", *Bangkok Post*, 4 October 2007; and "Ministry May Approve Maids from Pattani", *New Straits Times*, 1 November 2007.

[35] See "Samak and Abdullah to Discuss Rice Import" and "PM Invites Thais to Invest Up North", *New Straits Times*, 24 and 25 April 2008 respectively. Total bilateral trade between Thailand and Malaysia was US$15.66 billion in 2006 and $17.23 billion in 2007.

[36] "KL Asked to Contribute More", *New Straits Times*, 25 April 2008. Samak specifically mentioned Malaysian scholarships for students and teacher training as helpful contributions.
[37] In the most recent incident, Thai authorities requested Malaysian assistance in apprehending seven men suspected of involvement in bombing activities in the southern provinces. The suspects were believed to be hiding in the Malaysian states of Kelantan or Terengganu. See "Suspected Thai Bombers Believed Hiding in Malaysia", *New Straits Times*, 29 July 2008.

REFERENCES

Alagappa, Muthiah. "The Dynamics of International Security in Southeast Asia: Change and Continuity". *Australian Journal of International Affairs* 45, no. 1 (1991): 1–37.
"Allegations on Funds for Separatist Groups: We Don't Support Such Groups". *New Straits Times*, 10 December 2004.
Amer, Ramses. "Expanding ASEAN's Conflict Management Framework in Southeast Asia: The Border Dispute Dimension". *Asian Journal of Political Science* 6, no. 2 (1998): 41–42.
———. "The Association of South-East Asian Nations and the Management of Territorial Disputes". *Boundary and Security Bulletin* 9, no. 4 (2001/02): 81–82.
"Army Admits Southern Killings". *Bangkok Post*, 11 April 2007.
"Border Pass Now a Must For Weekend Travel". *New Straits Times*, 21 January 2008.
"Border Regiment to Monitor Security". *New Straits Times*, 30 January 2008.
Butcher, John G. "Why Do Thai Trawlers Get into So Much Trouble?" Unpublished manuscript, Western Australian Maritime Museum, 1999.
Buzan, Barry. "The Southeast Asian Security Complex", *Contemporary Southeast Asia* 10, no. 1 (1988): 1–16.
"Diplomatic Stalemate: KL Says It Won't Release Refugees". *New Straits Times*, 29 September 2005.
Farouk, Omar. "The Historical and Transnational Dimensions of Malay-Muslim Separatism in Southern Thailand". In *Armed Separatism in Southeast Asia* edited by Lim Joo Jock and S. Vani. Singapore: Institute of Southeast Asian Studies, 1984.
Fineman, Daniel. *A Special Relationship: The United States and Military Government in Thailand*. Honolulu: University of Hawai'i Press, 1997.
Ganesan, N. "Taking Stock of Post–Cold War Developments in ASEAN", *Security Dialogue* 25, no. 4 (December 1994): 457–68.
———. *Bilateral Tensions in Post-Cold War ASEAN*. Singapore: Institute of Southeast Asian Studies, 1999.

———. "Thailand's Relations with Malaysia and Myanmar in Post–Cold War Southeast Asia", *Japanese Journal of Political Science* 2, no. 1 (May 2001): 127–46.

———. "Malaysia in 2003: Leadership Transition with a Tall Shadow", *Asian Survey* 44, no. 1 (January/February 2004): 70–77.

———. "Thaksin and the Politics of Domestic and Regional Political Consolidation in Thailand", *Contemporary Southeast Asia* 26, no. 1 (April 2004): 26–44.

"Govts to Share ID Data on Citizens". *Bangkok Post*, 2 May 2007.

"It's War against Smugglers". *New Straits Times*, 11 April 2007.

"Joint Cabinet Meeting an Historic First". *Bangkok Post*, 12 December 2002.

"KL Asked to Contribute More". *New Straits Times*, 25 April 2008.

"KL Sees Light at the End of South Tunnel". *Bangkok Post*, 14 February 2007.

"KL Willing to Join Insurgent Peace Talks". *Bangkok Post*, 17 October 2006.

"Malaysia Asked to Help Track Militants". *Bangkok Post*, 17 August 2007.

"Malaysia, Thailand Plan Measures to End Southern Strife". *ChannelNewsAsia*, 23 March 2007.

"Malaysia to Form Patrol Regiment to Guard Border with Thailand". *Nation*, 3 August 2005.

McCargo, Duncan. "Thailand: A State of Anxiety". In *Southeast Asian Affairs 2008*, edited by Daljit Singh and Than, Tin Maung Maung. Singapore: Institute of Southeast Asian Studies, 2008.

"Military Abused Us, Say Fleeing Muslims". *Nation*, 19 March 2007.

"Ministry May Approve Maids from Pattani". *New Straits Times*, 1 November 2007.

"New Scanners at Border Checkpoints". *New Straits Times*, 1 November 2007.

"PM Invites Thais to Invest Up North". *New Straits Times*, 25 April 2008.

"PM: More Trade Will Boost KL-Bangkok Ties". *New Straits Times*, 22 August 2007.

"Prove Separatists Get Tom Yum Money". *New Straits Times*, 22 November 2006.

"Samak and Abdullah to Discuss Rice Import". *New Straits Times*, 24 April 2008.

Sean, Randolph R. *The United states and Thailand: Alliance Dynamics, 1950–1958*. Berkeley, CA: University of California Press, 1986.

"78 Perish in Custody". *Nation*, 27 October 2004.

Soegiarto, Aprilani. "Sustainable Fisheries, Environment and the Prospects of Regional Cooperation in Southeast Asia". Paper presented at the Nautilus Institute Workshop. East-West Centre, Honolulu. 23–25 September 1994.

"Subsidised Diesel Sold by Fishermen to Thais". *New Straits Times*, 15 April 2008.

"Sugar Trail to Thailand". *New Straits Times*, 23 January 2008.

"Surayud: Malaysia Net Funds Violence". *Bangkok Post*, 22 November 2006.

Suwanathat-Pian, Kobkhua. "Special-Thai Malaysian Relations", *Journal of the Malaysian Branch of the Royal Asiatic Society* 75, no. 282 (2002): 1–22.

"Tak Bai Crackdown: Global Outrage as Grim Details Emerge: PM Shows No Remorse". *The Nation*, 28 October 2004.
"Thai Fishing Vessel Seized". *New Straits Times*, 27 April 2007.
"Thai Foreign Minister Cuts Off Contact with Malaysia". *ChannelNewsAsia*, 19 October 2005.
"Thailand-Malaysia Bridge to Open in Dec". *Bangkok Post*, 4 October 2007.
"Thailand, Malaysia Cooperate Against Insurgency". *Bangkok Post*, 22 August 2007.
"Thailand, Malaysia Step Up Naval Accord". *Bangkok Post*, 14 July 2006.
"Thailand Must Stop 'Overflow' into Malaysia". *New Straits Times*, 20 October 2005.
"Thailand to Extend Security Wall on Malaysian Border". *The Nation*, 2 May 2007.
"Thai-Malaysian Ties on the Mend". *Nation*, 24 February 2006.
"Thaksin Outlines Thai Vision". *New Straits Times*, 11 July 2003.
"Ties with KL Have Improved, Says Surakiat". *Bangkok Post*, 12 August 2005.
Van der Kroef, Justus M. "ASEAN, Hanoi, and the Kampuchean Conflict: Between 'Kuantan' and a 'Third Alternative'", *Asian Survey* 21, no. 5 (1981): 515–35.
Vatikiotis, Michael. "Sea Worthy", *Far Eastern Economic Review* 157, no. 16 (1994): 80.
———. "Back-yard Bickering", *Far Eastern Economic Review* 157, no. 16 (1996): 22.

PART III

Case Studies — Maritime Southeast Asia

7

Malaysia-Indonesia Bilateral Relations: Sibling Rivals in a Fraught Family

Meredith L. Weiss

However close in proximity, Malaysia and Indonesia have not always been the best of neighbours. Relations reached their nadir with *Konfrontasi* in the early 1960s, when Indonesia violently contested Malaya's merger with Singapore, Sabah, and Sarawak as a neo-imperialist, nefarious plot.[1] But while Malaysia is less prone to pick fights with Indonesia than with long-since-ousted Singapore, tempers have flared before and since. The fact that overall, relations are amicable and symbiotic, though, puts less friendly moments in context. The two countries celebrated fifty years of diplomatic relations in 2006, and economic ties have never been closer. Between 2001 and 2005, bilateral trade doubled and Malaysian investments in Indonesia nearly quintupled, making Indonesia Malaysia's tenth largest trading partner and Malaysia, Indonesia's fourth largest investor. Moreover, around 1.2 million Indonesians work in Malaysia — more than in any other destination country. These workers represent a critical part of the labour force, comprising around seventy per cent of all foreign workers in Malaysia.[2] Moreover, despite the occasional sabre-rattling (whether symbolic or substantive), the two states cooperate militarily, for instance through a joint border committee and framework for exchange of maritime security information, and with more joint exercises than with other ASEAN states.[3] Indeed, the sheer depth and breadth of Malaysia-Indonesia ties — manifest not just in official statistics, but through a tangle of social, business, educational, and other connections — opens up a host of possible fault lines that have remained dormant. Any overblown grandstanding must thus be taken in stride. Overall, relations are good, yet the bilateral relationship is weakly-enough institutionalized that relatively small matters readily escalate into diplomatic crises. Moreover, the underlying flexibility and practicality of Malaysia and Indonesia's bilateral relationship has arguably discouraged greater recourse to multilateral institutions, despite the leading roles both play in ASEAN.

Ruhanas Harun links phases in Indonesia-Malaysia relations with major changes in Indonesia's regime: the launch of the New Order after 1966 brought a renewed sprit of brotherhood and close affinity after *Konfrontasi*, including ever-closer economic and security cooperation, then the fall of Suharto in 1998 brought a new focus on joint problem-solving.[4] Joseph Liow shifts the lens toward Malaysia, demarcating three periods: 1949–65, 1966–80, and 1981–2000;[5] we can add a fourth period to this rubric, beginning with the stabilization of a post-crisis political order from around 2000 on. The first period, the waning years of colonialism in both states, saw schemes for ethnic Malay unity rise and decline, then the angry spiral toward *Konfrontasi*. The second period saw broad agreement on establishing a regional security architecture, amid stepped-up language of "blood brotherhood", growing economic ties, and newly-shared, strident anti-communism and non-alignment.[6] By the third period, the countries were sparring for prestige, both economic and otherwise, amid revitalized and reshaped nationalist currents. Signposting this transition most clearly was the rise of fiercely ambitious, vocal, and Malay-chauvinist Prime Minister Mahathir Mohamad. The current period, following the crisis of 1997, has been marked by an economic focus and increasingly routinized diplomatic interactions (not least as the outsized personalities of Mahathir and Suharto receded from the scene), but with ramped-up regional and extra-regional connections constraining the field. Sporadic tensions punctuating symbiosis notwithstanding, in this period, shifts in the external environment, related both to economics and to security, have arguably mattered more to state priorities and strategies than changes in leadership.

A family metaphor is useful for conceptualizing Indonesia-Malaysia relations, not just for the cultural proximity of the two states: a straightforward realist approach is tempered by the possibility and discourse of shared norms, culture, and nationhood, and even testy relations at the centre may have little practical bearing on close personal ties among the states' long-intermeshed citizens. As Liow presents the underlying dilemma, "In the study of Indonesia-Malaysia relations, it appears that tensions have as much to do with conflicts of identity as they do with conflicts of interests".[7] Such tensions were most obviously manifest during the late colonial period, as schemes for a pan-"Malay" *Indonesia Raya* or *Melayu Raya* (Greater Indonesia or Malaya) were tabled, and ultimately rejected, on both sides. Importantly, the presumed pecking order within the "family" has always been contested, with Malaysia challenging Indonesia's "sense of regional entitlement".[8] The extent of common identity and purpose remains unclear today, affinities of language, religion, history, and geography notwithstanding. Relations between Malaysia and Indonesia are marked by very real strains, aggravated as much by how alluring a scapegoat each provides whenever one is needed as by the impossibility of disengagement. When matters get messy, political leaders step in, scold their naughty media and activists, and insist that all play nicely ... even when the underlying issues persist unabated.[9] Sturdy multilateralism may complement that sort of high-level, refereed approach, and might shift the balance of leverage in given disputes, yet most thorny spats develop one-on-one and are settled the same way.

The State of Bilateral Relations: Rosy, but Far from Golden

Overall, relations between Malaysia and Indonesia today are cordial and constructive. The two key areas of contention tend to be (relatively marginal) territorial disputes and issues related to labour migration, though cross-border environmental issues have gained increasing salience over the past decade as well, and Islam may represent a source either of common interest or aggravation.

While the major boundary contests between Indonesia and Malaysia subsided with the end of *Konfrontasi* — and Indonesia did not itself lay claim to Malaysian territory even then — flare-ups arise along the edges. Indonesia in particular has long been protective of its boundaries, asserting an Archipelagic Principle in 1957 laying claim to the water "surrounding, between and connecting the islands constituting the Indonesian state." Buttressing this doctrine were regulations on passage through these waterways, including 1962's Act of Innocent Passage, reinforcing Indonesia's construction of the whole area as a unified, and vulnerable, strategic defence system.[10] These rulings carried implications for waterways shared with Malaysia, especially the Strait of Malacca (declared international waters with the Anglo-Dutch Treaty of 1824), but also proposed how territorial seas should be defined from any national coastline. Malaysia and Indonesia signed an agreement acceding to Indonesian definitions of continental shelves in March 1970, but the status of the Strait of Malacca remained unclear, to Singapore's particular consternation. Further agreements followed. Though it generally yielded to a fairly recalcitrant Indonesia's demands, Malaysia remained concerned especially about channels between East Malaysia and the peninsula. Ultimately, Suharto and Tun Razak hammered out an agreement in late 1975, solidified in a 1976 memorandum on archipelagic principles of sovereignty and legitimate rights and interests — still not ratified by a dubious Malaysian Parliament.[11]

Indonesia and Malaysia's common borders, especially in petroleum-rich maritime areas, have since become a key source of contention. Most notable was the dispute over Sipadan and Ligitan islands in the Sulawesi (Celebes) Sea, off the coast of Sabah and Kalimantan. The islands themselves are not much to speak of. The territorial dispute only arose in 1969, when both sides began petroleum exploration along their respective continental shelves, and did not really heat up until Malaysia started developing tourism with a dive resort on Sipadan in the 1980s, then Indonesia sent troops to the area. From that point, tensions mounted quickly. Unable to reach an agreement after a series of bilateral negotiations — and apparently disinclined toward ASEAN mechanisms (see Solingen, this volume) — the disputants referred the case to the International Court of Justice (ICJ) in 1998. Drawing on ambiguous historical maps, treaty agreements, and activities and claims from the pre-colonial period onward, in December 2002, the court recognized Malaysia as sovereign. Indonesia accepted the judgement.[12] However amicably resolved, this dispute both presaged subsequent, similarly intractable disputes (over the Malaysia/Indonesia border in Borneo and especially over other islands) and demonstrated how much relations had deteriorated since the 1970s.[13]

The ICJ decision resolved sovereignty only over the two disputed islands, not the underlying maritime boundary.[14] Since then, tension has percolated over the Ambalat region, also in the Sulawesi Sea off the land border between East Kalimantan and Sabah, and its seabed, likewise claimed by both countries and believed to contain large deposits of petroleum and natural gas. Jakarta claims Ambalat was part of the Bulungan Sultanate, incorporated into the country with independence in 1945; Malaysia bases its claim to Ambalat and the unprepossessing Unarang Reef on a disputed 1979 map and the 2002 ICJ judgment. While the dispute was less closely covered in Malaysian media, anti-Malaysia rhetoric in the Indonesian press kept tensions high, especially in early 2005 after Malaysia's state-owned Petronas announced its granting of a concession for oil exploration of that area to Shell. The Indonesian Government protested, even mobilizing warships and fighter jets in the area and building a lighthouse on Unarang Reef, as Indonesian media assailed Malaysian cupidity. Malaysia, too, sent gunboats to protect its interests and harassed Indonesian interlopers, despite leaders' calls for a diplomatic solution. Invoking the spectre of 1963, youth groups mobilized a "crush Malaysia" campaign and the Indonesian press branded the conflict "Konfrontasi II",[15] while a bilateral "hactivist war" sparked up in cyberspace. An April 2005 brush-up between a Malaysian and Indonesian warship — resulting in minor damage to both vessels — ratcheted up even more intimations of looming armed conflict. After diplomatic protests on both sides and a squabble between Malaysian Deputy Prime Minister Najib Tun Razak and Indonesian newspaper *Kompas*, things settled down. Malaysian Prime Minister Abdullah Ahmad Badawi, Indonesian President Susilo Bambang Yudhuyono, and their Foreign Ministers issued joint statements, made goodwill visits, and expressed their intent to resolve matters amicably. Anxious to avoid the expense and hassle of international arbitration, the two sides considered a joint oil exploration deal — but tensions persist still, with periodic further grandstanding and incidents, from harassment of fishermen to breaches of airspace. Aggravating the dispute was the fact that the surge of nationalism was politically useful: it helped to mask popular disgruntlement over Indonesia's continuing weakness, from the after-effects of the Asian financial crisis and political transition to the tsunami of December 2004, at a time when Malaysia — zealously deporting several hundred thousand Indonesian workers — seemed notably unsympathetic.[16]

Meanwhile, Indonesia's own crises of territorial integrity have complicated relations with Malaysia. Most obvious was the long-standing secessionist struggle in East Timor. Tun Razak's government lent clear, consistent support to Indonesia's annexation of East Timor in 1975, asserting that the territory's fate lay with Indonesia and helping to broker an agreement the following year. The stance — which stood in contrast to Malayan support, however surreptitious, for anti-Jakarta elements in Sumatra and Sulawesi in the 1950s[17] — was both to maintain a strong post-*Konfrontasi* bilateral relationship and out of shared concern for communist insurgency in the case of Timorese independence, given that Portugal and Macau were then under communist governments.[18] The Malaysian Government hence disapproved of efforts by local civil society activists who joined regional counterparts in pressuring the Indonesian state. Matters came to a head with the Second Asia-Pacific Conference on East Timor, held in Kuala Lumpur in November 1996: it was broken up by thuggish members of the youth wings of the ruling United Malays National Organisation (UMNO) and its coalition partners, and more than one hundred conference participants were detained or deported.[19]

The secessionist conflict in Aceh, too, heightened an already-fraught situation. Many Malaysians were sympathetic to the Acehnese or themselves of Acehnese (or at least Sumatran) descent. Aspects of Islam, from Malaysians studying in Acehnese religious schools to shared aggravation with the downplaying of religiosity under Indonesia's New Order *Pancasila* ideology, only reinforced those ties, especially with rising Islamization in Malaysia. Indonesia suspected Malaysia of supporting the banned separatist Gerakan Aceh Merdeka (Free Aceh Movement, GAM) either indirectly, as by providing a safe haven, or more directly, as by training militia members — indeed, GAM leadership appears to have operated sometimes out of Malaysia.[20] Anxious both to maintain cordial ties with Indonesia and to avoid a tide of refugees (but also per its usual practice), Malaysia generally refused to acknowledge Acehnese illegally in the country as political refugees. Still, 112 Acehnese asylum-seekers who landed in Penang and Kedah in 1991, about to be deported as illegal immigrants, were given the option of staying in Malaysia; some, in fact, had dual nationality.[21] Subsequently, yielding to the UN High Commission on Refugees as well as domestic and international human rights groups, Malaysia allowed several hundred Acehnese to remain in the mid-1990s — but after forty sought asylum in foreign embassies in Kuala Lumpur in late 1996, the Home Ministry warned that all would have their status revoked and be forcibly repatriated in case of "further trouble". Soon after, Acehnese, including seven under the protection of the UN High Commissioner for Refugees (UNHCR), were among tens of thousands of undocumented Indonesians rounded up for deportation amid the financial crisis, with hollow assurances that the Indonesian authorities would allow their safe return. Again in early 1998, around a hundred Acehnese escaped from a Malaysian detention camp during a riot; twelve crashed the gate of the UNHCR's compound in a truck, begging asylum, then a week later, several dozen broke into the diplomatic compounds of France, Switzerland, Brunei, and the United States. The UNHCR sheltered the asylum-seekers pending investigation; the United States followed the UN's lead. The others embassies allowed Malaysian police to remove the Acehnese, deeming them social and economic rather than political refugees, notwithstanding the tensions then in their home province.[22] Malaysian and international human rights groups vehemently condemned the Malaysian government's actions.[23]

But Acehnese were not the only ones flocking to Malaysia. Migration — and particularly illegal migration — has been a source of bilateral tension since the late 1970s. Cross-border migration has been in train much longer, however; Malay aristocrats encouraged it, for instance, in the nineteenth century, favouring culturally-similar Indonesian workers to the Chinese and Indian labour imported by the British, while Malay leaders in the early years of independence still favoured Indonesian migration to help maintain numerical superiority of ethnic Malays over others in Malaya. Problems arose as the number of migrants involved mounted, first in agriculture, then in the construction and service sectors by the 1970s — and especially as awareness of and antagonism to undocumented labour surged.[24] Malaysia is Asia's largest receiving state for migrant workers, not just from Indonesia (other key sources are Bangladesh, the Philippines, Pakistan, and Thailand), and has one of the largest percentages of foreign workers in the world. The concatenation of an increase in these flows since Malaysia stepped up export-led industrialization in the 1970s,[25] the fact that undocumented workers now outnumber legal ones by probably close to fifty per cent, and an increase in civil societal activism in light of Malaysia's scant labour safeguards, has honed tensions. The government has always placed employers' interests above those of workers, let alone migrant ones. Moreover, migrants make an easy scapegoat when crime, unemployment, or other evils rise, though the usual pattern is to make a show of curbing migration and shipping workers home, even while allowing other workers still to come or remain. All in all, "Malaysia needs these workers, but does not want them".[26] As a result, despite the push and pull factors encouraging a constant flow of workers, increasingly, "There is a general feeling among Indonesian people of being humiliated and dishonoured by Malaysia."[27]

Indonesian workers in Malaysia are paid minimal wages (lower than the norm, for instance, in Hong Kong or Singapore), are not expected or encouraged to integrate into society or immigrate permanently, and may face various forms of abuse. Basic laws for social security and workers' compensation encompass legal migrants (except those in the "informal" domestic sector), supplemented by provisions for housing for foreign workers, but enforcement is minimal and workers who press claims are likely to be fired and lose their legal status. Irresponsible recruiters are another problem — around five thousand undocumented Indonesian migrants allegedly drowned in the Strait of Malacca between 1990–95 due to their recruiters' negligence, for instance, and few arrange for written contracts, safety standards, or benefits.[28] More dramatically, with Indonesian women comprising the majority of domestic workers, cases surface with some regularity of battered maids fleeing their employers, killed or suicidal, or otherwise tormented, each time exacerbating tensions;[29] notes a local human rights activist, "domestic workers are among the most abused people in Malaysia."[30] Overall, Indonesian workers are concentrated in "3-D", or "dangerous, discriminatory and degrading", jobs, feeding Malaysian stereotypes of Indonesians as a whole. (It bears mentioning, though, that however much Indonesian activists or leaders complain of working conditions in Malaysia, the Indonesian state has hardly been a friend to labour, especially under the New Order. Agitation over labour matters, at least at the central government level, may be less issue-driven than a convenient bogey.)

Malaysia and Indonesia signed their first bilateral agreement on labour in Medan in 1984. It established official channels for recruiting Indonesian workers, previously all undocumented. Totally ineffective, the Medan Agreement was rescinded four years later and replaced with one leaving it to the Indonesian Embassy in Kuala Lumpur to legalize the status of workers on arrival by granting them passports; this arrangement, too, proved too unwieldy to work. Meanwhile, the ranks of both documented and undocumented workers (preferred, since employers could avoid social security payments) continued to grow, however spasmodic official recruitment. The Malaysian Government announced an initial amnesty period for employers of illegal aliens to register them in 1991–92, along with a minimum wage and other improvements. In the same period, the government launched *Ops Nyah* (Operation Go Away) to prevent illegal entry and purge undocumented workers. Around ten thousand Indonesians were deported in the first phase and another thousand detained in the next. Similarly vacillating efforts continued through the financial crisis of 1997, spurred by Malaysian fears of a surge of Indonesians fleeing their own country's economic collapse, despite a Memorandum of Understanding in 1996 and Exchange of Notes in 1998 to clarify terms and procedures for employment of Indonesian workers. That December, the Malaysian Government announced a programme of massive expulsion — though again mixed with selective exceptions and another amnesty period. Punctuating the crackdown were riots, especially of Acehnese at the Semenyih detention camp in March 1998 in which at least eight detainees and one police officer were killed.[31] By 1999, Malaysia agreed to accept Indonesian workers of all skill levels again.[32]

Yet the cycle restarted in 2001. The Malaysian Government again increased penalties for illegal migrants and their employers, capped work permits for foreign workers (instantly "re-categorizing" thousands of Indonesians as illegal, some of whom then rioted in February 2002 at two detention centres), and announced plans to repatriate ten thousand illegal Indonesian migrants each month.[33] In early 2002, Deputy Prime Minister Abdullah Badawi announced a halt to the employment of Indonesians and their replacement by other workers, as Mahathir clarified that under a new "Hire Indonesians Last" policy, Indonesians would be confined to the domestic and agricultural sectors. The hastily-designed policy was unviable, however, causing an immediate forty per cent drop in the number of construction workers (since Indonesians comprised up to seventy per cent of workers in the sector, eighty per cent of them undocumented) and was rescinded — though not before angering Indonesians. Labour and non-governmental organization (NGO) activists protested outside the Malaysian Embassy in Jakarta, parliamentarians castigated Malaysians' high-handedness, and Indonesian media invoked *Konfrontasi* and urged retaliation. Malaysia issued a travel advisory for its citizens and demanded Indonesian authorities take action against those whose protests jeopardized bilateral relations.[34] Negotiations continued: Malaysian and Indonesian authorities established provisions, for instance, to help illegal Indonesian workers sue for unpaid back wages,[35] then signed a preliminary bilateral migrant worker agreement in Bali in mid-2006.

Labour and human rights activists on both sides charged that this latest agreement legalized "modern slavery", especially for domestic workers, and appealed for international intervention. These claims echoed a broader "rights-based" approach then informing the ASEAN Declaration on the Protection and Promotion of the Rights of Migrant Workers, signed in Cebu in January 2007.[36] The agreement addressed the transportation of workers into Malaysia and their terms of work (eventually to include minimum standards for pay and hours), but not their protection, nor would they be covered by Malaysian labour laws.[37] These issues are hardly trivial: the Indonesian Embassy in Kuala Lumpur documented around 1,200 cases of abuse just of Indonesian domestic workers in 2006[38] and grants refuge to an average of 150–200 migrant workers each month.[39] And yet Indonesia showed "almost no interest in the treatment of its citizens abroad", at least until the 2000s.[40] At that point, Malaysia's "securitization" of illegal Indonesian migrant workers, in the face of an increase in crime rates in the 1990s[41] as well as fears about regional terrorist networks,[42] sparked renewed vendettas against illegal migrants (including another slipshod mass expulsion in mid-2002) and protests in response among the Indonesian public, press, and politicians.[43] Malaysian Law Minister Rais Yatim fumed that "Malaysians in general cannot tolerate the violent behaviour of the Indonesians who are being too extreme and ungrateful"— even having "the cheek to wave the Indonesian flag".[44]

Most migrant workers report having been arrested at least once, regardless of immigration status;[45] complaints of ill-treatment by police are rife; and conditions in detention camps are notoriously poor.[46] Mahathir's suggestion that police brutality in Malaysia was at least less severe than in Indonesia hardly soothed the ill-will such incidents generated.[47] Indeed all along, neither side has been either particularly accommodating or effective in enforcing the complex bureaucratic agreements reached, though Malaysian authorities insist that they take cases of abuse seriously.[48] Such blunders amidst anti–illegal immigrant sweeps as the erroneous detention by Ikatan Relawan Rakyat Malaysia (Malaysian People's Volunteer Corps, RELA) of the wife of the Indonesian cultural attaché to Kuala Lumpur and abuses against the Chairman of the local Indonesian Students Association, or plainclothes police's arrest and beating of an Indonesian referee in town for the Asian Karate Championship, have made Indonesians take increasing note of how their nationals fare in Malaysia. Countering Indonesian calls for diplomatic action and boycotts have been efforts by the Malaysian media to play up crimes by Indonesians, giving the erroneous impression that rising, especially urban, crime may be substantially attributed to the extent of migrant labour. And so the tensions persist, bringing bilateral ties, per Indonesian parliamentarian Andreas Pareira, to their lowest point since the 1960s.[49]

Transboundary environmental issues — with a clear economic backstory — are also contentious. Most obvious is "the haze": air pollution traced to burning of forested areas especially in Indonesia's Kalimantan and Malaysia's Sabah and Sarawak, in part for swidden agriculture, but also on a much larger scale especially by oil palm plantations (many of them Malaysian joint ventures) and logging concessionaires. (Illegal logging remains a mutual concern, as well.) The haze reached seriously dangerous proportions in 1997–98 (with as much as eight million hectares burned, or an area over 120 times the size of Singapore), but had happened before and has recurred since, posing significant health risks and economic and ecological costs.[50] Supplementing a 1997 ASEAN division of labour and plan of action to combat the haze, that December, Malaysia and Indonesia (with Brunei, the hardest-hit) signed a memorandum of understanding for disaster relief, including action on the haze.[51]

Shared borders and threats have pushed Malaysia and Indonesia toward new joint initiatives in other areas as well. Most obviously, their recent cooperation in counterterrorism efforts highlights the extent of convergence in overall foreign policy orientations, including common collaboration with Western powers.[52] It is worth noting, though, that Islam has never been a major premise for bilateral cooperation in the past, and Islam takes on a different political timbre in each state. That said, Islamic resurgence among the populations of both may reinforce long-standing transnational links among Islamic organizations and networks. Pundits pounce upon any evidence of terrorist ties, but also see potential instrumental value to religion in countering strains and bolstering cohesion. While the secular nature of both governments works against Islam's providing a sturdy basis for renewed "kinship", the prominence of Islam as a factor in international politics heightens the sense of shared interest — so the dimension warrants watching.[53]

Management and Resolution of Contentious Issues

The key bones of contention between Malaysia and Indonesia have historically concerned resources and alignments, configured variously. Both states understand not only their own stature, but also their relationship with one another, in large part through a regional lens; they vie for status, yet also together form a crucial axis of support for initiatives from the Non-Aligned Movement to ASEAN. Still, the primary engine for conflict resolution between Indonesia and Malaysia has been and continues to be bilateral negotiation, often at the very personalized level of top leadership. Even on matters of multilateral agreements, by the early 1970s, the states had begun to consult in advance, to hammer out regional initiatives on which both could agree.[54] Particularly since both Indonesia and Malaysia are central boosters for regionalism, their apparent hesitance to commit more fully to a multilateral approach likely resonates, perhaps obstructing the development of more robust multilateral institutions and capacities or even of less personalized norms for engagement.

Bilateral ties centre on annual consultations between the countries' heads of state and joint commission meetings chaired by the two Foreign Ministers, supplemented by mechanisms such as the General Border Committee. Still, as the Malaysian Foreign Minister describes, thanks to "friendship and goodwill", the Malaysian premier and Indonesian President "had on many occasions, gone beyond the conventional diplomatic practice and communicated directly with each other over the telephone on a number of pertinent international issues whenever there was a need for such consultations".[55] Such personal ties made a key difference especially in the 1970s: Tun Razak was less suspicious of Indonesian, and especially Javanese, intentions than Tunku Abdul Rahman had been; Hussein Onn, who succeeded Razak upon his death in 1976, stayed the course, bringing the bilateral relationship to a new level of amity. Even extensive mechanisms for military cooperation developed under his watch, from joint exercises to training on each other's territory to collaborative arms production and technology exchange.[56] The pattern of informal "four-eyed" meetings (coupled with a degree of Malaysian deference to Indonesian preferences) ensured a high level of policy congruence and cordiality at least through the early 1980s. Mahathir, however, put less effort into such endeavours than did Tun Razak or Hussein Onn,[57] favouring a more businesslike approach.[58] The shift, explains Liow, was from "calculated deference" under Razak and Hussein to "diplomatic nonchalance" under Mahathir, substantially eroding the relationship.[59] By the same token, then-President Habibie, for instance, cancelled a planned visit to Malaysia and voiced his concern when his friend Anwar Ibrahim was ousted and detained in 1998.[60] Leaders on either side since have made less clear an imprint, though Abdullah Badawi and Susilo Bambang Yudhoyono seem more inclined to diplomacy than grandstanding and are reputedly on quite friendly terms.

Democratization in Indonesia may have complicated bilateral relationship maintenance. Popular opinion carries more weight than previously, and the media are far less fettered (as their role in the Ambalat dispute makes clear). Also salient, though, is the new Indonesian Government's uneven performance at job creation, poverty reduction, and general economic development since the financial crisis, which makes work in Malaysia so alluring an option. The current high levels of Malaysian investment in Indonesia may thus serve a dual purpose by boosting job creation to keep Indonesians from migrating, thus mitigating controversy. Still, despite recurrent nativist rhetoric, Malaysia relies upon a high number of Indonesian workers to keep its own economy afloat, and the problems of illegal migration began in the thick of Indonesia's boom years.[61]

Beyond the level of individual leaders, including at the less official or Track II level, bilateral mechanisms continue to develop, buttressing the formal relationship. The two countries launched a series of dialogues in the late 1980s and early 1990s, for instance the Indonesia-Malaysia Youth Dialogue, premised on a sense of close but unfocused kinship. Discussions in these forums, though, betrayed inconsistencies in participants' understanding of their countries' affinities and a degree of mistrust — apparent also in the lack of further development, for instance, of military exchanges.[62] The Institute of Strategic and International Studies, Malaysia and the Centre for Strategic and International Studies, Jakarta, too, hold a semi-regular Indonesia-Malaysia Colloquium[63] and have proposed extending exchanges between these institutes and among students, artists, chambers of commerce, and others. At the 2006 colloquium, for instance, Malaysia's Syed Hamid Albar described a series of meetings, including visits of the Malaysian Prime Minister to Jakarta

that July and of his Indonesian counterpart to Malaysia the following
month; between senior officials on matters of education, recruitment of
domestic workers, and commodities trading; and with delegations of
Indonesia's ruling Partai Demokrat in Malaysia and Malaysia's UMNO
in Indonesia. He recommended further such initiatives, encompassing
undergraduates, youth wings of political parties, artistes, athletes, and
corporations.[64]

Indeed, diplomatic negotiations have been only one of several channels
for expressing and resolving grievances. The states themselves are hardly
monolithic; positions and interests as defined by the centre are certainly
not consistent throughout society. Civil society plays a largely independent
role in calibrating relations between the two states and their citizens
— and indeed, the Malaysia-Indonesia relationship evokes unusually high
and enduring attention. Dating back to *Konfrontasi* — when Indonesian
students advocated for anti-Malaysia rebels in Brunei and petitioned
Nehru against deployment of Gurkha forces there, while railway worker
and oil workers' unions protested Britain's suppression of Azahari's
Kalimantan Utara movement,[65] even as Malaysian students clamoured
(successfully) for campus army units through which to defend Malaysia
to the death[66] — organized, non-governmental interests have interceded
on both sides. More recently, for instance, the primary respondents to
the haze of 1997–98 were NGOs, partly within the framework of ASEAN
(which explicitly incorporated NGOs and indigenous people in its 1994
Strategic Plan of Action on the Environment), but not entirely.[67]

It is personal ties and broad awareness, fostered in large part by shared
language and proximity, that have especially encouraged Malaysian NGOs
to put Indonesia-related issues at the forefront of their internationally-
oriented initiatives. The fact that a young Malaysian activist was among
those killed in the November 1991 Dili massacre, for instance, helped to
catalyze engagement among those who knew him. Moreover, Malaysian
media cover events in Indonesia, including related to contentious issues
such as East Timor and Aceh, relatively well.[68] Those factors that tend
to spur Malaysians to engage transnationally — a personal or vicarious
connection (i.e., if a friend or popular figure is involved), a Muslim
connection, or a connection by way of a large migrant or refugee
population present in Malaysia — all point to concern for Indonesian
affairs among Malaysian activists, and Malaysians' presumed or real
knowledge of and affinity with Indonesians grants them legitimacy in
speaking out.[69]

A key area for civil societal involvement is in advocating for the rights of migrant workers. There is some degree of activism on the domestic and regional levels — efforts by human rights NGOs and unions to engage migrant workers (who are forbidden to unionize), for instance, or the advocacy of migrant worker group Tenaganita on fair, enforced recruitment and labour practices, or of women's groups on protection for domestic workers.[70] Yet these efforts remain relatively shallow for now on the Malaysian side, limited by ethnicism, since concern for Malaysia's fragile "ethnic balance" politicizes and constrains debate on immigration, and cultural relativism, as asserting international labour standards may brand activists as pawns of the West.[71] Indeed, civil society in Malaysia wields limited influence on any foreign policy outcomes. NGOs may raise issues and public awareness, and some participate alongside the government in humanitarian exercises, but their influence is "questionable".[72]

All the while, multilateral venues have been expanding, even if bilateral negotiation remains the primary channel for resolution of Indonesia-Malaysia conflicts. Such options may be especially appealing among forum-shopping "third sector" activists, who can capitalize on support from regional counterparts and established or developing norms and covenants, however sidelined they may be in bilateral institutions and domestic contexts. Meanwhile, Mahathir's efforts to position Malaysia as a Muslim world and global South leader, for instance in the Organisation of the Islamic Conference (OIC), may have slighted the much larger Indonesia, just as the latter was shifting from an inward focus on national resilience and a dormant foreign policy to reclaiming a more significant place on the international stage.[73]

Importantly, even as ASEAN as an institution is institutionalizing its norms on human rights and labour, immigration issues in particular — including questions of labour migration — still tend to be seen as appropriately handled bilaterally.[74] Better cooperation between Malaysian and Indonesian police and immigration officers would go far to stem illegal migration and ensure adequate treatment of Indonesian workers en route to and in Malaysia, while enforced minimum wage policies and similar provisions would not only encourage legal rather than illegal migration, but improve conditions of work for Indonesian labour. Moreover, policies regarding levels of employment and repatriation would be more viable and less provocative if bilaterally determined rather than unilaterally imposed, and more conclusive than the series of ad hoc arrangements thus far.[75] Such mechanisms could usefully include personal connections between top government leaders and civil society activists alike, alongside more regularized bilateral and multilateral channels. At the same time, the increasing density of formal ties across states in the region may facilitate alliances a step beyond the bilateral level, as with cooperation among Malaysia, Indonesia, and the Philippines to counter extremism and terrorism.

Bilateral Relations Broadly: Choppy, but the Ship Sails On

Bombast notwithstanding, Malaysia and Indonesia do coexist peaceably, driven largely by the inevitability of geography and shared cultural and religious heritage, but anchored in common membership in ASEAN, economic ties, and more. Ironically, that very shared heritage gives rise to a certain sibling rivalry. Indonesia and Malaysia spar for "big brother" status with each other, in the region, and in the multilateral organizations of which both are members. As a result, nationalism at times obstructs common purposes and vision. For instance, Indonesia accuses Malaysia of claiming ownership of the folk song *Rasa Sayang* (which Malaysia denies, though it features the tune, long a local favourite, in a tourism advertisement), *batik* cloth, *wayang* puppets, and other cultural legacies. Calls to copyright anonymous folk songs to prevent further such cultural incursions suggest the extent of Indonesians' frustration.[76] Indeed, explains one analyst, "Today's Malaysia and today's Indonesia may well underestimate how much they have grown away from each other, despite the common language and some common cultural base."[77] Increasingly since the 1980s, it is accepted international norms that govern Malaysia-Indonesia relations rather than mere appeals to brotherhood, yet a degree of symbiosis is inevitable.[78]

Both sides identify to some extent as *bangsa serumpun*, nations with shared roots. However, too much focus on shared heritage "tends to create irrational expectations from both sides about each other" and lends knee-jerk sentiment too much credence. Malaysians stereotype Indonesians as illegal workers, uneducated maids, and criminals; Indonesians see Malaysians as arrogant and condescending. Broadly speaking, neither side takes sufficiently into account the other's distinct experiences and objectives.[79] Both, too, are ambitious, not only for their own nation's development, but on a more abstract, regional level. Kahin characterizes Indonesia's posture at the time of *Konfrontasi*: "Among Indonesians there has developed a widely-based belief that because of their country's size and armed power, and because it won its independence through revolution, it has a moral right to leadership in Asia".[80] Since then, and especially under the premiership of Mahathir Mohamad in the 1980s and 1990s, Malaysia has developed comparable expectations, based not least on sheer entitled chutzpah.

Despite mutual high-level reassurances, relations thus remain somewhat "brittle".[81] Bilateral ties are still more contingent than institutionalized, and neither side seems sure of the other's genuine goodwill or commitment to reciprocity — whether "bilateralism" really means something more than involving two parties.[82] Much as *Konfrontasi* has been ascribed at least in part to Sukarno's grandstanding style and the verbal jousting between him and Tunku Abdul Rahman, which left little room for compromise,[83] a change in domestic mood — especially a rise in non-negotiable, emotional nationalism — can still dangerously curtail policy options or public support for particular positions. Indonesian foreign policy has from the start been guided by an anti-(neo)colonial and "independent and active" (*bebas-aktif*) framework;[84] nationalism is neither new among the forces structuring bilateral relations nor superseded by regional commitments. Malaysia, too, has a nationalist edge, honed under Mahathir's *Malaysia boleh!* (Malaysia can!) ethos and approach. Subsequent Prime Ministers have been less outspoken, but Malaysia's aspirations have hardly dimmed.

In sum, bilateral mechanisms are necessarily more significant than multilateral ones to the everyday functioning and specific arrangement of Indonesia-Malaysia relations, yet norms and mechanisms remain relatively fluid. While the two countries share a strong commitment to ASEAN and regional mechanisms, and indeed jostle for pre-eminence within these, the issues most problematic or pressing beg bilateral solutions. Even when a broader structure, for instance the ICJ, is involved in dispute mediation, the decision to use and abide by that framework remains a bilateral one — as is, of course, the decision *not* to leave dispute resolution to ASEAN. Moreover, despite real contributions from ever-more institutionalized and routinized formal bilateral structures, high-level, personal ties remain paramount. This dimension dates back to early days: after the strain and mistrust of *Konfrontasi*, it was personal visits — by the Tunku to Indonesia in March 1968 and by Suharto to Kuala Lumpur two years later — that truly signalled a new phase in the bilateral relationship and a return to the kinship framework temporarily lost.[85] Even during *Konfrontasi,* future Malaysian Prime Minister Tun Abdul Razak negotiated behind the scenes with less-antagonistic elements from the Indonesian military and government, while sustaining personal friendships with Foreign Minister Subandrio and others. Razak's deference to Indonesian nationalism and interests laid the groundwork for a closer, friendlier relationship.[86]

Given economic interdependence, shared challenges, and simple expedience, government leaders are pragmatic: they have a mutual vested interest in not letting disputes spin out of control. ASEAN provides a stable overall framework, but the real work of relationship building, and the substantive issues that could endanger that prevailing balance, are at the bilateral level. Both states' commitment to the relationship and their much-vaunted "sibling" identity, built upon years of interactions and both instrumental and human connections, lends their relationship deep meaning — and sets an upper limit on how far either can press its agenda. In other words, while a realist lens reveals both the impetus behind contested decisions and where a bilateral approach falls short, a constructivist lens suggests the shared understandings that really hold things together, however poorly codified these norms might be. Economic imbalances, regime changes, and the steady elaboration of civil society continue to complicate Malaysia-Indonesia relations and negotiations, yet despite hawkish rhetoric, contentious issues are far more likely to be resolved now and in the foreseeable future by consultation than confrontation.

NOTES

[1] At issue were Indonesia's support both of a rebellion in Brunei (where Partai Rakyat leader A.M. Azahari sought a pro-Indonesia, independent Kalimantan Utara comprised of Brunei, Sarawak, and North Borneo [Sabah]) and of anti-Malaysia elements in the territories to be annexed; Britain's hand in the scheme and in Malaysia's future; and personality and other conflicts. Sources of tension included Malaya's offering asylum to Indonesian rebel leaders, the Tunku's awkward role in negotiations over West Papua in 1960, the relative status of ethnic Chinese, and especially Indonesia's toleration of communism and Soviet assistance (both anathema in Emergency-era Malaysia). Indonesia's anti-western standpoint rendered the Malaysia issue too fraught for consultation to work, especially given the presence of British and American troops ready to come to Malaysia's defence. Moreover, the

spectre of Malaysia offered Sukarno a convenient means to distract public attention from a host of domestic difficulties. Already then, too, Malaya and Indonesia were competitors economically and for regional status; Malaya was outpacing Indonesia and would advance even further as an expanded, anticommunist Malaysia. The newly-formed Malaysia severed diplomatic relations with Indonesia, which declined to acknowledge the state, on 17 September 1963. Thailand looked after Malaysia's interests in Indonesia, and Egypt after Indonesia's in Malaysia, for the duration of the conflict. Both sides suffered economic losses from the decline in trade and both accepted foreign military assistance, Malaysia from Britain, Australia, and New Zealand; Indonesia from the USSR, China, and France, while lobbying the Afro-Asian nations (with some success) to censure Malaysia. Attempts to negotiate a ceasefire failed until first Singapore left the federation in August 1965, then Sukarno was ousted by coup the next month and Suharto came to power. For more on this historical and political background, see J.A.C. Mackie, *Konfrontasi: The Indonesia-Malaysia Dispute, 1963–1966* (Kuala Lumpur/New York: Oxford University Press, 1974); Ruhanas Harun, "Kerjasama dan Konflik dalam Hubungan Malaysia-Indonesia", in *Malaysia's Foreign Relations: Issues and Challenges*, edited by Ruhanas Harun (Kuala Lumpur: University of Malaya Press, 2006), pp. 52–61; George McTurnan Kahin, "Malaysia and Indonesia", *Pacific Affairs* 37, no. 3 (Autumn 1964): 253–70; Justus M. van der Kroef, "Indonesia, Malaya, and the North Borneo Crisis", *Asian Survey* 3, no. 4 (April 1963): 173–81.

The conflict between Indonesia and Malaysia ended officially with an agreement signed in Bangkok in August 1966. However, Malaysia remained initially wary of Indonesia's intentions and the New Order regime's stability. Its lingering suspicion of Indonesian arrogance and aggression soured relations for some time. For details on Malaysian suspicions vis-à-vis Indonesia, see Marvin Ott, "Malaysia: The Search for Solidarity and Security", *Asian Survey* 8, no. 2 (February 1968): 130; and Joseph Chinyong Liow, *The Politics of Indonesia-Malaysia Relations: One Kin, Two Nations* (London: Routledge 2005), pp. 110–12.

Formal ties perked up almost immediately, though, with the restoration of diplomatic relations (and even more after 1970), including agreements on educational exchanges, trade, shipping, fishing, and more within just the first couple of years. See Ruhanas, "Kerjasama dan Konflik dalam Hubungan Malaysia-Indonesia", pp. 62–63.

[2] Data are relatively uncertain. One recent estimate puts around 40 per cent of the over 6 million Indonesians who work abroad (legally or not) in Malaysia — around 2.4 million workers. This figure comes from "RI, Malaysia Relationship Seen Surviving the Odd Bump", *Jakarta Post*, 5 October 2007. Another report offers a more plausible 1.5 million workers; see Devi

Asmarani and Carolyn Hong, "Indonesia and Malaysia Spats Expected to Blow Over", *Straits Times*, 12 October 2007. Probably around half are legal: a contemporaneous report cites "almost 600,000" documented workers, with probably around the same number undocumented; see Kalinga Seneviratne, "Class Clash Mars Malaysia-Indonesia Ties", Asia Times Online, 6 September 2007 <http://www.atimes.com/atimes/Southeast_Asia/II06Ae01.html> (accessed 1 March 2009). For more information on Indonesian workers in Malaysia, see Syed Hamid Albar, "Opening Address by the Hon. Dato' Seri Syed Hamid Albar Minister of Foreign Affairs of Malaysia at the Third Malaysia-Indonesia Bilateral Colloquium", organised by the Institute of Strategic & International Studies (ISIS) in Kuala Lumpur, Malaysia, 18 July 2006 <http://www.kln.gov.my/?m_id=25&vid=242> (accessed 1 November 2007).

3   Richard Stubbs, "Subregional Security Cooperation in ASEAN: Security and Economic Imperatives and Political Obstacles", *Asian Survey* 32, no. 5 (May 1992): 404–5.

4   For more on an Indonesian perspective of Indonesian-Malaysian relations, see Ruhanas Harun, ed., *Malaysia's Foreign Relations: Issues and Challenges* (Kuala Lumpur: University of Malaya Press, 2006).

5   For details on these three periods in Indonesian-Malaysian relations, see Joseph Liow, *The Politics of Indonesia-Malaysia Relations: One Kin, Two Nations* (London: Routledge 2005).

6   For instance, Liow describes a shared concern for Chinese influence (particularly as concentrated in Singapore), the establishment of a commission to unify language and orthography, joint efforts against communist remnants in Borneo under a March 1967 security agreement, and launch of a General Border Committee — all apparently sincere signs of goodwill. See Liow, *The Politics of Indonesia-Malaysia Relations*, pp. 108–9.

7   Ibid., p. 159.

8   Michael Leifer, *Indonesia's Foreign Policy* (London: Allen & Unwin for the Royal Institute of International Affairs, 1983) p. 173.

9   Stubbs, "Subregional Security Cooperation in ASEAN", pp. 397–98, extends the argument: the economic and security imperatives that push Malaysia, Indonesia, and Singapore toward integration, especially in defence, are counterbalanced by political ones. The result is perennial strains, but not severe enough to compromise ASEAN stability.

10 Liow, *The Politics of Indonesia-Malaysia Relations*, pp. 118–20.

11 Ibid., pp. 120–24.

12 Among the primary grounds for the decision were British colonial measures to protect turtles and their eggs on the islands in the early 1900s, establishment of a bird sanctuary on Sipadan in 1933, and construction of light towers on both islands, still maintained by Malaysia, in 1962 and 1963. For details,

see David A. Colson, "Sovereignty over Pulau Ligitan and Pulau Sipadan (Indonesia/Malaysia)", *American Journal of International Law* 97, no. 2 (April 2003): 403–4; and J.G. Merrills, "Sovereignty over Pulau Ligitan and Pulau Sipadan (*Indonesia v Malaysia*), Merits, Judgment of 17 December 2002", *International and Comparative Law Journal* 52, no. 3 (2003): 797–802.

13 Liow, *The Politics of Indonesia-Malaysia Relations*, pp. 143–46.

14 Colson, "Sovereignty over Pulau Ligitan and Pulau Sipadan (Indonesia/Malaysia)", p. 405.

15 According to Justus M. van der Kroef, "Indonesia, Malaya, and the North Borneo Crisis", *Asian Survey* 3, no. 4 (April 1963): 173, the term *Konfrontasi* denoted "a pattern of intense diplomatic pressure, press campaigns, mobilization of public opinion and threat of military force". While tensions remained far lower this time around, the term was not entirely inappropriate in terms of substance, but too symbolically-laden to be at all neutral in its implications.

16 Asmarani and Hong, "Indonesia and Malaysia spats expected to blow over", *Straits Times*, 12 October 2007; Yang Razali Kassim, "ASEAN Cohesion: Making Sense of Indonesian Reactions to Bilateral Disputes", *IDSS Commentaries* 15/2005, 6 April 2005 <http://www.rsis.edu.sg/publications/Perspective/IDSS152005.pdf> (accessed 1 March 2009); Mokhzani bin Zubir, "Malaysia-Indonesia Relations Surmount Negative Publicity", *AsiaMedia*, 11 May 2005 <http://www.asiamedia.ucla.edu/article.asp?parentid=24566> (accessed 1 March 2009); Bill Guerin, "Sulawesi Sea Row Dredges Up Defenses", *Asia Times Online*, 9 March 2005 <http://www.atimes.com/atimes/Southeast_Asia/GC09Ae02.html> (accessed 1 March 2009); and Kalinga Seneviratne, "Indonesia Tests Ties with 'Arrogant' Neighbor", *Asia Times Online*, 19 March 2005 <http://www.atimes.com/atimes/Southeast_Asia/GC19Ae03.html> (accessed 1 March 2009).

17 At stake were not just shared anti-communism, but also ethnic ties: most Malaysians were Sumatran, unlike the mutually-resented Javanese in Jakarta. See Joseph Liow, "Tunku Abdul Rahman and Malaysia's Relations with Indonesia, 1957–1960", *Journal of Southeast Asian Studies* 36, no. 1 (February 2005): 96–100.

18 Liow, *The Politics of Indonesia-Malaysia Relations*, p. 127.

19 Max Lane, "Conference on East Timor Attacked", *Green Left Weekly*, 13 November 1996, p. 254.

20 Liow, *The Politics of Indonesia-Malaysia Relations*, pp. 150–51.

21 Ibid., p. 150.

22 Most likely, some really were primarily economic refugees, yet all could face persecution upon repatriation, given the poor human rights situation in Aceh. At least five hundred returned from Malaysia in late March 1998, for instance, were held incommunicado by the Indonesian military for questioning

(possibly including torture) regarding possible links with GAM. (Hundreds of GAM members had fled to Malaysia as counter-insurgency efforts stepped up in the early 1990s.) The UN deemed the Acehnese political refugees and had been seeking access to detention camps to interview them for some time, without success. See Amnesty International, "Asylum-seekers at Risk in Mass Deportation of Economic Migrants", *ASA 28/09/98*, 2 April 1998 <http://web.amnesty.org/library/Index/ENGASA280091998?open&of=ENG-333> (accessed 2 November 2007); *International Herald Tribune*, 11 April 1998; South *China Morning Post*, 10 April 1998.

23 For instance, Amnesty International 1998; groups such as the Indonesian Solidaritas Perempuan (Women's Solidarity) and Malaysian human rights group Suara Rakyat Malaysia (Suaram, Voice of the Malaysian People) likewise issued statements.

24 Liow, *The Politics of Indonesia-Malaysia Relations*, p. 147.

25 Indeed, the Malaysian Agricultural Planters Association and United Planting Association of Malaysia lobbied the government in the 1980s to open the sector up to foreign workers. See Ruhanas, *"Kerjasama dan Konflik dalam Hubungan Malaysia-Indonesia"*, p. 67.

26 Amy Gurowitz, "Migrant Rights and Activism in Malaysia: Opportunities and Constraints", *Journal of Asian Studies* 59, no. 4 (November 2000): 863–65.

27 The Habibie Center's Wahyutama, quoted in Seneviratne, "Indonesia Tests Ties with 'Arrogant' Neighbour".

28 Gurowitz, "Migrant Rights and Activism in Malaysia: Opportunities and Constraints", pp. 867–68.

29 Diaz Hendropriyono, "Indonesian Military Might Will Win Malaysia's Respect", *Jakarta Post*, 25 October 2007; Dewi Anggraeni, "Indonesian Domestic Workers in Malaysia: Common Language Belies Cultural Differences", *Jakarta Post*, 8 February 2006.

30 Yap Swee Seng, quoted in Seneviratne, "Class Clash Mars Malaysia-Indonesia Ties".

31 At the time, the Malaysian Government claimed there were over 800,000 illegal foreign workers in Malaysia, but unofficial estimates were as high as 1.5 million according to the *International Herald Tribune*, 11 April 1998. Local and Acehnese activists claimed at least thirty Acehnese died during or as a result of the riots; the police said five died on the scene and three, during deportation. See *International Herald Tribune*, 31 March 1998. That month alone, Amnesty International's 1998 Report observed that 11,000 immigrants were deported (at least some — including the Acehnese who fought back — with the cooperation of the Indonesian Government, and transported on Indonesian naval vessels), with plans to deport another 10,000.

[32] Gurowitz, "Migrant Rights and Activism in Malaysia: Opportunities and Constraints", pp. 866–67; Joseph Liow, "Malaysia's Illegal Indonesian Migrant Labour Problem: In Search of Solutions", *Contemporary Southeast Asia* 25, no. 1 (April 2003): 55–56; and Greg Felker, "Malaysia in 1998: A Cornered Tiger Bares Its Claws", *Asian Survey* 39, no. 1 (January–February 1999), p. 51.

[33] Liow, "Malaysia's Illegal Indonesian Migrant Labour Problem: In Search of Solutions", p. 50).

[34] Ibid., p. 58. Indeed, as Liow points out, Indonesians were incorrect in deeming themselves singled out by the strict new policies: they applied to workers of other nationalities, as well. However, Indonesians have born much of the brunt, if only by dint of numbers, and Malaysian rhetoric has been distinctly unkind. See Liow, "Malaysia's Illegal Indonesian Migrant Labour Problem", pp. 53–54.

[35] Mathias Hariyadi, "Susilo and Badawi sign deal on illegal immigrants in Malaysia," *AsiaNews*, 15 February 2005 <http://www.asianews.it/index.php?art=2572&l=en> (accessed 1 March 2009).

[36] See Isagani de Castro, "Bilateralism and Multilateralism in Malaysia-Philippines Relations" in this volume.

[37] Ridwan Max Sijabat, "RI-Malaysia labor agreement meets strong opposition", *Jakarta Post*, 19 May 2006.

[38] "RI, Malaysia relationship seen surviving the odd bump", *Jakarta Post*, 5 October 2007.

[39] Seneviratne, "Class clash mars Malaysia-Indonesia ties".

[40] Gurowitz, "Migrant Rights and Activism in Malaysia", p. 871.

[41] Indonesian workers have been convicted of both petty and more serious crimes. In 2001 alone, 1,051 were arrested on such counts (which is not to say all were convicted), far more than from any other foreign community, and Malaysian officials have reportedly found weapons in illegal migrant settlements in the peninsula and East Malaysia. Periodic riots involving Indonesian workers in and around detention centres since 1987 have only added to the sense of threat. See Liow, "Malaysia's Illegal Indonesian Migrant Labour Problem", pp. 49–50.

[42] For instance, planning for the October 2002 Bali bombing apparently took place in Malaysia.

[43] Liow, "Malaysia's Illegal Indonesian Migrant Labour Problem", pp. 44 and 48–51.

[44] Quoted in ibid., p. 51.

[45] Gurowitz, "Migrant Rights and Activism in Malaysia", pp. 868–69.

[46] See, for instance, *Tenaganita* [Women's Force], "Abuse, Torture and Dehumanized Treatment of Migrant Workers at Detention Centers", *Asian Migrant* 8, no. 4 (1995): 114–16.

47 Liow, "Malaysia's Illegal Indonesian Migrant Labour Problem", p. 51. Given
    the relative homogeneity of Malaysian Malays, Indonesians stand out amongst
    them more than do Malays in larger and more ethnically diverse Indonesia,
    even just by their accent. See Diaz Hendropriyono, "Indonesian Military Might
    Will Win Malaysia's Respect"; and Dewi Anggraeni, "Indonesian Domestic
    Workers in Malaysia: Common Language Belies Cultural Differences". This
    disparity is especially the case for Indonesian Christians, some of whom use
    their common ethnicity and language to proselytize among Malay Muslims
    — a crime in Malaysia, where all ethnic Malays are constitutionally defined as
    Muslim. See Liow, "Malaysia's Illegal Indonesian Migrant Labour Problem",
    p. 49 for details.
48 "Indonesian President on Fence-Mending Malaysia Visit", *AFP*, 10 January
    2008.
49 "Indonesia-Malaysia Relations at Lowest Point", *ANTARA News*, 10 January
    2008.
50 James Cotton, "The 'Haze' over Southeast Asia: Challenging the ASEAN
    Mode of Regional Engagement", *Pacific Affairs* 72, no. 3 (Autumn 1999):
    331–51; and George J. Aditjondro, "Suharto's Fires", *Inside Indonesia* 65
    (January–March 2001), pp. 14–15.
51 Cotton, "The 'Haze' over Southeast Asia", pp. 342–44.
52 It was the "war on terror" that provided grounds for Mahathir to resuscitate
    U.S.-Malaysia relations after 2002, floundering to some extent since Vice
    President Gore praised anti-government *Reformasi* protesters at the APEC
    meetings in Kuala Lumpur in 1998, even as Indonesia still resisted growing
    American pressure to fall into line. See Gilbert Rozman and Noah Rozman,
    "The United States and Asia in 2002: Needing Help against 'Evil'," *Asian
    Survey* 43, no. 1 (January–February 2003): 3–4.
53 Liow, *The Politics of Indonesia-Malaysia Relations*, pp. 138, 151–54, and 170–71.
54 Ibid., p. 126. Liow continues by offering the example of the Zone of Peace,
    Freedom and Neutrality (ZOPFAN), first tabled by Malaysia. By the time of
    ZOPFAN's ratification in 1976, its "determining character had transformed
    from the external power guarantee and non-aggression pacts of the original
    Malaysian proposal to the notion of regional resilience, which was identified
    and accepted as Indonesia's prescription for regional order.... Malaysia's
    willingness to allow the dilution of its original proposal in order to
    accommodate Indonesian perspectives was telling of its willingness to defer
    to Indonesian proclivities."
55 Syed Hamid Albar, "Opening Address by the Hon. Dato' Seri Syed Hamid
    Albar Minister of Foreign Affairs of Malaysia at the Third Malaysia-Indonesia
    Bilateral Colloquium".
56 Liow, *The Politics of Indonesia-Malaysia Relations*, pp. 128–29.

57   The Tunku and Sukarno held one another in relatively low regard, but remained cordial; Razak went so far as to invite Indonesian Foreign Minister Adam Malik to stay at his home for the duration of a 1971 visit. Less confident of productive ties with Malay-nationalist Mahathir, the Indonesian Government asserted a preference for Ghazali Shafie, principle interlocutor in Malaysian negotiations with Indonesia since *Konfrontasi* and himself not only of Sumatran origin, but related to Adam Malik, to succeed Hussein Onn. Indeed, Mahathir and Suharto reportedly got along rather poorly. See Liow, *The Politics of Indonesia-Malaysia Relations*, pp. 118, 163, and 132–33 for details.

58   Liow "Malaysia's Illegal Indonesian Migrant Labour Problem", p. 55; and Liow, *The Politics of Indonesia-Malaysia Relations*, p. 132.

59   Liow, *The Politics of Indonesia-Malaysia Relations*, p. 134.

60   Felker, "Malaysia in 1998", p. 52.

61   Liow, "Malaysia's Illegal Indonesian Migrant Labour Problem", pp. 59–60.

62   Liow, *The Politics of Indonesia-Malaysia Relations*, pp. 138–39.

63   Held in 1988 and 1990, the colloquium was next reprised only in 2006. Jusuf Wanandi, "Steps to Fostering a Valuable Dialog with Malaysia," *Jakarta Post*, 31 August 2006.

64   Syed Hamid Albar, "Opening Address by the Hon. Dato' Seri Syed Hamid Albar Minister of Foreign Affairs of Malaysia at the Third Malaysia-Indonesia Bilateral Colloquium".

65   Van der Kroef, "Indonesia, Malaya, and the North Borneo Crisis", p. 178.

66   *Straits Times*, 23 September 1963, 17 December 1964, 17 February 1965, 23 March 1965.

67   Cotton, "The 'Haze' over Southeast Asia", pp. 342–43.

68   Meredith Weiss, "Transnational Activism by Malaysians: Foci, Tradeoffs and Implications", in *Transnational Activism in Asia: Problems of Power and Democracy*, edited by Nicola Piper and Anders Uhlin (London/New York: RoutledgeCurzon, 2004), p. 133.

69   Ibid., pp. 139 and 142.

70   Gurowitz, "Migrant Rights and Activism in Malaysia", pp. 870–73 and 882.

71   Ibid., p. 864.

72   K.S. Balakrishnan, "The Role of Civil Society in Malaysia's Foreign Policy", in *Malaysia's Foreign Relations: Issues and Challenges*, edited by Ruhanas Harun (Kuala Lumpur: University of Malaya Press, 2006), pp. 36–37 and 40–41.

73   Liow, *The Politics of Indonesia-Malaysia Relations*, pp. 135–36.

74   Gurowitz "Migrant Rights and Activism in Malaysia", p. 871.

75   Liow, "Malaysia's Illegal Indonesian Migrant Labour Problem", pp. 58–59.

76   "No Brotherly Love", *The Economist*, 13 October 2007, p. 47. Equally hot-headed, Diaz Hendropriyono in "Indonesian Military Might Will Win Malaysia's Respect", in the *Jakarta Post*, proposes military build-up and reform as a more

effective long-term deterrent, sure to "make the government of Malaysia and its citizens be more careful in their action toward Indonesia".

77 Dewi Anggraeni, "Indonesian Domestic Workers in Malaysia: Common Language Belies Cultural Differences".

78 Ruhanas, "Kerjasama dan Konflik dalam Hubungan Malaysia-Indonesia", pp. 71–72.

79 Rizal Sukma, "Relations with Malaysia Require a Realistic Approach", *Jakarta Post*, 3 September 2007.

80 Kahin, "Malaysia and Indonesia", pp. 260–61.

81 "No brotherly love," *The Economist*, 13 October 2007.

82 See Etel Solingen, "Multilateralism, Regionalism, and Bilateralism: Conceptual Overview from International Relations Theory", in this volume.

83 For instance, Mackie, *Konfrontasi: The Indonesia-Malaysia Dispute, 1963–1966*; and van der Kroef, "Indonesia, Malaya, and the North Borneo Crisis", pp. 178–79.

84 Sukma, "The Evolution of Indonesia's Foreign Policy".

85 Liow, *The Politics of Indonesia-Malaysia Relations*, pp. 113–14.

86 Ibid., 116–17.

REFERENCES

Aditjondro, George J. "Suharto's Fires". *Inside Indonesia* 65 (January–March 2001): 14–15.

Amnesty International. "Asylum-seekers at Risk in Mass Deportation of Economic Migrants". ASA 28/09/98, 2 April 1998 <http://web.amnesty.org/library/Index/ENGASA280091998?open&of=ENG-333> (accessed 2 November 2007).

Anggraeni, Dewi. "Indonesian Domestic Workers in Malaysia: Common language Belies Cultural Differences". *Jakarta Post*, 8 February 2006.

Asmarani, Devi and Carolyn Hong. "Indonesia and Malaysia Spats Expected to Blow Over". *Straits Times*, 12 October 2007.

Balakrishnan, K.S. "The Role of Civil Society in Malaysia's Foreign Policy". In *Malaysia's Foreign Relations: Issues and Challenges*, edited by Ruhanas Harun. Kuala Lumpur: University of Malaya Press, 2006.

Colson, David A. "Sovereignty over Pulau Ligitan and Pulau Sipadan (Indonesia/Malaysia)". *American Journal of International Law* 97, no. 2 (April 2003): 398–406.

Cotton, James. "The 'Haze' over Southeast Asia: Challenging the ASEAN Mode of Regional Engagement". *Pacific Affairs* 72, no. 3 (Autumn 1999): 331–51.

Felker, Greg. "Malaysia in 1998: A Cornered Tiger Bares Its Claws". *Asian Survey* 39, no. 1 (January–February 1999): 43–54.

Guerin, Bill. "Sulawesi Sea Row Dredges Up Defenses". *Asia Times Online*, 9 March 2005 <http://www.atimes.com/atimes/Southeast_Asia/GC09Ae02. html> (accessed 1 March 2009).

Gurowitz, Amy. "Migrant Rights and Activism in Malaysia: Opportunities and Constraints". *Journal of Asian Studies* 59, no. 4 (November 2000): 863–88.

Hariyadi, Mathias. "Susilo and Badawi Sign Deal on Illegal Immigrants in Malaysia". *AsiaNews*, 15 February 2005 <http://www.asianews.it/index. php?art=2572&l=en> (accessed 1 March 2009).

Hendropriyono, Diaz. "Indonesian Military Might Will Win Malaysia's Respect". *Jakarta Post*, 25 October 2007.

"Indonesia-Malaysia Relations at Lowest Point". *ANTARA News*, 10 January 2008.

"Indonesian President on Fence-mending Malaysia Visit". *AFP*, 10 January 2008.

Kahin, George McTurnan. "Malaysia and Indonesia". *Pacific Affairs* 37, no. 3 (Autumn 1964): 253–70.

Lane, Max. "Conference on East Timor Attacked". *Green Left Weekly* 254, 13 November 1996.

Leifer, Michael. *Indonesia's Foreign Policy*. London: Allen & Unwin for the Royal Institute of International Affairs, 1983.

Liow, Joseph. "Malaysia's Illegal Indonesian Migrant Labour Problem: In Search of Solutions". *Contemporary Southeast Asia* 25, no. 1 (April 2003): 44–64.

———. *The Politics of Indonesia-Malaysia Relations: One Kin, Two Nations*. London: Routledge, 2005.

———. "Tunku Abdul Rahman and Malaysia's Relations with Indonesia, 1957–1960". *Journal of Southeast Asian Studies* 36, no. 1 (February 2005): 87–109.

Mackie, J.A.C. *Konfrontasi: The Indonesia-Malaysia Dispute, 1963–1966*. Kuala Lumpur/New York: Oxford University Press, 1974.

Merrills, J.G. "Sovereignty over Pulau Ligitan and Pulau Sipadan (*Indonesia v Malaysia*), Merits, Judgment of 17 December 2002". *International and Comparative Law Journal* 52, no. 3 (2003): 797–802.

Mokhzani bin Zubir. "Malaysia-Indonesia Relations Surmount Negative Publicity". *AsiaMedia*, 11 May 2005 <http://www.asiamedia.ucla.edu/article. asp?parentid=24566> (accessed 1 March 2009)."No Brotherly Love". *The Economist*, 13 October 2007, p. 47.

Ott, Marvin. "Malaysia: The Search for Solidarity and Security". *Asian Survey* 8, no. 2 (February 1968): 127–32.

"RI, Malaysia Relationship Seen Surviving the Odd Bump". *Jakarta Post*, 5 October 2007.

Rozman, Gilbert and Noah Rozman. "The United States and Asia in 2002: Needing Help against 'Evil'." *Asian Survey* 43, no. 1 (January–February 2003): 1–14.

Ruhanas Harun. "Kerjasama dan Konflik dalam Hubungan Malaysia-Indonesia". In *Malaysia's Foreign Relations: Issues and Challenges*, edited by Ruhanas Harun. Kuala Lumpur: University of Malaya Press, 2006.

Seneviratne, Kalinga. "Indonesia Tests Ties with 'Arrogant' Neighbor". Asia Times Online, 19 March 2005 <http://www.atimes.com/atimes/Southeast_Asia/GC19Ae03.html> (accessed 1 March 2009).

————. "Class Clash Mars Malaysia-Indonesia Ties". Asia Times Online, 6 September 2007 <http://www.atimes.com/atimes/Southeast_Asia/II06Ae01.html> (accessed 1 March 2009).

Sijabat, Ridwan Max. "RI-Malaysia Labor Agreement Meets Strong Opposition". *Jakarta Post*, 19 May 2006.

Stubbs, Richard. "Subregional Security Cooperation in ASEAN: Security and Economic Imperatives and Political Obstacles". *Asian Survey* 32, no. 5 (May 1992): 397–410.

Sukma, Rizal. "The Evolution of Indonesia's Foreign Policy: An Indonesian View". *Asian Survey* 35, no. 3 (March 1995): 304–5.

————. "Relations with Malaysia Require a Realistic Approach". *Jakarta Post*, 3 September 2007.

Syed Hamid Albar. Opening Address by the Hon. Dato' Seri Syed Hamid Albar Minister of Foreign Affairs of Malaysia at the Third Malaysia-Indonesia Bilateral Colloquium. Organised by the Institute of Strategic & International Studies (ISIS) in Kuala Lumpur, Malaysia, 18 July 2006 <http://www.kln.gov.my/?m_id=25&vid=242> (accessed 1 November 2007).

Tenaganita [Women's Force]. "Abuse, Torture and Dehumanized Treatment of Migrant Workers at Detention Centers". *Asian Migrant* 8, no. 4 (1995): 114–16.

Van der Kroef, Justus M. "Indonesia, Malaya, and the North Borneo Crisis". *Asian Survey* 3, no. 4 (April 1963): 173–81.

Wanandi, Jusuf. "Steps to Fostering a Valuable Dialog with Malaysia". *Jakarta Post*, 31 August 2006.

Weiss, Meredith. "Transnational Activism by Malaysians: Foci, Tradeoffs and Implications". In *Transnational Activism in Asia: Problems of Power and Democracy*, edited by Nicola Piper and Anders Uhlin. London/New York: RoutledgeCurzon, 2004.

Yang Razali Kassim. "ASEAN Cohesion: Making Sense of Indonesian Reactions to Bilateral Disputes". *IDSS Commentaries* 15/2005, 6 April 2005 <http://www.rsis.edu.sg/publications/Perspective/IDSS152005.pdf> (accessed 1 March 2009).

8

Indonesia-Singapore Relations

Natasha Hamilton-Hart

The Singapore-Indonesia relationship is commonly described as being subject to sharp fluctuations, shifting between periods of tension and relatively close cooperation. A conventional schema would commence with the period of hostility during Indonesia's *Konfrontasi* (Confrontation) of Malaysia from 1963 to 1966, which also targeted Singapore by virtue of its temporary inclusion in Malaysia from 1963 until 1965.[1] Diplomatic relations improved with the change of regime in Indonesia, when President Sukarno was ousted by Suharto's New Order government in 1966, deteriorated sharply when Singapore executed two Indonesian marines in 1968, and returned to an increasingly close and cooperative footing from 1973 until the end of the New Order in 1998. Under four successive Indonesian Presidents since 1998, relations have been subject to a number of acerbic exchanges and occasionally obstructive policies, interspersed with declarations of cooperative intent and ongoing close relations in many functional areas.

The current state of bilateral relations appears to be somewhat prone to tension, beneath a veneer of official protestations to the contrary. As detailed below, a number of contentious issues remain outstanding, and progress towards resolving them has stalled since 2007. In the Indonesian press and Parliament, disputes with Singapore over seemingly mundane issues have frequently been magnified, and senior Indonesian politicians have accused Singapore of insincerity in its dealings with Indonesia. Singapore, for its part, has remained officially open to cooperation, but has taken a relatively inflexible line on several contentious issues. As noted with regard to Singapore's relations with its neighbours, bilateral issues "are often kept on hold merely to avoid open conflict".[2]

This chapter examines patterns of cooperation and conflict between Indonesia and Singapore with a view to understanding why the relationship appears prone to recurrent uneasiness and, during certain periods, difficulty in resolving matters of mutual interest. A number of different potential explanatory factors are examined. The first section asks whether Singapore is in a fundamentally vulnerable position with regard to Indonesia due to structural, historical, or demographic factors, and whether this might explain the apparent sensitivities surrounding the bilateral relationship. The second section looks at the role domestic political factors may play in driving the relationship, examining in particular the idea that the vagaries of Indonesia's domestic politics create tensions in the bilateral relationship during periods of political contestation or instability in Indonesia. The third section examines the structure of interests which link Indonesia and Singapore, asking whether irritants in the relationship are in fact out of line with the mix of complementary and competing interests that characterize the interlinked political economies of the two countries.

The principal arguments of this chapter can be briefly summarized. First, bilateral tensions are often magnified out of proportion, both by policymakers and by scholarly accounts that view irritants in isolation from the large areas of complementarity and cooperation that exist. Second, the bilateral relationship is not inherently prone to exceptionally high levels of tension and instability. Most of the structural and historical factors commonly assumed to influence the relationship are not, in fact, determinative. Certain structural tensions in the relationship do exist, but they have operated over a longer time period than the post-1965 era, and are not fundamentally rooted in culture or demographics. Third, the pattern of cooperation and contestation is driven as much by Singaporean strategies, aspirations, and politics as by Indonesian political shifts and leadership characteristics. Politicians on both sides have at times adopted a selective interpretation of the relationship, presenting it as more sensitive than it is, but the same fault need not be repeated in scholarly analyses.

It should be noted at the outset that an emphasis on the irritants in the relationship betrays a Singapore-centric orientation. The siege mentality which many accounts have attributed to Singaporean policymakers may capture the flavour of Singaporean self-representations with regard to its nearest neighbours, but the view of the bilateral relationship as seen from Indonesia is noticeably different. With a few exceptions, while Indonesia is depicted as presenting at least a latent threat for Singapore in work on Singapore's foreign relations, which tend to dwell on the irritants in the relationship, Indonesian accounts pay much less attention to the irritants and treat them as having much less significance. To take just one example, the pronouncement by Indonesian President Habibie that Singapore was a "little red dot" has been repeated ad infinitum in accounts of Singapore's foreign relations, and taken as an indicator of underlying ethnically-based hostility. Official Singaporean actors seem to have seized on the epithet with enthusiasm, using it as the title of a volume of quasi-official memoirs by Singaporean diplomats, and in speeches.[3] In contrast, most accounts of Indonesian foreign policy covering post-Suharto presidencies barely mention Singapore at all, and not in terms that suggest hostility.[4]

The Limits of Asymmetric Vulnerability

In most accounts of the bilateral relationship, the baseline around which relations have fluctuated is presented as fundamentally precarious, or inherently subject to tension, due to both history and "realist" structural factors such as size and relative power.[5] These inherent tensions are then seen as either skilfully contained or exploited, depending on domestic political shifts and leadership personality. But to what extent does the bilateral relationship between Singapore and Indonesia rest on structural characteristics that create a background of suspicion and potential instability? In the view of one of the most well-known scholars of Southeast Asian regional relations, the "inherent vulnerability" of Singapore is repeatedly emphasized as the essential driver of Singapore's foreign policy, a vulnerability that is presented as both objectively real — based on concrete asymmetries in territory, population, and resources — and psychologically embedded in the minds of Singapore's leaders.[6] In contrast, another major study of Singapore's foreign relations argues that "Singapore has outlived its archrealist outlook in foreign policy. Whereas the country remains small both in terms of land area and population size, there is a very real sense in which such smallness is compensated by its international linkages and presence."[7]

This section argues that Singapore is not exceptionally bound by imperatives for a defensive self-help posture, for reasons that include, but go beyond, being able to "compensate" for its geographic smallness. One reason is that asymmetries between the two countries are not as significant as they might at first glance appear. Of course, Indonesia is vastly bigger in terms of territory, natural resources, and population, and this makes possible (or, on some issues, requires) more inward-looking economic and security policies. However, other than the different degrees to which each country is impelled to look outwards, there are few necessary implications that follow from these structural asymmetries.

In terms of military power, the asymmetry is arguably not that great under most realistic scenarios. Singapore's military is vastly more modern, better equipped for conventional and high-technology warfare, and absorbs a much higher proportion of the national budget than Indonesia's.[8] The extremely small territorial size of the country, which means the lack of any option of strategic retreat when faced with an all-out attack aimed at territorial conquest, is undeniable. But the relevance of this vulnerability has to be assessed against the conceivable interest of either of Singapore's near neighbours in launching a military bid for Singapore's territory. War is far from being obsolete in the modern world system, but conditions which arguably make it unlikely — including an absence of natural resources, a knowledge and services-based economy, and shared fundamental interests in integration in a liberal international economy — apply in the case of Singapore and its neighbours.[9] This suggests that the international environment Singapore inhabits looks more like the world as envisaged by liberal international relations theorists than proposed by power-based realists, who see the self-help imperative as overriding. For other marked asymmetries between the two countries — in population and in economic wealth per capita — it is not clear why they should have a determinative influence on bilateral relations. Indeed, when other bilateral relationships involving close neighbours of very different size and wealth are considered, such asymmetries do not seem to be associated with particular tendencies towards instability or latent insecurity. Based simply on structural endowments, Brunei, rather than

Singapore, should be the Southeast Asian country with most reason to worry about its neighbours' intentions — and while Brunei did initially view Indonesia with a great deal of suspicion (Bruneian passports were not valid for travel to Indonesia until 1984), the rhetoric of insecurity does not heavily mark Brunei's foreign or security policies, or scholarly accounts of them.[10]

The idea that Singapore is inherently vulnerable vis-à-vis its neighbours frequently gains support through references to the effects of demographics and history. In this regard, two factors surface repeatedly in accounts of Singapore's relations with Indonesia: the differences in the ethnic and religious make-up of the two countries, and the legacy of Indonesia's *Konfrontasi* of Malaysia in the early 1960s. To what extent can either of these factors be seen as elements that make the relationship a fundamentally precarious one, framed by a background of insecurity? Here I argue that while both things do, at times, colour the relationship, they gain force not as exogenous factors confronting the two parties, but largely through a selective interpretation of history, active propagation of ideas about ethnically-based hostility, and certain features of Singapore's political economy. Neither demography nor history, on its own, is determinative.

In the case of the demographic characteristics of Singapore — the so-called "Chinese dot" in a "sea of green" — there seem to be two ways in which this "structural" factor has played out in the relationship with Indonesia. First is through the association drawn between ethnic Chinese and communism (and communist China) in the minds of many Indonesian policymakers, particularly influential military leaders, during the Cold War.[11] This belief clearly did circulate for some years, but its application to Singapore — a thriving capitalist hub where the political left had been sidelined since the early 1960s — is so at odds with reality that it cries out for explanation, rather than being a meaningful explanatory factor. This should be more apparent when we consider the second way in which ethnicity figures in the bilateral relationship — through an association with business enterprises seen by many in Indonesia as parasitic. The political marginalization and recurrent scapegoating of ethnic Chinese in Indonesia developed out of government policy in the late colonial era and deepened under Suharto's New Order.[12] Although much less pronounced after the deadly riots in Jakarta in May 1998, there remains some potential for Indonesian politicians to mobilize political support by resurrecting popular antagonism towards ethnic Chinese.

Such popular antagonism, however, cannot sensibly be considered a structural factor conditioning the Indonesia-Singapore relationship. First, anti-Chinese sentiments in Indonesia are clearly a political artefact, not an intrinsic element of Indonesian nationalism or culture. Second, any link to Singapore in the popular imagination is rooted less in perceptions of shared *ethnic* culpability linking Indonesian Chinese and Singapore than in the actual business relationships that have developed between the two countries. As discussed below, aspects of Singapore's political economy and the deliberate strategies adopted by both Singaporean and Indonesian players do generate conflicts of interest and resentment, but we have few reasons to see the association with ethnicity as anything other than partial and circumstantial. For the most part, racialized anti-Chinese sentiments in Indonesia have been directed at Indonesian Chinese, not Chinese in Singapore, Malaysia, or elsewhere. When tensions arise in the bilateral relationship, ethnicity sometimes becomes a convenient hook on which to hang grievances, but it is hard to find instances where it plausibly generated these grievances.

If we turn to a second necessarily perceptual factor, the historical legacy of Indonesia's *Konfrontasi* of Malaysia, again it makes more sense to this as a product of political and social action rather than an exogenous background factor conditioning the relationship. All historical events are open to competing interpretations, but *Konfrontasi* must rate as one where the "lessons" to be drawn from it are particularly contestable. What Singapore learnt from *Konfrontasi* may indeed have been that its neighbour has, at the very least, a potentially aggressive sense of entitlement in the region and, plausibly, strong expansionist impulses. However, *why* Singapore learnt this lesson should demand explanation, given several aspects of *Konfrontasi* that lend themselves to a very different interpretation of what the whole event meant for Singapore, and how it might have been remembered.

First, *Konfrontasi* was never aimed at Singapore per se. Sukarno's grievance was with the United Kingdom and Malaysia's Prime Minister Tunku Abdul Rahman. Second, Indonesia had in fact accepted the formation of Malaysia in principle, and Sukarno's later escalation of the conflict was sparked at least as much by obstinacy and bungling on the part of British officials (and the Tunku's weakness in dealing with them), as any exaggerated sense of pride or entitlement that Sukarno may have had.[13] Third, the military aspects of the conflict were very limited, particularly in terms of the impact on Singapore: Singaporean casualties were very low (extraordinarily low by the standards of interstate warfare), and the military effort by Indonesia was always half-hearted. Fourth, there is a strong case for arguing that the escalation of *Konfrontasi* was an outgrowth of Indonesian domestic politics at the time, rather than any enduring feature of the regional balance of power — and support for *Konfrontasi* by different Indonesian players rapidly diminished as domestic political payoffs from the venture began to crumble.[14]

While *Konfrontasi* does stand as a concrete instance of armed hostility experienced by Singapore, its place in the psyche of Singaporean policymakers (or some of those who write about them) is far from self-explanatory. Two points of comparison underscore the need to treat "history" as endogenous in the relationship between the two countries. First, while *Konfrontasi* is purposefully, and repeatedly, re-remembered with very selective filters, Singapore's role in the subversion of Indonesia led by the United States — which produced thousands of civilian casualties, as compared to the three who died in the bombing of a building by Indonesian marines in Singapore — is noticeably forgotten.[15] Second, the comparison with Israel, which Singapore has courted, should in fact serve to underscore the degree to which Singapore enjoys a secure international position.[16] Since it became an independent state in 1965 none of Singapore's neighbours have contested its right to exist, Singapore has fought no wars with its neighbours, and, since 1967, Singapore and Indonesia have been founding members of the region's most enduring organization, the Association of Southeast Asian Nations (ASEAN). The sharp difference on every point with Israel makes the comparison between the two countries both misleading and, when used by political leaders, provocative.

Although it remains contentious as to whether the kind of multilateralism enjoined by ASEAN has brought about a regional security community, in the sense of its members having stable expectations of peaceful dispute resolution among themselves, most accounts of the regional organization argue that it has served to embed shared interests, trust, and habits of cooperation.[17] In the early 1990s, a scholarly account persuasively argued that, "ASEAN has indeed become a security community in the sense that its members do not foresee the prospect of resorting to armed confrontation among themselves to resolve existing bilateral disputes."[18] Singapore's defence posture and some elements of regional arms acquisitions policies are clearly at odds with this idea, so there are potential grounds for scepticism about claims that ASEAN is actually a security community.[19] Nonetheless, shared membership of what on many indicators is one of the world's most successful regional organizations should underscore the degree to which it is unrealistic to see the Singapore-Indonesia relationship as shadowed by any threat to the sovereignty and survival of Singapore emanating from its neighbour.

Singapore as Hostage to Indonesian Politics?

The intermittent prominence of contentious issues on the bilateral agenda has led many accounts to imply that the rise and fall of tensions between the two countries has much to do with the state of Indonesian domestic politics. In this line of argument, the more Indonesian domestic politics are contested or unstable, the more disputes with Singapore are either created or become magnified, as challengers for power (or incumbents defending their position) seize upon disputes with Singapore to shore up their political position. There is some prima facie correspondence between periods of political contestation in Indonesia and heightened tensions with Singapore. Certainly, the long period of good bilateral relations during the authoritarian rule of President Suharto has often been noted, with an explicit link made not only with Suharto's personal leadership style but the "stability" (more accurately, enforced depoliticalization) of Indonesian politics under his rule.[20] An implication of such accounts is that the return of democratic politics in Indonesia since 1998 is not coincidently related to an increase in disputes and greater difficulty in cooperation on matters of mutual interest. However, while the cases discussed in this section do show some link to new opportunities for Indonesian actors to voice discontent since democratization, for the most part they do not suggest that democratic contestation in Indonesia is related to a more combative foreign policy orientation.[21]

The list of contentious bilateral issues that have led to acrimonious statements or obstructive actions in the last decade mostly relate to Indonesian grievances or complaints. Tensions in the relationship have arisen over government-linked Singaporean investments in Indonesia, complaints over exports of sand and granite from Indonesia to Singapore, Singapore's previous non-publication of trade statistics between the two countries (widely considered to reflect Singapore's concern not to advertise the extent of smuggling that occurs), the limited support Singapore provided Indonesia during the financial crisis of 1997–98, the use of Singapore as financial and medical haven by those accused of corruption in Indonesia, and cases of abuse of Indonesian domestic workers in Singapore.[22] The periodic problem of "haze" — smoke from forest fires in Indonesia that spreads to Singapore — has also been a somewhat contentious issue, as Singapore has pressed for the ratification by Indonesia of an ASEAN treaty on the prevention of transboundary haze before agreeing to more extensive technical and financial aid to Indonesia on the issue. While the treaty was drawn up in 2002, it has yet to be ratified, in part because some Indonesian lawmakers have wished to see the conclusion of a criminal extradition agreement with Singapore as a quid pro quo.[23]

At times, it looked as if progress was being made on these issues. For example, the longstanding Indonesian request for an extradition treaty with Singapore was in-principle agreed to in 2005, as part of a package that would include a Defence Cooperation Agreement (DCA). The extradition treaty and defence cooperation package was signed in April 2007 and would have provided extensive training facilities for Singapore's navy and air force in Indonesia as well as exchange of military technology. Opposition parties in the Indonesian Parliament, however, argued that the agreement would violate Indonesian sovereignty and allow Singapore to set up a military base in the country.[24] The issue remained mired in what were ostensibly disputes over how the training would be carried out, and featured prominently in the Indonesian press during the year. By October, the Indonesian Foreign Minister was reported as saying that the agreement had been "put aside" and talks on implementation would resume "after a cooling of diplomatic tension" over the issue.[25] The Indonesian Defence Minister had at times said that Singapore was deliberately stalling the agreement because it did not want the extradition treaty, and also claimed that it had been dropped by Singapore after Lee Kuan Yew's visit to Indonesia in mid-2007.[26] In turn, the Singapore Defence Minister claimed, "Singapore stands ready to honour this package of agreements", and implied that Indonesian domestic politics lay behind the delay:

> Unfortunately, this package has run into difficulties. We recognise that the domestic conditions in Indonesia may not allow for the package of agreements to be ratified at this time. Both Singapore and Indonesia have therefore agreed that the best option for both countries is to put the DCA and the ET [extradition treaty] aside for now.[27]

In several statements, the Singapore Government has repeatedly insisted that it remains willing to stand by the agreements, but is insistent that the DCA and extradition treaty cannot be treated as separate issues and that the government is not open to revising the contents of the agreements.

During 2007, the Indonesian press also gave a great deal of attention to calls for a buy-back of some Indonesian corporate assets which Singaporean Government–linked companies or investment funds had bought into in the wake of the financial crisis. At various times since these purchases were made, popular protests against the acquisitions had gained attention. While the street protests and political actors who criticized the deals focused on issues of possible job losses and sovereignty, it has been the decisions of Indonesian Government agencies that eventually led to projected sales of key purchases. These decisions involved a ruling by Indonesia's competition watchdog in November 2007 that accused Singapore-invested telecommunications companies of anti-competitive practices, and a regulation issued by the Indonesian central bank requiring a "single presence" by investors in the financial sector. As a result of the "single presence" policy, a subsidiary of Singapore's Temasek Holdings concluded an agreement to sell its majority stake in one of the large Indonesian banks it had invested in.[28] Another major sale of an Indonesian asset by a Singaporean Government–linked company was also announced during 2008, as an Indonesian court ruling in May upheld the competition watchdog's earlier finding of anti-competitive practices involving two Temasek-linked companies, SingTel and STT. Both of the Temasek-linked companies insisted they had not breached Indonesian laws and said they would make every effort to protect their interests in the two Indonesian telecommunications companies. However, STT did sell its large stake in an Indonesian telecommunications company, despite earlier filing an appeal to the Indonesian Supreme Court, arguing that, "Temasek has not broken any laws and will vigorously contest all allegations against us."[29]

At the governmental level, both sides insist that the relationship is good, and Indonesian Presidents since 2001 have refrained from making the kind of disparaging remarks about Singapore that the two short-serving Presidents after Suharto occasionally voiced. Is it reasonable to conclude, then, that interests basically are in alignment but that the relationship founders, at least somewhat, when political competition or instability in Indonesia lead to Singapore being used as a convenient scapegoat or lightening rod? This seems to accord with the broad pattern of ups and downs in the relationship, which was at its smoothest in the decades after Suharto consolidated his authoritarian hold on power (and therefore domestic political competition between contending players in Indonesia ceased to be a factor). As Singapore's former Prime Minister, Lee Kuan Yew, said in relation to the stalled DCA in 2007, "the difficulty is not between the Singapore government and the Indonesian government, the difficulty is within Indonesia's political process", with objections being played out as part of "political theatre" on the Indonesian side.[30] To some extent, this explanation of shifting levels of tension in the relationship also fits with the emphasis on personality and leadership that figures in many accounts.[31] As a Suharto-era former Indonesian Ambassador remarked, relations were "basically good, primarily due to the personal rapport between the two nations' leaders."[32]

Domestic politics or leadership personality-led explanations for periods of tension in the relationship assume an underlying popular antipathy towards Singapore, which is then either contained or exploited depending on the nature of political competition within Indonesia or idiosyncratic preferences of leaders. Certainly, while Singapore is a peripheral issue for most Indonesians most of the time, many might well concur with the view of a former Ambassador that, "Singapore tends to be self-centred, lacks empathy ... [and is] highly materialistic, is not a 'warm-hearted personality' and therefore views Indonesia only in terms of 'profit or no profit'."[33] Singapore has made efforts to redress this perception, increasing its support for the social sector, humanitarian relief, and a greater role for civil society contacts.[34] However, as shown by the willingness on the part of some Indonesian newspaper editors and politicians to market popular nationalism and create something of a furore over the proposed DCA, the mobilizing potential of the Singapore issue is clearly still alive.

What is less clear is how much this kind of focus on Indonesian politics explains elements of tension in the bilateral relationship. Many different players, both foreign and domestic, can and have served as lightening rods for popular discontent or mobilizing instruments for politicians. Disputes with Malaysia, for example, seem to offer just as much "mobilizing potential" in Indonesian domestic politics. It would be premature to write off such disputes as so much "political theatre" on the Indonesian side without examining the ways elements of tension are generated. It is also worth noticing that the recent forced divestments by Singapore Government–linked companies were not in any obvious way related to Indonesian domestic political competition: popular protests against the acquisitions had in fact been overridden earlier, and it was independent government agencies — the courts, anti-competition agency, and the central bank — which issued the rulings that eventually led to the divestments.

A focus on Indonesian politics also places Singapore in a curiously reactive role, making it appear that fluctuations in the relationship are determined primarily by *Indonesian* leadership and domestic political conditions. Certainly, there are clear differences between the two countries in terms of how domestic politics are likely to affect bilateral relations. Indonesia has undergone three major shifts in its system of government since the 1950s, and domestic pressures on its government have at times been significant. In contrast, Singapore's domestic political conditions have only minimally varied since 1965, and the governing party in power during the whole of this period has not faced any significant domestic challenges or rivals. Nonetheless, a focus on political conditions within Indonesia leaves unanswered key questions about Singapore's own priorities. Why, for example, has Singapore insisted on making an extradition treaty contingent on cooperation in defence matters?[35] Singapore's inflexible insistence that the two things must be treated as a package is in itself an unusual request, and it should prompt an examination of the role Singapore's interests, strategies, and actions play in determining the tenor of the relationship.

A "Normal" Mix of Competing and Complementary Interests?

The relationship between Indonesia and Singapore is not inherently precarious or prone to instability, but it remains that the interests of each are entwined in ways that throw light on the varying mix of cooperation and tension that marks the relationship. This section argues that a large area of complementarity between the national interests of both countries is complicated by some fundamentally competing political economy strategies at the national level, and the divergent capacities of each country to harness the interests and activities of private players to national goals.

Before detailing the ways in which there is some structural tension in aspects of the political economy of the bilateral relationship it is important to note the significant degree of alignment in the interests and perspectives of the two countries. On security issues, since the 1960s, both have shared a strong mutual interest in regional stability supported by the limited regionalism of ASEAN and predicated on an acceptance (in practice, if not in rhetoric) of the desirability of pro-Western security arrangements.[36] With the end of the Cold War, both countries endorsed the creation of mechanisms to anchor the United States in the region and incorporate China into a regional institutional framework.[37] In the early 1990s, it was noted that "the trends in the ASEAN region's security environment have generally served to emphasize the common interests of Malaysia, Indonesia, and Singapore", an observation reinforced by significant bilateral cooperation on defence matters since the 1980s.[38] As late as 1999, a review of bilateral tensions in Southeast Asia did not include the Singapore-Indonesia relationship in its list of sometimes-troubled relations.[39]

Economic trends since the 1980s, which saw a shift to a significantly more externally-oriented economy on the part of Indonesia, have also served to reinforce incentives for cooperation, including through the development of more powerful domestic economic constituencies whose interests are served by higher levels of economic openness and cooperation.[40] In most respects, the "new" items that have figured on the bilateral (and regional) agenda since the 1990s are also issues where national-level interests are, at bottom, shared. For example the recurrent transboundary "haze" problem arising from fires in Indonesia is a problem which, from a national perspective, Indonesia has at least as much of an interest in addressing as Singapore, given that the primary victims of the haze are Indonesian.[41] On another prominent issue, that of terrorism by non-state actors, both countries share fundamental interests in dealing with the problem and have proved ready to cooperate when appropriate. On both haze and terrorism, sub-national distributive and jurisdictional conflicts are more important obstacles to cooperation than bilateral differences.[42]

There are also, of course, many issues where Singapore and Indonesia are not in agreement. For example, they differ with respect to the role of third parties in addressing maritime piracy in the region, with Singapore favouring arrangements that would provide for U.S. involvement, while Indonesia has consistently argued that such a role would infringe its sovereignty.[43] The two countries have also taken markedly different rhetorical positions with regards to the American "war on terrorism" and attacks on Afghanistan and Iraq. However, differences over such macro-security arrangements have been relatively contained and do not normally intrude onto the bilateral relationship. Further, the contentious issues that have surfaced as bilateral irritants at various times, summarized in the previous section, are not core security issues that in any way threaten the survival or sovereignty of Singapore. They are, instead, largely mundane issues that have much more to do with the structural conflicts and competing interests arising out of the political economy through which the two countries are linked.

To identify aspects of tension within the political economy of bilateral relations, we must return to some of the complementarities between the two countries. Indonesia is a large, labour-abundant, capital-scarce economy in which primary commodity exports continue to play a critical role. Singapore is a labour-scarce entrepôt and financial centre that still owes a great deal of its prosperity to being able to act as a service hub and trading station. Although Singapore has developed a diversified industrial economy, it is very far from freeing itself from its traditional economic hinterlands, particularly Sumatra and Malaysia.[44] While the roles Singapore plays in the economies surrounding it are based on complementarities and mutual benefit for the parties involved, there is an enduring gap between, on the one hand, the private interests of the traders, investors, and bankers whose activities form the substance of longstanding links between Indonesia and Singapore and, on the other hand, the interests of successive governments in Jakarta. In both the colonial era and the post-independence period, the structure of Singapore's economy has placed it at odds with the interests of Jakarta-based governments in creating, and extending control over, a national economy. From their perspective, the line between a complementary and parasitic relationship has often been a thin one.

Tracing these competing interests — and the conflicts they have often spawned — to the colonial era should make us reconsider easy references to Indonesian nationalism and ethnic prejudice as fundamental drivers of tension in the relationship. The first point of note is that the Indonesian archipelago has for centuries been unevenly drawn into networks of trade and commerce involving Singapore. Not only was Singapore very much part of the "Malay world" in terms of cultural ties, as noted by an economic historian, Singapore has long played a key role in the economy of Indonesia.[45]

Reorienting economic activity away from the centripetal force exercised by Singapore was a fundamental objective of the Dutch colonial government, leading them to repeated clashes with the Straits Settlement Government based in Singapore. Redirecting the trade of the "Outer Islands" of the archipelago (i.e., outside of Java) from Singapore would require "very determined intervention, not only by commercial policy but also by force of arms".[46] The complaints registered by the Dutch colonial government against Singapore have an uncannily contemporary ring: they protested perennially about smuggling, about unfair competition from Singapore's free port, about counterfeiting and financial interference by merchants in Singapore, and about evasion from Indies law by fugitives who sought refuge in Singapore.[47]

During the Indonesian Revolution, Singapore's role in subverting the aims of the government of Jakarta served the interests of the republican cause, as "the British government in Singapore had surreptitiously encouraged local Chinese merchants to resume barter trade with Sumatra and Kalimantan by making available cheap ships that could slip through the Dutch blockade."[48] Singapore was in other ways a centre for revolutionary activity at this time.[49] The coincidence of interest between Singapore as a commercial trading centre and the Indonesian republicans wishing to resist and evade the controls of the Dutch was fortuitous, a product of the Indonesian Government during the revolution being more opposition-movement-cum-armed-rebellion than government. Once independence had been wrestled from the Dutch, Indonesia resumed efforts to develop a national economy, to redirect trade through its own ports, control its currency and develop its tax base — all efforts which put it at odds with the private actors on both sides, whose interests ran directly contrary to these goals. Their resistance — expressed in activities such as smuggling, illegal financial transactions, and capital flight — necessarily provoked official anger on the part of the Indonesian Government, which was, however, prevented from suppressing such activities by its own lack of enforcement capacities and weak organizational discipline.[50] These issues continue to surface: smuggling remains a problem, and Indonesia remains dissatisfied with Singapore's refusal to release data on individual traders through an electronic data exchange.[51] Singapore's continued strategy of acting as a financial hub and investment centre involves Indonesian actors to a considerable degree. According to estimates by investment bank Merrill Lynch and another private firm, "up to one third of the investors with assets of more than US$1 million in Singapore are of Indonesian origin; they number around 18,000 and have combined assets of US$87 billion."[52] Without any necessary implication that these funds have been illicitly acquired or are the fruits of corrupt practices in Indonesia, the legal and regulatory environment of that country invite suspicions.

Core features of the political economy of both countries have thus promoted mutually-enriching transborder economic exchanges, but often presented difficulties for the Indonesian Government in its role as guardian of the public sphere. Size, geographic location, and conscious economic strategy decisions have meant that Singapore looks outward — and very often to Indonesia — for everything from resources, trading commodities, financial sector clients, and labour. While there are genuine complementarities driving these exchanges, they also rebound in different ways in each country. Because of its economic endowments and a government system that has always been significantly prone to penetration and manipulation by private interests, Indonesia has been much less able to harness private economic activity to national goals. The form of economic integration that this has fostered differs markedly from the inward and outward internationalization of the Singapore economy, which has been closely tied to national purpose and regulatory objectives.[53]

Conclusions: Regime Maintenance and Bilateral Blowback

If the political economies and economic strategies of Indonesia and Singapore raise almost inevitable bilateral irritants, other, more contingent factors have aggravated mutual suspicions and tensions. These have been the domestic political strategies pursued to serve regime maintenance goals in both countries, and a paradoxical by-product of the so-called "ASEAN Way" of promoting regional stability. While neither is inescapable, they are both deeply entrenched.

The domestic political payoffs from playing up disputes with Singapore to serve diversionary or mobilizing ends during periods of political contestation in Indonesia have, as noted in the previous section, frequently been highlighted. To the extent that popular readiness to respond to such tactics is facilitated by the circulation of anti–ethnic Chinese stereotypes that have been encouraged by Indonesian governments, there is a link between regime maintenance and the potential for bilateral disputes to be magnified out of proportion. In this respect, it is important to note that the Indonesian Government policies and actions that have served to marginalize and stigmatize ethnic Chinese Indonesians were most pervasive during the height of Suharto's New Order, a time when the bilateral relationship was smooth. The fact that Suharto's interests led him to cultivate good relations with Singapore should not obscure the significance of this period in laying the ground for later expressions of antipathy and tension: it is not coincidental that several of the Indonesian grievances with regard to Singapore that surfaced after 1998 relate directly to connections between cronyistic Suharto-linked business players and Singapore.

On the Singaporean side, the representation of Indonesia as inherently threatening is consistent with specific political strategies adopted by the government since it came to power in 1959. Singaporean leaders have frequently, and publicly, underlined the supposed vulnerability of their country and the terms in which they have done so mean that Singapore's nearest neighbours are fairly clearly identified as the source of potential existential threats.[54] The usefulness of a foreign threat as a legitimizing mechanism for the regime and a mobilizing device to secure commitment to successive government impositions on its population has often been noted. Malaysian writer Zainuddin Bendahara argued that, "Lee Kuan Yew has been using the Malay bogeyman since he assumed leadership", a view echoed by other Malaysian commentators and political actors.[55] For Singaporeans, extending "the Malay bogeyman" — which neatly combines longstanding obsessions and anxieties with regard both to its northern neighbour and its own minority population — to Indonesia is a small step. In a country where government policy has consistently and deliberately perpetuated racialized visions of society, an image of Indonesia as a country dominated by "Malay-Muslims" is firmly lodged in both popular and official circles.[56]

If there are few reasons to believe that the Singapore-Indonesia relationship is shadowed by any inherent underlying suspicions, it does seem to be the case that both sides are subject to inflated sensitivities where the other is concerned. Singaporeans often read latent hostility into casual remarks by Indonesians, and Indonesians often seem to display an exaggerated sense of affront at actions by Singapore. Bilateral irritants which themselves involve relatively minor conflicts of interest therefore do sometimes escalate to the most senior political levels and may involve a surprising level of emotion. The explanation for this suggested by some accounts of both Indonesian and Singaporean foreign relations is that Indonesia is easily offended when its sense of entitlement to lead the region is not met.[57] It is not clear, however, why any aspirations for international leadership that Indonesia may have should take this form. It is therefore worth asking whether there are any other potential factors which might explain a sometimes exaggerated sensitivity.

While necessarily speculative, it is possible that a specific characteristic of the multilateralism of ASEAN, the so-called "ASEAN Way", has produced expectations of deference that predispose actors to taking offence when concerns or differences do arise.[58] The "ASEAN Way", with its emphasis on consensus, non-interference, and the avoidance of contentious issues has included an interpretation of "non-interference" that construes even comments on another member as illegitimate. To the extent that the "ASEAN Way" has become embedded as a core set of operating principles, the normative expectation that members will avoid all remotely negative or critical comment on fellow members has, arguably, created a sense of entitlement. Mock appeasement taken in the name of ASEAN solidarity generates further expectations of deference. Somewhat paradoxically, this mode of interaction may actually foster mutual suspicion and irritation, as shows of deference can be perceived not as exhibits of goodwill, but lack of trustworthiness. An example of how deference may backfire can be seen in Singapore's delayed establishment of diplomatic relations with China until after Indonesia restored ties with China, as late as 1990. The Singapore policy was universally accepted as something done in order to appease Indonesia. Yet this is remembered in at least some quarters in Indonesia as a sign of Singaporean insincerity and deviousness — of Singapore maintaining an official position at odds with actual practice. The multilateralized norm of outward deference that is part of the "ASEAN Way" may thus lead to a sense of betrayal — and elevated sensitivities at the bilateral level — when expectations are unmet.

NOTES

[1]   Indonesia's *Konfrontasi* policy, which included armed incursions into Malaysia and the detonation of bombs in Singapore, officially lasted until 1966 but in practice Indonesian officials had begun to scale down operations and discuss normalization with Malaysia from 1965. See Franklin Weinstein, *Indonesia Abandons Confrontation: An Inquiry into the Functions of Indonesian Foreign Policy* (Ithaca: Southeast Asia Program, Cornell University, 1969).

2   Chua Beng Huat, "Singapore in 2007: High Wage Ministers and the Management of Gays and Elderly", *Asian Survey* 48, no. 1 (2008): 57.

3   Tommy Koh and Chang Li Lin, eds., *The Little Red Dot: Reflections by Singapore's Diplomats* (Singapore: World Scientific and Institute for Policy Studies, 2005); Lee Hsien Loong, "A Little Red Dot and Tension across the Taiwan Strait", *Straits Times*, 23 August 2004 <http://yaleglobal.yale.edu/display.article?id=4403> (accessed 27 February 2009). As discussed in later sections, political interests on both sides have influenced the way the other country is presented to domestic audiences.

4   For example, Rizal Sukma, *Islam in Indonesian Foreign Policy* (London: Routledge 2003), pp. 83–120; Dewi Fortuna Anwar, "Key Aspects of Indonesia's Foreign Policy", in *Trends in Southeast Asia Series* 9 (Singapore: Institute of Southeast Asian Studies, 2003); Kai He, "Indonesia's Foreign Policy after Soeharto: International Pressure, Democratization, and Policy Change", *International Relations of the Asia-Pacific* 8 (2008), pp. 47–72.

5   Relatively few studies take the Singapore-Indonesia relationship as their primary focus, but relations between the two figure prominently in work on Singapore's foreign policy and generally receive some — albeit much less — attention in work on Indonesia's foreign relations. One of the few volumes to focus on the bilateral relationship is Lau Teik Soon and Bilveer Singh, eds., *Singapore-Indonesia Relations: Problems and Prospects* (Singapore: Singapore Institute of International Affairs, 1991). The major studies of Singapore's foreign policy and relations are N. Ganesan, *Realism and Interdependence in Singapore's Foreign Policy* (London: Routledge, 2005); Michael Leifer, *Singapore's Foreign Policy: Coping with Vulnerability* (London: Routledge, 2000); Bilveer Singh, *The Vulnerability of Small States Revisited: A Study of Singapore's Post-Cold War Foreign Policy* (Yogyakarta: Gadjah Mada University Press, 1999). Major works on Indonesian foreign policy and relations include Michael Leifer, *Indonesia's Foreign Policy* (London: Allen and Unwin, 1983); Dewi Fortuna Anwar, *Indonesia in ASEAN: Foreign Policy and Regionalism* (New York and Singapore: St. Martin's Press and Institute of Southeast Asian Studies, 1994); Leo Suryadinata, *Indonesia's Foreign Policy Under Suharto: Aspiring to International Leadership* (Singapore: Times Academic, 1996); Rizal Sukma, *Indonesia and China: The Politics of a Troubled Relationship* (London: Routledge, 1998); and Sukma, *Islam in Indonesian Foreign Policy*.

6   See Leifer, *Singapore's Foreign Policy: Coping with Vulnerability*.

7   See Ganesan, *Realism and Interdependence in Singapore's Foreign Policy*, p. 11.

8   See Tim Huxley, *Defending the Lion City: The Armed Forces of Singapore* (St Leonards, NSW: Allen & Unwin, 2000).

9   On the conditions which make war "obsolete", see John Mueller, "The Obsolescence of Major War", in *The Use of Force: Military Power and*

International Politics, edited by Robert J. Art and Kenneth N. Waltz (Lanham, MD: Rowman & Littlefield, 1999).

10 For a brief account of Brunei-Indonesia relations, see Anwar, *Indonesia in ASEAN: Foreign Policy and Regionalism*, p. 230.

11 See Sukma, *Islam in Indonesian Foreign Policy*.

12 For example, Takashi Shiraishi, "Anti-Sinicism in Java's New Order", in *Essential Outsiders: Chinese and Jews in the Modern Transformation of Southeast Asia and Central Europe*, edited by Daniel Chirot and Anthony Reid (Seattle: University of Washington Press, 1997), pp. 187–207; Yoshihara Kunio, *The Rise of Ersatz Capitalism in Southeast Asia* (Singapore: Oxford University Press, 1988).

13 See George Kahin, *Southeast Asia: A Testament* (London: RoutledgeCurzon, 2003), pp. 158–76. See also Greg Poulgrain, *The Genesis of Konfrontasi: Malaysia, Brunei, Indonesia 1945–1965* (Bathhurst: Crawford House, 1998) for an account that strongly contests the Singaporean (and Malaysian) narratives of *Konfrontasi*.

14 See Weinstein, *Indonesia Abandons Confrontation: An Inquiry into the Functions of Indonesian Foreign Policy*.

15 On the subversion policy of the United States in the late 1950s, see Audrey Kahin and George Kahin, *Subversion as Foreign Policy: The Secret Eisenhower and Dulles Debacle in Indonesia* (Seattle: University of Washington Press, 1995). Although Singapore's role was minor — and of course pre-dates the country's independence — it was used as a logistics and communications base.

16 On the comparison with Israel and Singaporean policymakers' perceptions, see Alan Chong, "Singapore's foreign policy beliefs as 'Abridged Realism': Pragmatic and Liberal Prefixes in the Foreign Policy Thought of Rajaratnam, Lee, Koh and Mahbubani", *International Relations of the Asia Pacific* 6, no. 2 (2006): 269–306.

17 See, for example, Amitav Acharya, "The Association of Southeast Asian Nations: 'Security Community' or 'Defence Community'?" *Pacific Affairs* 64, no. 2 (1991): 159–78; Amitav Acharya, *The Quest for Identity: International Relations of Southeast Asia* (Oxford: Oxford University Press, 2000). Even critical accounts of ASEAN tend to uphold the view that, whatever the organization's failings, it has contributed to maintaining intramural peace and stability. See, for example, Erik Kuhonta, "Walking a Tightrope: Democracy Versus Sovereignty in ASEAN's Illiberal Peace", *The Pacific Review* 19, no. 3 (2006): 337–58; David Martin Jones and Michael Smith, "Making Process, Not Progress: ASEAN and the Evolving East Asian Regional Order", *International Security* 32, no. 1 (2007): 148–84.

18 See Acharya, "The Association of Southeast Asian Nations: 'Security Community' or 'Defence Community'?" pp. 172–73.

[19] See Robert Hartfiel and Brian Job, "Raising the Risks of War: Defence Spending Trends and Competitive Arms Processes in East Asia", *Pacific Review* 20, no. 1 (2006): 1–22; Huxley, *Defending the Lion City: The Armed Forces of Singapore*.

[20] For example, Suryadinata, *Indonesia's Foreign Policy Under Suharto*; and Leifer, *Singapore's Foreign Policy*.

[21] See also He, "Indonesia's Foreign Policy after Soeharto", on Indonesia's post-1998 foreign policy more generally.

[22] See Ganesan, *Realism and Interdependence in Singapore's Foreign Policy*, pp. 88–98.

[23] See Chua Beng Huat, "Singapore in 2006: An Irritating and Irritated ASEAN Neighbour", *Asian Survey* 47, no. 1 (2007): 211.

[24] *Business Times*, 13 June 2007.

[25] *Straits Times*, 10 October 2007.

[26] *Kompas*, 4 February 2008.

[27] See "Speech by Mr Teo Chee Hean, Minister for Defence, at Committee of Supply Debate", 29 February 2008 <http://www.mindef.gov.sg/imindef/news_and_events/nr/2008/feb/29feb08_nr/29feb08_speech.html> (accessed 28 February 2009).

[28] *Business Times*, 27 March 2008. The sale, to a Malaysian bank, would be an extremely lucrative one for Temasek Holdings, as the deal valued Temasek's stake at about five times its purchase price. During 2008, it remained in question as a result of the Malaysian bank regulator dropping its approval for the purchase, arguing that a new takeover law in Indonesia might result in losses for the Malaysian bank. See *Business Times*, 26 August 2008. Later, the Malaysian central bank reinstated its permission for the sale after promises the Indonesian takeover law would be eased, but then appeared to raise further doubts. See *Business Times*, 17 September 2008.

[29] *Business Times*, 3 June 2008; AsiaOne.com, 8 June 2008.

[30] Quoted in *Business Times*, 28 July 2007.

[31] For example, Ganesan, *Realism and Interdependence in Singapore's Foreign Policy*, pp. 88–89; Leifer, *Indonesia's Foreign Policy*; Suryadinata, *Indonesia's Foreign Policy Under Suharto*.

[32] See Rais Abin, "Developments in Indonesia-Singapore Bilateral Relations: Politics", in *Indonesia-Singapore Relations: Problems and Prospects*, edited by Lau Teik Soon and Bilveer Singh (Singapore: Singapore Institute of International Affairs, 1991), p. 98.

[33] Ibid, p. 99.

[34] For example, Singapore International Foundation (SIF), *Gotong Royong: SIF Celebrates 15 Years of Friendship with Indonesia* (Singapore: SIF, 2007).

[35] This insistence on "bundling" issues together has also been a hallmark of Singapore-Malaysia negotiations on contentious issues. I thank N. Ganesan for this observation.

[36] See Shaun Narine, *Explaining ASEAN: Regionalism in Southeast Asia* (Boulder: Lynne Rienner, 2002), pp. 8–38.

[37] See Acharya, *The Quest for Identity*; Amitav Acharya, "Will Asia's Past be Its Future?" *International Security* 28, no. 3 (2003/2004): 149–64.

[38] See Richard Stubbs, "Subregional Security Cooperation in ASEAN: Security and Economic Imperatives and Political Obstacles", *Asian Survey* 32, no. 5 (1992): 401; and Acharya, "The Association of Southeast Asian Nations".

[39] See N. Ganesan, *Bilateral Tensions in Post–Cold War ASEAN* (Singapore: Institute of Southeast Asian Studies, 1999).

[40] See Stubbs, "Subregional Security Cooperation in ASEAN"; Richard Stubbs, "Signing on to Liberalization: AFTA and the Politics of Regional Economic Cooperation", *Pacific Review* 13, no. 2 (2000): 297–318; Etel Solingen, "ASEAN, Quo Vadis? Domestic Coalitions and Regional Cooperation", *Contemporary Southeast Asia* 21, no. 1 (1999): 30–54.

[41] See David Glover and Timothy Jessup, eds., *Indonesia's Fires and Haze: The Cost of Catastrophe* (Singapore: Institute of Southeast Asian Studies, 2006).

[42] See Tan See Seng and Krishna Ramakrishna, "Interstate and Intrastate Dynamics in Southeast Asia's War on Terror", *SAIS Review* 24, no. 1 (2004): 91–105; and James Cotton, "The 'Haze' over Southeast Asia: Challenging the ASEAN Mode of Regional Engagement", *Pacific Affairs* 72, no. 3 (1999): 331–51.

[43] See Ganesan, *Realism and Interdependence in Singapore's Foreign Policy*, pp. 87–88.

[44] See William Huff, *The Economic Growth of Singapore: Trade and Development in the Twentieth Century* (Cambridge: Cambridge University Press, 1994).

[45] See William Roff, "The Malayo-Muslim World of Singapore at the Close of the Nineteenth Century", *Journal of Asian Studies* 24, no. 1 (1964): 75–90; Howard Dick, "State, Nation-state and National Economy", in *The Emergence of a National Economy: An Economic History of Indonesia, 1800–2000*, by Howard Dick, Vincent Houben, Thomas Lindblad, and Thee Kian Wie (Honolulu: University of Hawai'i Press, Asian Studies Association of Australia, 2002), p. 11.

[46] See Dick, "State, Nation-state and National Economy", p. 21.

[47] See Eric Tagliocozzo, *Secret Trades, Porous Borders: Smuggling and States along a Southeast Asian Frontier, 1865–1915* (New Haven: Yale University Press, 2005); and Natasha Hamilton-Hart, *Asian States, Asian Bankers: Central Banking in Southeast Asia* (Ithaca: Cornell University Press, 2002), p. 35.

[48] See Dick, "State, Nation-state and National Economy", p. 30.

[49] See Yong Mun Cheong, *The Indonesian Revolution and the Singapore Connection, 1945–1949* (Leiden: KITLV Press, 2003).

50   See C.G.F. Simkin, "Indonesia's Unrecorded Foreign Trade", *Bulletin of Indonesian Economic Studies* 6, no. 1 (1970): 17–44; and Hamilton-Hart, *Asian States, Asian Bankers*, pp. 133–35.
51   Graeme Lang and Hiu Wan Chan, "China's Impact on Forests in Southeast Asia", *Journal of Contemporary Asia* 36, no. 2 (2006): 167–94; *Business Times*, 10 July 2003; and *Jakarta Post*, 10 September 2003.
52   See Chua, "Singapore in 2007", p. 57.
53   See Natasha Hamilton-Hart, "The Regionalization of Southeast Asian Business: Transnational Networks in National Contexts", in *Remapping East Asia: The Construction of a Region*, edited by T.J. Pempel (Ithaca: Cornell University Press, 2005), pp. 170–91.
54   See Leifer, *Singapore's Foreign Policy*.
55   Quoted in *Straits Times*, 9 August 2002.
56   See Chua Beng Huat, "Racial Singaporeans: Absence after the Hyphen", in *Southeast Asian Identities: Culture and the Politics of Representation in Indonesia, Malaysia, Singapore, and Thailand*, edited by Joel S. Kahn (New York and Singapore: St. Martin's Press and Institute of Southeast Asian Studies, 1998); David Brown, *The State and Ethnic Politics in Southeast Asia* (London: Routledge, 1994). An Indonesian who became a Singaporean permanent resident — and was therefore required to have a "race" on his identity card — describes the difficulty he met in requesting that he not be described as "Malay". See <http://www.indrani.net/blogger/2005/04/how-to-change-your-race-legally.html> (accessed 28 February 2009).
57   For example, Suryadinata, *Indonesia's Foreign Policy Under Suharto*.
58   On the "ASEAN Way", see Narine, *Explaining ASEAN*; Acharya, "Will Asia's Past be Its Future?"; and Anwar, *Indonesia in ASEAN*.

REFERENCES

Acharya, Amitav. "The Association of Southeast Asian Nations: 'Security Community' or 'Defence Community'?" *Pacific Affairs* 64, no. 2 (1991): 159–78.
———. *The Quest for Identity: International Relations of Southeast Asia*. Oxford: Oxford University Press, 2000.
———. "Will Asia's Past be Its Future?" *International Security* 28, no. 3 (2003/04): 149–64.
Anwar, Dewi Fortuna. *Indonesia in ASEAN: Foreign Policy and Regionalism*. New York and Singapore: St. Martin's Press and Institute of Southeast Asian Studies, 1994.
———. "Key Aspects of Indonesia's Foreign Policy". *Trends in Southeast Asia Series*, no. 9. Singapore: Institute of Southeast Asian Studies, 2003.

Brown, David. *The State and Ethnic Politics in Southeast Asia*. London: Routledge, 1994.

Chong, Alan. "Singapore's Foreign Policy Beliefs as 'Abridged Realism': Pragmatic and Liberal Prefixes in the Foreign Policy Thought of Rajaratnam, Lee, Koh and Mahbubani". *International Relations of the Asia Pacific* 6, no. 2 (2006): 269–306.

Chua, Beng Huat. "Racial Singaporeans: Absence after the Hyphen". In *Southeast Asian Identities: Culture and the Politics of Representation in Indonesia, Malaysia, Singapore, and Thailand*, edited by Joel S. Kahn. New York and Singapore: St. Martin's Press and Institute of Southeast Asian Studies, 1998.

———. "Singapore in 2006: An Irritating and Irritated ASEAN Neighbour". *Asian Survey* 47, no. 1 (2007): 206–12.

———. "Singapore in 2007: High Wage Ministers and the Management of Gays and Elderly". *Asian Survey* 48, no. 1 (2008): 55–61.

Cotton, James. "The 'Haze' over Southeast Asia: Challenging the ASEAN mode of regional engagement". *Pacific Affairs* 72, no. 3 (1999): 331–51.

Dick, Howard. "State, Nation-state and National Economy". In *The Emergence of a National Economy: An Economic History of Indonesia, 1800–2000*, by Howard Dick, Vincent Houben, Thomas Lindblad, and Thee Kian Wie. Honolulu: University of Hawai'i Press, Asian Studies Association of Australia, 2002.

Ganesan, N. *Bilateral Tensions in Post–Cold War ASEAN*. Singapore: Institute of Southeast Asian Studies, 1999.

———. *Realism and Interdependence in Singapore's Foreign Policy*. London: Routledge, 2005.

Glover, David and Timothy Jessup, eds. *Indonesia's Fires and Haze: The Cost of Catastrophe*. Singapore: Institute of Southeast Asian Studies, 2006.

Hamilton-Hart, Natasha. *Asian States, Asian Bankers: Central Banking in Southeast Asia*. Ithaca: Cornell University Press, 2002.

———. "The Regionalization of Southeast Asian Business: Transnational Networks in National Contexts". In *Remapping East Asia: The Construction of a Region*, edited by T.J. Pempel. Ithaca: Cornell University Press, 2005.

Hartfiel, Robert and Brian Job. "Raising the Risks of War: Defence Spending Trends and Competitive Arms Processes in East Asia". *Pacific Review* 20, no. 1 (2007): 1–22.

He, Kai. "Indonesia's Foreign Policy after Soeharto: International Pressure, Democratization, and Policy Change". *International Relations of the Asia-Pacific* 8 (2008): 47–72.

Huff, William. *The Economic Growth of Singapore: Trade and Development in the Twentieth Century*. Cambridge: Cambridge University Press, 1994.

Huxley, Tim. *Defending the Lion City: The Armed Forces of Singapore*. St Leonards, NSW: Allen & Unwin, 2000.

Jones, David Martin and Michael Smith. "Making Process, Not Progress: ASEAN and the Evolving East Asian Regional Order". *International Security* 32, no. 1 (2007): 148–84.

Kahin, Audrey and George Kahin. *Subversion as Foreign Policy: The Secret Eisenhower and Dulles Debacle in Indonesia*. Seattle: University of Washington Press, 1995.

Kahin, George. *Southeast Asia: A Testament*. London: RoutledgeCurzon, 2003.

Koh, Tommy and Chang Li Lin, eds. *The Little Red Dot: Reflections by Singapore's Diplomats*. Singapore: World Scientific; Institute for Policy Studies, 2005.

Kuhonta, Eric. "Walking a Tightrope: Democracy Versus Sovereignty in ASEAN's Illiberal Peace". *Pacific Review* 19, no. 3 (2006): 337–58.

Lang, Graeme and Cathy Hiu Wan Chan. "China's Impact on Forests in Southeast Asia". *Journal of Contemporary Asia* 36, no. 2 (2006): 167–94.

Lau Teik Soon and Bilveer Singh, eds. *Singapore-Indonesia Relations: Problems and Prospects*. Singapore: Singapore Institute of International Affairs, 1991.

Lee Hsien Loong. "A Little Red Dot and Tension across the Taiwan Strait". *Straits Times*, 23 August 2004 <http://yaleglobal.yale.edu/display.article?id=4403> (accessed 28 February 2009).

Leifer, Michael. *Indonesia's Foreign Policy*. London: Allen and Unwin, 1983.

———. *Singapore's Foreign Policy: Coping with Vulnerability*. London: Routledge, 2000.

Mueller, John. "The Obsolescence of Major War". In *The Use of Force: Military Power and International Politics*, edited by Robert J. Art and Kenneth N. Waltz. Lanham, MD: Rowman & Littlefield, 1999.

Narine, Shaun. *Explaining ASEAN: Regionalism in Southeast Asia*. Boulder: Lynne Rienner, 2002.

Rais Abin. "Developments in Indonesia-Singapore Bilateral Relations: Politics". In *Indonesia-Singapore Relations: Problems and Prospects*, edited by Lau Teik Soon and Bilveer Singh. Singapore: Singapore Institute of International Affairs, 1991.

Roff, William. "The Malayo-Muslim World of Singapore at the Close of the Nineteenth Century". *Journal of Asian Studies* 24, no. 1 (1964): 75–90.

Simkin, C.G.F. "Indonesia's Unrecorded Foreign Trade". *Bulletin of Indonesian Economic Studies* 6, no. 1 (1970): 17–44.

Singapore International Foundation (SIF). *Gotong Royong: SIF Celebrates 15 Years of Friendship with Indonesia*. Singapore: SIF, 2007.

Singh, Bilveer. *The Vulnerability of Small States Revisited: A Study of Singapore's Post–Cold War Foreign Policy*. Yogyakarta: Gadjah Mada University Press, 1999.

Solingen, Etel. "ASEAN, Quo Vadis? Domestic Coalitions and Regional Cooperation". *Contemporary Southeast Asia* 21, no. 1 (1999): 30–54.

Stubbs, Richard. "Subregional Security Cooperation in ASEAN: Security and Economic Imperatives and Political Obstacles". *Asian Survey* 32, no. 5 (1992): 397–410.

———. "Signing on to Liberalization: AFTA and the Politics of Regional Economic Cooperation". *Pacific Review* 13, no. 2 (2000): 297–318.

Sukma, Rizal. *Indonesia and China: The Politics of a Troubled Relationship*. London: Routledge, 1998.

———. *Islam in Indonesian Foreign Policy*. London: Routledge, 2003.

Suryadinata, Leo. *Indonesia's Foreign Policy under Suharto: Aspiring to International Leadership*. Singapore: Times Academic Press, 1996.

Tagliocozzo, Eric. *Secret Trades, Porous Borders: Smuggling and States along a Southeast Asian Frontier, 1865–1915*. New Haven: Yale University Press, 2005.

Takashi Shiraishi. "Anti-Sinicism in Java's New Order". In *Essential Outsiders: Chinese and Jews in the Modern Transformation of Southeast Asia and Central Europe*, edited by Daniel Chirot and Anthony Reid. Seattle: University of Washington Press, 1997.

Tan, See Seng and Kumar Ramakrishna. "Interstate and Intrastate Dynamics in Southeast Asia's War on Terror". *SAIS Review* 24, no. 1 (2004): 91–105.

Teo Chee Hean. "Speech by Mr Teo Chee Hean, Minister for Defence, at Committee of Supply Debate 2008", 29 February 2008 <http://www.mindef.gov.sg/imindef/news_and_events/nr/2008/feb/29feb08_nr/29feb08_speech.html> (accessed 28 February 2009).

Weinstein, Franklin. *Indonesia Abandons Confrontation: An Inquiry into the Functions of Indonesian Foreign Policy*. Southeast Asia Program, Cornell University, 1969.

Yong Mun Cheong. *The Indonesian Revolution and the Singapore Connection, 1945–1949*. Leiden: KITLV Press, 2003.

Yoshihara Kunio. *The Rise of Ersatz Capitalism in Southeast Asia*. Singapore: Oxford University Press, 1988.

9

Bilateralism and Multilateralism in Malaysia-Philippines Relations

Isagani de Castro, Jr.

The Philippines and Malaysia have had an "abnormal"[1] bilateral relationship over the past four decades. The two countries have had to close down their embassies several times since full diplomatic relations were established in May 1964. The main reason for this development is the territorial dispute over Sabah. As the current Philippine Ambassador to Malaysia Victoriano Lecaros said, "there is nothing in our relations with other countries that comes to the nature of Sabah."[2] The dispute over this large, 76,115 square kilometre property has been the thorn in the history of Philippines-Malaysia bilateral relations. The Sabah claim initiated or complicated two major contentious issues in the bilateral relationship which have persisted to this day: the Muslim separatist rebellion in the southern Philippines and Filipino labour migration to Sabah. The other contentious bilateral issue tackled in this chapter is the conflicting claims of the two countries over territories in the South China Sea.

Through the years, the two countries have been using bilateralism to manage the contentious issues in their relationship. In the case of Malaysia, bilateralism is the primordial way of dealing with the Philippines. Being the economically-stronger nation, bilateralism has enabled Malaysia to strengthen its position on the various contentious issues vis-à-vis the Philippines.

The Philippines, on the other hand, has been using bilateralism and multilateralism in managing contentious issues with Malaysia. The Philippines has sought to raise the dispute over Sabah in the United Nations International Court of Justice (ICJ) but has not got Malaysia's consent.

With regard to its problem with Muslim separatists in the south, the Philippines allowed the Organisation of the Islamic Conference (OIC) to play a key role in resolving the conflict with one faction of the Muslim separatists, the Moro National Liberation Front (MNLF). It has also invited Malaysia to broker the peace negotiations with the other separatist group, the Moro Islamic Liberation Front (MILF). Other nations are now also involved in the peace process.

On the problems faced by Filipino migrants in Sabah, the Philippines has resorted to both bilateral and multilateral means in managing this tension. On the Spratlys dispute, the Philippines has used the Association of South East Asian Nations (ASEAN) as a forum to try to force the six claimant countries into a status quo position.

Both Malaysia and the Philippines have never considered using ASEAN's dispute settlement mechanism to resolve the Sabah dispute. Sabah is seen as a purely bilateral concern. It is a problem best left out of ASEAN. Diplomats from the two countries said bringing in other ASEAN members would just complicate the issue. ASEAN's policy of non-interference is also a cardinal principle being followed.

Historically, the Philippines' multilateral option has been to bring it to the ICJ since it is basically a legal dispute which requires a judicial decision from the world court. For Malaysia, it has so far been successful in basically forcing the Philippines to give up its claim. After the overthrow of the Marcos dictatorship in 1986, Malaysia has been taking advantage of the Philippines' weakness so that the Philippines would have no leg left to stand on to defend its claim. It has called on the Philippines to establish a consulate in Sabah, the last nail in the coffin that would finally bury the Philippines' long-dormant claim.

Malaysia's unilateral actions in the disputed Spratly islands, such as its occupation of the Investigator Shoal and Erica Reef in 1999, protested by the Philippines, have also strengthened its position vis-à-vis the other claimants. However, when dealing with the bigger claimant, China, Malaysia takes a common position with ASEAN.

According to a veteran Filipino diplomat, the absence of an ASEAN Charter was one factor why disputes have not been brought before ASEAN's dispute settlement mechanisms, as "there was no legal basis with force of law to comply".[3] Singapore's Ambassador-at-large Tommy Koh has said that only around one-third of ASEAN "pledges and commitments" have been implemented, and he expressed hope that the signing of an ASEAN Charter would "rectify the situation".[4]

Some diplomats also said that the ASEAN High Council on the Treaty of Amity and Cooperation (TAC) is not seen as an appropriate body to bring disputes such as Sabah or Spratlys to since it is not a judicial body that can settle legal questions. It is also seen as merely a body that can recommend ways of solving disputes. There is also no precedent to assess the value of the High Council since no dispute has ever been brought to it.

Brief History of Philippines-Malaysia Relations

The two countries established diplomatic relations in 1959 when the Philippines established a legation in Kuala Lumpur. Full diplomatic ties were established on 18 May 1964. According to the two governments, bilateral ties have not been able to be fully developed due to the territorial dispute over Sabah. "Bilateral relations have been cordial but had been prevented from reaching its full potential due to the question of Sabah", said the Department of Foreign Affairs in numerous official releases.

Bilateral relations between the Philippines and Malaysia can be divided into these historical periods:

1959–86: Macapagal-Marcos — Troubled Bilateral Relations

The years 1959 to 1986 have been described as the "troubled" period "due to both countries' conflicting claims to sovereignty over Sabah (North Borneo)."[5] Various attempts to "resolve this claim peacefully through diplomatic negotiations were unsuccessful."[6] Datuk Eman Haniff, a former Malaysian Ambassador to the Philippines, traced the start of the problem to June 1962 when the Philippines officially filed her claim to Sabah.[7] Then President Diosdado Macapagal, the father of the current

Philippines President Gloria Macapagal-Arroyo, filed the Philippine claim of sovereignty with the United Kingdom. From September 1963 to May 1964, diplomatic and consular relations were suspended.

In 1968, relations ruptured and reached their lowest point. Two events were responsible for this. First, the "Philippines institutionalized the claim through the enactment of Republic Act 5546 incorporating Sabah as part of the territory of the Philippines."[8] And second, also in 1968, a covert military operation seeking to destabilize and take over Sabah — Project Merdeka — was implemented by the Marcos government.[9] Thereafter, Malaysia lodged a formal protest with the Philippines "over the report of the existence of a Philippine special force to conduct infiltration, subversion and sabotage in Sabah."[10] Malaysia arrested twenty armed Filipinos in Sabah. Sabah's Chief Minister Tun Mustapha assailed the Marcos government for "irresponsible adventurism".[11] Malaysia then pulled out its embassy in Manila while the Philippine embassy in Kuala Lumpur closed on 29 November 1968. Malaysia "also ended its participation in regional meetings that involved the Philippines."[12]

The Jabidah massacre cannot be overemphasized because it was the turning point in the escalation of the Muslim separatist movement in the Philippines. As two investigative journalists on the Muslim rebellion put it, "it was the spark that lit the Muslim rebellion."[13] The Malaysians also consider it a critical event since it convinced them that President Marcos could not be trusted. The Malaysians then gave the Muslim separatists safe haven in Sabah, funds, and other kinds of support which led to the escalation of armed conflict in the southern Philippines, a war that remains only partly resolved to this day.

1986–98: Repairing Troubled Ties with Malaysia

The fall of the Marcos regime in February 1986 provided an opportunity to repair damaged ties with Malaysia. By this time, the Philippines was faced with many internal problems — a divided military, a communist rebellion, two Muslim separatist movements, a large foreign debt, and widespread poverty.

The Aquino government then laid a new foundation in settling the issue over Sabah. The Malaysians were willing to settle the private claims of the heirs of the Sultan of Sulu, but it wanted the Philippines to take steps to drop the claim by revising its baselines law and removing the paragraph that provided for a reservation on the Sabah question. The Aquino administration tried to take this step by introducing a new baselines law, but it failed to pass Congress.

Former President Fidel Ramos built on the foundation laid by his predecessor. He reached an agreement with Malaysian Prime Minister Mahathir Mohamad to set aside or shelve the Sabah dispute. The goal was to not let the dispute become an obstacle to improving economic ties. Senator Blas Ople said Ramos was able to "de-ice this frosty relationship of three decades."[14] This was followed by the signing in 1993, during President Ramos' visit to Malaysia, of a memorandum of understanding establishing the Philippines-Malaysia Joint Commission for Bilateral Cooperation. The commission sought to intensify political, economic, social, and cultural cooperation between the two countries.

It was during the Ramos administration that economic relations developed rapidly. Malaysian investments to the Philippines went up from only US$7.6 million in 1993, the year the joint commission was established, to $169 million the following year. Malaysian investments in the Philippines reached a record high during the Ramos presidency. The Philippines also got Malaysia, Indonesia, and Brunei to agree to establish a new growth area called the East ASEAN Growth Area (EAGA). Its goal was to develop the backwater areas of the four countries. Although not as successful as other regional growth areas, these four countries now hold regular BIMP-EAGA meetings, some of them during ASEAN ministerial meetings. This growth triangle has provided impetus to strong ties among the four countries.

1998–January 2001: Strained Bilateral Ties

Bilateral relations between the Philippines and Malaysia soured during the brief reign of President Joseph Ejercito Estrada. Although Estrada continued the foreign policies of Ramos, Estrada's personal friendship and expression of support for former Malaysian Deputy Prime Minister Anwar Ibrahim caused a strain in the otherwise close and vibrant ties achieved by Ramos. Estrada's all-out-war policy against the separatist MILF reversed the peace policy of the Ramos administration.

It was during the Estrada government that Malaysia occupied two islets in the disputed Spratly Islands, Investigator Shoal and Erica Reef, and caused a diplomatic row.

January 2001–Present: Malaysia Facilitates Peace in the South

President Gloria Macapagal-Arroyo, who took over from President Estrada in January 2001 following a military-backed people's revolt, has similar policies to the Ramos administration. First, instead of an all-out-war policy against the MILF, President Arroyo pursued peace talks. Arroyo invited Malaysia to facilitate peace negotiations with the MILF. Since 2001, Malaysia has been hosting and facilitating the peace talks. It led the International Monitoring Team for the ceasefire between the Philippine Government and the MILF until it completely withdrew in November 2008 after the collapse of the peace talks. Arroyo also gave priority to Ramos' BIMP-EAGA initiative and gave it fresh impetus. At the 13th ASEAN Summit in Singapore, BIMP leaders held their fourth summit.

Trade between the Philippines and Malaysia has also grown under the Arroyo government. After falling to $2.1 billion in 2001, total merchandise trade went up to $3.1 billion in 2002, and to $4.7 billion in 2004. However, Malaysian investments have fallen in recent years.

There have been several high-level exchanges under the Arroyo administration. President Arroyo had a state visit in August 2001, just six months into her presidency. According to the Department of Foreign Affairs, that visit "allowed the Philippines to forge closer ties with Malaysia, which had been strained by old as well as new issues that emerged under the previous administration."[15] These visits have allowed the two leaders to "establish rapport and personal friendship."[16]

Four contentious issues are taken up in this chapter. It discusses how these problems are managed. It also explains why ASEAN's dispute settlement mechanisms were not used. The four bilateral contentious issues are: (1) the Sabah dispute, (2) Muslim separatists, (3) Filipino migrants in Sabah, and (4) dispute in the South China Sea.

Sabah: Bilateralism Weakens the Philippines' Hand

This chapter will give priority to the Sabah dispute since it is the biggest, and most serious, bilateral issue. Malaysia's diplomatic strategy on Sabah is to let the status quo persist and to use bilateralism to weaken the Philippines' claim to Sabah. The non-resort to multilateralism, including not going to the ICJ or ASEAN's dispute settlement mechanism, has been advantageous to Malaysia.

The Sabah dispute is essentially a legal dispute. The Philippines contends that it acquired sovereignty over Sabah from the Sultanate of Sulu. Sulu is one of the Muslim provinces of the Philippines. Malaysia's position is that it acquired sovereignty from the United Kingdom and that Sabah has been ceded to the entities that have ruled Sabah. Various electoral exercises have also confirmed that the people in Sabah want to be with Malaysia.

Marcos Government Creates a Thorn in Bilateral Ties

President Marcos' diplomacy involved bilateral and multilateral means to address the issue of Sabah. However, the disclosure in 1968 of the Jabidah massacre showed that he also discreetly opted for a military solution to strengthen the Philippines claim.

The Sabah dispute was the first major political-security crisis of ASEAN. The exposé of the Jabidah massacre incident, where Filipino-Muslim trainees were summarily killed in an aborted attempt to destabilize Sabah, just seven months after ASEAN's establishment in August 1967, threatened ASEAN's union. Former ASEAN Secretary-General Rodolfo Severino said the ASEAN member-states tried to prevent the dispute from affecting the newly-formed ASEAN. He said ASEAN decided to "keep the bilateral dispute officially out of ASEAN in order to protect it." The Philippines, he said, tried to "internationalize the issue by bringing it to the United Nations and other multilateral forums."[17]

In 1977, President Marcos, reflecting the importance he thought of ASEAN, said at an ASEAN Summit in Kuala Lumpur that as a "contribution … to the future of ASEAN", he was taking "definite steps to eliminate one of the burdens of ASEAN — the claim of the Philippine Republic to Sabah."[18] However, from 1977 until Marcos' fall from power in February 1986, the Sabah dispute remained unresolved.

The late Senator Blas Ople said he once asked Marcos why he "reneged on his promise" to take steps to drop the claim. Marcos told him that "Malaysian leaders had not taken steps … to honour the promised quid pro quo. One of the reasons was that Kuala Lumpur had been less than forthcoming on the private claims of the heirs of the Sultan of Sulu."[19]

Aquino Government Takes Major Step to Drop Sabah Claim

The democratic government of President Aquino, faced with a legacy of economic bankruptcy, widespread poverty, communist rebellion, and

Muslim separatism left by the Marcos dictatorship, took the first major step to drop the Philippine claim to Sabah. In 1987, just less than two years into her presidency, Aquino adopted a policy to drop the Philippine claim, but this had to be done through the legislature. On 19 November 1987, then Senator Leticia Ramos-Shahani, an administration upper house legislator, filed a bill dropping the Philippine claim to Sabah. The bill delineated the archipelagic baselines of the Philippines, which excluded Sabah. Aquino certified them as urgent bills in the hope that they could be passed before the 14–16 December 1987 ASEAN Summit in Manila. However, the bill was opposed by Muslim legislators since it supposedly "endangers" the propriety rights over Sabah by the Sultanate of Sulu.[20]

Prior to the ASEAN Summit in Manila in December 1987, Philippine and Malaysian diplomats secretly met in Kuala Lumpur to work out drafts of a Treaty of Friendship and Cooperation and an agreement on Joint Border Patrol and Border Crossing. These were the quid pro quo for the dropping of the claim. Foreign Affairs Undersecretary Jose Ingles said the proposed border agreement was intended to "prevent Muslim secessionists from seeking sanctuary in Sabah."[21] It was also meant to prevent arms smuggling to Mindanao. The joint border patrol sought to regulate the flow of people and goods across the Philippine-Malaysian border. However, Congress failed to pass the joint resolution dropping the claim due to opposition from legislators. A report in *Newsbreak* magazine said a Filipino politician wanted a share of a proposed US$70 million settlement with the heirs, which thus scuttled the agreement.[22]

Despite the non-passage of the bill or the resolution dropping the Sabah claim, Mahathir did attend the ASEAN Summit in Manila. Mahathir was quoted as having told Malaysian journalists that "he was not disappointed that Congress did not pass the bill in time for the summit." He felt that Aquino was "really sincere" in settling the territorial dispute.[23] Then Foreign Affairs Secretary Raul Manglapus said the government had "done its best" to get the bill approved but "nothing is really predictable."[24] Senator Blas Ople, who was then head of the Senate Foreign Relations Committee, said the Aquino government "could not muster the political support to effect a statutory change."[25]

Ramos Government Follows Through on Predecessor's Attempts

President Ramos pursued the initiative of the Aquino government to drop the claim a step further. Former Philippine Ambassador to Malaysia

Rodolfo Severino said the "Malaysians thought they could do business with Ramos."[26] Thus, Mahathir reversed the policy of prohibition of high-level visits to the Philippines outside of ASEAN events. Mahathir adopted a more accommodating posture with the Ramos government.

As then Senator Ople, who was part of the Philippine delegation to Ramos' visit to Malaysia in 1993, said: "Kuala Lumpur reconsidered its long-standing position that the bilateral relationship would not go forward without the formal dropping of the Sabah claim by legislative action.... Dr Mahathir indicated that he understood the political necessity in the Philippines to undertake further consensus-building on this question."[27]

Interpreting Malaysia's new attitude, Ople said "Malaysia believed that by strengthening economic cooperation, the Sabah question will somehow resolve itself."[28]

JCM: Stronger Bilateralism Subverts Philippines' Claim

One of the major outcomes of the new era of vibrant bilateral relations under the Ramos regime was the establishment of the Philippines-Malaysia Joint Commission for Bilateral Cooperation (JCM) in July 1993. This strengthened bilateralism in Philippines-Malaysia relations. According to Victoriano Lecaros, the current Philippine Ambassador to Malaysia, the JCM is "the highest level of interaction short of a summit."[29] It is a high-level delegation led by the Foreign Affairs Ministers of the two countries. Former Philippine Ambassador to Malaysia Jose Brillantes described the JCM as a "safety valve" which prevents tensions and disputes from boiling over.[30]

The JCM has "triggered" the creation of other working groups that have become "another safety mechanism", Brillantes said.[31] Each working group "handles and anticipates certain problems hoping that what happened before is not going to recur."[32]

The Philippines and Malaysia have held six JCM meetings since 1993. These have focused mainly on boosting trade, economic cooperation, and social issues like labour and migration. The dispute over Sabah is not officially on the agenda of these meetings since this is a "special case" that needs "special negotiation", Lecaros said.[33] However, in some JCM meetings, Malaysian officials have urged the Philippines to establish a consulate in Sabah so that the Philippines can better attend to the needs of Filipinos there. Lecaros said the JCM also does not officially take up the Spratlys dispute because this is "not a bilateral issue".[34]

Some analysts believe it is the Ramos government that has done the most to subvert the Philippines claim to Sabah. This is because it was during the Ramos era (1992–98) that the Philippines entered into several bilateral agreements with Malaysia which imply "de facto" recognition of Malaysian sovereignty over Sabah. One example is the BIMP-EAGA growth triangle, launched in 1993, where Sabah is one of the areas — the other is Sarawak — defined as part of Malaysia's contribution to the growth triangle.

During his state visit to Malaysia in January 1993, Ramos discussed with Mahathir "the establishment of a Philippine consular office in East Malaysia", but he was given legal advice that it would mean dropping the claim.[35] Ramos informed Mahathir that his government was still trying to "reach a national consensus on the issue".[36] For this purpose, Ramos created the Joint Bipartisan Legislative-Executive Advisory Council on Sabah that was to form a national policy on the disputed territory. However, the council failed to come up with a unified policy under the Ramos government. Instead of a consulate, the Ramos government set up four temporary offices in Kota Kinabalu, Tawau, Sandakan, and Labuan so that passports could be issued to undocumented Filipinos who availed of Malaysia's 1997 Regularization Program for Illegal Immigrants from Indonesia and the Philippines. As a result, around 110,000 Filipinos were issued work permits in 1997. The Philippine Government said the setting up of these offices was "welcomed by the Malaysian authorities".[37] These offices have helped strengthen Malaysia's position on Sabah.

Relations between the two countries soured due to Estrada's expression of support for Anwar Ibrahim. However, the Department of Foreign Affairs bureaucrats followed the Ramos government's policy that pursuing the claim was already unrealistic. At the JCM held in March 2000, the Philippine side "reiterated the Philippine Government's commitment to establish a consulate in Sabah."[38] However, it also noted the continued absence of a national consensus on the issue and the fact that other sectors believed this would "jeopardize the Philippine sovereignty claim".[39]

Despite Closer Ties, Sabah Still Unresolved

Consistent with its bilateral approach in pushing the Philippines to drop its claim, Malaysia continued to encourage the Philippines to establish a consulate in Sabah. This was reportedly secured by Mahathir in a one-on-one meeting during one of Arroyo's early visits to Malaysia. But when Arroyo returned home, opposition from some legislators prompted Arroyo to backtrack and change her mind, which reportedly displeased Mahathir.

In her state visit to Malaysia in 2002, Arroyo was advised by the Department of Foreign Affairs that if Mahathir would raise the issue of establishing a Philippine consulate in Sabah, she would "note that the Philippine government is still trying to reach a national consensus on the issue."[40]

Relations between the Philippines and Malaysia under Arroyo have been restored to the vibrant state reached during the Ramos administration. Since 2001, Malaysia has been brokering the peace talks with the other separatist group, the MILF.

In September 2002, following the controversy over the mass deportation of Filipinos from Sabah, Arroyo reconstituted the legislative-executive committee that was tasked by Ramos to arrive at a national policy on the Sabah claim. However, such a national policy remains elusive until today.

Keeping Multilaterals Out Helps KL

Bilateralism has been the preferred mode by Malaysia in dealing with the dispute over Sabah. Keeping multilateral institutions, including ASEAN, out of the picture has been advantageous to Malaysia's interests. As Mercado Abad, Head of the ASEAN Regional Forum (ARF) Secretariat said: "Malaysia seems to be assured the status quo works in its favour. This is a case of pragmatic bilateralism."[41] Former ASEAN Secretary-General Rodolfo Severino said that for ASEAN as a whole, "there are some things that are better dealt with bilaterally because involving others may just add complication to the matter."[42] Severino said each country would have to find the best way of settling a particular dispute. "For legal disputes, you go to the ICJ or the Tribunal of the Law of the Sea." This is what Malaysia and Indonesia did with respect to the Sipadan-Ligitan dispute. "If it's bilateral, if it requires elevation to the ICJ, whatever works, you follow", he said.[43] As early as 1968, then Foreign Affairs Secretary Narciso Ramos had already said that the "dispute is a legal dispute".[44] Under Article 36, paragraph 3 of the United Nations Charter, he said "legal disputes are as a general rule referred to the ICJ for decision." The ICJ, he said, is the "best body to handle such a complex issue."[45] In the case of territorial disputes such as Sabah or

Sipadan-Ligitan between Malaysia and Indonesia, Severino said ASEAN is better left out of these. "What would be the added value of having ASEAN deal with it? It was satisfactorily dealt with in the ICJ."[46] Severino said that the Philippines, as early as the sixties, proposed to bring the Sabah dispute to the ICJ, but Malaysia has opposed it "on the supposition that agreeing to have this done at the World Court would mean that there's some doubt as to the legality of Malaysia's position."[47] But since decades have passed, he suggested that perhaps, "it's time for Malaysia to rethink its position."[48]

Likewise, the Malaysian view is that it would be best to keep ASEAN out of the dispute. For them, this is a domestic problem that should not involve outside powers such as the United States. Then President Marcos tried to get the United States involved and to support it on the dispute, but the United States chose to be neutral.

For the Malaysians, the issue of Sabah is already settled. It is no longer a territorial dispute but a proprietary issue that must be settled with the heirs of the Sultan. Malaysia has been consistent in rejecting a multilateral solution, for instance, by agreeing to bring the issue to the ICJ. Malaysia also understands that it would be very costly politically for the incumbent leader to drop the Sabah claim as it would shatter confidence in the government and would even be seen by some as tantamount to political suicide.

Absence of National Consensus and Lack of Political Will Hinder Conflict Resolution

An analysis of the attempts by various Philippine Governments to drop the Sabah claim also shows that the policymaking system in the Philippines makes it difficult to negotiate the Sabah claim in a multilateral setting. The Philippines presidential system of government vests in Congress the power to pass laws, while the executive branch executes the laws. Although foreign policy is vested mainly with the executive branch, foreign policies which may affect the Constitution and national laws would require congressional approval. If the Philippines had a parliamentary system of government, perhaps it would have been easier for the Aquino or the Ramos administration to drop the Sabah claim. The multiparty system that developed after the restoration of democracy in 1986 has also made it more difficult for the ruling party to get multiparty support for a major bilateral initiative such as dropping the Sabah claim.

The fact that the Sabah claim is hardly even discussed during national elections also means there is no opportunity to rally voters' support for a shift in diplomatic policies. There is no constituency calling for the dropping of the Sabah claim, and this means its importance as a political-electoral issue is quite low. Since the restoration of democracy, three administrations — Aquino, Ramos, Arroyo — have attempted to get an executive-legislative consensus on dropping the claim. None has succeeded. There is already a committee whose goal is to come up with a national consensus, but it has so far not been able to come up with it. Diplomats and analysts from both countries also agreed that it would be quite politically costly for any Philippine President to give up the claim. He or she may be accused of treason, culpable violation of the Constitution, and subject to impeachment.

It has been the failure of the executive and legislative branches of government to gather enough political will to drop the claim, which has proved to be a stumbling block in finally settling this dispute. In addition, the forces of nationalism — including the heirs of the Sultan of Sulu — have thus far been able to get enough support in Congress, particularly the older generation of politicians, to block the effort to drop the claim.

It cannot be said, however, that the executive and the legislative branches of government often fail to move forward on bilateral issues. There have been bilateral initiatives in the past which were approved by the Senate, the legislative body that ratifies treaties. For instance, the controversial Visiting Forces Agreement between the United States and the Estrada administration was surprisingly approved by the Senate in 1999. And in 2008, another controversial bilateral accord, the Japan-Philippines Economic Partnership Agreement, just got enough votes needed — sixteen — to be ratified by the Senate.

Another problem is the heirs of the Sultan of Sulu. Malaysia wants the heirs to speak with one voice so that she can deal with them collectively. But it has been difficult to get all the heirs to have a common stand. To Malaysia, Sabah is no longer a territorial dispute but a proprietary issue which has to be settled with the heirs.

This year, Malaysia and the Philippines will be submitting their respective baselines with the UN Convention on the Law of the Sea. Under the draft bill endorsed by the Arroyo government to Congress, the Philippine archipelagic baseline excludes Sabah, but the Philippine position is that this is without prejudice to its claim. Based on the official administrative map of the Philippines released by the National Mapping and Resource Information Authority, the country's central mapping agency, Sabah is not within the Philippines' international boundaries. It is simply part of the large island of Borneo. In time, however, the two countries may be able to put a close to this issue as the younger generation of Filipinos and Filipino leaders adopt a more practical approach in resolving this dispute. This stand is reflected in President Arroyo's preference to drop the claim. She was fifty-three years old when she assumed office in January 2001. Politicians seen as blocking this effort are around twenty years older, and many of them no longer hold key public posts.

The prospect of finding jobs in Malaysia, the problems of Filipinos in Sabah, and the weak military capability of the Philippines are factors that will continue to weaken the Philippines position on Sabah vis-à-vis Malaysia.

Muslim Separatist Movement: OIC, Not ASEAN, Key to Conflict Resolution

In response to the Marcos government's covert plan to infiltrate and destabilize Sabah in 1968, Malaysia responded by giving support to the Filipino Muslim separatists in the southern Philippines. Soliman Santos, an expert on the Muslim separatist movement, citing an account of one of the MNLF founders, summarized the international involvement in the conflict:

> Foreign support, including in the form of arms and military training, as early as 1969 to the emerging MNLF, which was formed as an immediate response to the Jabidah Massacre of 18 March 1968.... The first 90 Moro mujahideen (warriors), including Misuari and the MNLF's first Central Committee, were given military training in Pulau Pangkor island, Perak, Malaysia, arriving via Sabah in 1969.[49]

Citing other historical accounts, Santos said, "Sabah's Chief Minister Tun Datu Mustapha Harun allowed Sabah to be used as a training camp, supply depot, communications centre, and sanctuary for the MNLF from 1972 to 1976."[50] A peace agreement brokered by Libya was reached in 1976.

Malaysia has never admitted these allegations and has said that the conflict in the southern Philippines is a domestic affair. The conflict has been defined as one between the Muslim separatist movement in the southern Philippines and the government. Thus, it would have been difficult and unrealistic to bring this problem before ASEAN for dispute settlement. ASEAN's principle of non-interference is one reason for its mere secondary role in the peace process with the Muslim separatists.

In the resolution of this conflict between the Philippines and the Muslim separatists, Santos said it was the OIC, and not ASEAN, which played a key role, although ASEAN or "Asian diplomacy" would later play a crucial role when Indonesia assumed a leadership role in the peace process.[51] The OIC's leverage as the Philippines' major source of oil was a factor in its influential role.

Through the efforts of the OIC, a peace agreement was reached in Tripoli, Libya in 1976. However, the Marcos government was accused by the OIC of not complying with the accord, negotiations broke down, and conflict resumed until the Marcos regime fell in 1986.

Peace negotiations with the MNLF resumed under the democratic regime of President Aquino. By this time, there were already two separatist movements, the MNLF and the breakaway MILF.

The Ramos government pursued the peace negotiations with the MNLF until a final peace agreement was reached with the MNLF in September 1996. Libya and Indonesia played a key role in convincing Misuari to accept the Ramos government's formula, "even if it deviated from the Tripoli Agreement".[52]

Malaysia's Peace Brokering Weakens the Philippines' Hand

The Aquino government initiated peace talks with the other separatist group, the MILF, but no agreement has been reached. The Ramos administration built on its achievement in concluding a peace agreement with the MNLF by signing a ceasefire agreement with the MILF in 1997. The Estrada government reversed these gains after it launched an all-out war against the MILF and successfully captured its permanent camps.

President Arroyo adopted the same strategy as Ramos and pursued peace talks with the MILF. She invited Malaysia to help broker a peace accord with the MILF. Thus, from giving Muslim separatists safe haven in Sabah in the 1970s, Malaysia has now assumed the role of a "third-party facilitator"[53] in the peace talks between the Philippine Government and another separatist group, the MILF. Malaysia has hosted all the meetings in Kuala Lumpur.

Santos said Malaysia's "role of facilitation is moving towards mediation."[54] This includes "devising or promoting a solution, loosening the tension between the parties, creating an atmosphere conducive to negotiation, being an effective channel of information, and providing the parties with suggestions."[55]

The Malaysians' "prosper thy neighbour" policy is the guiding principle that has prompted Malaysia to play a prominent role in the peace talks. The Sipadan hostage crisis in 2000 and the growing problems caused by Filipino migrants have also pushed Malaysia to take a more active role in the peace process. From October 2004 to November 2008, Malaysia led the sixty-member International Monitoring Team for the government-MILF ceasefire. Other countries have been included in the International Monitoring Team, namely Brunei, Libya, and Japan. The IMT's composition was expanded to "include the participation of other nations in monitoring the rehabilitation and development work related to the peace process".[56]

Peace talks collapsed in September 2008 after the Arroyo government backed out of signing an agreement on an expanded and more powerful Muslim ancestral homeland that was set on 5 August in Kuala Lumpur. Concluding a peace deal between the Arroyo government and the MILF is now unlikely since the Arroyo government wants disarmament of the separatists even before a final peace settlement is reached. It also wants a peace deal that would be in line with the Philippine Constitution, which is a major obstacle to resolving the demands of the separatists.

Some analysts have said internationalization of the Muslim separatist problem actually weakens the hand of the Philippines. Malaysia has now become a guarantor of peace in the south. In contrast, if the Philippines could resolve the conflict through military and development means, it would diminish the influence of Malaysia over the Philippines.

The late former MILF Chairman Hashim Salamat once expressed the view that the quid pro quo in Malaysia's brokering the peace negotiations is Sabah. "Malaysia is hoping that if she could play an important role in ending the conflict ... the Sabah claim may be dropped or delayed indefinitely", he said.[57]

Filipino Migrants in Sabah: Exploiting the Philippines' Weak Hand

The Muslim separatist movement caused a large migration of Filipinos to Sabah who fled the war. Between 50,000 to 80,000 Filipinos were believed to have fled to Sabah. The UN High Commissioner for Refugees (UNHCR) once estimated it at 100,000. Based on a Malaysian Census in 1990–91, 57,197 were counted as refugees. This refers to "Filipinos who arrived in Sabah between 1970 and 1977 during the escalation of hostilities in Southern Philippines between government forces and Muslim secessionists."[58] Filipino refugees were allowed to stay and work "without any time limitation in Sabah and Labuan" under an order signed in 1972. Many of them are already voters in Sabah and are used by politicians in Sabah to help them get elected.

Sabah has also attracted migrant workers from the Philippines, Indonesia, and other neighbouring countries. Sabah is dependent on migrant labour to run its economy. A large proportion of the foreign workers are in agricultural estates and plantations. In 2001, out of 147,447 legal foreign workers in Sabah, 93 per cent were Indonesians; 6 per cent were Filipinos. In 2003, 44 per cent of Malaysia's foreign population were in Sabah; 23 per cent of Sabah's population were non-Malaysian citizens.

Through the years, these foreigners have posed various problems for Sabah. The kidnapping of tourists in Sipadan in 2000 by the Abu Sayyaf terror group did a lot of damage to Malaysia's tourism industry. From 1999 to 2001, around one-fourth of criminal cases involved immigrants. Squatter colonies of undocumented migrants are also perceived to be "havens for criminals and other undesirable elements and illegal activities."[59]

Malaysia has taken several steps to address these issues. Among the steps taken have been: strict border control and checks; arrest and deportation of irregular immigrants; regularization programmes; penalties for employers who hire foreign workers without a valid work permit; penalties for those who shelter or bring in undocumented workers; a levy on foreign workers; voluntary repatriation of foreigners; destruction of squatter colonies.

The problems faced by Filipino migrants in Sabah has been a growing contentious issue between the two countries. Arrests and large-scale deportations have caused bilateral conflicts. In particular, the large-scale deportation implemented by Malaysia in 2002 was a major diplomatic problem. In response, then Foreign Secretary Blas Ople summoned the Malaysian Ambassador in August 2002 and handed him a diplomatic note conveying Manila's concern over the "inhuman treatment" of deportees.[60] Then Malaysian Ambassador Taufik Mohamed Noor said he too was "shocked about the appalling conditions of the deportees" and "promised to convey the Philippine government's concerns to Kuala Lumpur."[61]

President Arroyo sent a delegation to Malaysia which asked Malaysia to reduce the number of Filipino deportees. From February 2002 to April 2002, just three months, nearly 9,000 Filipinos were deported. Most of them had been living in Sabah, Labuan, or Sarawak for more than ten years. Around half of them came from the nearby Muslim provinces of Sulu and Tawi-Tawi. The Philippines Government asked Malaysia to reduce the number of deportees to 200 a month, extend the deadline, and to find ways to let them return to Malaysia as legal workers. These requests were eventually granted. Then Ambassador to Malaysia Jose Brillantes said that following the filing of the diplomatic protest, "the situation has vastly improved".[62] A few civil society groups and some politicians raised a howl over Malaysia's treatment of Filipino deportees.

Kuala Lumpur Uses Bilateralism to the Full

The Philippines and Malaysia have used bilateral means to manage these migration-related problems. These have become a major topic in the Joint Bilateral Commission (JCM). Two other bilateral committees have been formed to address the migration issues: the Republic of the Philippines–Malaysia Working Group on Migrant Workers, and the Republic of the Philippines–Malaysia Joint Committee on Sabah Repatriates. These groups are headed by senior officials of the two countries. The working group, which has met at least three times, was established as a "mode for constructive engagement and effective collaboration on matters affecting the lot of Filipino migrants in Malaysia."[63]

Malaysia has also used bilateral negotiations to try to extract more concessions from the Philippines on the Sabah dispute. At the sixth JCM, for instance, Datuk Rastam Mohd Isa, Secretary-General of the Ministry of Foreign Affairs of Malaysia called on the Philippines to establish a consulate in Sabah in order to better attend to the needs of Filipinos there. He said:

> I strongly believe that the establishment of the Philippines Consulate General in Sabah is the right start in addressing the problems faced by Filipino nationals in the state and in the process, this *bold step would bring a permanent solution to this irritant in our bilateral ties.*[64]

The establishment of a Consulate-General's office in Sabah would make it easier for the Philippine Government to better serve Filipino migrants there.

Few Gains in the Philippines' Multilateral Approach

On the part of the Philippines, diplomats have been using ASEAN as a forum to advance its agenda on Filipino migrants. Indonesia and other sending states have supported the Philippines in this endeavour.

At the twelfth ASEAN Summit in 2006/2007 in Cebu City, for instance, the Philippines initiated the ASEAN Declaration on the Protection and Promotion of the Rights of Migrant Workers. The agreement defines the obligations of receiving states, sending states, and the commitments of ASEAN as a regional community. It is a "rights-based approach to protection of rights of migrant workers and promotion of their welfare".[65]

Spratlys Dispute: The Philippines Maximizes Multilateral Options

The territorial dispute in the Spratlys in the South China Sea is essentially a multilateral dispute involving the six claimant countries — Brunei, Malaysia, the Philippines, Vietnam, Taiwan, and China.

This section focuses on one incident, basically a bilateral dispute between Malaysia and the Philippines in mid-1999, when Malaysia occupied Investigator Shoal and Erica Reef. Philippine diplomats I interviewed could no longer recall this dispute and how it was resolved. Thus, for the facts about this incident, this chapter is relying heavily on the 2004 doctoral thesis, "The Spratly Islands Dispute: Decision Units and Domestic Politics" by Christopher Chung.[66]

Investigator Shoal is around 460 kilometres from the Philippines province of Palawan, and around 250 kilometres from Kota Kinabalu, Sabah, Malaysia. It is in an area claimed by Malaysia, the Philippines, Taiwan, and China. The shoal has an area of 205 square kilometres.

In June 1999, it was discovered that Malaysia had built a two-storey concrete building, helipad, pier, and radar antenna on Investigator Shoal. Malaysia also occupied and built a two-storey building and helipad on Erica Reef, which lies around 525 kilometres from Palawan. After these were discovered, the Philippines, China, and Vietnam protested

Malaysia's actions. The Philippines filed a diplomatic protest saying that Investigator Shoal was "part of Philippine territory and within the country's exclusive economic zone."[67] It also complained that Malaysia violated the 1992 Manila Declaration on the South China Sea, which prescribed a status quo, meaning no new occupation and construction, in the disputed areas.

After the occupation and construction on Erica Reef, the Department of Foreign Affairs filed a diplomatic protest on 20 August 1999.

In response to Malaysia's actions, President Joseph Estrada said the Philippines would also build structures on islands that it claims. But this was opposed by Foreign Affairs Secretary Domingo Siazon who did not want the conflict to escalate. Siazon's position eventually prevailed in the Cabinet.

After its unilateral occupation, Malaysia "kept a low profile" and eventually, the dispute died down. Henceforth, Malaysia "did not occupy any further features, contrary to media reports". [68]

Neither Malaysia nor the Philippines used ASEAN's dispute settlement mechanisms to resolve this dispute. Severino said it is best to use the Law of the Sea Tribunal to settle such legal disputes.[69] Since the dispute actually involves four of the ten ASEAN members and two non-ASEAN countries — China and Taiwan — ASEAN's dispute settlement mechanism would not be appropriate for it. However, the Philippines used ASEAN as a forum to ventilate its sentiments and to urge compliance with ASEAN declarations on the South China Sea that commit signatories not to use force and to exercise restraint. It reminded other countries about such commitments as provided in the 1992 Manila Declaration on the South China Sea.

The Philippines has also pushed for a regional code and bilateral codes of conduct. It concluded bilateral codes of conduct with China and Vietnam in August 1995 and in November 1995 respectively. As Severino said, the Philippines objective is to "obtain a Chinese commitment not to pull another Mischief Reef".[70] These codes of conduct commit the countries to "strive for peaceful settlement of disputes by diplomatic means, to take cooperative measures to prevent conflict, to build trust, and to promote the joint exploration, development and exploitation of the resources therein."[71]

In July 1996, ASEAN Foreign Ministers endorsed the need for a regional code of conduct, that is, between ASEAN and China. According to Severino, ASEAN and China started to negotiate the code in March

2000. However, disagreements among ASEAN countries "held up the conclusion of the code".[72]

At the 1999 meeting of ASEAN Foreign Ministers, Malaysia "opposed any discussion of its occupation of Investigator Shoal and Erica Reef".[73] Malaysia's position was that bilateral issues should be "discussed bilaterally".[74] In that meeting, Malaysia "successfully opposed the Philippines' call to include in the foreign ministers' communiqué a statement urging all claimants to halt occupation and construction in disputed areas of the South China Sea".[75] It merely "recognized that several issues remained a source of concern".[76]

Indonesia, a non-claimant country, has hosted three sessions of Workshops on Managing Potential Conflicts in the South China Sea. These have been conducted outside of ASEAN. Indonesia's attempts at dispute settlement in the Spratlys were made as a goodwill gesture and delivered as a non-claimant state. Indonesia, as *primus inter pares* in ASEAN, was uniquely placed to offer such good offices. Were it not for these two important considerations, its role as a broker would have been difficult.

Kuala Lumpur's Unilateralism Works to its Advantage

Based on how the 1999 incident played out, Malaysia's unilateral action has helped strengthen its position in the South China Sea. The country's move to occupy Investigator Shoal and Erica Reef was apparently a pre-emptive move for the code of conduct agreement that was to be agreed upon with China. In line with what China did on Mischief Reef in 1995 and 1998, Chung said Malaysia's occupation "demonstrated the benefits of pro-activity".[77] He said: "In seizing a contested feature and building permanent structures, the reality of possession makes dislodgement by diplomatic, legal, military or moral pressure a difficult task."[78]

Chung's thesis is that "while Malaysia's approach emphasized occupation of contested features, the Philippines concentrated on diplomacy to internationalize its position."[79] He added:

> A weak economy and low military capability to handle external threats severely constrained Manila's options to defend its claim. Diplomacy at bilateral and multilateral levels was the only realistic instrument of statecraft available to shore up its claim.[80]

However, when dealing with China, Malaysia took a common position with the Philippines and the rest of the ASEAN countries.

As Mecardo Abad, head of the ARF secretariat, said:

> The multilateral code of conduct and other forms of bilateral arrangements are political expressions of peaceful outlook. This is a case where a group of relatively smaller countries have used a multilateral approach to join forces to advance their collective interest vis-à-vis a major power.[81]

Conclusion: Non-resort to ASEAN Mechanisms for Conflict Resolution Explained

The contentious issues between the Philippines and Malaysia have never been raised before the ASEAN High Council in the Treaty of Amity and Cooperation (TAC). In fact, no political or security related dispute has ever been brought to the ASEAN High Council. Several reasons were put forward for this.

Then Foreign Affairs Assistant Secretary for ASEAN Affairs Luis Cruz said that "so far, they [ASEAN] haven't identified a regional issue that will merit the attention of the High Council."[82]

Severino said the ASEAN High Council on the TAC is an "expression of ASEAN's determination to resolve disputes by peaceful means." He said the fact that ASEAN has not used the council "is of no importance".[83] Severino said that it is important to note that the council is "not a dispute settlement mechanism". He added:

> If you read the Treaty, it says there this High Council will recommend ways of solving disputes. It doesn't say it will solve the dispute. That's why it's not an adjudicating body. The High Council is not a court of justice. It is just a political body that will recommend ways of solving things, so if it's not used, that means there are no disputes.[84]

Severino said that if the bilateral dispute is essentially a legal dispute, the best recourse would still be the ICJ, not ASEAN. "For legal disputes, you go to the ICJ or to the Tribunal of the Law of the Sea, which is what Malaysia and Singapore did."[85]

Will the adoption of the ASEAN Charter at the end of 2009 mean that ASEAN members will soon be using ASEAN's dispute settlement mechanisms? Will the Philippines and Malaysia be using these mechanisms to resolve their disputes?

Ambassador Rosario Manalo, the Philippines representative to the high-level task force on the ASEAN Charter, said the approval of the

ASEAN Charter could prompt ASEAN to make use of the High Council for managing disputes. She said the Charter will force member states in the TAC to develop the council's operation. Prior to the approval of the Charter, "there was no legal basis with force of law to comply". But now, "there is, it's rules-bound".[86]

The ASEAN Charter has three separate dispute settlement mechanisms: one for the political community, another for the economic community, and a third for the social community. For a political-security dispute, parties are referred to the High Council on the TAC or the ASEAN Summit.

Manalo said the Charter provides for dispute settlement mechanisms, "including arbitration". However, she pointed out that ASEAN does not have a "judicial agency or a court because we don't have the capacity to do that". This means that a dispute that requires judicial action cannot be resolved by ASEAN. But she said there will be arbitration panels. If a dispute still remains unresolved at ministerial levels or by arbitration, the dispute "shall be referred to the ASEAN Summit for its decision". She said the leaders "still have the ultimate say". If unresolved at the level of leaders, the "UN is still the last resort".

Outgoing ASEAN Secretary-General Ong Keng Yong said that when it comes to political-security disputes, the High Council on the TAC is available and can be activated.[87] But he believed that eventually, for territorial disputes, leaders will have the final say. For very legal issues, the best recourse would be the ICJ. "In certain disputes, maybe you require political [decision]. On certain disputes, you require legal. It will depend on the dispute and the nature", he said.

"Many of these territorial disputes have a lot of political implications. So I think the way the drafters of the charter look at it is that many of these political-security disputes are likely to be handled first by our ministers and our leaders before they activate any other mechanism. So it is all a political issue", Ong said.[88]

Severino said he does not think the adoption of the ASEAN Charter would "change [the] character of ASEAN". Asked if ASEAN members will now resort to the various dispute settlement mechanisms in the charter, Severino said: "No. They will have to willingly do it. They will be willing to do it only if they recognize that it's good for them to do it.... The willingness to do so would have to come from the member states."[89] And this willingness, "will take time", he said.

NOTES

1   This term was used by Datuk Emam Mohd. Haniff in a speech delivered before the Philippine Council for Foreign Relations, 28 September 1989, Ateneo de Manila University, Philippines.
2   Long-distance telephone interview with Philippine Ambassador to Malaysia, Victoriano Lecaros, 27 October 2007.
3   Interview with Ambassador Rosario Manalo, Philippines representative to the high-level task force on the ASEAN Charter.
4   Ling Chang Hong, "Only a third of ASEAN pledges implemented", *Sunday Times* (Singapore), 18 November 2007, p. 10.
5   Estrella Solidum, "Philippine External Relations with Southeast Asia", Philippines Centennial Vista, Foreign Service Institute–Department of Foreign Affairs, 1998, p. 126
6   Ibid.
7   Haniff, Speech before the Philippine Council for Foreign Relations, p. 175.
8   Ibid., p. 175.
9   Marites Vitug and Glenda Gloria, *Under the Crescent Moon: Rebellion in Mindanao* (Quezon City: Ateneo Center for Social Policy and Public Affairs and Institute for Popular Democracy), pp. 2–23.
10 Ibid., p. 20.
11 Ibid., pp. 20–21.
12 Ibid., p. 20.
13 Ibid., p. 2.
14 Blas Ople, "A Breakthrough in Kuala Lumpur", *Manila Bulletin*, 2 February 1993 (published in Ople's monograph, *Going Beyond Sabah: RP–Malay Solidarity*, 3 February 1994).
15 Department of Foreign Affairs, *Overview of Philippines-Malaysia Relations*, 2002.
16 *Ibid.*
17 Rodolfo Severino, *Southeast Asia in Search of an ASEAN Community: Insights from the Former ASEAN Secretary-General* (Singapore: Institute of Southeast Asian Studies, 2006), pp. 164–65.
18 Ibid., pp. 165–66
19 Blas Ople, "Will Ramos Drop Sabah?" *Manila Bulletin*, 15 October 1992 (reprinted in Ople's monograph, *Going Beyond Sabah: RP–Malay Solidarity*, 3 February 1994).
20 Wilson Bailon, Marites Sison, and Sonora Ocampo, "Stormy Debate on Sabah Looms", *Manila Chronicle*, 25 November 1987, p. 1.
21 Ibid.
22 Glenda Gloria, "An Old Wound Called Sabah", *Newsbreak*, 30 September 2002, p. 28.

23   "Mahathir: Cory Sincere on Sabah", *Manila Chronicle*, 16 December 1987, pp. 1–2.

24   Ibid., p. 2.

25   Blas Ople, "Our Bilateral Ties: A New Unfolding", Privilege speech delivered on the Senate floor, Manila, Philippines, 3 February 1994 (reprinted in Ople's monograph, *Going Beyond Sabah: RP–Malay Solidarity*, 3 February 1994).

26   Long-distance interview with Rodolfo Severino, former ASEAN Secretary-General, 1 October 2007.

27   Blas Ople, "Our Bilateral Ties: A New Unfolding", p. 4.

28   Blas Ople, "Our Place in Southeast Asia", *Philippine Graphic*, 18 February 1993. (reprinted in Ople's monograph, *Going Beyond Sabah: RP–Malay Solidarity*, 3 February 1994, p. 12).

29   Long-distance interview with Philippine Ambassador to Malaysia, Victoriano Lecaros, 27 October 2007.

30   Long-distance interview with former Philippine Ambassador to Malaysia, Jose Brillantes, 22 October 2007.

31   Ibid.

32   Ibid.

33   Ibid., and interview with Victoriano Lecaros, 27 October 2007.

34   Ibid.

35   Confidential briefing paper for President Gloria Macapagal-Arroyo's Working Visit to Malaysia, Department of Foreign Affairs, 7 May 2002.

36   Ibid.

37   Office of the Press Secretary, Overview of Philippine-Malaysia Relations (backgrounder), 2005, part of a briefing kit for media for President Gloria Macapagal-Arroyo's visit to Kuala Lumpur, Malaysia to attend the Eleventh ASEAN Summit and related summit meetings, December 2005.

38   Confidential briefing paper for President Gloria Macapagal-Arroyo's Working Visit to Malaysia, Department of Foreign Affairs, 7 May 2002.

39   Ibid.

40   Ibid.

41   Email interview with Medardo Abad, head of ASEAN Regional Forum Secretariat-Jakarta, October 2007.

42   Interview with Rodolfo Severino, former ASEAN Secretary-General, 1 October 2007.

43   Ibid.

44   Narciso Ramos, "Philippines Brings the Sabah Dispute to the UN", text of statement delivered before the UN General Assembly during its Twenty-third Session in New York (Manila: Department of Foreign Affairs, 15 October 1968).

45   Ibid.

46   Interview with Rodolfo Severino, former ASEAN Secretary-General, 1 October 2007.

47   Ibid.
48   Ibid.
49   Soliman Santos, Jr., "The Philippines-Muslims Dispute: International Aspects from Origins to Resolution", *World Bulletin: Bulletin of the International Studies Institute of the Philippines* 16, nos. 1–2 (2000): 7. Santos' paper explains the reasons why the OIC, rather than ASEAN, was able to play a key role in brokering a peace agreement with the Moro separatists.
50   Ibid.
51   Ibid., p. 36.
52   Ibid., pp. 34–35.
53   Soliman Santos, "Malaysia's Role in the Peace Negotiations between the Philippine Government and the Moro Islamic Liberation Front", unpublished paper shared by the author (May 2003), p. 2.
54   Ibid., p. 6.
55   Ibid.
56   Office of the Press Secretary, "Overview of Philippine-Malaysia Relations," 2005.
57   Santos, Malaysia's Role, p. 12.
58   Bilson Kurus, "Undocumented Immigrants in Sabah: Reality, Trends and Response", *Asian Migrant* (July–September 2002), p. 69.
59   Ibid., p. 70.
60   "Manila Protests KL's Treatment of Filipinos", *Inq7.net* (Philippines), 27 August 2002.
61   Ibid.
62   "Arroyo to Send Ramos to Malaysia to Discuss Deportation Issue", 2 September 2002 <http://findarticles.com/p/articles/mi_m0WDQ/is_2002_Sept_2/ai_91081481>.
63   Department of Foreign Affairs, Manila, Philippines, "Joint Statement, Third Meeting of the RP–Malaysia Working Group in Migrant Workers", 16 June 2006.
64   Opening remarks by H.E. Datuk Rastam Mohd Isa, Secretary-General of the Ministry of Foreign Affairs of Malaysia at the Senior Officials Meeting of the Sixth Joint Commission Meeting between Malaysia and the Republic of the Philippines, Kuala Lumpur, 27–28 April 2006; emphasis added.
65   Interview with Foreign Affairs Undersecretary for Migrant Workers, Esteban Conejos, 10 January 2007.
66   Christopher Chung, "The Spratly Islands Dispute: Decision Units and Domestic Politics" (Ph.D. dissertation, University of New South Wales, 2004).
67   Ibid., p. 121.
68   Chung, "The Spratly Islands Dispute", p. 128.
69   Interview with Rodolfo Severino, former ASEAN Secretary-General, 1 October 2007.

70 Rodolfo Severino, *Southeast Asia In Search of an ASEAN Community*, p. 186.
71 Fidel V. Ramos. "Spratlys: Oil on Troubled Waters", *Manila Bulletin*, 4 September 2005, p. 18.
72 Rodolfo Severino, *Southeast Asia In Search of an ASEAN Community*, p. 186.
73 Christopher Chung, "The Spratly Islands Dispute", p. 145.
74 Ibid., p. 163.
75 Ibid.
76 Ibid.
77 Ibid., p. 125.
78 Ibid.
79 Ibid., p. 116.
80 Ibid.
81 Interview with Medardo Abad, Head of ASEAN Regional Forum Secretariat-Jakarta, October 2007.
82 Interview with Foreign Affairs Assistant Secretary for ASEAN Affairs Luis Cruz, 31 August 2007.
83 Interview with Rodolfo Severino, former ASEAN Secretary-General, 1 October 2007.
84 Ibid.
85 Ibid.
86 Interview with Ambassador Rosario Manalo, Philippines representative to the High Level Task Force on the ASEAN Charter, 7 November 2007.
87 Interview with ASEAN Secretary-General Ong Keng Yong, 8 September 2007.
88 Ibid.
89 Interview with Rodolfo Severino.

REFERENCES

Abad, Medardo. "Prospects for Conflict Mediation in ASEAN". Remarks at the Asia Mediators' Retreat, presented at Sentosa, Singapore, 22 November 2005.
Arguillas, Carol. "Ten Years After". *Newsbreak*, 11 September 2006, p. 20
"Arroyo to send Ramos to Malaysia to Discuss Deportation Issue". *Kyodo News International*, 29 August 2002 <http://findarticles.com/p/articles/mi_m0WDQ/is_2002_Sept_2/ai_91081481> (accessed 28 February 2009).
———. Draft as of 7 December 2006.
"ASEAN Declaration on the Protection and Promotion of the Rights of Migrant Workers". Draft endorsed by ASEAN Foreign Ministers, 12 January 2007 <http://www.aseansec.org/19264.htm> (accessed 28 February 2009).
Bailon, Wilson. "Shahani Files Bill Dropping Sabah Bid". *Manila Chronicle*, 20 November 1987, pp. 1 & 7.

Bailon, Wilson, Marites Sison, and Sonora Ocampo. "Stormy Debate on Sabah Looms". *Manila Chronicle*, 25 November 1987, pp. 1 & 6.

Chung, Christopher. "The Spratly Islands Dispute: Decision Units and Domestic Politics". Ph.D. dissertation, School of Politics, University of New South Wales, 2004.

Constantine, Greg. "The Lost Boys of Sabah". *The Irrawaddy*, 5 October 2007.

Dacanay, Ceferino B. "An Assessment of the Philippine-Malaysia Border Cooperation Agreement". M.A. dissertation, National Defense College of the Philippines, 2001.

De Castro, Isagani, Jr. "Nightmare in Mindanao". *Newsbreak*, 27 May 2002.

Department of Foreign Affairs, "Overview of Philippines-Malaysia Relations". Manila, Department of Foreign Affairs, 2002.

————. "Confidential briefing paper for President Gloria Macapagal-Arroyo's Working Visit to Malaysia". Manila, Department of Foreign Affairs, 7 May 2002.

————. "Joint Statement, Third Meeting of the RP-Malaysia Working Group in Migrant Workers". Manila, Department of Foreign Affairs, 16 June 2006.

————, "Overview of Philippines-Malaysia Relations". Manila, Department of Foreign Affairs, 2007.

Ganesan, N. *Bilateral Tensions in Post-Cold War ASEAN*. Singapore: Institute of Southeast Asian Studies, 1999.

Gloria, Glenda. "An Old Wound Called Sabah". *Newsbreak*, 30 September 2002, p. 28.

Haniff, Datuk Eman Mohd. "Malaysia-Philippine Relations". *Foreign Relations Journal* (December 1989): 174–83.

Kurus, Bilson. "Undocumented Immigrants in Sabah: Reality, Trends and Response". *Asian Migrant* (July–September 2002) p. 69.

Ling, Chang Hong. "Only a Third of ASEAN Pledges Implemented". *Sunday Times* (Singapore), 18 November 2007, p. 10.

"Mahathir: Cory Sincere on Sabah". *Manila Chronicle*, 16 December 1987, p. 1.

Mangahas, Malou. "Gov't Set to Formalize Dropping of Sabah Bid". *Manila Chronicle*, 4 December 1987, pp. 1 & 8.

"Manila Protests KL's Treatment of Filipinos". Inq7.net, 27 August 2002.

Office of the Press Secretary (Philippines). "Overview of Philippines-Malaysia Relations". Part of a briefing kit for media for President Gloria Macapagal-Arroyo's visit to Kuala Lumpur, Malaysia for the Eleventh ASEAN Summit and other related summit meetings, December 2005.

"OFW Alliance Presses Boycott of Malaysian Services, Goods". Inq7.net, 31 August 2002.

Opening remarks by H.E. Datuk Rastam Mohd Isa, Secretary-General of the Ministry of Foreign Affairs of Malaysia at the Senior Officials Meeting of the Sixth Joint Commission Meeting between Malaysia and the Republic of the Philippines, Kuala Lumpur, 27–28 April 2006.

Ople, Blas. "Will Ramos drop Sabah?" *Manila Bulletin*, 15 October 1992.

———. "A Breakthrough in Kuala Lumpur". *Manila Bulletin*, 2 February 1993.

———. "Our Place in Southeast Asia". *Philippine Graphic*, 18 February 1993.

———. "Our Bilateral Ties: A New Unfolding". Privilege speech delivered on the Senate floor, 3 February 1994.

———. "The Burden of Sabah". *Manila Bulletin*, 26 January 2003.

"Philippines-Malaysia Relations". A Research Project of the Center for International Relations and Strategic Studies–Foreign Service Institute (Department of Foreign Affairs), August 1996.

Ramos, Fidel V. "Spratlys: Oil on Troubled Waters". *Manila Bulletin*, 4 September 2005.

Ramos, Narciso. "Philippines Brings the Sabah Dispute to the UN, Department of Foreign Affairs". Text of statement delivered before the UN General Assembly during its Twenty-third Session in New York, 15 October 1968.

"RP Readies Raps Versus Malaysian Illegals". Inq7.net, 29 August 2002.

"Sabah's Perfect Storm". *Asian Migrant*, (July–September 2002): 57

Santos, Soliman, Jr. "The Philippines-Muslims Dispute: International Aspects from Origins to Resolution". *World Bulletin: Bulletin of the International Studies Institute of the Philippines* 16, nos. 1–2 (2000).

———. "Malaysia's Role in the Peace Negotiations between the Philippine Government and the Moro Islamic Liberation Front". Unpublished paper, May 2003.

Severino, Rodolfo. *Southeast Asia in Search of an ASEAN Community: Insights from the former ASEAN Secretary-General*. Singapore: Institute of Southeast Asian Studies, 2006.

Sison, Marites and Wilson Bailon. "Manglapus Picked as Sabah Heirs' Negotiator". *Manila Chronicle*, 5 December 1987, pp. 1 & 6.

Solidum, Estrella. "Philippine External Relations with Southeast Asia". In *Philippine External Relations, a Centennial Vista*. Foreign Service Institute, Department of Foreign Affairs, 1998.

Vitug, Marites Danguilan. "The Road to Kuala Lumpur: The Inside Story of How President Arroyo got the MILF Back to the Peace Table". *Newsbreak*, 18–25 April 2001, p. 21.

Vitug, Marites and Glenda Gloria. *Under the Crescent Moon: Rebellion in Mindanao*. Quezon City: Ateneo Center for Social Policy and Public Affairs and Institute for Popular Democracy, 2000.

10

Malaysia-Singapore Relations: A Bilateral Relationship Defying ASEAN-style Multilateralist Approaches to Conflict Resolution

K.S. Nathan

Introduction: The Persistent Influence of Realism

In an anarchic world such as ours — comprised as it is of about 195 state-units whose interactions are still governed by Westphalian notions of sovereignty — the primary goal of foreign policy is to ensure state survival. Once the state develops confidence in managing national security, and by extension, defending itself against external threats, its leadership invests a higher degree of trust in international cooperation, including strengthening ties with neighbours with whom it has

This paper is a revised and updated version of an earlier work, which appeared as "Malaysia-Singapore Relations: Retrospect and Prospect", *Contemporary Southeast Asia* 24, no. 2 (August 2002): 385–410.

outstanding historical, territorial, political, ideological, economic, and resource disputes. As such, this chapter takes the view that the key issues in Malaysia-Singapore relations are better analyzed and evaluated within the framework of political realism. The American political scientist, Sheldon Simon, has made very pertinent observation in this regard on Southeast Asian international relations:

> Realism (or self-help) will continue as an important analytical framework for understanding Southeast Asian security because individual states still have unresolved conflicts with each other and because no consensus exists whether external threats to regional order exist or who they may be.[1]

Foreign policies pursued essentially within a state-centric framework tend to endorse the realist paradigm, while efforts to build regional political, economic, and security institutions for mutual gain, although at an incipient stage, suggest also that neo-liberalist tendencies coexist with the realist approach to national security and regional advancement.[2] This coexistence of apparently divergent political perspectives — the former stressing politics as a zero-sum game and the latter focussing more on state capabilities and potential to achieve security and prosperity through cooperation rather than conflict — tends to better explain the dynamics of Malaysia-Singapore relations. The foreign policy interests, strategies, and expected outcomes of these two Causeway neighbours, and especially for the island republic since independence in 1965, reflect an appreciation based on power considerations as in this anarchic world the best and historically proven approach has been self-help. As Michael Leifer, a well-known British specialist on Southeast Asia observes:

> The rhetoric of government [in Singapore] registers a belief in the premises of the realist paradigm in International Relations, whereby states are obliged to fend for themselves as best they can in an ungoverned and hostile world.[3]

While international institutions and diplomacy do provide some measure of comfort, they are secondary instruments to policies and capabilities designed to ensure national security and survival. Realists believe that weak states are not capable of security leadership or managing regional order except through balance of power strategies in partnership with major external powers.[4] Even if Malaysia does not wholly subscribe to this view, the Singaporean strategic perspective is much closer to the realist perspective.

This chapter therefore proceeds from the realist and perhaps sceptical premise that the regional states in Southeast Asia support multi-lateralism in principle but tend to prioritize bilateralism (intra-regional and extra-regional) in practice as the region has yet to evolve into a "security community".[5] The all-inclusive ASEAN Regional Forum (ARF) instituted in 1994 is at best still a forum for multilateral security dialogue and cooperation without binding commitments and enforcement machinery. Thus bilateral issues, such as those affecting Malaysia-Singapore relations, continue to be handled bilaterally and not via the multilateral ARF structure. The chapter will conclude with the observation that national interests are approached and addressed essentially from a realist perspective — an approach that is particularly salient in Singapore's foreign policy strategy given its miniscule size and the geopolitical realities obtaining in its immediate neighbourhood, with a Malay/Muslim dominant Malaysia to the north, and a huge archipelagic state with an overwhelming Muslim population to the south.

Given its geo-political size and location, Singapore's survival strategy tends to focus on a very strong and robust deterrence to any threats arising from what it sees as a Malay/Muslim world in its immediate vicinity. Thus, analysts of Singapore's foreign policy have tended to use criteria that are more appropriate to the realist paradigm of international politics with its focus on elements of national power. For instance, N. Ganesan stresses the importance of Singapore's immediate regional environment in the Malay Archipelago as a determining factor shaping its national (internal and external) outlook. These factors include (1) geographical proximity, (2) historical interactions, (3) transnational linkages, (4) leadership perceptions, and (5) the country's differing socio-economic texture and level of development.[6]

Evidently, these criteria are equally relevant to Malaysian foreign policy formulation, but with the exception that while Singapore's quest for survival identifies its immediate "Malay" neighbours as threats, Malaysia predicates its survival and advancement in a broader balance of power terms. In other words, while Singapore might fear being swallowed up one day by Malaysia, the same logic does not apply vis-à-vis Singapore on the Johor side of the Causeway. For Malaysia, the logic of political realism dictates that while Singapore might be an irritant from time to time, economic interdependency and broader regional/global interests which are of greater concern to Malaysia require that bilateral relations and issues be downplayed and managed to mutual benefit.

Although Malaysia is committed to good neighbourly relations with its ASEAN neighbour, it can be argued that the Malay-dominant state has not quite come to terms with the loss of Malay power to what it considers to be the only sovereign state (historically known as Temasik) in the Malay archipelago and Southeast Asia controlled solely by a recent wave of Chinese immigrants. This Malay perception of Chinese-dominant Singapore can be surmised in reverse from former Singapore premier Lee Kuan Yew's own comment: that Singapore is the only place in Southeast Asia where the overseas Chinese can hold their heads high.[7] This dichotomy in worldview and political ideology is reflected by Malaysia's advocacy of *Bumiputeraism* (i.e. special preferences for the proclaimed indigenous Malay community) as opposed to Singapore's propagation of meritocracy and multiracialism. Arguably, the political economy of these two ideologies tends to be diametrically opposed to the conduct of cordial relations on a sustained basis, resulting in sometimes occasional as well as frequent hiccups in the bilateral relationship.

The UMNO (United Malays National Organisation) ideology of *Bumiputeraism* emphasizing state patronage, protection, and privileges for "indigenous" people would arguably find favour with the nearly fifteen per cent of Singapore Malays, while the People's Action Party (PAP) ideology focusing on meritocracy would arguably be well received by the approximately twenty-five per cent of Malaysian Chinese. Nevertheless, political pragmatism on both sides has prevailed over the last forty-four years to ensure that these irritations are contained for the greater good of mutual economic prosperity and regional stability within the framework of the Association of Southeast Asian Nations (ASEAN). In short, differences over various issues point to the existence of functional tension in Malaysia-Singapore relations (i.e. their conflict precludes the prospect of close and cordial relations), but permits the possibility of pursuing a certain level of political, economic, and security cooperation for mutual benefit. Their functional tension is clearly arising both from the political economy of their relationship, which include differences in ethnic composition and economic performance, as well as the structural character of regional and global international relations in which the power calculus imposes certain constraints and creates certain opportunities. In this regard, the Asian economic crisis since July 1997, which triggered an economic downturn in Southeast Asia, also contributed to the exacerbation of bilateral tensions.

Political Economy of Bilateral Relations: Competition and Complementarity

The political dimensions of economic activity in the international sphere are now subsumed under the subject of international political economy — an area of investigation that has become a vital if not critical component in the study of international relations as a discipline. Malaysia has a population of 27 million spread over 130,000 square miles of territory covering Peninsular Malaysia and the East Malaysian states of Sabah and Sarawak. In stark comparison, Singapore is an island state, more correctly a city state, occupying an area about 240 square miles and with a population of over 4.8 million in 2008 (of which over 3.6 million are Singapore citizens/permanent residents). Both territorial size and population pressure in Singapore provide crucial inputs into bilateral relations. Malaysia has the history, space, time, and territory to develop its resources, whereas the island state must feel the constant pressure of performing to stay ahead in order to safeguard national survival. Whilst Malaysia is abundant in natural resources, Singapore has to survive largely on the ingenuity of its human capital. Heavy dependence on the external economic environment and consequently on foreign investment, proof of performance, and capacity to maintain its status as a first world economy cumulatively impose a high premium on internal political and social stability for the island republic — with consequences for type of regime and style of governance most suited to achieving these goals. As noted by one writer, "dependence on foreign investment also increases the need of the government to control and modify many aspects of social and economic life and behaviour in order to ensure a continued favourable climate for investors."[8] The PAP government which has now been in power for 50 years (1959–2009), has established an undisputable record of political stability and economic growth, and has been strongly committed to rooting out corruption to boost efficiency and economy at all levels. The multiracial and meritocratic philosophy of the PAP stems from the doctrinal assumption that racism breeds corruption. Hence the conflict of perspective and philosophy with Malaysia's model of preferential rights and racial discrimination in favour of the fifty-five per cent Malay population officially termed as *Bumiputera* (the remaining five per cent is constituted by the other "indigenous races" in Sabah and Sarawak). The PAP would maintain that its multiracial ideology from this standpoint continues to conduce to the emergence of a united, non-racial, and egalitarian society whereas UMNO's bifurcation of Malaysian society into two artificial and politically and racially-motivated categories of *Bumiputera* and non-*Bumiputera* ultimately deepens ethnic divisions and does not conduce to the emergence of a "Malaysian Malaysia".

Singapore's resource scarcity is immediately revealed by its dependence on water supply from Malaysia — an issue that surfaces whenever strains develop in other areas of bilateral relations. Yet Singapore's economic productivity has an impact on Malaysian economic growth, especially vis-à-vis the southern state of Johor, separated from the island republic by a mere one-quarter mile Causeway. Rising levels of economic interdependence and the economic as well as political spinoffs in terms of enhanced governmental capacity to realize social expectations could only be ignored to one's own peril. Strong economic relationships and partnerships across the Causeway, built over the decades, are difficult to unhinge given scheduled commitments to meet productivity deadlines.

The sound economic basis of interdependence enables the political rhetoric to operate at a certain superficial level to accommodate the political contingencies of incumbent leaderships. It is therefore not surprising that election time in Malaysia is paralleled by bilateral spats. Volatile elements in Malaysian politics are certainly greater compared to Singapore's fairly monolithic political leadership. Malaysia is politically a more complex society, with the government playing the role of intermediary in ethnic relations, dispenser of largesse to silence political disaffection as well as reward political loyalty, custodian of proper Islamic thinking and practice in a multi-religious society, and suppressor of all forms of societal activity deemed to be extremist and threatening national security.

In the economic sphere, such mutual dependence does invariably shape political realities and options for both parties. The direction of trade statistics underscores the importance of Malaysia and Singapore as each other's vital trading partner. Annual two-way trade exceeds US$40 billion, with Malaysia emerging as Singapore's top trading partner in 2000 — a position it has maintained to the present. In 2007 alone, bilateral trade totalled $110 billion.[9] Also, in 2008, Singapore ranked as Malaysia's second largest trading partner after the United States, accounting for 14.6 per cent of Malaysia's total trade.[10] The republic is also Malaysia's second largest export destination, and third largest source of imports.[11] Malaysia accounts for over 20 per cent of Singapore's exports, while Singapore takes over 40 per cent of Malaysian exports, mostly through re-export. The direction of trade of these two countries points to a strong dependence on export markets in the United States, Japan, Hong Kong, Korea, Germany, and the United Kingdom. These countries, together with Taiwan, are major foreign investors in Malaysia, Singapore, and the ASEAN region as a whole. Singapore's main imports were integrated circuits and semiconductors, assembled printed circuit boards and computer parts, as well as telecommunications equipment. The republic's main exports to Malaysia comprised integrated circuits and semiconductors, refined petroleum, and telecommunications equipment.

Singapore was also the top investor in Malaysia in 2003 in terms of the total value of approved projects, at RM 1.2 billion. According to the Malaysian Industrial Development Authority, the city state's investments were largely concentrated in electrical and electronic products, plastics, and fabricated metal products. Leadership change has also been reflected in the flow of money, further complementing economic activities on both sides of the Causeway. In 2004 alone, Singapore's investment arms have poured nearly US$800 million into Malaysia. State holding company Temasek Holdings bought 5 per cent of Telekom Malaysia for US$422 million in March, and 15 per cent of Alliance Bank Malaysia for US$125 million in July. In June, Government Investment Corporation bought 70 per cent of a shopping mall for US$123 million and 5 per cent of infrastructure developer Gamuda for US$53 million. Then in July, Government Investment Corporation paid US$28 million for a 5 per cent equity in Shell Refining Malaysia.[12] One analyst notes, "The sudden easing of restrictions on Singapore government acquisitions in Malaysia underscores the improvement in bilateral relations since November 1 [2004] when Abdullah Ahmad Badawi took over as prime minister from Mahathir Mohamad."[13]

The inauguration of the 2,217 square-kilometre Iskandar Development Region (now renamed Iskandar Malaysia) has added a new dimension to the political economy of the relationship between the two Causeway neighbours — with both opportunities and constraints. The opportunities clearly arise from economic interdependence and strong cultural ties. To date, Singapore companies have invested nearly S$1 billion (RM 2.5 billion) worth of projects in the mega

Iskandar Malaysia project in Johor. Since the Iskandar Malaysia project kicked off in 2005, Singapore companies have been involved in some 220 projects there,[14] thus taking advantage of local knowledge, cultural affinity, capital, and entrepreneurship from the republic combined with plentiful supply of human resources and labour to fuel economic development on both sides of the Causeway. The downside of this otherwise optimistic scenario is to be found in the vagaries of Malaysian/ Johor politics. UMNO politicians under the banner of Malay/Malaysian nationalism are quick to capitalize on bilateral spats and issues from time to time — a trend that can negatively effect the extent to which bilateral relations can widen and deepen. Notably, a diplomatic retreat (meeting between Malaysian PM Abdullah Badawi and Singapore PM Lee Hsien Loong) was held in mid-May 2007 in the Malaysian northern resort of Pulau Langkawi, which resulted in agreement to establish a joint ministerial committee to oversee economic cooperation in the Iskandar Development Region. However, a Malaysian political analyst succinctly observed, "some rumblings by detractors of the Abdullah Badawi government, not least of all the former premier Mahathir, have already dubbed the project as a 'sell-out' to Singaporean interests."[15]

The trade structure of both countries serves as a political impetus for the formulation of economic policies favourable to foreign investment. Hence the national economic plans provide a clue to the political economy of their relationship — tending towards both competition and complementarity. But, according to one source, the real impetus is business and realpolitik. The two economies are obviously facing mounting pressure as multinationals move manufacturing from their nations to cheaper plants in China, India, and other low-cost sites. This trend has prompted Malaysian Foreign Minister Syed Hamid Albar to remark that the change of leadership in both countries (Abdullah Badawi in Malaysia and Lee Hsien Loong in Singapore), "allows us to leave old baggage behind and move forward to forge a new partnership that takes into account the new realities in our region and around the world."[16] In this direction, the Malaysia-Singapore Third Country Business Development Fund valued at US$2.63 million was launched in Kuala Lumpur in July 2004 to jointly identify projects in developing countries with a view to expanding their operations in the growing context of globalization.

Malaysia's major goal in the next twenty years is to reduce the heavy dependence on Singapore as a re-export centre for Malaysian merchandise. This necessarily entails upgrading the country's technological and industrial base, its seaports and airports, educational infrastructure, transportation networks, and transforming the commodity composition of bilateral (with Singapore) and international trade from low value-added to high value-added, especially manufactured goods and electrical and electronic products. Another major area of transformation lies in the structure of Malaysian overseas investments, including Singapore — from the real estate sector to financial, business, and capital-intensive manufacturing industries. Singapore has traditionally been a major financial and services hub for the Asia-Pacific region.

Singapore's national development strategy has always been underpinned by the need to stay ahead as the best method of survival. Singapore's Strategic Economic Plan covering a forty-year period from 1991–2030 is directed towards achieving developed country status and, by extension to create a "first world economy". The target for Singapore is to catch up with the Netherlands by 2020 and the United States by 2030. The eight-fold objectives of the plan are: (1) enhance human resources, (2) promote national teamwork, (3) become internationally oriented, (4) create a conducive climate for innovation, (5) develop manufacturing and service clusters in line with industrial strategy, (6) spearhead economic development as part of industrial strategy, (7) maintain international competitiveness to promote economic resilience, and (8) reduce vulnerability as an integral element of economic resilience.[17]

In comparing the national development objectives of both countries, one does notice a similar basic thrust in the economic field — hence the element of competition stemming from the quest for the same basket of foreign investments, and from the ability of both countries to provide similar services to that portion of the international economy that is engaged in Southeast Asia. Competition and complementarity thus provide the backdrop to bilateral issues that emerge from time to time, or which perpetuate strains due to non-resolution. However, the significance of political will in resolving them is evidenced by the latest agreements in principle reached by both sides during then Senior Minister Lee Kuan Yew's visit to Malaysia in September 2001. We turn next to these issues.

Key Bilateral Issues: Influence of Competition and Complementarity in Conflict Management and Resolution

Water

Singapore suffers from a major resource scarcity: water. Assured water supply at certain levels for a lengthy period of time from its nearest hinterland (Johor in Malaysia) has invariably become an increasingly contentious issue in bilateral relations. Perceptual as well as substantive differences have already emerged regarding the type and quantity of water to be supplied to Singapore — whether raw or treated. As Malaysia's industrial capacity expands, the rationale to supply raw water to Singapore and purchase back treated water at a higher price would be more difficult to sustain. Competitive industrialization on both sides of the Causeway is but one factor explaining the difference of approach by the two governments.

The Malaysian proposal to supply only treated water to Singapore after the 1961 and 1962 agreements expire in 2011 and 2061 respectively, takes into account Malaysia's own expanded requirements of water usage based on a growing population, and the need to achieve a balance between commercial and private consumption. Currently, Malaysia sells raw water to Singapore at 3 sen per 1,000 gallons (3,785.3 litres), and buys treated water from the republic at 50 sen per 1,000 gallons.[18] The agreements provide for review of the price structure after a lapse of twenty-five years. Hence, since the mid-1980s, the water issue has resurfaced, and it became politically tainted especially on the Malaysian side as to whether Kuala Lumpur was getting a fair price for the sale of raw water to and purchase of purified water from the republic. Malaysian Prime Minister Mahathir Mohamad unequivocally stated that change is the order of the day with respect to the water issue. The present water agreement was drawn up during colonial times by the British specifically to favour Singapore. It does not reflect Malaysia's national interests as an independent nation. In Mahathir's view, "it simply does not make sense for Singapore to take our money and pay us back three sen. It makes good sense for Malaysia to supply Singapore with treated water when the present agreement ends." However, at the moment, if Malaysia raises the price of raw water above the three sen level, Singapore could also legitimately raise the cost of treated water above the current rate of 50 sen per 1,000 gallons.

The island republic's perspective is quite naturally informed by its role as a global city state whose access to vital natural resources must be guaranteed to enable it to function as an international port and service centre. As Singapore's opposition Member of Parliament pointedly remarked in response to demands by some Malaysian politicians to stop the supply of water to Singapore, "This issue is very serious. I mean, it is not a case of sacrificing an opportunity to bathe ourselves. It's our lifeblood. It's like declaring war on Singapore if they cut off water."[19] Singapore clearly dismisses the Malaysian Government's perception that it is profiteering from the sale of treated water to Johor, arguing that it costs the republic RM 2.40 sen to treat 1,000 gallons of water which it sells to Johor at 50 sen per 1,000 gallons. The republic is already feeling the pressure of securing additional water supply well before the 2061 cut-off point. Under an agreement with Johor, Singapore draws about 1.527 billion litres of raw water daily, or less than forty per cent of the republic's daily requirements.

Awareness on both sides has grown substantially — that the water problem, if left unresolved, would almost certainly complicate other bilateral issues so that any long-term resolution would require a settlement on the basis of a comprehensive package covering other contentious issues and irritants in the bilateral relationship. To this end, then Senior Minister (SM) Lee made two visits to Kuala Lumpur — in August 2000 and again in September 2001. This latter visit was evidently undertaken with greater urgency stemming from Lee's perception of future trends in Malaysian politics carrying the prospect, even if remote at this stage, of an Islamic-oriented PAS (Parti Islam SeMalaysia) government taking control of federal power in future elections. It was Lee's considered assessment that a more stable and fair deal could be struck with the UMNO-led government of Mahathir Mohamad than with a future theocratic government whose national and international priorities could be radically different, thus rendering the relationship more "problematic".[20] He also expressed concern that a future government in Kuala Lumpur that is more favourably disposed towards growing Islamic militancy "will not deliver".[21] Lee also took the view that it was his personal responsibility as Singapore's first premier of over thirty-years standing, to reach some form of finality on this matter with a Malaysian leader with whom he had become acquainted since 1965 prior to Singapore's separation from Malaysia. Settling the water issue as part of a comprehensive package would clearly help prevent the burdens of the past revisiting successor governments on both sides of the Causeway while enabling them to adopt a more constructive and perhaps less emotional approach to fostering good bilateral relations both in the spirit of ASEAN and in the context of globalization. For Malaysia's part, former premier Mahathir has always maintained that the water issue must be resolved together with other outstanding bilateral issues as a comprehensive package — an approach reflecting convergence of national interests of the two Causeway neighbours.

The skeletal agreement signed on 4 September 2001 in Kuala Lumpur guarantees the supply of water from Malaysia beyond 2061 (upon expiry of the 1961 agreement) — at 1.33 billion litres per day compared to Singapore's request for 2.85 billion litres a day. However, the price of water will increase fifteen-fold in the near future costing Singapore an additional RM 45 million each year. Malaysia, however, has asked for 60 sen per 1,000 gallons. Beyond 2061, Malaysia has offered to supply 350 million gallons a day (mgd), although this is less than the 750 mgd requested by SM Lee. Singapore has agreed to the lower figure although the ratio of raw water to treated water is yet to be finalized. Prime Minister Mahathir has offered 100 mgd of raw water and 250 mgd of filtered water. However, SM Lee's request is for 150 mgd of raw water and 200 mgd of treated water, which will be supplied by a joint venture between Johor and the Public Utilities Board of Singapore. The 1990 agreement between Johor and the Public Utilities Board will serve as a basis for determining the price of filtered water. Raw water will be sold at 60 sen per 1,000 gallons, and will be reviewed after every five years.[22]

In addition, Singapore is obliged to give Malaysia twelve parcels of land as a "bonus" for the guaranteed water supply. There is little doubt that concerns over Malaysia's shifting political landscape coupled with economic recession in the republic provided sufficient incentives for Senior Minister Lee to broker a "less than balanced" agreement in Malaysia's favour as he was convinced that the comprehensive pact was a sufficiently good trade-off for long-term security.[23] Nevertheless, the devil is in the detail, and it would take a good deal of give-and-take by officials on both sides to iron out a durable compromise that reflects mutual confidence for the promotion of mutual interests. The last round of discussions over water in Kuala Lumpur in July 2002 has underscored basic differences of approach in resolving this issue, especially in relation to the price mechanism. Malaysia wishes to delink the pricing aspect from other issues in the comprehensive package, while Singapore prefers to resolve all outstanding bilateral issues as a package. Kuala Lumpur has in recent times hinted more than once that the price paid by Singapore for raw water from Johor is too low, pointing to the sale of water by China to Hong Kong at RM 6.80 per 1,000 gallons.[24] Singapore holds to the view that any formula to fix the price of water supplied by Malaysia to the republic, would apply only to future agreements, and cannot be retrospectively applied to the 1961 and 1962 agreements.[25]

It should also be noted that Singapore in the meantime had developed a realistic approach to water security by exploring all other options to boost self-sufficiency, especially in times of crisis. To the extent that Singapore succeeds in significantly reducing its dependence on Malaysian supplies, the scope for politicking over water would most certainly be narrowed. Arguably, the pressure on Malaysia would be relaxed and the penchant for Malaysian politicians to manipulate the bilateral relationship to serve narrower political agendas would also cease to exist. Thus, the degree of success of Singapore's water management strategies might prove crucial in minimizing the leverage politicians across the Causeway claim to have on the republic. One writer on the subject has persuasively argued that the water issue has already been "desecuritized" in the light of Singapore's long-term strategic approach including the following measures: (1) optimizing domestic water yields from its three major reservoirs — MacRitchie, Peirce, and Seletar/Bedok; (2) implementing conservation measures through use of low capacity flushing cisterns, price manipulation, and public education; and (3) developing access to alternative water supplies through recycling waste water, desalination, and sourcing from Indonesia.[26]

On the Malaysian side, the republic's efforts toward water self-sufficiency would not only be welcomed, but also viewed as a positive step towards strengthening partnership and cooperation on all aspects of bilateral relations in the decades ahead. Such efforts would also "facilitate a more pragmatic and rational approach towards mutually agreed pricing arrangements with respect to the supply of raw water from Malaysia and treated water by either partner".[27] More recent efforts by Singapore to achieve water self-sufficiency are apparently producing positive results which would further "desecuritize" this issue from the overall relationship.

In July 2002, Singapore unveiled its reclaimed water or NEWater initiative. NEWater will become an important part of the Singapore government's strategy to double the country's source of water while reducing the dependence on water imports from Malaysia. Indeed, by 2010 the government expects NEWater factories to meet 15–20 per cent of Singapore's needs.[28] In September 2005, the republic also opened its first desalination plant in Tuas, with Prime Minister Lee Hsien Loong proudly remarking, "Singapore has managed to turn its water challenge from a vulnerability into a strength", adding also that "desalination for Singapore, an island in the sea, is a natural solution".[29] On the Malaysian side, the government's efforts to centralize water management and to privatize its supply, in line with current global trends regarding management of this critical resource, are measures apparently undertaken "to harangue Singapore into paying fair-market rates for Malaysian water".[30]

Malayan Railway (KTM) Land, CIQ, and Tanjong Pagar

In the present world of international relations characterized by international anarchy, each sovereign state survives, defends, and propagates itself on the basis of self-help. It uses the legal notion of political, territorial, and constitutional sovereignty to strengthen its psychological survival as an independent state. Threats to national sovereignty have to be immediately rebuffed if not challenged as the core values of sovereign existence need to be defended through all the means at its disposal. International law becomes a useful weapon to pursue territorial and sovereignty claims as it provides an empirical basis of defence. In this context, the Tanjong Pagar Customs, Immigration, and Quarantine (CIQ) issue, tied as it is to Malaysian ownership of railway land in Singapore, touches on the core issue of national sovereignty, especially for the island republic.

The entire issue should be located in a broader historical context. Malayan Railway land covering over 217 hectares and stretching 20–30 kilometres into Singapore territory was acquired under a 1918 colonial ordinance specifically for use by Malayan Railway (Keretapi Tanah Melayu or KTM) for a period of 999 years. The same ordinance limits the use of this land which is now prime property in Singapore. However under a separate bilateral arrangement on 27 November 1990 known as the Points of Agreement or POA, the two countries decided to depart from the 1918 Railway Ordinance to facilitate joint redevelopment of the Tanjong Pagar Railway Station and the lands adjacent to the track owned by KTM. Malaysia's reluctance to go ahead with the 1990 agreement is based on the fear that it might eventually be forced to give up proprietary control over some or all of KTM's land in Singapore.[31]

This issue has invariably become linked to the CIQ issue for reasons that remain unclear. Singapore has argued that the two issues are separate: ownership of KTM land as opposed to exercising sovereign rights by another state on Singapore's sovereign territory. The republic has maintained using international conventions and legal practice that any exercise of sovereign rights by Malaysia on Singapore's territory, such as stamping passports, can only be done with the sufferance of the Government of Singapore. Since both parties had agreed to move the CIQ facilities to Woodlands commencing 1 August, 1998, it was viewed by the republic as highly improper for Malaysia to retract from the agreement, as it did in June 1997, by insisting that it would continue to operate at Tanjong Pagar after 1 August 1998. Foreign Minister S. Jayakumar informed the Singapore Parliament on 31 July 1998 that in a 17 July meeting between officials of both sides, the Malaysian delegation fully understood that the CIQ and POA are separate issues, hence there was no question of Singapore taking back KTM land merely by relocating its CIQ in Woodlands.[32]

The 1990 POA states that the KTM railway station would be moved either to Bukit Timah first, or directly to Woodlands. In exchange, under the 1990 POA, three parcels of railway land — at Tanjong Pagar, Kranji, and Woodlands — would be jointly developed on a 60:40 basis with the Malaysian Government having the larger share. However, three years later, Mahathir expressed his displeasure with the POA as it failed to include a piece of railway land in Bukit Timah for joint development.

The September 2001 comprehensive agreement was aimed at resolving this thorny issue which always provided sufficient latitude to be exploited for political purposes in times of economic or political difficulties. Both governments have reached an understanding on the Malaysian immigration checkpoint on the Kuala Lumpur–Singapore railway line, which is to be moved from Tanjong Pagar to Kranji on the northern border. The issue over Malayan Railway land — a very sensitive issue for Kuala Lumpur — appeared to have been resolved by Singapore's agreement to offer Malaysia another twelve plots of land in Bukit Timah (as mentioned earlier). However, the agreement was suspended when bilateral relations nose-dived in 2002 and 2003.

Singapore also agreed in principle to Malaysia's request to build a new bridge to replace the Johor-Singapore Causeway (which was to be demolished in the year 2007), and to build an underground tunnel at Malaysia's cost to link a newly electrified service to the Kranji station

in Singapore.[33] But relations soured in 2002–3 when Malaysia decided
to de-link the water issue from the overall package to the point that old
wounds tended to reopen, with entrenched bureaucrats on both sides
regaining ascendancy by asserting traditionally-held fixed views on all
the outstanding issues. In the event, Singapore too withdrew concessions
made in the context of a package under the Lee-Mahathir agreement in
2001. The impasse appeared to have been broken following a change
in Malaysian leadership from Mahathir Mohamad to Abdullah Badawi
on 31 October 2003. Since then ties have warmed based on the good
personal rapport between Abdullah and then Prime Minister and later
(from 12 August 2004) Senior Minister Goh Chok Tong. Kuala Lumpur
is keen to replace the Causeway with a bridge arguing that the existing
link is a bottleneck for growing road traffic, while a new high bridge
would allow small ships to pass through. Indeed, Malaysia's enthusiasm
— and Singapore's reluctance — in this matter must be viewed in the
context of growing competition in port facilities offered by both sides,
with Malaysia's Port of Tanjung Pelepas offering attractive discounts for
similar services provided by the republic. The old Causeway apparently
blocks potential customers to the Malaysian facility which opened in
2000, and is not only the fastest growing port but also ranks among the
world's top twenty ports.[34] Shipping analysts expect the competition
between Port of Singapore Authority Corporation, operator of the
world's second-busiest port and Tanjung Pelepas to intensify in the
years ahead.[35]

Central Provident Fund (CPF) Withdrawals

The withholding of pension funds of Malaysian employees in Peninsular
Malaysia by the Singaporean authorities has not helped in reducing
bilateral friction. Malaysia fails to understand why employees from
Sabah and Sarawak are able to withdraw their CPF (a mandatory pension
plan) savings upon completing their contracts whereas those from
Peninsular Malaysia are unable to do so under similar circumstances.
Singapore prefers to deal with this problem as part of an overall package
that would bring about greater stability to bilateral relations. The
republic uses the historical factor of long-standing close links between
Peninsular Malaysia and Singapore to justify differential treatment. The
current practice allows a Peninsular Malaysian to withdraw his CPF
savings in full if he is at least fifty years old, and has left permanently
to reside in Peninsular Malaysia. The same employee is also entitled

to withdraw his pension from age fifty onwards provided he has not worked in Singapore for two years. Malaysian workers from Sabah and Sarawak, as well as other foreigners, can withdraw their CPF savings any time after they leave Singapore.

It is estimated that there are over 200,000 Malaysians presently working in Singapore.[36] Malaysian workers affected by the Singapore ruling feel that they have been short-changed by the vagaries of Causeway politics as Singapore has linked the CPF withdrawal issue to the resolution of two other issues: the supply of water and the transfer of the CIQ checkpoint from Tanjong Pagar to Woodlands.[37] To date, nearly S$2 billion of Peninsular Malaysia employees' funds are being withheld by Singapore on the argument that Singaporeans themselves can only withdraw their CPF upon reaching the age of fifty-five, and also because many Peninsular Malaysian workers tend to return to Singapore to find work after having left earlier. Geographic proximity enables many workers to shuttle frequently across the Causeway. The republic says that this is not the case with East Malaysians from Sabah and Sarawak, who are therefore entitled to their pension funds prior to departure from Singapore.

In any event, the fact that issues such as the CPF withdrawals get intertwined with other more important issues testify to the high level of sensitivity that exists in the bilateral relationship especially when it turns sour. This realization informed the comprehensive package approach to bilateral dispute resolution during Lee's September 2001 visit to Kuala Lumpur. Singapore adopted a more conciliatory approach by allowing Malaysians to withdraw their CPF savings after they have stopped working in the republic rather than waiting until they turn fifty-five. Upon achieving final agreement, Singapore will permit withdrawal of CPF funds over a period of two years. Pending final agreement, it appears that the republic still views resolution of the pension funds issue in quid pro quo terms. Senior Minister Goh representing the Singapore Government at bilateral talks in Putra Jaya (Malaysia's administrative capital) in late 2004 stated that on a reciprocal basis, Singapore would release the CPF funds of Malaysians and consider the joint development of additional pieces of Malayan Railway land in the republic if Kuala Lumpur would allow Republic of Singapore Air Force (RSAF) aircraft to use Malaysian airspace for training.[38]

Use of Malaysian Airspace by RSAF Aircraft

On 18 September 1998, Malaysia formally revoked permission for the RSAF to use its airspace in southern Johor — a decision that has obviously been taken in the context of worsening relations following the imposition of capital controls earlier that month. Ordinarily, RSAF "intrusions" into Malaysian airspace would have been ignored given the general cordiality, interdependence, mutual benefit, and pragmatic approaches that govern interstate relations across the Causeway. In the wake of the Asian economic crisis, accompanied as it was by a major internal political episode involving the sacking (2 September 1998), and arrest and detention (20 September 1998) of Deputy Prime Minister Anwar Ibrahim, unresolved bilateral issues, or those that have a potential for conflict, become favourably disposed to the vagaries of domestic politics, especially those involving UMNO. It cannot be denied that in times of internal political crisis, the resort to politics of diversion is a fortuitous strategy employed by politicians anywhere in the globe.

Malaysia decided that it was time to expose the airspace intrusions to justify cancellation of previous arrangements that enabled Singaporean military aircraft to overfly Malaysian airspace with little or no formality. As of 18 September 1998, the withdrawal of the use of Malaysian airspace by the RSAF covered five major aspects of hitherto ongoing bilateral military cooperation: (1) to withdraw the waiver of the requirement to apply for diplomatic clearance for the RSAF fixed-wing aircraft based at the Payar Lebar Airbase when transiting South Johor to and from the Singaporean training area in the South China Sea; (2) to withdraw the clearance granted to all types of RSAF aircraft to conduct training within the Royal Malaysian Air Force (RMAF) Low Flying Area; (3) to terminate the arrangement for the RSAF to conduct navigational training over the airspace of the Peninsula, Sabah, and Sarawak; (4) to terminate the combined search and rescue operations and exercises, i.e. arrangements which were formalized through RMAF and RSAF Combined Search and Rescue Operating Procedures; and (5) all RSAF aircraft to cease entry into Malaysian airspace after taking off from Tengah airbase.[39] Henceforth the RSAF would need to give fourteen days written notice seeking approval from Wismaputra (Malaysia's Foreign Ministry) to use Malaysian airspace.

Mutual reactions to the Malaysian decision have been highlighted by the local media in both countries in a manner that has not led to improving relations, let alone limiting whatever additional damage has been caused by other linked issues. The problem acquired greater salience when a British Navy helicopter crashed in the South China Sea during a planned naval exercise between British and Singapore forces. Singapore blamed the delay in the search and rescue operations on Malaysia. Defence Minister Syed Hamid Albar retaliated by saying that the RSAF was capable of using an alternative route which was only twelve minutes longer to launch its search and rescue operation.[40]

The withdrawal by Malaysia of clearance rights to the RSAF coincided with rising concern over alleged increased airspace intrusions by a neighbour whose military power has expanded significantly in the past decade. The RSAF is known to operate a fleet of thirty-five F-5E/F Tiger IIs, fifty-two A-4s Super Skyhawks, and eighteen F-16 Fighting Falcons for its fighter operations training in Malaysian airspace. It also operates a fleet of 109 helicopters, fourteen transport/air tankers, five maritime aircraft, and four E-2C Hawkeye airborne early warning aircraft.[41]

Strategic analysts view the Malaysian decision as a major setback for the republic, which is now obliged to train its pilots in faraway places like the United States and Australia.[42] In this regard, Malaysia has gone a step further to request the International Civil Aviation Organisation to revert to Malaysia control of airspace in the southern peninsula (stretching from Negeri Sembilan to Johor), now handled by Singapore since it gained independence in 1965. The fact that Kuala Lumpur was piling the pressure on Singapore only days after the closure of the Malaysian CIQ checkpoint in Tanjong Pagar was indicative of how a chain reaction could be set in motion in a relationship involving two very close neighbours. Sovereignty in exercising immigration control for one side is as vital as sovereignty in resuming full control of air, sea, and land space for the other. Yet, political will and pragmatism on both sides enable deals to be made that circumvent so-called sovereignty-sensitive issues, provided they are not seen to be impinging on the core interests that could impact upon national survival and security.

Mutual concessions in the September 2001 agreement included restoration of Singapore's facility to use Malaysia's military airspace, i.e. a return to the access regime for RSAF aircraft prior to the withdrawal decision announced by Malaysia on 18 September 1998. However, as a comprehensive final settlement has yet to be reached, the issue of Singapore military aircraft using Malaysian airspace has remained suspended to date.

Since 2005, attempts to re-negotiate the issue has run into "nationalist roadblocks" set up by Johor politicians who insist that the federal government should not trade sovereignty for Singapore's consent to build the new bridge to replace the old Causeway. A senior and outspoken Johor politician, Johor Baru Member of Parliament, Shahrir Samad, who is also the leader of the Barisan Nasional backbenchers in Parliament, expressed strong resentment over Singapore Foreign Minister George Yeo's claim that Malaysia has no right to unilaterally demolish its side of the Causeway as it is an international facility.[43] Nevertheless, both governments have decided not to discuss the matter in public while negotiations are in progress to resolve the matter. The republic's position, however, is that the building of the new bridge to replace the Causeway must reflect "a balance of benefits to both sides".[44] This apparent linkage between "bridge" and "airspace" would obviously require a good deal of political wisdom on both sides to avert a stalemate in an otherwise improving relationship under the two new prime ministers.

Bridge to Replace Causeway

The "bridge saga" began in 1996 when Mahathir announced that Malaysia will go ahead with building a half-bridge/crooked bridge/ scenic bridge and wait for Singapore to complete its portion of the bridge, to replace the existing Causeway, which would be demolished. However, Singapore has argued that there has to be a "balance of benefits" for it to go along with Malaysia's proposal. Singapore wanted Malaysia to supply sand for twenty years to support its land reclamation projects in exchange for consent to build the new bridge — a proposal that was stridently opposed by Johorean politicians as a violation of national sovereignty.

Meanwhile, the foundation work for the "scenic bridge" had already begun in Johor Baru, but faced obstacles following the handover of power from Mahathir to Abdullah Badawi in November 2003. Prime Minister Abdullah, who has been downsizing and cancelling Mahathir's mega projects since he took office, finally decided to abandon the bridge project, citing that it was uneconomical and also would lead to many legal complications with Singapore. The Bridge Project was formally abandoned on 12 April 2006 with compensation paid to Malaysian companies involved in the aborted project. This "bridge saga" provided further evidence that bilateralism in Malaysia-Singapore relations continues to have an unsettled trajectory, despite joint cooperation being enhanced in respect of Singapore's award of the US$3.4 billion Singapore Integrated Resort project at Sentosa to Malaysian company Genting International, and assurances by Prime Minister Abdullah that Singaporean participation in the Iskandar Development Region in southern Johor will have no adverse effects on Malay rights and privileges under the *Bumiputera* policy.[45] Additionally, the Iskandar Development Region, now renamed "Iskandar Malaysia" could well provide a future source of friction in bilateral relations arising from political economy considerations on the Malaysian side: (1) Malaysia's lack of capacity to handle mega projects,[46] and (2) manipulation of Malay nationalist feelings by demagogues who stake their political fortunes on whipping up anti-Singapore rhetoric rather than address serious issues of governance, corruption, and mis-management of the nation's wealth under the well-intentioned but poorly implemented New Economic Policy.

Sovereignty Disputes over Maritime Territory

The fact that Both Malaysia and Singapore have resorted to international arbitration by the Hague-based International Court of Justice (ICJ) is highly suggestive of deep-seated mutual suspicions about each other's intentions. Malaysia and Singapore both assert sovereignty over Pulau Batu Putih (Pedra Branca). Located some twenty-four nautical miles to the east of Singapore, Pedra Branca commands the entire eastern approach to the Singapore Strait, through which almost 900 ships pass daily. Pedra Branca, meaning "White Rock" in Portuguese and named as such on sixteenth century Portuguese maps, is also called Pulau Batu Putih by the Malaysians. Sitting at the eastern entrance of the Singapore Strait, it houses the Horsburgh Lighthouse, the oldest feature on the island, which was built by the British between 1847 and 1851. The island also comprises Middle Rocks, which are two clusters of rocks situated 0.6 nautical miles south of Pedra Branca, and South Ledge, a rock formation that can be seen only at low-tide, which sits 2.1 nautical miles to the south.

In 1979, Malaysia published a map claiming the island. In response, Singapore lodged a formal protest with Malaysia in early 1980.[47] After some acrimonious debate through the media stemming also from the conflation of other bilateral issues, the issue was submitted to the ICJ for resolution in 2003. During the ICJ submissions in November 2007, Singapore accused Malaysia of making baseless claims arising from incomplete records, whereas Malaysia has expressed concern over the negative impact on the stability of Malaysia-Indonesia relations, as well as on environmental and navigational security in the event the island republic gains legal sovereignty.[48]

After receiving final submissions by both sides, the ICJ delivered its judgment without appeal on 23 May 2008. The decision went in favour of Singapore's claim to Pedra Branca, while sovereignty over Middle Rocks was awarded to Malaysia. However, with respect to South Ledge, the ICJ concluded that sovereignty over that maritime feature belongs to the state in the territorial waters of which it is located. Significantly the Court observed that for all practical purposes, by 1980 when the dispute crystallized, sovereignty over Pedra Branca/Pulau Batu Putih had passed to Singapore.[49]

The ICJ decision brought to a close the twenty-eight-year-old territorial dispute between both countries, and was immediately described as a "win-win" outcome by Foreign Minister Datuk Seri Dr Rais Yatim, who led the Malaysian side at The Hague where the court is located. Despite the matter being fully resolved at the hands of the ICJ, Malay nationalist feelings remain unsettled, with the Sultan of Johor stating that he would reclaim sovereignty over Pulau Batu Putih even if it took another hundred years.[50] At issue undoubtedly is the fact that Singapore's sovereignty over Pedra Branca legally extends the coordinates of Singapore's territorial sea and Exclusive Economic Zone to the disadvantage of Malaysia's fishing and other economic interests.

Conclusion: Malaysia-Singapore Relations — Bilateralism or Multilateralism for Conflict Management and Resolution?

Malaysia and Singapore are two relatively new countries which are knit together by historical, familial, cultural, political, economic, and strategic ties. Their relationship is truly characterized by interdependence, with perhaps Singapore relying more heavily on Malaysia for a resource vital to the republic's survival: water. Any successful negotiation leading to mutual benefits with respect to future water supplies by

Malaysia beyond 2061 is bound to affect mutual perceptions on all other outstanding issues that are targeted for further discussion and resolution.

To be sure, ethnicity is a factor that invariably operates in providing a certain character and dynamic to the relationship. From the days of merger, to separation and beyond, the spectre of ethnicity has been directly if not indirectly raised by both sides during periods of friction. Malaysia is more inclined to take the view that Singapore opts for a rather over-legalistic approach that conveys the impression that the city state is insensitive to the cultural milieu in which it finds itself. Kuala Lumpur tends to view such an approach as antagonistic and confrontational, and not in keeping with the general consensual approach based on *musjawarah* (deliberation) and *mufakat* (consensus). Singapore, on the other hand, prefers to hold steadfastly to formal commitments that have issued from negotiations as its own survival and prosperity are firmly based on strategic planning to fulfil the aspirations of its citizenry and to remain competitive internationally. Singapore's reaction to the Asian financial crisis vis-à-vis Malaysia in terms of pushing up interest rates which in turn caused an exodus of Malaysian currency to the republic was seen as contrary to good neighbourly relations, and contravening the apparent mutual commitment by both leaders (Mahathir and Goh Chok Tong) to the policy of "prosper thy neighbour" as opposed to "beggar thy neighbour".

Singapore, on its part, has since the late 1960s adopted a national strategy of survival based on military and economic strength. The city state's defence policy and rapid growth of its arms industry are viewed with concern if not suspicion in Kuala Lumpur. Malaysia is aware of Singapore's military power, especially its air superiority, even if these elements project a purely defensive orientation. Nevertheless, Malaysia is less concerned about the military dimension as Malaysia's national priorities focus more on socio-economic development rather than military power as an index of national strength. This rather relaxed attitude vis-à-vis Singapore perhaps should mitigate the security dilemma for the city state, as Malaysia has clearly no aggressive designs on the republic, considering the fact that the island state received its independence from Malaysia some forty years ago.

A final resolution of other, less critical issues such as Tanjong Pagar, CPF withdrawals, access by Singapore's military aircraft to Malaysian airspace and the like would no doubt help to build a more conducive environment for the progress of bilateral relations. Indeed, the existence of both competition and complementarity, tied as they are to broader issues of national survival and advancement, creates some uniqueness in the bilateral relationship. Issues that give rise to occasional friction, tension, and strain, are either neutralized or marginalized by more important issues of "rice and curry", i.e. the commitment by both leaderships to improve the material welfare of their own societies. Thus, it can be argued that the evidence of the past forty-four years suggests that this bilateral relationship is characterized by functional tension and cooperation — with the desire and momentum to cooperate taking precedence over perceptual and structural differences. Both leaderships have adopted a pragmatic approach to substantive issues without allowing issues that have a localized political content to scuttle meaningful cooperation. Indeed, it is possible to conclude that the dictates of both realism and neorealism oblige the two Causeway neighbours to adopt a pragmatic and business-like approach to bilateral relations — as seen in the joint development projects in Singapore Integrated Resorts at Sentosa and Marina Bay Sands and Iskandar Malaysia.

Ultimately, the national interest can be best advanced by the reign of pragmatism over sentimentalism. Current trade and investment statistics further highlight the degree of interdependence between the two countries. Bilateral Malaysia-Singapore trade alone accounts for fifty per cent of intra-ASEAN trade. And based on Malaysian projections, Singaporeans are expected to contribute half of the tourism dollars that Malaysia earns every year. There is little doubt that the character of bilateral relations reflects ongoing historical, geographic, and cultural ties.

It is in this context that the two countries' involvement in ASEAN, Asia-Pacific, and other world fora should be viewed. Both are obviously committed to membership and development of ASEAN which protects the sovereignty of individual member states as well as promotes their individual and collective welfare. ASEAN is valuable to both as a forum for development, security, and regional cooperation. It is a useful multilateral mechanism for promoting best practices in resolving bilateral issues. Recent developments following the 11 September 2001 terrorist attacks in the United States have clearly energized Malaysia-Singapore bilateral relations in the security dimension. Both countries have cooperated very closely to meet the threat of international terrorism that may be linked to Al-Qaeda operatives in this region. Whatever might be the evidence, both governments have taken the view that the threat of religious terrorism is real, and the need to pool resources ever more urgent. Malaysia's Anti-Terror Pact with the United States (14 May 2002), appears to be a follow-up of the Tripartite Anti-Terrorism Pact signed by three ASEAN members — Malaysia, Indonesia, and the Philippines — on 7 May 2002 in Putra Jaya.[51] Singapore's own security links with the United States, and Manila's cooperation with U.S. Special Forces for anti-terrorism operations in the southern Philippines, all attest to a higher security presence and cooperation with ASEAN in the post–11 September era. At a broader regional level, both Singapore and Malaysia have been instrumental in the establishment of the ASEAN Regional Forum (ARF) as a mechanism for security dialogue and cooperation involving extra-regional powers. For Malaysia, as for Singapore and other ARF members in Southeast Asia, the ARF is a confidence-building institution even if the process of erecting a regional multilateral security structure is problematic at this stage.

The operative factors that shape domestic and international policy on both sides of the equation significantly affect the types of mechanisms available and the compromises that can be reached. For Singapore, the determining factors include its strategic geography, demographic size and character, resource scarcity, perceptions of vulnerability especially vis-à-vis immediate neighbours, preservation of territorial sovereignty, and economic survival through interdependence and globalization of trade, commerce, finance, and services. On the basis of similar criteria, the determinants of Malaysia's domestic and foreign policy can be stated as follows: (1) national sovereignty with particular emphasis on political integrity and territorial unity of the Malaysian Federation; (2) economic development and social justice in the context of a multiracial society; (3) preservation of constitutional monarchy, Islam, and the special rights of the Malays; (4) a firm commitment to ASEAN and promotion of other forms of economic regionalism that advance national interests; (5) promotion of regional stability and security via the Zone of Peace, Freedom and Neutrality (ZOPFAN); and (6) commitment to promote South-South cooperation aimed at enhancing the economic welfare of the less developed world including the fifty-six member OIC (Organisation of the Islamic Conference) countries, and support for human rights and social justice at the global level.

Malaysia's rapid industrialization is yet another source of growing competition for Singapore — in such areas as port facilities, container services, airports, and infrastructure projects — all of which could have removed if not reduced the cutting edge enjoyed by the republic in the past two decades. In recent years, Malaysia's Kuala Lumpur International Airport has attempted to provide a package of incentives to fifty airlines in an attempt to lure them away from Singapore's Changi Airport — options such as waiver of landing and parking fees, tax breaks, and passenger pick-up and drop-off rights (known as "fifth freedom rights").[52] The rising stature of Malaysia's ports had emboldened former Deputy Transport Minister Ramli Ngah Talib to suggest that "Malaysian ports have grown to match Singapore's efficiency and productivity, and would be very soon the top 10 in world container traffic."[53] Yet, the changing global economic and political environment also creates opportunities for the two Causeway neighbours to enjoy mutual gains by complementing their efforts thereby strengthening ASEAN regionalism. Singapore's former premier Goh Chok Tong, with reference to the bilateral spats, underscored the need to put aside differences, and work to strengthen regional cooperation by expediting the mechanism available in ASEAN.[54] The management by both sides of the territorial claim over Pedra Branca is a reflection of both political maturity and respect for mutual sovereignty, as the issue was finally resolved by the International Court of Justice on 23 May 2008. Whatever the outcome, both neighbours would in all probability respect it in the true ASEAN spirit of give-and-take. Likewise, they have shown similar restraint over the issue of Singapore's land reclamation works at Pulau Tekong. While Malaysia has claimed, and Singapore has denied, that the land-starved city state's reclamation works were aimed at narrowing the shipping lanes to Malaysian ports (Tanjung Pelepas and Pasir Gudang), the conflict was finally resolved in April 2005 with modifications to the contested area of the island, after submissions made to the International Tribunal for the Law of the Sea.

Finally, competition and complementarity would continue to govern the bilateral relationship in the new millennium in the context of a changing international political economy. The impact of the Bali bombings in 2002 and 2005 should indeed spur region-wide efforts towards acting collectively to defeat the scourge of international terrorism while encouraging member states to adopt more conciliatory and pragmatic approaches to resolving bilateral issues. The ASEAN states provided a collective response to combating terror — an indication that where national interests converge on a commonly perceived threat, the prospects for multilateralism are enhanced.[55] The momentum of ASEAN regionalism would invariably engender member states to focus on common goals and to resolve bilateral issues within the framework of the Bali Treaty (ASEAN Concord I, 1976; and ASEAN Concord II, 2003). The signing of the ASEAN Charter at the Singapore Summit on 20 November 2007, despite the serious problem of human rights violations in Myanmar, could well signal the birth of a new phase of multilateralism in which the ASEAN Secretariat has been more empowered. The Charter, which has been ratified by all ten signatories within the stipulated one-year period, obliges ASEAN members to adhere to the rule of law, good governance, the principles of democracy and constitutional government, show respect for fundamental freedoms, as well as promote and protect human rights and social justice.[56] Yet, realist thinking is still exercising a strong influence on policymakers as sovereignty issues and disputes over territorial and resource claims are not being channelled into the ASEAN machinery for dispute resolution. Besides, laggard Myanmar challenges ASEAN coherence in a rather striking manner: Yangon's ratification of the ASEAN Charter has not necessarily signified any change in attitude by the ruling State Peace and Development Council in demonstrating substantial progress towards political accommodation and democratic reform to ASEAN and the international community — a point made emphatically by the brutal suppression of pro-democracy protests in September 2007.[57]

The rise of China and India, and the rapid pace of globalization are critical factors in ensuring the effective participation of each of its ten members to enhance ASEAN's relevance. In this regard, leadership changes on both sides of the Causeway are enabling the two neighbours to better appreciate the geopolitical context of realism, by managing and resolving conflicts through pragmatism, and the opportunities presented by neoliberalism, in strengthening institutional cohesion to promote regional security and prosperity. Yet, this essay should end, as it began, on a note of cautious optimism on the prospects for Asian multilateralism in general, and for security multilateralism in Southeast Asia. N. Ganesan argues that the 1997 Asian financial crisis "significantly weakened regional multilateral institutions and made states more inward-looking to attend to immediate domestic matters".[58] Additionally, Rueland observes that day-to-day decision-makers have only hesitantly accepted the consequence of the shift from realist to liberal, cooperative, comprehensive and human security in terms of the need for a deepening of institutions, allocation of scarce resources, and redefinition of national sovereignty.[59] In light of the current global economic meltdown, both countries have a unique opportunity to marshal resources for cooperative endeavours to alleviate the economic hardships faced by their citizenry. In this context, as multilateral approaches to economic integration and conflict resolution in Southeast Asia are still in the early stages of maturity, bilateral mechanisms to resolve problems are still preferred — and have a better chance of success, both at the intra-ASEAN and extra-ASEAN levels of interaction — notwithstanding recent efforts to empower the ASEAN Secretariat.

NOTES

[1] Sheldon W. Simon, "International Relations Theory and Southeast Asian Security", *Pacific Review* 8, no. 1 (1995): 7.

[2] For a concise and interesting account of the role of realism and neo-liberalism in Southeast Asian foreign policies, see ibid., pp. 5–24.

[3] Michael Leifer, *Singapore's Foreign Policy: Coping with Vulnerability* (London: Routledge, 2000), p. 15.

[4] For a more detailed discussion on this subject, see Amitav Acharya, *Regionalism and Multilateralism: Essays on Cooperative Security in the Asia-Pacific* (Singapore: Eastern Universities Press, 2003), pp. 278–80.

[5] Among the requirements of a security community are: (a) the absence of a competitive military build-up or arms race involving the regional actors, and (b) a high degree of political and economic integration. For details, see Amitav Acharya, *Regionalism and Multilateralism*, pp. 152–78.

[6] N. Ganesan, *Realism and Interdependence in Singapore's Foreign Policy* (London: Routledge, 2005), p. 56.

[7] T.S. George, *Lee Kuan Yew's Singapore* (London: Andre Deutsch, 1984), p. 169.

[8] Linda Y.C. Lim, "The Foreign Policy of Singapore", in *The Political Economy of Foreign Policy in Southeast Asia*, edited by David Wurfel and Bruce Burton (New York: St. Martin's Press, 1990), p. 134.

[9] Government of Singapore, "Trade with Major Trading Partners", *Statistics Singapore*, February 2008 <http://www.singstat.gov.sg/stats/visualiser/trade/trade.html> (accessed 22 February 2009).

[10] Zakaria Abdul Wahab, "Trade between Malaysia and Singapore will Increase Despite Global Uncertainty", Bernama, 12 April 2008 <http://www.bernama.com/bernama/v5/newsindex.php?id=352316> (accessed 2 March 2009).

[11] See Singapore Business Federation Report on Third Malaysia-Singapore Business Forum 2005 <http://www.sbf.org/public/event/details/event20051122.jsp> (accessed 22 February 2009).

12 "Malaysia and Singapore: A New Détente", *BusinessWeek*, 6 September 2004 <http://www.businessweek.com/magazine/content/04_36/b3898081.htm> (accessed 2 March 2009).

13 S. Jayasankaran, "Friends United: Singapore's Purchase of a Stake in Telekom Malaysia Could Herald Improved Bilateral Ties", *Far Eastern Economic Review* (hereafter cited as *FEER*), 11 March 2004, p. 16.

14 "Singapore Firms Invest Nearly S$1 billion in Iskandar Malaysia Project", *ChannelNews Asia*, 19 January 2009 <http://www.iskandarmalaysia.com.my/media-news.aspx?mid=7&smid=28&cid=0&itmid=320&title=Singapore%20Firms%20Invest%20Nearly%20S$1b%20In%20Iskandar%20Malaysia%20Project> (accessed 2 March 2009).

15 Johan Saravanamuttu, "Malaysia-Singapore Relations: Economic Diplomacy and the IDR", OpinionAsia, 1 June 2007 <http://www.opinionasia.org/EconomicDiplomacyandtheIDR> (accessed 2 March 2009).

16 "Malaysia and Singapore: A New Détente", *BusinessWeek*, 6 September 2004 <http://www.businessweek.com/magazine/content/04_36/b3898081.htm> (accessed 2 March 2009).

17 Sharon Ong, "Singapore-Malaysia Bilateral Economic Relations: Competition and Complementarity" (B.A. Thesis, National University of Singapore, March 1997), pp. 14–17.

18 *The Star* (Malaysia), 5 June 1999, pp. 1–2.

19 *The Sun* (Malaysia), 8 June 1997.

20 *FEER*, 20 September 2001.

21 "Malaysia, Singapore Progress on Rifts Straining Relations", Agence France Presse (hereafter cited as *AFP*), 6 September 2001.

22 *Straits Times*, 15 September 2001, p. 24.

23 *South China Morning Post*, 5 September 2001.

24 *Straits Times*, 3 July 2002, p. 1.

25 *Straits Times*, 18 June 2002, p. 4.

26 For details, see Joey Long, "Desecuritizing the Water Issue in Singapore-Malaysia Relations", *Contemporary Southeast Asia* 23, no. 3, (December 2001): 504–32.

27 K.S. Nathan, "Malaysia-Singapore Relations: Retrospect and Prospect", *Contemporary Southeast Asia* 24, no. 2 (August 2002): 400.

28 "Reclaimed Water: Singapore Introduces NEWater", International Water and Sanitation Centre, 13 August 2002 <http://www.irc.nl/page/2133> (accessed 2 March 2009).

29 *Today* (Singapore), 14 September 2005, p. 4.

30 S. Jayasankaran, "Splashing Out: Kuala Lumpur is to Take Control of the Nation's Water Supply and Invest Heavily in the Future", *FEER*, 4 September 2003, p. 18.

31 *See Asiaweek*, 14 August 1998, pp. 28–30.

[32] "Jawapan oleh Menteri Ehwal Luar Prof. S. Jayakumar di Parlimen pada 31 Julai 1998 kepada Soalan-Soalan Tambahan", Ministry of Foreign Affairs (Singapore) Press Release, Admin Page, p. 1.

[33] *FEER*, 20 September 2001.

[34] Anthony L. Smith, "Malaysia-Singapore Relations: Never Mind the Rhetoric", in *Asia's Bilateral Relations*, edited by Satu P. Limaye (Honolulu, Hawaii, USA: Asia-Pacific Center for Security Studies, Special Assessment, October 2004), Chapter 14 <http://www.apcss.org/Publications/SAS/AsiaBilateralRelations/AsiasBilateralRelationsComplete.pdf> (accessed 1 March 2009).

[35] *FEER*, 13 March 2003, p. 19.

[36] *Business Times*, 3 June 1998.

[37] *Berita Harian*, 14 September 1998.

[38] Clarence Fernandez, "Malaysia, Singapore, Jumpstart Stalled Relations", *Reuters*, 13 December 2004 <http://www.signonsandiego.com/news/world/20041213-0059-malaysia-singapore.html> (accessed 2 March 2009).

[39] *The Star*, 18 September 1998.

[40] *New Straits Times*, 30 September 1998.

[41] *New Straits Times*, 19 September 1998.

[42] For instance, Bruce Gale of the *Political and Economic Consultancy* regional newsletter remarked that the matter would be viewed more seriously in Singapore than in Malaysia. See *The Star*, 18 September 1998.

[43] "JB Opposes Opening up Airspace to Singapore", *Straits Times*, 26 October 2005, p. 16.

[44] Ibid.

[45] "Genting Wins Bid for Second Casino", *Bloomberg News*, 11 December 2006 <http://www.iht.com/articles/2006/12/11/bloomberg/sxgenting.php> (accessed 2 March 2009).

[46] Johan Saravanamuttu, "Malaysia-Singapore Relations: Economic Diplomacy and the IDR". On whether foreign (Singapore's) participation in IDR is a threat to Malay rights, Prime Minister Abdullah said, "the presumption that the IDR will harm Malays is an insult to the ability of Malays to compete on the global stage." See PM's Opening Speech at Fifty-eighth UMNO General Assembly, 7 November 2007 <http://yeinjee.com/malaysia/pm-opening-speech-at-umno-general-assembly-2007/> (accessed 1 March 2009).

[47] "Background on Pedra Branca", *ChannelNews Asia*, 6 November 2007 <http://www.channelnewsasia.com/stories/singaporelocalnews/view/309953/1/.html> (accessed 2 March 2009).

[48] "Malaysia's Claim Baseless, Singapore DPM Tells Court", *New Straits Times*, 20 November 2007, p. 10.

[49] ICJ's Judgement on Pedra Branca, 23 May 2008 <http://www.asiaone.com/News/Asiaonet+News/Singapore/Story/A/Story2008053-66727.html> (accessed 25 May 2008).

[50] Farik Zolkepli, "Johor Sultan Finds Ways and Means to Reclaim Batu Puteh", *The Star*, 19 June 2008.

[51] *Straits Times*, 8 May 2002, p. 1.

[52] *Straits Times*, 11 April 2002, p. S12.

[53] *Straits Times*, 19 March 2002, p. A1. The *Straits Times* adds that Malaysian ports handled 7.3 million containers in 2001, and were forecast to move 10 million containers in 2002. Singapore handled 15.5 million boxes in 2001. Malaysia's port infrastructure would be raised to handle 380 million tonnes of cargo a year, from 220 million tonnes in 2000. And Johor's port of Pelabuhan Tanjung Pelepas (PTP) has pulled the Danish shipping line Maersk from Singapore. Taiwan's biggest shipping line, Evergreen Marine, has also signed with PTP. It will move over eighty-five per cent of its Singapore transhipment volumes to the Malaysian port from August 2002. See *Business Times* (Singapore), 5 July 2002, p. 1–2.

[54] *Straits Times*, 3 May 2002, p. 1.

[55] K.S. Nathan, "Southeast Asian Responses to Arms and Terror", in *Controlling Arms and Terror in the Asia Pacific: From Bali to Baghdad*, edited by Marika Vicziany (Cheltenham, UK: Edward Elgar Publishing Limited, 2007), pp. 160.

[56] "Abdullah: Charter will be a Boon for Southeast Asia", *New Straits Times*, 21 November 2007, p. 2.

[57] "Nine Killed as Myanmar Junta Cracks Down on Protests", *AFP*, 26 September 2007 <http://afp.google.com/article/ALeqM5jkMCKEq7yPbP20x3UjDZH9DbaJIQ> (accessed 1 March 2005).

[58] N. Ganesan, *Realism and Interdependence in Singapore's Foreign Policy*, p. 123.

[59] Jurgen Rueland, "Traditionalism and Change in the Asian Security Discourse", in *Asian Security Reassessed*, edited by Stephen Hoadley and Jurgen Ruland (Singapore: Institute of Southeast Asian Studies, 2006), p. 363.

REFERENCES

Abdullah Badawi. "Malaysian Prime Minister's Opening Speech at Fifty-eighth UMNO General Assembly", 7 November 2007 <http://yeinjee.com/malaysia/pm-opening-speech-at-UMNO-general-assembly-2007/> (accessed 1 March 2009).

"Abdullah: Charter will be a Boon for Southeast Asia". *New Straits Times*, 21 November 2007, p. 2.

Abdul Wahab, Zakaria. "Trade between Malaysia and Singapore will Increase Despite Global Uncertainty", Bernama, 12 April 2008 <http://www.bernama.com/bernama/v5/newsindex.php?id=352316> (accessed 2 March 2009).

Acharya, Amitav. *Regionalism and Multilateralism: Essays on Cooperative Security in the Asia-Pacific*. Singapore: Eastern Universities Press, 2003.

"Background on Pedra Branca". Channel News Asia, 6 November 2007 <http://www.channelnewsasia.com/stories/singaporelocalnews/view/309953/1/.html> (accessed 2 March 2009).

Fernandez, Clarence. "Malaysia, Singapore, Jumpstart Stalled Relations", Reuters, 13 December 2004 <http://www.signonsandiego.com/news/world/20041213-0059-malaysia-singapore.html> (accessed 2 March 2009).

Ganesan, N. *Realism and Interdependence in Singapore's Foreign Policy*. London: Routledge, 2005.

"Genting Wins Bid for Second Casino", Bloomberg News, 11 December 2006 <http://www.iht.com/articles/2006/12/11/bloomberg/sxgenting.php> (accessed 2 March 2009).

George, T.S. *Lee Kuan Yew's Singapore*. London: Andre Deutsch, 1984.

Government of Singapore. "Trade with Major Trading Partners". *Statistics Singapore*, February 2008 <http://www.singstat.gov.sg/stats/visualiser/trade/trade.html> (accessed 22 February 2009).

"Jawapan oleh Menteri Ehwal Luar Prof. S. Jayakumar di Parlimen pada 31 Julai 1998 kepada Soalan-Soalan Tambahan". Ministry of Foreign Affairs (Singapore) Press Release, (31 July 1998?).

Jayasankaran, S. "Splashing Out: Kuala Lumpur is to take Control of the Nation's Water Supply and Invest Heavily in the Future", *Far Eastern Economic Review*, 4 September 2003, p. 18.

—————. "Friends United: Singapore's Purchase of a Stake in Telekom Malaysia could herald Improved Bilateral Ties". *Far Eastern Economic Review*, 11 March 2004, p. 16.

"JB Opposes Opening up Airspace to Singapore". *Straits Times*, 26 October 2005, p. 16.

Leifer, Michael. *Singapore's Foreign Policy: Coping with Vulnerability*. London: Routledge, 2000.

Lim, Linda Y.C. "The Foreign Policy of Singapore". In *The Political Economy of Foreign Policy in Southeast Asia*, edited by David Wurfel and Bruce Burton. New York: St. Martin's Press, 1990.

Long, Joey. "Desecuritizing the Water Issue in Singapore-Malaysia Relations". *Contemporary Southeast Asia* 23, no. 3, (December 2001): 504–32.

"Malaysia and Singapore: A New Détente". *BusinessWeek*, 6 September 2004 <http://www.businessweek.com/magazine/content/04_36/b3898081.htm> (accessed 2 March 2009).

"Malaysia's Claim Baseless, Singapore DPM Tells Court". *New Straits Times*, 20 November 2007, p. 10.

"Malaysia, Singapore Progress on Rifts Straining Relations", Agence France Presse (hereafter cited as AFP), 6 September 2001.

Nathan, K.S. "Malaysia-Singapore Relations: Retrospect and Prospect". *Contemporary Southeast Asia* 24, no. 2 (August 2002): 385–410.

————. "Southeast Asian Responses to Arms and Terror". In *Controlling Arms and Terror in the Asia Pacific: From Bali to Baghdad*, edited by Marika Vicziany. Cheltenham, UK: Edward Elgar, 2007.

"Nine Killed as Myanmar Junta Cracks Down on Protests", *AFP*, 26 September 2007 <http://afp.google.com/article/ALeqM5jkMCKEq7yPbP20x3UjDZH9D baJIQ> (accessed 1 March 2005).

Ong, Sharon. "Singapore-Malaysia Bilateral Economic Relations: Competition and Complementarity". B.A. thesis, Department of Economics and Statistics, National University of Singapore, 1997.

"Reclaimed Water: Singapore Introduces NEWater", International Water and Sanitation Centre, 13 August 2002 <http://www.irc.nl/page/2133> (accessed 2 March 2009).

Rueland, Jurgen. "Traditionalism and Change in the Asian Security Discourse". In *Asian Security Reassessed*, edited by Stephen Hoadley and Jurgen Ruland. Singapore: Institute of Southeast Asian Studies, 2006.

Saravanamuttu, Johan. "Malaysia-Singapore Relations: Economic Diplomacy and the IDR". *OpinionAsia*, 1 June 2007 <http://www.opinionasia.org/ EconomicDiplomacyandtheIDR> (accessed 2 March 2009).

Simon. Sheldon W. "International Relations Theory and Southeast Asian Security". *Pacific Review* 8, no. 1 (1995): 5–24.

Singapore Business Federation Report on Third Malaysia-Singapore Business Forum 2005 <http://www.sbf.org/public/event/details/event20051122.jsp> (accessed 22 February 2009).

"Singapore Firms Invest Nearly S$1 billion in Iskandar Malaysia Project". *ChannelNews Asia*, 19 January 2009 <http://www.iskandarmalaysia.com.my/ media-news.aspx?mid=7&smid=28&cid=0&itmid=320&title=Singapore%20Fir ms%20Invest%20Nearly%20S$1b%20In%20Iskandar%20Malaysia%20Project> (accessed 2 March 2009).

Smith, Anthony L. "Malaysia-Singapore Relations: Never Mind the Rhetoric". In *Asia's Bilateral Relations*, edited by Satu P. Limaye (Honolulu, Hawaii, USA: Asia-Pacific Center for Security Studies, Special Assessment, October 2004) <http://www.apcss.org/Publications/SAS/AsiaBilateralRelations/ AsiasBilateralRelationsComplete.pdf> (accessed 1 March 2009).

Zolkepli, Farik. "Johor Sultan Finds Ways and Means to Reclaim Batu Puteh", *The Star*, 19 June 2008.

11

Bilateral Relations between Indonesia and the Philippines: Stable and Fully Cooperative

Ikrar Nusa Bhakti

Unlike bilateral relations between Indonesia and Malaysia or Indonesia and Singapore, there has been no "hot or big issues" between Indonesia and the Philippines. In other words, since the establishment of diplomatic relations between Indonesia and the Philippines on 24 November 1949,[1] the two countries' bilateral relations have never undergone any turbulence. Perhaps the only strained issue in the two countries' bilateral relations happened during the late 1950s, when U.S. Military Bases in Subic and Clark were used by U.S. President Eisenhower's administration to undertake Central Intelligence Agency clandestine military operations to support the Pemerintahan Semesta (Permesta) secessionist rebellion in Sulawesi from 1957 to 1959.[2]

The foundation of bilateral relations between Indonesia and the Philippines was initially set up in the 1950s by top leaders of the two countries through personal arrangements, mutual courtesy visits, or meetings of senior officials. In order to strengthen the bilateral relationship, the two countries signed several agreements, most of them related to border management, such as the Treaty of Friendship signed in Jakarta on 21 June 1951, Immigration Agreement between the Government of the Republic of Indonesia and the Government of the Republic of the Philippines signed in Jakarta on 4 July 1956, followed by Joint Directives and Guidelines of Implementation of the Agreement signed in Manila on 14 September 1965, Exchange of Notes on 31 January 1966, The Implementing Rule and Regulation on the Border Crossing on 1 July 1975, Agreement on Border Trade between the Government of the Republic of Indonesia and the Government of the Republic of the Philippines signed on 1 August 1974, and Agreement on Defence and Security Cooperation between the Government of the Republic of Indonesia and the Government of the Republic of the Philippines in 1997.

The change of governments both in Indonesia and the Philippines have never changed cordial and fully cooperative relations between the two countries in handling issues related to border crossing, undocumented Indonesian nationals in the Philippines, or transnational crime. Indonesia and the Philippines have a history of helping each other in solving separatist pressures and problems.

The purpose of this chapter is to describe and analyse Indonesia-Philippine relations since 1975. Although the main focus of this chapter is how both countries handled the bilateral relationship after the end of the Second Indochina War, it is necessary to trace a little from the past. Consequently, before analysing the contentious issues and how both countries solved those issues, it is necessary to describe similarities and differences between Indonesia and the Philippines and why the legacy of the Sukarno-Macapagal relationship has served as a guide in promoting the bilateral relationship.

The chapter is divided into a total of five sections. The first identifies the similarities and differences between Indonesia and the Philippines, followed by the second section on the legacy of the Sukarno-Macapagal relationship. The third section deals with the contentious issues in the bilateral relationship and how Indonesia and the Philippines handle those issues. The fourth section describes and analyses development cooperation between the two countries through the BIMP-EAGA (Brunei-Indonesia-Malaysia-Philippines East ASEAN Growth Area) arrangement, while the last section looks at the importance of ASEAN in supporting bilateral relations within the Southeast Asian region.

Similarities and Differences between Indonesia and the Philippines

Indonesia and the Philippines are neighbouring archipelagos, perhaps even once part of the same land mass. While the Philippines lies generally northward and eastward of Indonesia, their climates are much the same. Both countries have a variety of racial/ethnic groups and languages, but in both the Malay stock and linguistic roots predominate.[3] Overall density of population is much the same: Indonesia has some 234,693,997 people (estimation in July 2007) and an area of 735,355 square miles;[4] the Philippines has 88,706,300 people and an area of 115,831 square miles.[5] Indonesia and the Philippines have problems of separatism in their own countries.

Both countries achieved independence after World War II following more than three centuries of colonial rule, Indonesia through Dutch colonization and the Philippines through Spain and the United States. The Philippines was granted independence from the United States on 4 July 1946, and Indonesia proclaimed its independence on 17 August 1945 followed by a revolutionary period until the Dutch transferred sovereignty to Indonesia on 27 December 1949. In other words, the Philippines gained its freedom by evolution and Indonesia by revolution. This development may well explain why Indonesia, in particular during the Sukarno presidency, was very anti-colonial and anti-imperialist. It was also anti-Western in its foreign policy orientation, while the Philippines was aligned with the United States and generally pursued pro-Western policies.

While Indonesia in the early 1960s inclined towards internationalist perspectives, such as the establishment of the Non-Aligned Movement and Conference of the New Emerging Forces, the Philippines was actually the first Southeast Asian country to introduce regionalism in the mid-1950s. President Macapagal was very active in establishing regionalism among the three Malay states, Malaysia, Indonesia, and the Philippines, popularly known as Maphilindo in the early 1960s. The association however had been inactive because of the Indonesian policy of *Konfrontasi* towards the establishment of the Malaysian Federation between 1963 and 1966. Although Indonesia and the Philippines both opposed the establishment of the Malaysian Federation (due to their differences in colonial history and foreign policy orientations), they responded differently to this new entity. Indonesia launched *Konfrontasi* against Malaysia, while the Philippines used diplomatic channels in dealing with the issue, specifically its claim to the state of Sabah in the island of Borneo.

Apart from these differences, whoever is President in Indonesia, with either a civilian or military background, will always be closer to Vietnam (which has been regarded by Indonesia as a nationalist rather than a communist state, with a similar history to Indonesia) which gained independence through revolution. During the Sukarno period, when the leader of Communist Vietnam, Ho Chi Minh, made a courtesy call to Indonesia, he was famous among Indonesian people as "Paman Ho" (Uncle Ho). During the Vietnam War, Indonesia supported Vietnam in the maintenance of its national integration, while the Philippines became an ally of the United States. On 8 August 1967, Indonesia and the Philippines became two of the five founding countries in Southeast Asia to establish the Association of Southeast Asian Nations (ASEAN).

Legacy of the Sukarno-Macapagal Relationship

As mentioned above, from 1950 to 1966, Indonesia and the Philippines had broadly divergent foreign and defence policies. Indonesia was one of the promoters of the Non-Aligned Movement and closer to the Soviet Union and China, and even attempted to forge a "Jakarta-Phnom Penh-Beijing-Hanoi-Pyongyang" axis in order to combat the so-called "Neocolonialism, Colonialism and Imperialism" (Nekolim).[6] At the same time, the Philippines was one of the U.S. allies in the Southeast Asian region (even though the Philippines was also a member of the Non-Aligned Movement).[7] However, those differences in foreign policy orientation had never been an impediment for the leaders of the two countries to develop a cordial relationship based on perceived brotherhood. During his seven-day official visit to the Philippines, which started on 28 January 1951, President Sukarno tried to establish cordial relations with President Elpidio Quirino and discussed how to promote the bilateral relationship in the future. As a result, on 21 June 1951 in Jakarta, Indonesia and the Philippines signed a treaty of friendship which became the foundation of the future relationship between Indonesia and the Philippines.[8] Sukarno visited Manila many times to chat with Philippine Presidents, from Elpidio Quirino, Ramon Magsaysay Jr., to Carlos P. Garcia and Diosdado P. Macapagal. During those periods, the two countries signed quite a number of agreements, such as a cultural agreement, an agreement on the abolition of visa requirements, and a border crossing agreement.[9]

From a political perspective however, Sukarno and Macapagal can be regarded as the two leaders who laid down a cornerstone of the bilateral relationship, namely how to solve their bilateral problems peacefully and how to use each other for communication to a third party for the benefit of the other. A good example of this approach is how Sukarno and Macapagal were of the same opinion that Asian problems must be solved by the Asians themselves through Asian-styled consultations. During Sukarno's visit to Manila in November 1962, President Macapagal assured Sukarno that the Philippines would not be used as a U.S. base against Indonesia. In return, Sukarno assured Macapagal that he would not solicit communist military assistance while confronting Malaysia.[10] It is interesting to note that during the Sukarno-Macapagal period, Indonesia and the Philippines opposed the establishment of the Malaysian Federation, although with different motives, political interests, and methods — Indonesia through confrontation with Malaysia, the Philippines through diplomacy.[11] However, during his visit to the United States in October 1964, in order to get military assistance from the United States Government, Macapagal stressed the Philippines' dramatic shift in attitude toward Indonesia by describing the importance of increasing Philippine military strength in Mindanao (its large southern island) so as to discourage known Indonesian penetration or expansionism.[12]

The change of government in Indonesia from Sukarno to Suharto did not have any negative impact on the bilateral relationship, in fact the relationship became much better compared to the Sukarno-Macapagal era. Under President Suharto, Indonesia's foreign relations after 1966 were generally moderate, inclined towards the West, regionally focused,[13] and they were matched with the Philippine foreign policy under President Ferdinand Marcos. Indonesia also implemented good neighbourly relations with its Southeast Asian neighbours. The policy by Indonesia to end the politics of *Konfrontasi* against Malaysia in 1966 opened the gate for the establishment of ASEAN on 8 August 1967. During the Suharto-Marcos period, Indonesia became a mediator for the Philippines and Malaysia to end "temporarily" the Philippine claim over Sabah for the sake of ASEAN and its unity.

When Corazon Aquino took power after the fall of the Marcos government through "People's Power" in 1986, Jakarta was the first capital visited by the new Philippine President. A trip to Jakarta before a trip to Washington D.C. was certainly unprecedented. During Aquino's visit to Jakarta, President Suharto took the opportunity to press the urgency of defeating the New People's Army which had become an issue not only to Philippine internal security, but also for the stability of the region. To show support for Aquino's government, Suharto insisted that the 1987 ASEAN Manila Summit meeting go forward despite apprehensions in other ASEAN capitals about the security situation in the Philippines.[14]

A change of government in the Philippines from Aquino to Fidel Ramos in 1992 had a positive impact on the bilateral relationship. This was because Ramos, as chief of staff of the Armed Forces of the Philippines during the Marcos period and later Secretary of National Defence, was well-known to the senior leadership of the Indonesian Armed Forces. As a result, Indonesia and the Philippines shared the same views on the dangers of communist and Islamic rebellions.[15] On 20 September 1993, President Fidel V. Ramos arrived in Jakarta for a five-day state visit. During his visit, Indonesia and the Philippines signed a memorandum of understanding on the establishment of an Indonesia-Philippines joint commission. The commission has undertaken several meetings since 1995, either in Jakarta or in Manila, to discuss problems in the bilateral relationship and how to solve them.[16]

After the fall of Suharto in May 1998, which signalled a new reform era in Indonesia, bilateral relations between Indonesia and the Philippines, in particular in the political and security areas, fared extremely well. This assessment is evidenced by the high frequency of visits from the presidential level to government officials, entrepreneurs, non-governmental organizations (NGOs), and even ordinary people. For example, on 29 June 2001, President Abdurrahman Wahid made a one-day working visit to Manila. President Megawati Sukarnoputri as the eldest daughter of Sukarno had built a personal relationship with President Gloria Macapagal-Arroyo (the daughter of President Diosdado Macapagal) and made several courtesy calls to Manila. Her first official visit was to Manila. President Susilo Bambang Yudhoyono also visited Manila many times either to improve the bilateral relationship or to attend ASEAN meetings. Both Megawati had, when she was in power, and now Yudhoyono has a hotline with Gloria Macapagal-Arroyo.

During Yudhoyono's visit to Manila on 20–23 June 2005, Indonesia and the Philippines strengthened their bilateral cooperation on combating terrorism and other transnational crime, issues related to the South China Sea, Indonesia's support for the Philippines to become an observer at the Organisation of the Islamic Conference (OIC), Philippines policy on undocumented Indonesians, determination (delimitation) of the borderlines of the two countries' maritime territory, cooperation on energy, interfaith dialogues, and mutual support for an East Asian Community, ASEAN, Asia-Africa Summit, and the UN.[17]

Contentious Issues

There are several contentious issues between Indonesia and the Philippines, but so far the two countries have managed the issues bilaterally through formal diplomatic channels or through actual cooperation in the field.

Miangas (Island of Palmas) Case

Indonesia has no territorial boundary dispute with the Philippines related to Miangas Island. However, it has a minor problem related to border crossers from Miangas to Cape San Agustin in Davao Oriental. Ownership over Miangas was settled before the International Court of Justice (ICJ) at The Hague in 1928, when the Dutch presented a stronger case than the U.S. contender.[18] The decision of the ICJ was included in the protocol on the Extradition Treaty between Indonesia and the Philippines signed in Jakarta on 10 February 1976.[19] Yet Indonesia and the Philippines, as successor states, have not pursued the matter of bilaterally defining the exact coordinates of the fluid sea border connecting the two countries. And so, although Miangas is nominally part of Indonesia, the waters surrounding it are silently claimed by the Philippines in a border dispute that is, to all intents and purposes, inactive.

Miangas is Indonesia's northernmost island. Interestingly, the island with a population of just 982 persons is about 324 miles away from North Sulawesi's provincial capital of Manado, while Davao City is just 78 miles away. In order to arrange for traditional border crossers, the two countries signed a special border crossing arrangement in 1975. Residents of the border area have the privilege of crossing the border without passports to visit family, celebrate religious occasions, or engage in petty trading. For these reasons, and to avoid illegal border crossing or smuggling, the Philippines and Indonesia have built border crossing stations on adjacent islands on both sides of the border, including Miangas.[20]

In early February 2009, however, the issue related to Miangas emerged as a hot issue discussed at the coordination meeting on how to secure Indonesia's border areas. The meeting was held by the National Central Bureau and Interpol Indonesia at the National Police Headquarters in Jakarta on 11 February 2009. Indonesia has land borders with three countries — Malaysia, Timor Leste, and Papua New Guinea — and maritime borders with ten countries — Malaysia, Papua New Guinea, Timor Leste, India, Thailand, Vietnam, Singapore, the Philippines, Palau, and Australia. Those border areas have become places of serious criminal activities such as terrorism, human smuggling/trading, narcotics smuggling, oil and gas smuggling, smuggling of daily necessities, smuggling small weapons, illegal fishing, illegal logging, illegal sand reclamation, cyber-crimes, and maritime piracy. Apart from these transnational organized criminal activities, Indonesia's most-outer islands could have easily been claimed by other countries. According to Deputy Head of North Sulawesi Regional Police, Commissioner John Kalangi, there was a map published by the Philippines Tourism Authority which included three of Indonesia's northern-most islands in Sangihe and Talaud Regencies — Miangas, Marore, and Marampit — as part of the Philippines. In the future, this will create territorial boundary disputes between Indonesia and the Philippines. There are at least four issues related to the Indonesia-Philippines maritime border: firstly, the ideological conflict between the Moro Islamic Liberation Front (MILF) and the Philippine government will have a negative impact on the people of Sangihe-Talaud in Sulawesi; secondly, islands in Sangihe and Talaud regencies may become one of the transit locations for actors of terrorism who undertake military training in the Philippines; thirdly, islands in Sangihe-Talaud have also been detected as sea lanes of communication for smuggling of illicit small weapons and bomb materials; fourthly, the islands of Miangas, Marore, and Marampit in Sangihe-Talaud regencies were depicted on the Philippine tourism map as part of the Philippines.[21] Indonesia's Foreign Affairs Minister Hassan Wirayudha, however, has brushed off rumours of a takeover of Indonesia's northernmost island of Miangas by the Philippines, saying Manila was fully aware Miangas was Indonesian territory. Wirayuda said that making a fuss about Miangas was a waste of time since the

Philippines government has not even officially claimed anything yet. It means that there has been no territorial dispute between Indonesia and the Philippines related to who possesses Miangas Island since that issue was solved by the ICJ in 1928. Foreign Ministry spokesman, Teuku Faizasyah, told *The Jakarta Post* that a private sector error might be blamed for the controversy.[22] It is indeed possible that suspicions of the Indonesian police are owing to ignorance regarding tourist cooperation between Indonesia and the Philippines in accordance with the terms of the BIMP-EAGA.

Until now (2009), Indonesia and the Philippines have been discussing the delimitation of maritime boundaries between the two countries. Since 2003, the two countries have organized meetings of the Joint Permanent Working Group on Maritime and Ocean Concerns either in Jakarta, Manila, Davao, or Bogor. The Working Group is divided into three sub-working groups, namely the Sub-working Group on Delimitation of Common Maritime Boundaries, Sub-working Group on Safety and Security of Navigation, and Sub-working Group on Fisheries Conservation and Management. Related to delimitation of common maritime boundaries, Indonesia and the Philippines accepted the principle of archipelagic states in accordance with the United Nations Law of the Sea Conference (UNCLOS) 1982. Although there have been differences between the two countries in solving maritime boundaries, they agreed to use the principle of the median line. In order to calculate the equidistant line, Indonesia has always used base point and baseline methods while the Philippines used the coastline method. Apart from that, delimitation of the two countries' maritime boundaries is more complicated because it is also related to their maritime borders with a third party, namely Malaysia to the west and Palau to the east.[23]

Since UNCLOS I in 1958, Indonesia tried to get international recognition for the principle of the archipelagic state in accordance with the Djuanda Declaration of 1957. Indonesia's diplomacy to get that recognition failed during the UNCLOS I and II in 1958 and 1960 respectively. It was not until over two decades later, in UNCLOS III in December 1982, the regime of "archipelagic state" was finally recognized by the international community, as signified by its incorporation in UNCLOS 1982. The Djuanda Declaration stated:

> The government declares that all waters surrounding, between and connecting the islands constituting the Indonesian state, regardless of their extension or breadth, are integral parts of the territory of the Indonesian

state and therefore, parts of the internal or national waters which are under the exclusive sovereignty of Indonesian state.... delimitation of territorial sea (the breadth of which is 12-miles) is measured from baseline connecting the outermost points of the islands of Indonesia.[24]

Following the Djuanda declaration, Indonesia has always used the method of baseline to discuss delimitation of maritime boundaries with other countries, including with the Philippines. Between 1957 and 1966, Indonesia's archipelagic doctrine was determined by symbolic and strategic consideration, but since the beginning of the New Order era to the present (1966 till now) an economic consideration has been added. According to Dino Patti Djalal these are of:

- *symbolic consideration*, because the territorial model is perceived to bear relevance to the theme of national unification;
- *strategic consideration*, because it involves an attempt to control foreign maritime territories and, especially, naval movements within the archipelago;
- *economic consideration*, because it significantly relates to the resource exploitation (mainly oil) in offshore areas.[25]

During the liberal democracy period in Indonesia (1949–57), one of the domestic issues was primarily related to national unity (civil wars in particular in Sumatra and Sulawesi and the struggle to regain West Irian/Papua from the Dutch). During the Suharto period up until now, symbolic, strategic, and economic considerations taken together have been very important in formulating the Indonesian archipelagic doctrine. Apart from that, Indonesia is not only facing traditional threats, such as infiltration or invasion from foreign countries, but also non-traditional threats such as illegal fishing, illegal logging, human smuggling, small weapons smuggling, narcotics smuggling, and so forth.

Illegal Entry and Undocumented Indonesian Citizens in the Southern Philippines

According to the census data taken by the Indonesian Consulate General in Davao in 2004, there are about 7,946 undocumented Indonesian citizens in Davao, General Santos, Sarangani Island, Glan, Isulan, Kabacan-Kidapawan, Kiamba, Tikang, Pagang, Balut Island, Santa Maria, and Makdung. Most of them came from Sangir-Talaud, North Sulawesi, Indonesia's island closest to the Philippines. They have been living in the Mindanao area for at least three generations and have intermarried with Filipinos. Interactions among Filipinos and Indonesians in the border areas have been going on for a long time. The two countries are still trying to solve this problem by giving those involved an option, either to maintain Indonesian citizenship or to become Philippine citizens.[26]

From a historical perspective, interaction between people in North Sulawesi and those from the southern Philippines began several centuries ago. Most of the time, their interactions have been positive in tone, but sometimes conflict has also occurred between them. Such conflicts have even found their way into the names of a few areas in North Sulawesi, for example, the meaning of Tinakareng is "the area guarded by fences", because during the early period, people from Mindanao accidentally attacked this area. Another example is Miangas, the northernmost island of Indonesia, which means "open for the sea pirates" because it used to be visited by pirates from Mindanao. Quite a few of the inhabitants in Miangas speak Bisaya, Tagalog, or even English, because several decades ago they cultivated land in Mindanao and had business relationships with residents in the southern Philippines. During the Kingdoms era in the early 1590s, there were wars between the kingdoms in Sangihe-Talaud and the kingdom in Mindanao.[27]

Population mobility of people from Sangihe-Talaud to the southern Philippines is caused by a few factors, such as the geographical proximity of the area, social kinship among people of the area, population pressures in Sangihe-Talaud Islands, the lack of natural resources, and other economic and political reasons. Some people from Sangihe-Talaud undertook permanent migration, but others only undertook circular mobility. Until the early twentieth century, people from Sangihe-Talaud migrated to the southern Philippines in order to improve their economic prosperity, either to cultivate the land in Mindanao, undertake illegal trade between the two regions, or to work in plantations and harbours in the Philippines. These crossings have caused bilateral problems between Indonesia and the Philippines. As a result, the Philippine Government undertook forced extradition of 200 Indonesian families from 1963 to 1965. It is also why Indonesia and the Philippines signed a border agreement in 1965.[28]

In order to improve bilateral relations between the two countries the Indonesian Government, in 1963–65, sponsored the return migration of about 3,216 Sangir people from the southern Philippines. In the mid-1970s, quite a number of people from Sangihe-Talaud also returned to Indonesia because of severe political conditions in the southern Philippines. In 1983–91, some 1,234 people returned to Indonesia at their own expense.[29]

Mobility of people from North Sulawesi to the southern Philippines and vice versa depended on economic, political, and security conditions in those areas. If economic, social, and security conditions in the southern Philippines were better than in North Sulawesi, people migrated to the former, and if not, it was the other way around. For example, during the mid-1960s, when the conditions in Indonesia worsened after the so-called Indonesian Communist Party coup, quite a number of people from North Sulawesi migrated to the southern Philippines. However, when conditions in the southern Philippines deteriorated in the 1970s due to radical Islamic activities in the region, Sangihe-Talaud people undertook permanent migration to Indonesia, particularly to North Maluku. However, when ethnic conflict occurred in Maluku and North Maluku, the Sangihe-Talaud people became internally displaced persons in Manado and several places in North Sulawesi, such as in Minahasa and Bitung.[30]

Illegal Fishing

Illegal fishing by Filipinos has become a minor problem between the two countries. In order to avoid it, Indonesia and the Philippines signed a Memorandum of Understanding (MOU) on Marine and Fisheries Cooperation on 23 February 2006. This agreement will be valid effectively for a five year period. This MOU replaced the previous MOU or Republic of the Philippines–Republic of Indonesia Arrangement on Utilization of Part of the Total Allowance Catch in the Indonesian Exclusive Zone. Based on this 2006 MOU, permission to fish within the Indonesian Exclusive Economic Zone will only be given to Philippine fisheries companies that have established joint ventures with Indonesian companies.[31]

Problems Related to Terrorism and Islamic Militancy

There have been some reports during the 1980s that 115 members of the Free Aceh Movement (Gerakan Aceh Merdeka, GAM) were trained in the Philippines by Muslim guerillas in Mindanao,[32] and that Indonesia-based members of Jemaah Islamiah (JI) had ties with the Moro Islamic Liberation Front (MILF) to undertake military training and terror activities in the southern Philippines.[33] While the MILF is trying to distance itself from partnership with the extremist JI, it has pushed individual JI members increasingly towards the Abu Sayyaf Group. The JI and Abu Sayyaf are working increasingly with the Rajah Solaiman Movement, while new militant converts to Islam based in Manila and northern Luzon serve as a conduit for more experienced terrorist groups to move into the Philippine urban heartland.[34] It was also reported that illicit small arms smuggling has been going on from the southern Philippines to the conflict areas in Indonesia using areas where the Indonesian security patrols are infrequent.

JI members and other Islamic militant groups from Indonesia were sent to the Philippines for military training using a route from Kalimantan Timur to Sabah (Malaysia), thence to Tawi-Tawi (Philippines), and Sulu/Mindanao (Philippines). This led the three countries of Indonesia, Malaysia, and the Philippines to sign in May 2002 a tripartite agreement to combat transnational crime and terrorism.[35] The Philippines Government also forced all vessels to use designated sea lanes along the borders with Malaysia and Indonesia to deny Islamic militants easy access to its restive Muslim areas.[36] In addition, the increasing threat of terrorism has prompted the Philippines and Indonesia to review their existing border agreement signed in 1975. The review was proposed during the twenty-third Philippines-Indonesia border committee vice-chairmen's conference in Davao City in December 2002. Among other measures, the joint border committee proposed a more efficient monitoring and restriction of border crossers within a twenty-five-mile radius from their residential address. They also discussed the possible inclusion of the maritime police and immigration agencies in border crossing activities which the navy and the coastguard are currently undertaking.[37] During his visit to Manila in July 2007, Indonesian Foreign Minister Hassan Wirayuda and the State Secretary of the Philippines Alberto G. Romulo told a press conference that both countries had concerns about the sea border between the southern Philippines and eastern Indonesia and would intensify patrols in the area.[38] The two countries have also agreed to expand intelligence sharing and patrols along their porous border to keep up pressure on Islamic militants.[39]

It is a fact that in order to combat terrorism and transnational crime in general, Indonesia and the Philippines have already signed an agreement on cooperative activities in the field of defence and security

in August 1997, several MOUs between the Indonesian National Police
and the Philippine Police in November 2005, including the establishment
of a Joint Technical Working Group in March 2006, and a document
on Standard Operating Procedures Joint Operation in November 2006.
In June 2007, the two national police forces undertook a Joint Training
Design Group meeting that has produced some agreement on hot pursuit
in the border areas, handing over of suspects by the national police, and
administration of training between the two national police forces.

Indonesia became a broker between the Philippine Government and the
Moro National Liberation Front (MNLF) to end decades of violence and
give Moro Muslims substantial autonomy in the four-province Autonomous Region of Muslim Mindanao with an agreement signed on 2 September 1996.[40] It is interesting to note that while Indonesia has always
supported the Philippines Government in its treatment of separatism
in Mindanao, Indonesia was actually at the same time learning how to
give special autonomy status to Aceh so as to stop separatism in that
westernmost province of Indonesia. The Philippines, on the other hand,
also took part in finding a comprehensive solution to the Aceh conflict by
sending its military observer during the implementation of the Cessation
of Hostilities Agreement between the Government of Indonesia and GAM.
The Philippines also became a member of The Aceh Monitoring Mission
after the Helsinki Peace Accord was signed on 15 August 2005.

Indonesia and the Philippines have the same political interest to
cooperate in anti-terrorism activities because such activities in the southern
Philippines and the use of Indonesia's northernmost islands by terrorists
as sanctuary or a place for military training could have a negative impact
on the stability and national unity of both countries.

Development of BIMP-EAGA

The Brunei Darussalam, Indonesia, Malaysia, the Philippines-East ASEAN
Growth Area (BIMP-EAGA or simply EAGA) was established in 1994.
It provides an alternative model of sub-regional cooperation in order
to develop border areas between countries. It covers the provinces of
eastern Indonesia (North Sulawesi, North Maluku, Maluku, and Papua),
the eastern part of Malaysia (Sabah and Sarawak), the southern part
of the Philippines (Mindanao), and Brunei Darussalam. The success
of BIMP-EAGA depends on the leadership in the four countries, their
respective economic policies and conditions, as well as the political and

security problems in the provinces in the border areas. BIMP-EAGA has attempted to develop trade, investment, and tourist activities in what are some of the most troubled areas of both Indonesia and the Philippines. The Indonesia-EAGA (I-EAGA) provinces, particularly Poso (Central Sulawesi), Ternate and Bacan (North Maluku), and Ambon (Maluku) were the scenes of communal, religious, and violent conflicts during the late 1990s and early 2000s, while Papua and West Papua provinces have witnessed vertical conflicts or separatism since the early 1960s. On the Philippine side, Mindanao (the largest island of the southern Philippines) is the major area of the Philippines-EAGA project (P-EAGA), but Mindanao is the site of an ongoing armed conflict between the Moro Islamic groups and the Armed Forces of the Philippines.

During the Ramos presidency (1992–98), the Philippine Government took the lead of the BIMP-EAGA development programmes in order to solve the problem in Mindanao through military force instead of poverty eradication through economic activities. It brought a relatively positive impact to Mindanao following the 1996 peace agreement that suspended the armed conflict. EAGA unfortunately lost its most eminent backer during the Estrada presidency (1998–2001) when it was downgraded by an all-out-war policy against the Moro insurgency. Estrada's successor, President Gloria Macapagal-Arroyo gave signs that the growth area should be revived, but this approach has fallen victim to circumstances.[41]

Indonesia-Philippine cooperation to develop the least-developed border areas of both countries have been hampered by the political and security conditions in those areas. It is understandable that cooperation between the two countries has been mostly focused on maintaining security and order in their border areas. It depends on the leadership in the provinces of the southern Philippines and eastern part of Indonesia to undertake province-to-province cooperation in order to reduce uneven development between centre and periphery and unified development of the border areas.

The Importance of ASEAN

We cannot separate bilateralism and multilateralism in this case study because ASEAN member states believe they are complementary. It is true that ASEAN cannot be used as a vehicle to solve overlapping territorial claims between two or more member states. ASEAN leaders have even tried to sweep those issues under the carpet or use the ICJ to decide which country has legitimate claim over a disputed territory. For example, Indonesia and Malaysia solved the issue of their overlapping claims over the islands of Sipadan and Ligitan in 2002 via the ICJ. Until now ASEAN has also kept the spirit of the ASEAN Way that includes the principle of non-interference in the domestic affairs of individual member states. This principle has in turn been successful in maintaining the unity of ASEAN. The Annual Meeting of the ASEAN Foreign Ministers or ASEAN Summit Meetings, however, can be used by two or more member states to discuss contentious issues faced by those countries and how to resolve those issues. And because ASEAN is moving towards becoming a security community, it is much easier for its member states to maintain good neighbourly relations.

Conclusion

Bilateral relations between Indonesia and the Philippines have been stable and cooperative since the establishment of diplomatic relations in 1949. President Sukarno and President Macapagal laid down the foundation of the two countries' bilateral relations in the 1960s.

Although there have been mutual problems faced by the two countries, these have always been resolved successfully through dialogue between the heads of governments. Any urgent issues such as security in the border areas can also be solved at the ministerial level or through cooperation between the militaries and the police forces. Indonesia and the Philippines have also signed several agreements and memoranda of understanding in the field of defence and security as umbrellas to undertake military and security cooperation.

Indonesia-Philippines relations have never been as close as the relationship between Indonesia and Malaysia or Indonesia and Singapore. However, by contrast, Indonesia and the Philippines have never experienced any turbulence in their relationship compared to Indonesia's bilateral relationship with Malaysia and Singapore. Yet, it is important to ask why Indonesia and the Philippines, the two archipelagic states in ASEAN, have had difficulty in economic cooperation. Is it because they have different historical backgrounds, their economies are not complementary, or they have insufficient funds, or because the central governments in Jakarta and Manila have no interest to develop their border areas, or because previous attempts have been hampered by political and security considerations in the southern Philippines and the eastern part of Indonesia? The leaders of the two countries should realize that if they do not develop economic cooperation they will be left out of the economic development of Southeast Asia, since other ASEAN countries will reap benefits from the development of mainland Southeast Asia, in particular through their cooperation with China and India.

NOTES

1   The Philippines formally accorded *de jure* recognition to the Republic of Indonesia on 27 December 1949. This is the same date that the Dutch recognized Indonesian independence as per the Hague Roundtable Conference.
2   Audrey R. Kahin and George McT. Kahin, *Subversion as Foreign Policy: The Secret Eisenhower and Dulles Debacle in Indonesia* (New York: New Press, 1995); for the full story of CIA Operations in Sulawesi and Maluku, see Tom Cooper and Marc Koelich, "Clandestine US Operations: Indonesia 1958, Operation 'Haik'", *Publication of Air Combat Information Group*, 1 September 2003 <www.acig.org/artman/publish/article_175.shtml> (accessed 17 September 2007).
3   Benjamin Higgins, "Development Problems in the Philippines: A Comparison with Indonesia", *Far Eastern Survey* 26, no. 11 (November 1957): 161.
4   "Republic of Indonesia", Wikipedia, the free Encyclopaedia <http://en.wikipedia.org/wiki/Indonesia> (accessed 17 September 2007).
5   "Republic of the Philippines", Wikipedia, the free Encyclopaedia <http://en.wikipedia.org/wiki/Philippines> (accessed 17 September 2007).
6   "Sukarno's Foreign Policy", Country Studies <http://www.country-studies.com/indonesia/sukarno's-foreign-policy.html> (accessed 17 September 2007).
7   "Filipina", Indonesian Wikipedia, the free Encyclopaedia <http://id.wikipedia.org/wiki/Filipina> (accessed 17 September 2007); see also, "[Philippines] Relations with Asian Neighbors", U.S. Library of Congress <http://countrystudies.us/philippines/93.htm> (accessed 17 September 2007).
8   Office of the Press Secretary (Philippines), "Chronology of Philippines-Indonesia Relations" <http://www.ops.gov.ph/indonesia2001/backgrounder.htm> (accessed 17 September 2007); Names of the Philippines Presidents were quoted from "Philippines History. Presidents & Vice Presidents of the Philippines" <http://philippine-history.philsite.net/presidents.htm> (accessed on 18 September 2007).
9   Ibid.
10 "The Sukarno years: 1950–1965", *Sejarah Indonesia* <http://www.gimonca.com/sejarah/sejarah09.shtml> (accessed 17 September 2007).

11   For more discussion on this issue, see for example, Charles A. Fisher, "The Malaysian Federation, Indonesia and the Philippines: A Study in Political Geography", *Geographical Journal* 129, no. 3. (September 1963): 311–28; see also, U.S. Department of State, Office of the Historian, "Sukarno's Confrontation With Malaysia (January–November 1964)", in *Foreign Relations 1964–1968, Volume XXVI, Indonesia; Malaysia-Singapore; Philippines*, Documents 1–24 <http://www.state.gov/r/pa/ho/frus/johnsonlb/xxvi/4425.htm> (accessed 18 September 2007).

12   U.S. Department of State, Office of the Historian, "Philippines", *Foreign Relations 1964–1968, Volume XXVI, Indonesia; Malaysia-Singapore; Philippines*, Documents 294–318 <http://www.state.gov/r/pa/ho/frus/johnsonlb/xxvi/4426.htm> (accessed 18 September 2007).

13   "Foreign Policy Under Suharto", Country Studies <http://www.country-studies.com/indonesia/foreign-policy-under-suharto.html> (accessed 18 September 2007).

14   "The Philippines", Country Studies <http://www.country-studies.com/indonesia/the-philippines.html> (accessed 18 September 2007); for more details, also see, Donald E. Weatherbee, "The Philippines and ASEAN: Options for Aquino", *Asian Survey* 27, no. 12 (December 1987): 1223–39.

15   During the Suharto period, communism was regarded as *Ekstrem Kiri* or "Extreme Left" while Islamic radicalism as *Ekstrem Kanan* or "Extreme Right".

16   Departemen Luar Negeri Republik Indonesia, "Hubungan Bilateral Indonesia-Filipina" [Bilateral relations Indonesia–the Philippines] <http://www.dfa-deplu.go.id/?category_id=13&country_id=&news_bil_id=403&bilateral=asia timur> (accessed 20 April 2008).

17   Indonesian Embassy in Manila, "Hubungan Bilateral Indonesia-Filipina" [Bilateral relations Indonesia-Philippines], n.d.

18   See, Island of Palmas (Miangas) Case. Netherlands v. United States. Permanent Court of Arbitration (1928). Sole Arbitrator: Max Huber. 2U.N. Rep. Int'l Arbitral Awards 829 <http://ksumail.kennesaw.edu/~cli/palm.htm> (accessed 19 September 2007); see also, "Island of Palmas Case", Wikipedia, the free Encyclopaedia <http://en.wikipedia.org/wiki/Island_Palmas_Caseber 19> (accessed on 19 September 2007).

19   See "UU 10/1976 tentang Pengesahan Perjanjian Ekstradisi Antara Republik Indonesia dan Republik Philipina serta Protokol" [Law No.10/1976 on the ratification of Extradition Treaty between the Republic of Indonesia and the Republic of The Philippines), Jakarta, 26 July 1976.

20   Djorina Velasco, "Between Manado and Davao: How the Indonesian island of Miangas is making use of its Philippines ties", *Newsbreak*, 11 February 2007 <http://www.newsbreak.com.ph/index.php?option=com_content&Itemid=88889064&task=view&id=23> (accessed 17 September 2007).

21 "Perbatasan Tak Terurus. Lintasan Surga bagi Aktivitas Kejahatan Tingkat Tinggi", *Kompas* (12 February 2009), pp. 1 and 15.

22 "Border Dispute: Private Mapmaker Suspected in Border Blunder", *Jakarta Post*, 14 February 2009, p. 4.

23 See for example, "Laporan hasil rapat interdep Kelompok Teknis Delimitasi Batas Maritim RI-Filipina" [Report on the result of interdepartmental meeting Technical Group on Delimitation of Maritime Boundary Indonesia-Philippines] (Jakarta: Markas Besar Tentara Nasional Indonesia [Indonesian Military Headquarters], March 2004); "Laporan Hasil Pertemuan ke-5 JPWG-MOC RI-Filipina" [Report on the result of the fifth JPWG-MOC Indonesia–the Philippines] (Jakarta: Markas Besar Tentara Nasional Indonesia, Staf Teritorial [Indonesian Military Headquarters, Territorial Staff], March 2007).

24 See Dino Patti Djalal, *The Geopolitics of Indonesia's Maritime Territorial Policy* (Jakarta: Centre for Strategic and International Studies, 1996), pp. 29 and 42.

25 Ibid., p. 1.

26 Embassy of the Republic of Indonesia, "Background information about the Philippines and Bilateral Relations between Indonesia–The Philippines", n.d.

27 Aswatini Raharto et al., *Mobilitas Penduduk dan Pembangunan Daerah Perbatasan (Kasus Kabupaten Sangihe Talaud, Daerah Perbatasan Indonesia-Filipina)* [Population Mobility and Development of the Border Area. Case study of Sangihe-Talaud, Border Area between Indonesia and the Philippines] (Jakarta: Puslitbang Kependudukan dan Ketenagakerjaan- Lembaga Ilmu Pengetahuan Indonesia [PPT-LIPI], 1997), p. 9.

28 Aswatini Raharto, ed., *Migrasi Kembali Orang Sangir-Talaud Dari Pulau-Pulau di Wilayah Filipina* [Return Migration of the people of Sangir-Talaud from Islands in the Philippines] (Jakarta: Puslitbang Kependudukan dan Ketenagakerjaan — Lembaga Ilmu Pengetahuan Indonesia [PPT-LIPI], 1995), pp. 1–2.

29 Suko Bandiyono, "Mobilitas Penduduk Sangihe" [Mobility of Sangihe people], in *Dinamika Mobilitas Penduduk di Wilayah Perbatasan* [The dynamic of population mobility in the border area], edited by Mita Noveria et al. (Jakarta: Pusat Penelitian Kependudukan — Lembaga Ilmu Pengetahuan Indonesia [PPT-LIPI], 2007), pp. 77–99.

30 Ibid., p. 98.

31 Embassy of the Republic of Indonesia, "Background information about the Philippines and Bilateral Relations between Indonesia–The Philippines", n.d.

32 See ICG Asia Report No. 17, *Aceh: Why Military Force Won't Bring Lasting Peace*, (Jakarta/Brussels: International Crisis Group, 21 June 2001), p. 3 <http://

www.internal-displacement.org/8025708F004CE90B/(httpDocuments)/
C2EB3F86C3AAD411802570B700593FF5/$file/ICG_ACEH_June01.pdf>
(accessed 3 March 2009).

[33] See ICG Asia Report No. 80, *Southern Philippines Backgrounder: Terrorism and the Peace Process* (Singapore/Brussels: International Crisis Group, 13 July 2004) <http://www.reliefweb.int/library/documents/2004/icg-phl-13jul.pdf> (accessed 3 March 2009).

[34] For a good analysis see, ICG Asia Report No. 110, *Philippines Terrorism: The Role of Militant Islamic Converts* (Jakarta/Brussels: International Crisis Group, 19 December 2005).

[35] "Malaysia, Indonesia, Philippines Sign Agreement on Terrorism", Xinhuanet, 7 May 2002 <http://news.xinhuanet.com/english/2002-05/07/content_383299. htm> (accessed 19 September 2007).

[36] "Philippines Says Plans to Tighten Southern Border", Reuters, 13 March 2006 <http://asia.news.yahoo.com/060313/3/2h925.html> (accessed 19 September 2007).

[37] "Philippines, Indonesia Review Border Agreement amid Terror Threats", *Asia Africa Intelligence Wire*, 19 December 2002 <http://www.accessmylibrary. com/comsite5/bin/pdinventory.pl?pdlanding=1&referid=2930&purchase> (accessed 19 September 2007).

[38] "Indonesia, Philippines vow to beef up surveillance on Border", *People's Daily Online*, 17 September 2007 <http://english.people.com.cn/90001/90777/ 6215336.html> (accessed 19 September 2007).

[39] "Indonesia, Philippines to expand security ties", *Khalleej Times Online*, 13 July 2007 <http://www.khaleejtimes.com/DisplayArticleNew.asp?xfile=data/ theworld/2007/July/theworld_July32> (accessed 19 September 2007).

[40] See for example, "Indonesia Brokers Philippines Peace Bid", *Inside Indonesia* 50 (April–June 1997) <http://insideindonesia.org/content/view/886/29/> (accessed 19 September 2007).

[41] For a good description and analysis of BIMP-EAGA see, for example, Adriana Elisabeth, "The Role of the Philippines in the BIMP-EAGA Growth Triangle and the Dynamics of ASEAN Political Economy" (Ph.D. dissertation, University of Wollongong, 2008).

REFERENCES

Bandiyono, Suko. "Mobilitas Penduduk Sangihe" [Mobility of Sangihe people]. In *Dinamika Mobilitas Penduduk di Wilayah Perbatasan* [The Dynamic of population mobility in the border area], edited by Mita Noveria et al. Jakarta: Pusat Penelitian Kependudukan — Lembaga Ilmu Pengetahuan Indonesia (PPT-LIPI), 2007.

"Border Dispute: Private Mapmaker Suspected in Border Blunder". *Jakarta Post*, 14 February 2009, p. 4.

Cooper, Tom and Marc Koelich. "Clandestine US Operations: Indonesia 1958, Operation 'Haik'". *Publication of Air Combat Information Group*, 1 September 2003 <www.acig.org/artman/publish/article_175.shtml> (accessed 17 September 2007).

Departemen Luar Negeri Republik Indonesia [Ministry of Foreign Affairs of the Republic of Indonesia]. "Hubungan Bilateral Indonesia-Filipina" [Bilateral relations Indonesia–the Philippines] <http://www.dfa-deplu.go.id/?category_id=13&country_id=&news_bil_id=403&bilateral=asiatimur> (accessed 20 April 2008).

Djalal, Dino Patti. *The Geopolitics of Indonesia's Maritime Territorial Policy*. Jakarta: Centre for Strategic and International Studies, 1996.

Elisabeth, Adriana. "The Role of the Philippines in the BIMP-EAGA Growth Triangle and the Dynamics of ASEAN Political Economy". Ph.D. dissertation, Department of History and Politics, University of Wollongong, 2008.

Embassy of the Republic of Indonesia. "Background information about the Philippines and Bilateral Relations between Indonesia–The Philippines", n.d.

Fisher, Charles A. "The Malaysian Federation, Indonesia and the Philippines: A Study in Political Geography". *Geographical Journal* 129, no. 3 (September 1963): 311–28.

"Foreign Policy Under Suharto". Country Studies <http://www.country-studies.com/indonesia/foreign-policy-under-suharto.html> (accessed 18 September 2007).

Higgins, Benjamin. "Development Problems in the Philippines: A Comparison with Indonesia". *Far Eastern Survey* 26 no. 11 (November 1957): 161–69.

Indonesian Embassy in Manila. "Hubungan Bilateral Indonesia-Filipina" [Bilateral relations Indonesia-Philippines], n.d.

"Indonesia Brokers Philippines Peace Bid". Inside Indonesia 50 (April–June 1997) <http://insideindonesia.org/content/view/886/29/> (accessed 19 September 2007).

"Indonesia, Philippines to Expand Security Ties". *Khalleej Times Online*, 13 July 2007 <http://www.khaleejtimes.com/DisplayArticleNew.asp?xfile=data/theworld/2007/July/theworld_July32> (accessed 19 September 2007).

"Indonesia, Philippines Vow to Beef Up Surveillance on Border". *People's Daily Online*, 17 September 2007 <http://english.people.com.cn/90001/90777/6215336.html> (accessed 19 September 2007).

International Crisis Group. "ICG Asia Report No. 17. *Aceh: Why Military Force Won't Bring Lasting Peace*". Jakarta/Brussels: International Crisis Group, 21 June 2001 <http://www.internal-displacement.org/8025708F004CE90B/(httpDocuments)/C2EB3F86C3AAD411802570B700593FF5/$file/ICG_ACEH_June01.pdf> (accessed 3 March 2009).

———. "ICG Asia Report No. 80. *Southern Philippines Backgrounder: Terrorism and the Peace Process*". Singapore/Brussels: International Crisis Group, 13 July 2004 <http://www.reliefweb.int/library/documents/2004/icg-phl-13jul.pdf> (accessed 3 March 2009).

———. "ICG Asia Report No. 110, *Philippines Terrorism: The Role of Militant Islamic Converts*". Jakarta/Brussels: International Crisis Group, 19 December 2005.

Island of Palmas (Miangas) Case. Netherlands v. United States. Permanent Court of Arbitration (1928). Sole Arbitrator: Max Huber. 2U.N. Rep. Int'l Arbitral Awards 829 <http://ksumail.kennesaw.edu/~cli/palm.htm> (accessed 19 September 2007).

Kahin, Audrey R. and George McT. Kahin. *Subversion as Foreign Policy: The Secret Eisenhower and Dulles Debacle in Indonesia*. New York: New Press, 1995.

"Malaysia, Indonesia, Philippines Sign Agreement on Terrorism". Xinhuanet, 7 May 2002 <http://news.xinhuanet.com/english/2002- 05/07/content_383299.htm> (accessed 19 September 2007).

Markas Besar Tentara Nasional Indonesia [Indonesian Military Headquarters]. "Laporan hasil rapat interdep Kelompok Teknis Delimitasi Batas Maritim RI-Filipina" [Report on the result of interdepartmental meeting Technical Group on Delimitation of Maritime Boundary Indonesia-Philippines]. Jakarta: Markas Besar Tentara Nasional Indonesia, March 2004.

Markas Besar Tentara Nasional Indonesia, Staf Teritorial [Indonesian Military Headquarters, Territorial Staff]. "Laporan Hasil Pertemuan ke-5 JPWG-MOC RI-Filipina" [Report on the result of the fifth JPWG-MOC Indonesia–the Philippines]. Jakarta: Markas Besar Tentara Nasional Indonesia, March 2007.

Office of the Press Secretary (Philippines). "Chronology of Philippines-Indonesia Relations" <http://www.ops.gov.ph/indonesia2001/backgrounder.htm> (accessed 17 September 2007).

"Perbatasan Tak Terurus. Lintasan Surga bagi Aktivitas Kejahatan Tingkat Tinggi". *Kompas*, 12 February 2009), pp. 1 and 15.

"The Philippines". Country Studies <http://www.country-studies.com/indonesia/the-philippines.html> (accessed 18 September 2007).

"Philippines, Indonesia Review Border Agreement amid Terror Threats". *Asia Africa Intelligence Wire*, 19 December 2002 <http://www.accessmylibrary.com/comsite5/bin/pdinventory.pl?pdlanding=1&referid=2930&purchase> (accessed 19 September 2007).

"Philippines Says Plans to Tighten Southern Border". Reuters, 13 March 2006 <http://asia.news.yahoo.com/060313/3/2h925.html> (accessed 19 September 2007).

Raharto, Aswatini, et al. Migrasi Kembali Orang Sangir-Talaud Dari Pulau-Pulau di Wilayah Filipina [Return Migration of the people of Sangir-Talaud from islands in the Philippines]. Jakarta: Puslitbang Kependudukan dan Ketenagakerjaan — Lembaga Ilmu Pengetahuan Indonesia (PPT-LIPI), 1995.

————. Mobilitas Penduduk dan Pembangunan Daerah Perbatasan (Kasus Kabupaten Sangihe Talaud, Daerah Perbatasan Indonesia-Filipina) [Population mobility and development of the border area. Case study of Sangihe-Talaud, border area between Indonesia and the Philippines]. Jakarta: Puslitbang Kependudukan dan Ketenagakerjaan- Lembaga Ilmu Pengetahuan Indonesia (PPT-LIPI), 1997.

"Sukarno's Foreign Policy". Country Studies <http://www.country-studies.com/ indonesia/sukarno's-foreign-policy.html> (accessed 17 September 2007).

"The Sukarno Years: 1950–1965". *Sejarah Indonesia* [History of Indonesia] <http:// www.gimonca.com/sejarah/sejarah09.shtml> (accessed 17 September 2007).

U.S. Department of State, Office of the Historian. "Sukarno's Confrontation with Malaysia (January–November 1964)". In *Foreign Relations 1964–1968, Volume XXVI, Indonesia; Malaysia-Singapore; Philippines*, Documents 1–24 <http://www. state.gov/r/pa/ho/frus/johnsonlb/xxvi/4425.htm> (accessed 18 September 2007).

————. "Philippines", *Foreign Relations 1964–1968, Volume XXVI, Indonesia; Malaysia-Singapore; Philippines*, Documents 294–18 <http://www.state.gov/r/ pa/ho/frus/johnsonlb/xxvi/4426.htm> (accessed 18 September 2007).

U.S. Library of Congress, "[Philippines] Relations with Asian Neighbors". Country Studies <http://countrystudies.us/philippines/93.htm> (accessed 17 September 2007).

"*UU 10/1976 tentang Pengesahan Perjanjian Ekstradisi Antara Republik Indonesia dan Republik Philipina serta Protokol*" [Law No. 10/1976 on the ratification of Extradition Treaty between the Republic of Indonesia and the Republic of The Philippines), Jakarta, Indonesia, 26 July 1976.

Velasco, Djorina. "Between Manado and Davao: How the Indonesian Island of Miangas is Making Use of its Philippines Ties". *Newsbreak*, 11 February 2007 <http://www.newsbreak.com.ph/index.php?option=com_content&Itemid=8 8889064&task=view&id=23> (accessed 17 September 2007).

Weatherbee, Donald E. "The Philippines and ASEAN. Options for Aquino". *Asian Survey* 27, no. 12 (December 1987): 1223–39.

Conclusion

12

Conclusion

N. Ganesan and Ramses Amer

This conclusion summarizes the book's main findings. This will be followed by a broader discussion on the relationship between multilateralism and bilateralism in the Southeast Asian context. The broader discussion will also specifically link Etel Solingen's theory chapter at the start of the book to the country studies. This linkage will assist in placing the case studies within a broader context as well as bring the book full circle. The conclusion also addresses the importance of key factors influencing the bilateral relationships in the Southeast Asian region and their impact on regional collaboration and ASEAN.

Main Findings

Etel Solingen's chapter makes it clear that there are many different forms of international cooperation with different meanings attached to them. She then goes on to identify seven different core concepts in the international relations literature dealing with the subject. The term multilateralism itself became a focus of analysis in the 1990s. Central to the concept of multilateralism is a set of protocols demanding that states forego some of their own narrow interests in order to achieve general organizing principles in relationships characterized by diffuse reciprocity. Different schools of thought such as neorealism, neoliberal institutionalism, and constructivism employ different approaches to the study of multilateralism that in turn highlight different core variables and constraints. Solingen thinks that a convergence of domestic coalitional strategies among dominant actors favouring internationalization provides a powerful incentive for multilateralism, and it was such convergence that spurred ASEAN. There was a synergy between economic and security interests in ASEAN. Nonetheless, states like Indonesia, the Philippines, and Singapore tended to favour bilateral cooperation with external countries on security matters despite their common fears. Dominant internationalizing coalitions favour any arrangements, multilateral or otherwise, that promise both domestic political and macroeconomic, as well as regional, stability; these, in turn, enhance attractiveness to foreign investment and access to global markets, technology, and capital required for sustained economic growth and domestic political survival.

Regionalism may be also driven by ideas and identity in a constructivist sense; the impetus for them may not necessarily be state-led. Regionalism is a policy or project, while regionalization may be both process and product. The latter is also likely to be a "bottom up societally driven process". Networks, on the other hand, arise out of commonly held ideas or agendas and may operate in a number of fora. The attention or focus of study for networks is the relationship itself rather than a country. The concept of forum shopping, of much more recent vintage, emphazises the choice of platform for dealing with a given issue in the international arena. In other words, just like individuals, states consciously exercise choice in their selection of venues to further their interests. The literature draws extensively from political economy but has deeper roots in legal studies.

In contrast to multilateralism, bilateralism appears to cater to specific reciprocity. While acknowledging the utility of bilateralism, there are many scholars who regard bilateralism as a transactional form that complicates and undercuts multilateralism, especially in the domain of economics and trade. Such arrangements are viewed by some scholars as having a deleterious effect on liberalizing tendencies in international trade. Other scholars however take a much more nuanced view as to whether bilateralism and multilateralism are mutually inclusive or exclusive.

Sheldon Simon's chapter examines the evolution of multilateralism in Southeast Asia. While ASEAN has achieved much in the international arena in the 1980s, he argues it has been severely challenged in the 1990s. These challenges stem from the organization's inability to deal with sub-regional problems and the problems spawned by the Asian financial crisis in 1997. His central argument is that ASEAN's institutional evolution has been stymied by a lack of "collective intersubjective identity" central to multilateralism. He regards this identity as central to movement away from the non-interference rule characterizing ASEAN in the 1990s, leading in turn to its loss of purpose and inability in dealing with problems affecting member states. Simon also believes that the ASEAN Charter adopted at the 2007 summit meeting will go some way in establishing this necessary identity. He attributes the late establishment of this identity to ASEAN's concern with soft or regime security. He then identifies a core pool of genuine security concerns he believes ASEAN states should collectively address. These include issues like terrorism, weapons smuggling, maritime security, diseases, and the withdrawal of support for countries like Myanmar for its poor political record and violence.

Whereas Simon thinks that the Charter and its ratification is an important first step in overcoming some of the structural hurdles of the organization, he appears sceptical as to how much progress will be made on the basis of the Charter. He then cites an official who argues that the Charter should be viewed more as a statement of declaratory intent rather than a commitment to a course of actions that include sanctions for non-compliance. Other obstacles that he cites to the Charter's utility include the retention of the non-interference principle and the consensual decision-making rule that effectively allows a single state to veto a collective decision, the poor guidelines for the implementation of democracy and human rights, and the absence of enforcement mechanisms against countries that violate the Charter's provisions. Simon also looks at issues ASEAN can collectively address and some of the progress made in the areas of transnational crime and intelligence sharing. He concludes the chapter by arguing that security cooperation at the regional level is generally weak because ASEAN has been unable or unwilling to deal with core security issues. He deems the consensual decision-making rule to be the greatest impediment to such cooperation because that rule obliges all decisions to be mutually acceptable to all member states.

In his chapter on the relationship between Vietnam and Thailand, Nguyen Vu Tung argues that the relationship between the two countries is extremely important. He does so by highlighting the importance of mainland Southeast Asia in Vietnamese foreign policy. He also reminds readers that this relationship served as a barometer of Vietnam's relations during the Cold War as well as the period following the normalization of relations between the two countries in 1976. Despite previous hostilities, the 1980s marked a significant turnaround in the bilateral relationship. This development was due to the relaxation of international and regional tensions as well as domestic political and policy changes in Vietnam and Thailand. Tung begins his chapter by highlighting some of the historical and cultural affinities between the Vietnamese and Thai peoples. However, differences in worldview and conflicting national interests undermined these affinities. Vietnam was also influenced by Thai involvement in the Indochina Wars, and had viewed both Thailand and ASEAN as serving American interests in the wider region. Consequently, Thailand was viewed as "anti-communist, reactionary and above all, a country of opposing ideology". This situation was complicated by Vietnam's self-perception as the victor in the Indochina Wars whereby it had a corresponding right to order regional relations. Vietnam's interest in retaining influence in Cambodia and Laos also complicated relations with Thailand. Vietnam's subsequent so-called invasion and occupation of Cambodia worsened relations with Thailand, and by extension, ASEAN. Vietnam's changed foreign policy priorities and its acceptance of the ASEAN method of regional cooperation were especially important for improved relations with Thailand in the 1990s. Its growing emphasis on diplomacy in foreign policy and greater attention to developing the local economy also helped bilateral relations. Tung argues that Vietnam has also been much more committed to improving relations with all Southeast Asian countries. Confidence-building measures, especially in the area of defence cooperation with Thailand, are also viewed as helpful. Finally, both countries have successfully concluded an agreement demarcating the overlapping seas zone related to continental shelf and Exclusive Economic Zone boundaries in the disputed area in the Gulf of Thailand to the south-west of Vietnam and north-east of Thailand. The first meeting of the high-level Joint Committee on Fisheries and Marine Order took place and the two countries inked an agreement on cooperation in maintaining order at sea and in the joint development of marine resources. These arrangements have significantly minimized maritime-related disputes between Vietnam and Thailand.

Trade appears to be one of the areas where the two countries have some tensions. Indeed, the two countries are described as competitors for a number of export products, including rice and marine resources. However, the bilateral trade balance is significantly in Thailand's favour. Similarly, they also compete for foreign direct investments. Thailand is seen as playing up its economic competition with Vietnam in order to serve a domestic constituency. Political relations are described as having suffered from Thailand's refusal to extradite two Americans of Vietnamese origin accused of terrorist acts in Vietnam. Consequently, political and security cooperation has been downgraded since 2006 and the ministerial level Joint Consultative Mechanism has also been cancelled. But within a broader context, the ongoing political difficulties and regime transition in Thailand have been holding up bilateral relations. And in the final analysis, increased bilateral cooperation supported by the ASEAN multilateral cooperative mechanisms has improved relations between Vietnam and Thailand, thus raising the hope that this currently friendly relationship can be long lasting.

Ramses Amer's chapter deals with the Cambodia-Vietnam bilateral relationship. He begins the discussion by examining the deterioration of the bilateral relationship that eventually led to the Vietnamese military intervention in Cambodia in 1978–79. This conflict, that also involved China and the Soviet Union, started the relationship on an extremely bad footing where both countries viewed each other with enmity. Following international brokerage and containment of the civil war, the issue of ethnic Vietnamese returnees became an issue. Nonetheless, a number of agreements demarcating land and maritime borders were signed between the two countries to stabilize the relationship. The issue of hostilities involving ethnic Vietnamese however continued into the late 1990s. After both countries signed the Supplementary Border Treaty in 2005, their relations improved significantly. This in turn led to a large number of elite visits between the two countries.

The bilateral relationship is described as being historically plagued by Cambodian negative perceptions of ethnic Vietnamese. Amer argues that Cambodian political elites of all persuasions have highlighted the Vietnamese as "the other". This historical hangover is said to have derived from the "pro-Thai part of the Khmer royalty" that emerged victorious with external support in the early nineteenth century. There are differences in both countries' perceptions of history. For instance, Cambodia takes the view that Vietnamese territorial expansion in the Mekong Delta occurred at the expense of Cambodian territory. There have also been Cambodian accusations of Vietnamese involvement in its internal affairs. These perceptions have in turn complicated the issue of the resolution of territorial claims between both countries. Then First Prime Minister Norodom Ranarridh is seen to be especially prone to such assertions in his bid to secure and enhance his political legitimacy.

Other major issues in the bilateral relationship are identified as ethnic Vietnamese in Cambodia and ethnic Khmer in Vietnam. The former in particular were subjected to repeated attacks in the past, but such attacks have now subsided. While ethnic Khmers in Vietnam have attracted the interest of the Cambodian elite, Amer argues that Vietnam has consistently sought to treat them fairly and inclusively. The Cambodian perceptional hangover is believed to render any resolution to the two important issues of territorial claims and ethnicity difficult. Despite this obstacle, relations between the two countries have indeed improved recently. Thus, Amer sees far greater commitment on the part of the elites of both countries to resolve outstanding issues, as exemplified by the progress in managing the land border issue. The maritime disputes remain unresolved and the two countries have not managed to find a solution despite ongoing negotiations.

Pavin Chachavalpongpun's chapter examines the bilateral relationship between Thailand and Myanmar. Pavin posits that Thailand tradition-ally antagonizes the different Myanmar regimes by using history to construct a negative perception of the country. For its own national reasons, Thailand propagates widely held Thai perceptions of Myanmar as the aggressor state that twice invaded the old Siamese capital, Ayuttaya. Despite the British colonization of Burma, the Thai elite continue to characterize Myanmar as an enemy to justify its policies. In so doing, the Thai elite has considerably marred its bilateral relationship with Myanmar. This situation was worsened by the Thai buffer policy supporting the "anti-Rangoon, anti-communist ethnic minorities along the common border" with Myanmar. While many of these insurgent armies have signed ceasefire agreements with the existing Myanmar Government, both Thailand and Myanmar continue to regard each other with suspicion. This is so much so that Thailand has accused the Myanmar Government of complicity in the problems of illegal migration, refugees, infectious diseases, transnational crime as well the manufacture and inflow of drugs.

Pavin also points out that bilateral relations between the two countries were especially poor when the Democrat Party was in power in Thailand. The Democrat Party had a very clear anti-Rangoon stance and capitalized on its democratic credentials to draw attention to the military authoritarian regime in Myanmar. This policy was in contrast to the previous one which emphasized economic issues as the mainstay of the Thailand-Myanmar relationship. ASEAN too has multilateral interest in the continual engagement and inclusion of Myanmar so as to prevent it from falling under the Chinese sphere of influence. According to Pavin, the golden period of Thailand-Myanmar relations occurred during the premiership of Thaksin Shinawatra in Thailand whereby both countries mutually benefitted from improved economic relations. There was significant growth in bilateral trade and investments during this period from 2001 to 2006. While the September 2006 coup in Thailand caused some temporary disarray in their bilateral ties, the subsequent governments led by the People's Power Party followed Thaksin's lead in foreign policy.

Pavin highlights the dysfunctional relationship between the Thai military elite who have a negative perception of Myanmar, and the political elite who have economic interests at heart. Thai politics is therefore characterized as the power play of elite interests, both domestically and internationally. Present day contentious issues in the bilateral relationship include the Myanmar ethnic minorities residing in the border areas, Myanmar troops along the common border, Thai illegal fishing and logging in Myanmar, Myanmar illegal workers and migrants, and the flow of illegal drugs into Thailand. Despite their mutual mistrust, Thai and Myanmar military officers regularly discuss these bilateral problems in their meetings. Civil society groups and NGOs play a role in the resolution of some issues by drawing attention to the negative impact of border developments on Myanmar. Systematic resolution of outstanding issues is supposedly dealt with by the Thailand-Myanmar Joint Commission on Bilateral Relations and a Joint Trade Commission for economic matters. However, Pavin regards both organizations as incompetent and details how problems are typically resolved by elites at the personal level. Moreover, a number of bilateral military channels exist to enhance strategic cooperation between the two countries. He concludes his study by noting that not all contentious issues are resolved, and some are specifically retained to serve as leverage in future negotiations.

The chapter by N. Ganesan deals with Thailand-Malaysia bilateral relations. This relationship is a historically friendly one that survived the bilateral turbulence in the 1990s. Owing to common perceptions of domestic and external threats, both countries have benefitted significantly from the convergence of their foreign and defence policies during the Cold War. The elites from both countries have traditionally regarded each other as friendly neighbours, and have accordingly pursued accommodative policies with each other. Consequently, both countries address mutual problems and discuss their differences without the animosity marking Thailand-Myanmar relations.

Traditionally, Malaysia's and Thailand's foreign policies emphasize their different interests within Southeast Asia. Thailand has better ties with its mainland Southeast Asian neighbours, while Malaysia has closer relations with its maritime neighbours. However, the common border between Malaysia and Thailand means that bilateral ties between these two countries are centred on the four northern provinces of peninsular Malaysia and the four southern provinces of Thailand. Between 1989 and 2005, Malaysia-Thailand bilateral relations deteriorated. Ganesan argues that their ties deteriorated along with the dismantling of the structural dictates of the Cold War. As a result of this disengagement, threat perceptions changed and a number of new non-traditional threats rose to the fore. These included overlapping territorial claims, illegal fishing and migration, and smuggling. More recently, the outbreak of political violence in southern Thailand has also become an issue, leading Thailand to complain that Malaysia tacitly supported such activities. However, for the most part, both countries have collaborated to deal with this security issue.

Both countries resolve territorial and demarcation issues through joint border committees. Malaysia and Thailand have used these committees to great effect in the past to deal with common security issues like the communist insurgency. At the lower level, regional border committees deal with similar issues. Serious problems are resolved at the bilateral level during ministerial meetings and the many regional multilateral fora of which they are members. Some issues may be conflated with others, and may therefore require the involvement of multiple agencies. Illegal fishing is a classic case in point, for there are a great many discrete organizations in Thailand involved in the fishing industry. Both countries have undertaken measures to resolve overlapping territorial claims. The first of these was a memorandum of understanding in February 1979 on the delimitation of their continental shelf boundary in the Gulf of Thailand. Resources in disputed areas were subsequently resolved through mutual cooperation. It was in this spirit that both countries established the Malaysia-Thailand Joint Authority. In October 1979, both countries also signed a treaty regarding their territorial sea delimitations in the Gulf of Thailand and the Strait of Malacca. In May 1990, both countries reached an agreement on the matters pertaining to the Malaysia-Thailand Joint Authority. While this relationship is generally characterized by structural quid pro quos, government agencies also play an important role in determining bilateral ties. For instance, Mahathir is often described as considerate in his dealings with Asian countries while Thaksin prefers to make highly charged and nationalistic pronouncements.

Meredith Weiss examines the relationship between Indonesia and Malaysia. She claims that relations between the two countries are generally good and symbiotic despite some previous tensions over the Indonesian *Konfrontasi* in the 1960s. Better bilateral relations followed when Sukarno's revolutionary foreign policy was replaced with a development oriented one by Suharto's New Order government. The latter government was much more committed to friendly relations with Malaysia, as evinced by the reduction of its revolutionary rhetoric and its movement towards a regionally-centred security architecture. While the new Suharto government also rendered its relationship with Malaysia more competitive, the two countries' large number of shared cultural norms and ideas have tempered the realist appraisals of the relationship.

Although their relationship is by and large cordial and constructive, territorial disputes and labour migration have been known to cause some friction between them. Weiss also identifies cross-border environmental issues as a new point of contention between Malaysia and Indonesia. Territorial disputes involving Indonesia are tricky due to the country's extensive claims and the sheer expanse of the Indonesian archipelago. The problem is further accentuated by the fact that areas jointly claimed by Indonesia and Malaysia often hold oil and gas deposits. The first overlapping claim emerged over the islands of Ligitan and Sipadan. It was resolved by the International Court of Justice (ICJ) in Malaysia's favour in 2002. Since then, issues involving overlapping claims have become increasingly contentious and the Indonesian media has whipped up local emotions over the issue. Similar claims to Ambalat between both countries rose to the fore after Malaysia granted a concession for oil exploration. In subsequent developments, the navies of both countries were deployed, leading to an incident whereby two warships grazed each other. Swift intervention by political elite diffused the situation although several overlapping claims continue to exist.

The issue of migration is conflated with illegal migration as well as Malaysian sympathy and support for Acehnese migrants fleeing the fighting between the military and the secessionist insurgency movement. Indonesia was unhappy with what it perceived as Malaysian support for Acehnese independence. This is because Indonesia believes Malaysia had gone out of its way to initiate an asylum policy for Acehnese refugees. Broadly put, migration, specifically illegal migration, has been a source of tension since the 1970s. Despite providing cheap and much needed manpower to labour intensive industries in Malaysia, illegal immigrants are not welcome and are often rounded up and deported. In turn, this is a source of some embarrassment and shame for Indonesia. Some of these illegal immigrants are also involved in criminal activities. Additionally, Indonesia provides a large number of domestic helpers who are sometimes subjected to abuse in Malaysia. Trans-boundary pollution also occurs due to forest burning in Kalimantan and Sumatra and sometimes in the East Malaysian states of Sabah and Sarawak. This has led to greater cooperation between the two countries in issues touching on the environment, counter-terrorism, and intelligence sharing.

The resolution of contentious issues between the two countries is typically undertaken at both the bilateral level and the personal level between elites. Joint commission meetings and general border committees also routinely deal with problems as well as benefit from "friendship and goodwill". Democratization in Indonesia has however made elite resolution of problems much more difficult. Personal ties and broad awareness between both countries have also opened up issues to the scrutiny of NGOs. Some of these organizations are involved in activism, especially for labour rights. Other multilateral channels such as ASEAN have also come to encompass the expansion of relations between both countries. Weiss concludes by noting that both countries are committed to coexisting peacefully, adding that there is clear awareness of ethno-cultural similarities and worldviews encapsulated in the Malay phrase, *bangsa serumpun*.

Ikrar Nusa Bhakti's chapter on Indonesia-Philippines bilateral relations essentially argues that the relationship is generally stable and positive and not prone to the kind of turbulence that characterize some of the other relationships examined. The relationship is said to have received a lasting tone from the original positive personal relationship between Presidents Sukarno of Indonesia and Macapagal of the Philippines. Some of the more contentious issues are said to include the ambiguity of the status of Miangas Island owing to its geographical proximity to the Philippines but ownership by Indonesia. Another issue is the presence of some 8,000 illegal and documented Indonesian nationals residing in the southern Philippines. There appears to be a migration of these people depending on the general climate of security and economic opportunities available. So for example, owing to the outbreak of ethnic hostilities in Maluku at the turn of the century, there is a current preference for these migrants to live in the southern Philippines. Illegal fishing that also used to be a major problem is described as being better managed through a 2006 memorandum of understanding between the two countries. Joint exploration of marine resources has also been mooted as a way out of this problem.

Terrorism and Islamic militancy in the southern Philippines is another troubling issue in the bilateral relationship. Since this issue is common to both countries, there has generally been security cooperation aimed at dealing with it collectively. Indonesia is also said to have learnt some valuable lessons from the Philippines while helping to broker peace talks between the Moro National Liberation Front (MNLF) and the Philippine Government. These lessons were apparently put to good use when Indonesia negotiated to end the violence in Aceh. Finally, the East ASEAN Growth Area (EAGA) is seen as an important link in bringing together disparate territories from Brunei, Indonesia, Malaysia, and the Philippines. However, the area has border and security-related challenges that need to be dealt with in the first instance. Ikrar concludes the chapter by arguing that ASEAN fulfils a critical role in the bilateral relationship and Indonesian foreign policy in general. Consequently, both bilateralism and multilateralism are viewed as complementary policy options.

In her chapter, Natasha Hamilton-Hart argues that the Indonesia-Singapore relationship is subject to sharp fluctuations of tension and peaceful cooperation. The relationship is conventionally regarded as having been poor in the 1960s and early 1970s with significant improvement after the firm establishment of the New Order regime and its commitment to local development and regional cooperation. Relations became rockier after the Suharto government collapsed in 1998. Despite a veneer of calm and protestations of a positive relationship, tensions lurk below the surface. The tensions are "magnified out of proportion as a result of viewing them in isolation from the large areas of complementarities and cooperation that exists". Political elite from both countries are viewed as selectively interpreting the relationship, and hence subjecting it to more sensitivity than necessary. There is also a noticeable gap between Indonesia and Singapore's perceptions of irritants, with the latter tending to play it up as a threat to Singapore.

The structural asymmetries between Singapore and Indonesia do not necessarily empower Indonesia and disadvantage Singapore. Hamilton-Hart is of the opinion that Singapore's endowments and economic calibration are of insufficient interest to larger neighbouring countries to warrant a military invasion. Additionally, she regards the inherent differences in size and demography as well as previous historical tensions as not determinative of the relationship. Similarly, negative stereotypes and violence towards the Chinese are argued as strictly directed towards Indonesian Chinese rather than the ethnically Chinese per se. Historically, *Konfrontasi* was also never directed against Singapore, and the island's involvement and casualties were marginal. Common membership in ASEAN is viewed as embedding common interests, trust, and habits of cooperation. The process of democratization in Indonesia is viewed as opening the bilateral relationship to greater scrutiny. However, this development is not necessarily associated with a more combative foreign policy orientation.

Most contentious bilateral issues are viewed as complaints originating from Indonesia. These include the status of Singapore Government–linked investments in Indonesia, complaints over exports of sand and granite, the sensitiveness of trade statistics covering the issue of widespread smuggling of goods, the use of Singapore as a medical and financial haven by those accused of corruption, and the treatment of Indonesian domestic workers in Singapore. Pollution from Indonesian forest fires is also an issue. Disagreements have emerged over an extradition treaty between the two countries and an agreement tied to defence cooperation. Some unhappiness had also arisen over the Singapore Government's investments in the Indonesian telecommunication industry. The Indonesians perceive Singapore as a cold-hearted and highly materialistic country. However, this assessment has been tempered by Singaporean social and humanitarian aid to Indonesia. Finally, Indonesian domestic politics often paints Singapore as a purely reactive partner in their relationship, which is far from true. If anything, it should be noted that Singapore, as a country with a single political party in power for more than forty years, has its own priorities.

The Singapore-Indonesia relationship is a largely complementary one, despite their historical competition in trade matters. Indonesia's vast expanse and the inability of the government to police it effectively, and Singapore's outward orientation towards Indonesia for all sorts of commodities and services, have led to several problems. Singapore's recourse to maintaining the stance of acknowledging a clearly identifiable existential threat in its immediate periphery is also regarded as serving regime interests. Attention is then drawn to how ASEAN norms of interaction and deference to Indonesia's proprietary sense of entitlement in the region have spawned unhappiness when expectations are unmet.

In Isagani de Castro's chapter on Malaysia-Philippines relations, he argues that the two countries have had an "abnormal" bilateral relationship, with both countries closing down their embassies several times since full diplomatic ties were established in 1964. Much of the friction between the two countries has traditionally involved the Philippines' claim to the Malaysian state of Sabah. Other irritants in the relationship include the status of Filipino migrants in Sabah and overlapping claims over parts of the Spratly Islands in the South China Sea. De Castro argues that Malaysia has traditionally resorted to bilateral venues to resolve its problems with the Philippines, while the latter resorts to an admixture of bilateral and multilateral fora. The multilateral arenas have included ASEAN mechanisms and the ICJ.

The first period of this bilateral relationship is described as having lasted from 1959 to 1986 when the Marcos government fell. This first period was marked by testy ties as a result of claims over Sabah and the discovery of a plot by the Philippines to infiltrate Sabah. The offer of Malaysian sanctuary for Philippine Muslim rebels in Sabah was also a major issue. During the next period, from 1986 to 1998, there were clear attempts to salvage the relationship. Especially important in this regard was the establishment of the Philippines-Malaysia Joint Commission for Bilateral Cooperation under the Ramos government in 1993. For a brief period after the Ramos government, relations were strained as a result of President Estrada's support for Anwar Ibrahim. However, from 2001, the relationship became much better under the Arroyo government whereby

Malaysia helped to deal with the Muslim insurgency in the southern Philippines. Trade and investment ties have also been enhanced.

The Arroyo administration is described as having improved the bilateral relationship between the Philippines and Malaysia. Nonetheless, Arroyo has been unable to deal with the Sabah issue since legislators in the Philippines tend to obstruct her efforts to drop the claim. The bilateral resolution of problems and the retention of the status quo are seen as working in Malaysia's favour. Malaysia also appears to regard the Sabah issue as settled — that it is a proprietary rather than a territorial claim. Consequently, the remaining issue is only one of compensation to the heirs of the Sulu Sultanate. De Castro argues that the lack of a national consensus and the absence of political will have tended to obstruct the resolution of bilateral problems from the Philippine side. Problems arising from the Muslim insurgency in the south are traditionally arbitrated by the Organisation of the Islamic Conference (OIC) with Malaysia playing a mediating role between the Philippine Government and the Moro Islamic Liberation Front (MILF). However, in so doing, Malaysia weakens the position of the former party. The situation regarding the treatment of illegal immigrants in Sabah improved following Philippine diplomatic intervention. NGOs and civic organizations are also involved in monitoring the welfare of such workers in Sabah. The Philippines' occasional resort to multilateralism is viewed as having yielded very few gains in comparison to Malaysia's resort to bilateralism on most issues and unilateralism on the overlapping claims to the Spratly Islands. Although there are common bilateral mechanisms for the resolution of contentious issues, the Philippines has sometimes unsuccessfully sought to pursue multilateral options.

In his chapter, K.S. Nathan explores the bilateral relationship between Malaysia and Singapore. While he argues the relationship is best viewed through a realist prism, he acknowledges that Singapore's anxieties vis-à-vis Malaysia are much less relevant for Malaysia in that it predicates survival within a wider arena and a balance of powers. Despite a seemingly large number of unresolved issues, Malaysia tends to downplay tensions and work the bilateral relationship to mutual benefit. He notes that Malay elites have not yet come to terms with the loss of Singapore and view Singapore as the only regional country that is controlled by migrants. This seeming historical tension in the perception of the one country towards the other is described as an important component in the relationship that in turn informs it.

Subsequently, Nathan looks at some of the historical origins of tensions between the two countries.

The political economy of the two states is described as being at once complementary and competitive. Singapore's external reliance for many things coupled with its small size and desired status is said to exact a toll on regime type and socio-political conditions that favour investments. The resource scarcity has also led Singapore to rely on Malaysia for many necessities, including potable water — the pricing and continued supply of which has been a thorn in bilateral relations. Other sensitive issues include disputes on how to develop Malayan Railways' land bank, the retention of the pension contribution of Malaysian workers by Singapore authorities, Malaysian low flight over-space access for Singapore military aircraft, and sovereignty disputes over Pedra Blanca/ Pulau Batu Putih, Middle Rocks, and South Ledge that were resolved by the ICJ in May 2008. Despite competition in attracting foreign investments, both countries are also described as being heavily dependent on each other for trade, with a general view to maintaining positive bilateral relations.

Most sensitive issues are described as being negotiated and settled within a bilateral framework, with overlapping territorial claims referred to and arbitrated by the ICJ. Ethnicity is viewed as an issue that affects how sensitive issues are resolved. Nathan argues that Singapore tends to adopt a cold rational-legalistic approach while Malaysia prefers a consultative and consensual approach. Singapore's approach to survival is characterized as premised on economic and military strength. Malaysian concerns over Singapore's military assets and capabilities notwithstanding, it is deeply committed to socioe-conomic development in general. Despite primarily utilizing bilateral fora to resolve tensions, both countries are supportive of regional multilateral fora for development, security, and cooperation in a wider context. Nonetheless, elements of competition, especially in the area of infrastructure facilities and service industries, is regarded as contributing to healthy competition within the bilateral relationship.

Broader Discussion

The case studies analysed in this book have documented that bilateralism is a well-established policy response in Southeast Asian international relations. Bilateralism is a useful mechanism with substantial historical precedence in the resolution of problems between geographically proximate states. In many instances, bilateralism preceded the onset of multilateralism in Southeast Asia. Nonetheless, we stake no claim that such interactions are only useful among geographically proximate states. All states may avail themselves to the usefulness of bilateralism as a policy tool. Nonetheless, in the Southeast Asian case, it is a truism that bilateralism is significantly enhanced among geographically proximate states.

There appear to be a large number of reasons privileging bilateralism over multilateralism, especially among geographically proximate states. From our findings, it is clear that history has privileged bilateralism and provided policy formulators with an established practice and venue in dealing with immediately adjacent states. This historical imperative in turn derived from the geographical necessity of coping with dense transactions and interactions. Consequently, history and geography combine to provide the most forceful evidence in favour of bilateralism. The accumulated interactions and knowledge derived from bilateralism subsequently serve to undergird the practice and establish it as a preferred medium through which international relations may be conducted. Additionally, the case studies also indicate the ready and regular availability of structures permitting bilateral interactions. These may take the form of joint border committee meetings as in the case of Malaysia, Myanmar, Thailand, and Vietnam or ministerial meetings as in the case of Indonesia, Malaysia, and Singapore. This difference in turn raises two important questions: Do countries with common land borders have an established pattern of bilateral transactions derived from geographical imperatives? If so, how do they differ from maritime states where similar geographical imperatives preclude such border committees?

Apart from the convenience of continuing with an established practice, there are many other factors privileging bilateralism. Bilateralism appears to allow for the resolution of problems that are unique to two countries or appear to involve them the most. In this regard and returning to Etel Solingen's theoretical considerations, it may be argued that levels of compliance in bilateralism was likely to be higher and attendant transactional costs significantly lower than when like issues are negotiated within a multilateral setting. The scope of such agreements also tends to be lesser and the arrangements are significantly more flexible, taking into account idiosyncratic considerations that are often extremely important in the region. Additionally, there is the existence of a strongly held normative belief in Southeast Asia that bilateral avenues provide the best forum to resolve conflicts or coordinate policies, as argued by T.J. Pempel.

Bilateralism may involve specific and traditional security discourse markers like overlapping territorial claims as well as non-traditional threats like illegal migration and environmental pollution. The utilization of such fora seems to buffer the issue at hand from excessive publicity that may in turn lead to political posturing. Such posturing is certainly not uncommon in developing countries and Asia where the notion of "face" and propriety often complicate international relations. Posturing often significantly complicates the situation from rational resolution and opens up the possibility of pandering to important domestic political constituencies. When such posturing occurs, a simple issue often becomes conflated with many others. Additionally, it is likely to escalate tensions and often leads to the overall deterioration of bilateral relations. Consequently, quiet and contained bilateral diplomacy is often the forum of choice for neighbouring countries. The bilateral relationships examined in this volume do tend to suggest that security issues take priority over economic issues at the outset. In other words, there does appear to be sequential logic favouring security matters in the first instance. Conversely, it may be noted that when bilateral security relations are poor between geographically proximate countries, economic activities tend to suffer. This spillover effect is most clearly demonstrated in the case of Malaysia-Singapore and Thailand-Myanmar bilateral relations. In the former case, Malaysia unilaterally acted against Singapore's economic interests in 1998 when relations with Singapore were poor following the Asian financial crisis. Similarly, at the peak of Myanmar's tensions with Thailand, border trading zones were typically closed, much to the chagrin of Thailand. On the other hand, when the security environment is favourable, bilateral economic relations tend to be expansive as is the case between Vietnam and Thailand, Malaysia and Thailand, and Malaysia and Singapore recently.

Nonetheless, it should be noted that such fora often privilege larger and more powerful countries as well. In other words, smaller countries with less power and fewer policy instruments may suffer from bilateralism during the negotiation process. In this regard, multilateral fora offer greater protection for smaller states than bilateral ones as the former are more likely to adhere to rational-legal principles rather than power considerations. The most recent example of such disagreement occurred between Cambodia and Thailand over the land surrounding the UNESCO-designated historical Preah Vihear Temple Complex in 2008. Both countries deployed additional troops along the common border and clashes occurred. Additionally, Thailand was itself in a political crisis with a weak government as well as a military allied with the traditional elite and opposed to the elected government. Prime Minister Hun Sen in Cambodia faced the uncertain prospects of a national election. Further exacerbating the matter was the fact that both countries were involved in a good measure of political posturing. The issue has been dealt with through bilateral contacts and talks and Thailand in particular stressed its preferences for a purely bilateral approach to dealing with both tensions and disputes. Thus, the Cambodia-Thailand dispute and the heightened tension in 2008 display the pre-eminence of bilateralism in dealing with both border issues and tension between the countries of Southeast Asia.

It should be noted at this juncture that bilateralism and multilateralism are not mutually exclusive enterprises. In fact, as Etel Solingen points out in the theoretical chapter, states often engage in forum shopping or pick and choose where they deal with a particular issue. Naturally, there are many considerations that go into such venue selection. All else held constant, the likelihood of securing the greatest benefit in an issue is likely to be a strong motivation. Alternatively, states may and indeed often do deal with a number of fora simultaneously. Such a practice may involve the bundling of issues on the basis of positive outcomes or for legal or normative reasons. Another way to conceptualize the relationship between bilateralism and multilateralism is to think of them as avenues in a layered process where states retain a core of bilateral transactions that are then supplemented by increasingly larger fora as the arena radiates outward, not unlike the latticed approach mentioned by Christopher Dent. In such a scenario, states may quite simply reinforce their choices in larger domains to secure preferred outcomes. Whatever the case may be, it is clear that states do not necessarily regard bilateralism and multilateralism as mutually exclusive policy options.

In fact, there are quite a few instances where the failure of a bilateral forum to resolve an issue resulted in the issue being brought to a larger multilateral forum. This seems to be the case especially where the issues have legal implications in international law. Overlapping territorial claims provide the best example of just such a development. In 2002, the ICJ ruled on the question of sovereignty over the disputed islands of Ligitan and Sipadan between Indonesia and Malaysia. Similarly, in 2008, the ICJ determined the ownership of Pedra Blanca/Pulau Batu Putih and Middle Rocks between Malaysia and Singapore. Both these cases display the limitations of the regional approach to solving important bilateral issues and the seeming irrelevance of regional mechanisms. On a more positive note, however, disputing countries were able to agree on the utilization of an international dispute settlement mechanism and agree to abide by the terms of its judgement.

The end of the Second Indochina War in 1975 marked a major watershed in Southeast Asian international relations. The same may be said of the Third Indochina War involving the conflicts between Cambodia and Vietnam, which led to the Vietnamese military intervention in 1978–79 and the subsequent regional polarization in the Cambodian Conflict. Case studies chapter writers were also asked to identify the most important and sensitive issues in the bilateral relationship they were examining. Afterwards, they were tasked to identify how these issues were typically dealt with at the bilateral level and whether there was recourse to multilateralism. The discussion required an identification of the venues utilized in the resolution of disputes as well as the importance of both structural and agency factors in dispute resolution and bilateral relations. While broad structural imperatives generally shaped bilateral policy output, agency reasons also exerted an important influence in bilateral relationships. In other words, political elites in the countries involved were often responsible for setting the general tone and temper for bilateral relations with neighbouring countries. Similarly, political personalities were as important as historical episodes such as the outbreak of conflict or previous hostilities in the shaping of bilateral relations. The historical hangover is still clearly evident in the case of Cambodia-Vietnam, Thailand-Myanmar, Thailand-Malaysia, Indonesia-Malaysia, and Malaysia-Singapore relations. In this regard, it may be surmised that history has a powerful impact on formative perceptions in bilateral relations. This formative impact may then be reinforced or altered by elites.

Elites in Asian countries often exercise power that is disproportionate to their office. Rational-legal power is often buttressed by powerful constituencies, clientelism, and tremendous access to public and natural resources. Consequently, their imprint on policy output is significantly enhanced. Since many of these countries have political systems with little diffusion of power, decisions made by elites are strictly top-down. As a result, good and bad relations are amplified many times over. Another clear demonstration of the impact of elites in the state of bilateral relations is their impact on the periodization of the relationship. This impact is very clear in many of the relationships, especially if regimes had remained in power for a long period of time. Hence, the idiosyncratic imprint of the likes of Ferdinand Marcos in the Philippines, Lee Kuan Yew in Singapore, Mahathir Mohamed in Malaysia, Ne Win in Burma, and Suharto in Indonesia are clearly visible. If two such elites disliked each other, the impact on bilateral relations would have been profound. For example, it was common knowledge in diplomatic circles that Mahathir and Suharto disliked each other intensely. This bad chemistry in turn had a very negative impact on Malaysia-Indonesia bilateral relations. Fortunately, Suharto was restrained by his Javanese aristocratic ways and the ASEAN structural framework that limited Indonesian hegemony. Mahathir was equally restrained by rational-legal considerations, a firm faith in Asian values, and a resolve to deal with regional problems in a cooperative way. Perhaps the sobering and positive outcome of frayed bilateral relations is this: Rational structural imperatives blunt the potentially damaging impact of agency factors.

Structural imperatives have had a definitive impact on Southeast Asian international relations. Until 1991, the dynamics associated with the Second and Third Indochinese Wars had a formative impact on regional international relations. The Second Indochina War spilled over from the dynamics of the Cold War wherein the United States sought to contain the spread of communism in Southeast Asia as well as the policies of China and the Soviet Union. In turn, China and the Soviet Union were opposed to U.S. military intervention in the Indochinese countries. After the conclusion of the Second Indochina War in 1975, the Sino-Soviet rivalry in the Asia Pacific came to the forefront. Ironically, the emergence of the Third Indochina War was characterized by rivalry among the communist-ruled Asian countries of Cambodia-Vietnam and China-Vietnam respectively. The collapse and subsequent implosion of the Soviet Union in 1991 had a profound impact on regional structures that modelled themselves on either the communist or non-communist side of the Cold War divide. The broader developments led in turn to the resolution of the Cambodia Conflict, the full normalization of relations between China and Vietnam, as well as between Vietnam and ASEAN. These developments allowed ASEAN to shed its Cold War origins and interests and expand to incorporate the three Indochinese states and Myanmar. Hence, structural imperatives have a great deal of impact on regional developments. They have informed and conditioned regional international relations as well as the form and agenda of multilateral institutions in Southeast Asia. In this regard, idiosyncratic policy output was often restrained by structural conditions.

The looser structural conditions of the post–Cold War period have in turn allowed for far more discretion in the evolution of regional organizations and the regional agenda. In fact, this structural loosening led to the dispersion of the previously convergent foreign and defence policies of the ASEAN states. The new environment brought about new challenges and with it, new problems, and new perceptions of threat. Hence, it is no coincidence that bilateral relations between geographically proximate states deteriorated substantially in the 1990s. Not only did the new environment bring about new challenges, it also allowed for much more idiosyncratic foreign policy output. This was not necessarily a negative development because regional states acquired far more independence and latitude in policy output than before. However, it marked the start of a new learning curve. This curve challenged and tested the limits of the informal arrangements and accommodation that multilateralism had brought to regional relations. It also tested the limits to which state sovereignty became an issue in the regional management of regional problems. The political violence that followed in Cambodia, Myanmar, and Timor Leste all became issues testing ASEAN's mettle. The absence of procedural protocol in dealing with internal problems within ASEAN was a liability that attracted much negative attention. Yet, this informality and the absence of enforcement mechanisms for compliance spelled the loss of significant gains that had been made earlier. Moreover, there is precious little regional multilateral organizations can do when the situation within a country or between countries deteriorated. The non-intervention principle also returned the members to basic principles of power and influence in dealing with each other. There were attempts to remedy this problem through the formation of an ASEAN Troika in the 1990s but it has proved to be of little use thus far. It is to be hoped that ASEAN members and their major dialogue partners accede to the Treaty of Amity and Cooperation (TAC) lodged with the United Nations. Hopefully, TAC will provide sufficient deterrence against the outbreak of conflict between member states. TAC requires that signatories agree to resolve differences between states without resort to violence. Nonetheless, when relations were frayed between Myanmar and Thailand, and more recently between Cambodia and Thailand, there was no mention of TAC or the promise to avoid conflict. States involved in those situations merely attended to domestic constituencies and concerns.

Do these developments mean that ASEAN will lack relevance in an area where it is much needed, i.e. in dispute settlement? The question is complex and the assessment depends on what role is being assigned to ASEAN. If ASEAN is expected to actively settle interstate disputes among its members then its track record is weak. If ASEAN is expected to be more a norm creator that provides its members with a framework for improved relations and mechanism that the member states can utilize for the management and eventual settlement of their disputes, then ASEAN's role and performance appears to be a positive one. An additional issue to consider is whether bilateral dispute settlement among the ASEAN member states is a sign of weakness of the regional ASEAN approach and framework for dispute settlement or if it is in fact an integrated part of it. The goal of ASEAN is a peaceful and cooperative Southeast Asia and if this is promoted through bilateral dispute settlement that is in line with the regional framework then it is not a sign of ASEAN weakness. An example has been the progress in settling Vietnam's border disputes since the early 1990s. This has been done primarily through bilateral approaches but in line with the ASEAN principles and mechanism for dispute settlement.[1] In fact what is potentially more damaging to the regional approach and mechanisms, is that when bilateral negotiations could not settle the disputes between Indonesia and Malaysia and between Malaysia and Singapore, they were referred to the ICJ, thus bypassing the regional mechanisms, in particular the High Council of the TAC. This bypassing appears to suggest that ASEAN practices what Robert Keohane has called contract rather than foundational multilateralism devoid of deep organization, mutual recognition, and interaction. The domestic environments in countries involved in security disputes are simply not sufficiently permissive to allow for the utilization of untested regional mechanisms. In this regard Etel Solingen is accurate in suggesting that the ASEAN Troika and High Council are unlikely to evolve to become the principal mechanisms of dispute settlement.

Structural deficiencies within the regional framework will have to be redressed. The ASEAN Charter committing its members to observe certain protocols is now in place, as is its attempt to create an ASEAN

Community. These are initiatives that are clearly meant to consolidate the gains ASEAN has already made in regional relations. It is also an attempt by regional countries to take greater charge of regional concerns and problems. There is no doubt that many countries signed the Charter because it required minimal commitment and even less actual compliance. The ASEAN Charter therefore could deteriorate into that which an ASEAN politician once referred to the Zone of Peace, Freedom and Neutrality (ZOPFAN) — a statement of declaratory intent. Nonetheless, it seems that two specific obstacles will have to be overcome in order to achieve the intended goals. The first of these is that ASEAN states need to redirect their perceptions of threat away from each other. This was the precondition that Karl Deutsch wrote about in his formative work on security communities. The second and much more practical problem is that ASEAN may have to move away from Indonesian leadership of the organization. This move is required in order for ASEAN to be independent of individual member states. It may be remembered that immediately after the downfall of the Suharto government in 1998, ASEAN was left without a rudder. However, there is an inherent problem with this proposition. Indonesian foreign policy privileges Southeast Asia and in particular ASEAN. In fact, this is the reason for its impassivity vis-à-vis the structural dynamics of the East Asia Summit and East Asian Community. Both these larger institutions will overshadow Indonesia within a larger footprint. Consequently, the enthusiasm shared by China and Malaysia regarding the former was certainly not forthcoming in Indonesia. In contrast to the Indonesian policy formulators' complaints of the structural confines of ASEAN in the early 1990s, the current thinking appears to confine ASEAN's potential within the region as a whole.

The type of multilateralism that is practiced by ASEAN is clearly regionalism rather than regionalization. There is little doubt that ASEAN is in the main an elite-led enterprise. Attempts at informing the wider audience of the association's utility and mandate are few, and in fact ASEAN leaders have in the past explicitly refused to deal with civil society activists from their own countries during official meetings. Some such elite, especially those from non-democratic states, have insisted that such activists be denied the opportunity to attend formal meetings. In this regard it will be interesting to note whether Indonesia, which is traditionally regarded as *primus inter pares* in ASEAN, will lead in the development of a much more democratic culture in the region given its own astounding transformation within such a short period of time.

Finally, it might be noted that different networks have obtained and prevailed at different times in ASEAN's political evolution. The association's early embeddedness in the Malay Archipelago often led to Indonesia, Malaysia, and Singapore as part of the early network determining the trajectory of ASEAN. This network was extended to include Thailand after the conclusion of the Second Indochina War in deference to Thai security concerns, albeit at that time both Indonesia and Malaysia regarded China rather than Vietnam as the threat to regional security. All three countries collectively elevated the importance of the Indochina security complex for the purpose of regional unity. Later in the 1990s, following the resolution of the Cambodian situation, Vietnam, Laos, and Cambodia, that joined ASEAN much later, often acted as part of a network and tended to vote collectively on many issues. Similarly, in the 1990s, the Philippines and Thailand acted as members of a democratic network to attempt to bring Myanmar in line with more regional norms of governance.

The one final thing that is often overlooked but needs to be noted is that there exist domestic coalitions in Southeast Asia that actively resist internationalization. Myanmar's military bureaucracy may be cited as one that has never responded favourably to the application of international norms of governance. Similarly, the Philippines has a domestic coalition that retains oligarchic control of the country's politics and economy. Consequently, regardless of formal commitments, it is often unable to live up to these commitments after accession to binding protocols.

Howsoever ASEAN may evolve in the future, there is little doubt that bilateralism will continue to be an important forum within ASEAN. As mentioned at the outset, our preliminary evidence indicates that almost all ASEAN states have privileged bilateralism over multilateralism. This privileging appears to be especially true when difficult or contentious issues are involved. This practice, to all intents and purposes, is likely to persist in the foreseeable future.

NOTES

[1]   For details on the progress in managing and settling Vietnam's border disputes see Ramses Amer and Nguyen Hong Thao, "Vietnam's Border Disputes — Assessing the Impact on its Regional Integration", in *Vietnam's New*

Order: International Perspectives on the State and Reform in Vietnam, edited by Stéphanie Balme and Mark Sidel (Basingstoke: Palgrave Macmillan, 2007), pp. 71–87; and Ramses Amer and Nguyen Hong Thao, "Vietnam's Border Disputes: Legal and Conflict Management Dimensions", in *The Asian Yearbook of International Law, Vol. 12 (2005–2006)*, edited by B.S. Chimni, Miyoshi Masahiro, and Thio Li-ann (Leiden: Martinus Nijhoff, 2007), pp. 111–27.

REFERENCES

Balme, Stéphanie and Mark Sidel. *Vietnam's New Order: International Perspectives on the State and Reform in Vietnam*. Houndmills, Basingstoke, Hampshire and New York: Palgrave Macmillan, 2007.

Chimni, B.S., Miyoshi Masahiro, and Thio Li-ann. *The Asian Yearbook of International Law, Vol. 12 (2005–2006)*. Leiden and Boston: Martinus Nijhoff Publishers, 2007.

Index

Vietnam War, xvi
  end of, 67
  Thailand's involvement, 71, 72
Vietnam-Thailand relations, 67–91
  building mutual trust, 79
  improved relations, 74–79
  missed opportunities, 68–74
  substantializing bilateral
      cooperation, 81–82
Vietnamization, 96
Visiting Forces Agreement
  United States and Philippines, 237
Vo Van Duc, 82
Vo Van Kiet, 100
Vu Khoan, 79

W
war on terror, 42, 211

water
  Malaysian-Singapore relations,
      263–267
Western powers
  collaboration with, 181
World Court, 236
World Trade Organization, 16

Y
yaa baa, 120
Yettaw, John, 126
Youn, 112

Z
Zainuddin Bendahara, 215
Zone of Peace, Freedom and
      Neutrality (ZOPFAN), 48, 278,
      335

www.ingramcontent.com/pod-product-compliance
Lightning Source LLC
Chambersburg PA
CBHW021846020426
42334CB00013B/214